D1562914

ORGANIZE OR PERISH

ORGANIZE OR PERISH

America's Independent Progressives, 1913–1933

EUGENE M. TOBIN

CONTRIBUTIONS IN AMERICAN HISTORY, NUMBER 114

GREENWOOD PRESS

New York • Westport, Connecticut • London

Library of Congress Cataloging in Publication Data

Tobin, Eugene M.
  Organize or perish.

  (Contributions in American history, ISSN 0084–9219 ;
no. 114)
  Bibliography: p.
  Includes index.
  1. Progressivism (United States Politics)   2. United
States—Politics and government—1865–1933.   3. Liberal-
ism—United States—History—20th century.   I. Title.
II. Series.
E743.T59   1986   973.91   85–11452
ISBN 0–313–25013–8 (lib. bdg. : alk. paper)

Library of Congress Catalog Card Number: 85–11452
ISBN: 0–313–25013–8
ISSN: 0084–9219

First published in 1986

Greenwood Press, Inc.
88 Post Road West
Westport, Connecticut 06881

Printed in the United States of America

The paper used in this book complies with the
Permanent Paper Standard issued by the National
Information Standards Organization (Z39.48–1984).

10 9 8 7 6 5 4 3 2 1

Copyright Acknowledgments

We gratefully acknowledge permission to reprint materials from the following sources:

Howard Yolen Papers, Minnesota Historical Society

Lynn Haines Papers, Minnesota Historical Society

Hiram W. Johnson Papers, by permission of the Bancroft Library, University of California at Berkeley, and Philip B. Johnson

W. Jett Lauk Papers, by permission of the University of Virginia Library

William Kent Papers, by permission of the Yale University Library

Harry Slattery Papers, by permission of the Duke University Library

Theodore Roosevelt to Charles E. Merriam, November 23, 1912, Charles E. Merriam Papers, Box 22, The University of Chicago Archives

Amos R. E. Pinchot Papers (Library of Congress), by permission of Antoinette Pinchot Bradlee

"Direct Action and Conscience: The 1913 Paterson Strike as Example of the Relationship Between Labor Radicals and Liberals," *Labor History* 20:1 (Winter 1979): 73–88

John Nevin Sayre Papers, A. J. Muste Papers, the American Union Against Militarism collection, and the People's Council of America collection, by permission of the Swarthmore College Peace Collection

Brookwood Labor College Papers, by permission of the Archives of Labor History and Urban Affairs, Walter P. Reuther Library, Wayne State University

Oswald Villard Papers, by permission of the Houghton Library, Harvard University

For my mother
CLARA TOBIN
and the memory of my father
HYMAN TOBIN

Contents

Acknowledgments

When I first started the research for this book I was twenty-nine years old, unmarried, and already something of an academic gypsy. Now, almost a decade later, as the manuscript is being readied for publication, I am happily married, the father of two children, and I no longer wake up in the morning wondering what state I live in. Much has happened over the last ten years, and I am pleased to have the opportunity to acknowledge the support and assistance of those who helped me along the way.

The book began as a research proposal in a yearlong post-doctoral seminar led by Dewey W. Grantham at Vanderbilt University. As a National Endowment for the Humanities (NEH) Fellow-in-Residence, I joined eight new colleagues in an intensive and rewarding analysis of twentieth-century American political culture. Dewey Grantham inspired us, scolded us, encouraged us, and taught by example. He has remained a wonderful colleague and friend, and I am deeply grateful for the generosity, graciousness, and support he has given me over the years. His sympathetic understanding, constant encouragement, and wise counsel have been invaluable. He has been a teacher in the most profound and best sense of that word. I would also like to thank three alumni of that NEH seminar, Milton S. Katz, John A. Dittmer, and Ralph B. Levering, whose encouragement and friendship, not to mention their athletic abilities, made the year in Nashville a memorable one.

This project would have been difficult to pursue without the assistance of the many archivists and librarians who eased my labor and patiently answered my many questions. I would especially like to thank James H. Hutson, Chief of the Manuscript Division at the Library of Congress and his marvelous colleagues; Judith Ann Schiff, Sterling Memorial Library, Yale University; Dione Miles, Archives of Labor and Urban Affairs, Walter P. Reuther Library, Wayne State University; Estelle Rebec and Bonnie Hardwick, The Bancroft Library, University of California, Berkeley; Bernice B. Nichols and Jean R. Soderlund, Swarthmore College Peace Collection; Dallas R. Lindgren, Minnesota Historical Society; and Saundra Taylor, The Lilly Library, Indiana University. Closer to home, Joan T. Wolek and Karolyn G. Crockett of Hamilton College's Burke Library fulfilled my numerous interlibrary loan requests with accuracy and speed.

Complying with the provisions of contemporary copyright law is sometimes frustrating, but in my case it has been most rewarding. I would like to thank Philip B. Johnson and The Bancroft Library for permission to publish portions of correspondence in the Hiram W. Johnson Papers; the University of Virginia Library for permission to quote from the Papers of W. Jett Lauck; Yale University Library for the right to publish extracts from the William Kent Papers; Duke University Library for permission to include quotations from the Harry Slattery Papers; the University of Chicago's Joseph Regenstein Library for permission to publish material from the Charles E. Merriam Papers; and Houghton Library, Harvard University for the opportunity to include portions of correspondence from the Oswald Garrison Villard Papers. It is a special pleasure to acknowledge the encouragement offered by Antoinette Pinchot Bradlee and her permission to publish portions of correspondence from the Amos R. E. Pinchot Papers (Library of Congress). I would also like to express my appreciation to editor Daniel J. Leab and *Labor History* for permission to use material (in chapter three) which first appeared in that journal ("Direct Action and Conscience: The 1913 Paterson Strike as Example of the Relationship Between Labor Radicals and Liberals." *Labor History* 20:1 [Winter 1979]: 73–88).

Friends, colleagues, and teachers also provided helpful suggestions and encouragement during various stages of this project. Among the many who helped me to keep going, the following have my thanks and gratitude: Morton Keller provided me with solid graduate training and set an example of the historian as craftsman; Richard Lowitt and J. Leonard Bates turned brief breaks at the Library of Congress into a postdoctoral seminar on twentieth-century American politics. Robert H. Zieger, Stanley Shapiro, David P. Thelen, William H. Harbaugh, and my old friend Michael H. Ebner, all read portions of the manuscript and offered valuable criticism and support. I am especially indebted to Nancy F. Cott who graciously and unselfishly shared with me the results of her own research on the role of the Woman's Committee for Political Action during the 1924 campaign. Her generous display of collegiality made the culmination of my work personally and intellectually rewarding.

At different points but in similar ways, two fine scholars challenged me with their probing and penetrating critiques. Alan Havig gave an earlier draft of the manuscript the close reading and often painfully frank criticism that every author dreads and needs so desperately. LeRoy Ashby read a later version and offered a chapter by chapter analysis that forced me to make my arguments more coherent and sustained. Had I taken full advantage of all the excellent comments and advice offered, this might have been a better book. I am responsible, of course, for all errors of fact and interpretation that remain.

I would also like to acknowledge the contributions of past and present colleagues. At Miami University (Ohio), Michael J. Hogan, Jack T. Kirby, Ronald E. Shaw, Jeffrey P. Kimball, David M. Fahey, and Richard M. Jellison welcomed me as a visiting assistant professor and made my two years in Oxford, Ohio pleasant and rewarding. Richard S. Kirkendall and Maurice Baxter gave me the opportunity to spend a year teaching twentieth-century American history at Indiana University as well as the time to begin writing this manuscript. At Hamilton College it has been my good fortune to work with two distinguished department chairs, Edwin B. Lee and David R. Millar, who encouraged my teaching and research interests in American liberal and labor politics. C. Duncan Rice, first as Dean of the College and more recently as a departmental colleague, offered his constant encouragement and wise counsel. I have also benefited from the friendship and intellectual stimulation of Alfred H. Kelly and Robert L. Paquette whose own commitment to scholarship and teaching have served to inspire and motivate me.

A number of agencies and institutions have offered encouragement in a variety of ways. A National Endowment for the Humanities Fellowship gave this project an indispensable start. Grants from the New Jersey Historical Commission and the Penrose Fund of the American Philosophical Society facilitated research trips across the country. A summer faculty research appointment from Miami University (Ohio) made possible an extended stay at the Library of Congress. Faculty research support from Hamilton College has been constant and extraordinarily generous. I am particularly appreciative of the financial assistance provided through the Williams-Watrous-Couper Endowment Fund for faculty research.

Typing for this book began in draft form at Indiana University under the astute supervision of Libby Gitlitz. Three fine typists at Hamilton College, Debbie Barnes, Laurie Moses, and especially Maitland Alferieff, met my deadlines with skillful, good-natured efficiency. During one particularly discouraging period, Maitland and her husband Basil provided some much needed moral support and encouragement.

The professionals at Greenwood Press have treated this book with the care and attention every writer hopes for but only occasionally receives. Executive Vice President James T. Sabin smoothly initiated an anxious author into the publishing business; Series Editor Jon L. Wakelyn offered valuable criticisms at several key points; editorial assistant Maureen Melino patiently explained the mysteries of the copyright law; copyeditor Pat Garnett judiciously used her red pencil in a skillful and meticulously detailed fashion, while Production Editors Douglas Gall and Loomis Mayer worked closely with an expectant author during the various stages of the publication process.

My major debt, however, is to my wife Beverly, who while leading her own very busy life, managed to juggle the responsibilities of a two-career marriage. Her superior editorial skills saved me from numerous errors of grammar, syntax, and style, which if not worthy of Yogi Berra, were personally embarrassing. She read the manuscript more times than even I care to admit and helped prepare the index. Her most important contribution was never allowing me to make publication of this book a more important event than it deserved or our family's well-being could bear. My children also helped by providing a proper sense of perspective. David's confidence in my expertise as a historian was best revealed by seeking his mother's advice for his History homework. Leslie, who first became aware of "the book" around her fourth birthday, reminded me that she already had "written" two books and hers had pictures!

Finally, I am most grateful to my parents, to whom this book is dedicated. Words are inadequate to express my love and gratitude. My parents created an atmosphere of trust, mutual respect, and intellectual curiosity, and encouraged me to grow as an individual. They have always been there when I needed them. I hope I can do as much for my children.

My major disappointment is that my father did not live to see the final results of this work. His obvious joy and pride in my career and his constant words of encouragement will always remain a personal source of comfort and satisfaction. I will miss him very much.

ORGANIZE OR PERISH

I

Introduction

In 1924, when columnist William Hard challenged the readers of the *Nation* to answer the question "What is Progressivism?" they might have been permitted a moment's hesitation or even nostalgia.[1] For in the six years since the end of the Great War, neither the United States nor the world seemed "safe for democracy" much less reform. The American people and their elected representatives thoroughly repudiated the wartime idealism of one president and then proceeded to embrace the benign platitudes of his successor. The League of Nations, purportedly the cornerstone of postwar collective security, was the victim of personal pride and domestic politics. The repression of dissent and nonconformity, which had been implemented under the guise of wartime solidarity, continued after the Armistice as a security blanket against internal enemies. Prohibition, women's suffrage, and immigration restriction, ironically the most visible remnants of a now-twisted progressive tradition, were passed in a surge of misplaced idealism. But the Eighteenth Amendment proved unenforceable; the enfranchisement of women proved only that the sexes were more alike than was commonly acknowledged; while the restrictive legislation of the early twenties made "100 percent Americanism" synonymous with racial hysteria.

But let us not overstate the case—too much. Progressivism was not totally moribund, nor were its advocates inactive. Social welfare reformers greeted the passage of the Sheppard-Towner Maternity and Infancy-Protection Act (1921) with pleasure, though both its duration and appropriation were limited.[2] But even that modest triumph was tempered by Supreme Court decisions in the next two years which overturned a national child labor law and a state minimum wage statute for women. Efficiency experts, however, could point to the continuance of another side of reform—the nonpartisan regulatory commission—when Congress created the Federal Power Commission and the Railroad Labor Board in 1920. Unfortunately, as was the case with such earlier governmental bodies as the Interstate Commerce Commission and Federal Trade Commission, these new agencies were transformed by the appointive process into protectors—rather than watchdogs—of the industries they had been created to regulate.

Moreover, the bold, innovative wartime experiments in public housing, social insurance, and government operation of the railroads—which so many progressives envisioned as the opening wedge in the reconstruction of postwar society—were themselves abandoned with the coming of the Armistice.[3] This sudden suspension of federal spending, the liquidation of government contracts, and the worldwide economic dislocation created by the war led to a severe recession in 1920–1921 as farm prices collapsed and unemployment reached 12 percent. Though the country emerged from the recession by 1924, neither farmers nor workers ever fully recovered their pre–1921 purchasing levels.

The Harding administration's efforts to aid the farmer through passage of high protective tariffs, regulation of grain exchanges and stockyards, and the availability of more and larger loans to farm cooperatives all proved inadequate to the task. Rather than suffer stoically, the American farmer sent a message to Washington in the 1922 congressional elections. The arrival of several insurgent legislators, or "Sons of the Wild Jackass" as critics disparagingly labeled them, made the farm bloc an increasingly powerful political force, but one whose concerns reflected the specialized, often narrow needs of a single interest group.

Labor militancy, on the other hand, declined precipitously during the early twenties in the face of the government's willing use of injunctions to suppress strikes and its tacit support of the open shop. Over one and a half million workers dropped off union membership rolls between 1920 and 1923, partly discouraged by government coercion, but partially seduced by such blandishments of welfare capitalism as company unions and employee profit-sharing plans.[4] Even the emergence in 1922 of the Conference for Progressive Political Action, a reform coalition spearheaded by the railroad labor brotherhoods in uneasy alliance with socialists and middle-class intellectuals, failed to sustain the revival of political progressivism beyond Robert M. La Follette's presidential candidacy in 1924. That campaign and the tenuous relationship between liberal and labor leaders suggested, however, that progressives would have to lay aside cherished beliefs in a classless society and recognize labor as the dominant partner in any sustained struggle.

Given the mildly reactionary intellectual and political climate of the early twenties, one might ask whether anyone, including the progressives themselves, really cared to answer William Hard's question "What is Progressivism?" much less devote a lifetime's struggle to its achievement. That some reformers were willing to do so, even at the risk of abandoning their own class, was evident in the career of Frederic C. Howe, whose revealing autobiography appeared in 1925. "I believed that the things that I wanted would come about in time," he wrote in a chapter entitled "Unlearning"; "that they would be brought about by liberals—liberals as represented by the *Nation*, the *New Republic*, the insurgent group in Congress. We liberals had the truth." But Howe, a gifted scholar-activist whose careers were distinguished by their breadth and commitment to social justice, finally concluded that his own class was not interested in freedom, democracy, or equality of opportunity. "I still wanted all of this. But I had been wrong about the way to get it. ... The place for the liberal was in labor's ranks."[5] There were few progressives as active as Frederic C. Howe between 1920 and 1925 and fewer still who embraced the cause of labor.

One year later a now-famous symposium in *Survey*, voice of the social welfare movement, seemed to capture the national mood and with it the future historical debate. "Where are the Pre-War Radicals?" beseeched the editors.[6] A number of well-known reformers were paraded forth testifying to their loss of faith, or was it will? A generation later the question received professional legitimacy with publication of Arthur S. Link's seminal essay "What Happened to the Progressive Movement in the 1920s?" The composite picture which emerged pointed to several deficiencies in postwar progressivism: it simply had run its course; its ideas, never totally adequate even in their own time, were now sterile and obsolete. Its leaders were either dead or incapacitated by infirmities. Some progressives found the movement's postwar legacy—immigration restriction and prohibition—embarrassing if not forbidding. Others were unable to accommodate themselves to the New Era's emphasis upon the special needs of producing groups at the expense of an earlier belief in a classless society. In short, the movement, except for surviving pockets of resistance among insurgents in Congress and scattered social welfare advocates, was dead, and few mourned its passing.[7]

One remarkable aspect of this interpretation is that it runs counter to the evidence. Biographical and organizational studies documenting the existence of genuine progressive activity during the twenties abound, yet few historians have countered successfully the apparent impregnability of this earlier argument. Clearly, liberalism or progressivism, and contemporaries used the terms interchangeably, were far from triumphant after the war, and public awareness of reform activities paled in comparison with the prewar era. Reformers, however, stayed out of the closet long enough to engage in a number of efforts at coalition politics, especially with elements of organized labor. We need to examine the activities of such groups if we are to understand the direction of progressivism after the war.

In recent years a number of historians have provided clear evidence of political reform during the twenties involving the railroad labor brotherhoods, congressional insurgents, farmer-labor party supporters, and the familiar middle-class intellectuals which attests to the survival of a strong progressive tradition.[8] One unintended, and I believe, unfortunate consequence of this excellent work has been the emergence of an interpretation which implicitly focuses on the displacement of the allegedly cautious, genteel, middle-class reformers of the prewar era by a putatively hard-nosed, class-conscious, street-wise group of urban liberals clearly linked to the New Deal. According to this interpretation, the progressivism of the earlier years had failed. Middle-class reformers were either too fainthearted or overly committed to the survival of capitalism to consider challenging the system.

In *An Encore for Reform: The Old Progressives and the New Deal*, Otis L. Graham, Jr., offered an interpretation which significantly buttressed the earlier view of progressivism as having been practically nonexistent during the 1920s. His examination of prewar reformers' attitudes toward the New Deal suggested that the contribution even of the minority who approved of liberalism's new direction was minimal. Most surviving prewar progressives bitterly opposed the New Deal, displeased by its intellectual sterility and imprecise planning. The attitudes of reformers in the thirties can be best appreciated, according to Graham, with reference to events of *that* decade "and the situation of individuals in those years, taken against the stubborn persistence of social attitudes and a social education begun and largely completed many years before." The crucial point is his contention that most progressives passed through the 1920s with their ideas unchanged. It seems surprising, in view of his primary concern with the progressive rather than the New Deal "mind," that Graham should cast only a cursory glance toward the period of 1912 to 1932. "This is not to say," as he admits, "that [these] years are of no importance. . . . But they rarely stimulated in an old reformer a change in basic ideals."[9] These "tired radicals," one might conclude, were too old to fight, too ill-equipped to meet the exigencies of the postwar era, and too uninvolved in public life's pressures and responsibilities to have anything constructive to offer.

This thesis is compelling, provocative, and convincing—up to a point. It is one thing to lament the absence of reform accomplishments in the postwar years and quite another to ignore tangible evidence of progressives' struggles. Graham was more sensitive to this issue in a later work. "It needs to be emphasized," he wrote in *The Great Campaigns: Reform and War in America, 1900–1928*, "that the eclipse of reform in the 1920s was never total . . . and if these efforts are forgotten simply because they were beaten back, we then exaggerate the placidity and consensus of the [decade]."[10] Conceding the soundness and relevance of most postwar progressive ideas, Graham's language evoked the mood of an earlier generation when he acknowledged the continued responsibility of reformers in the 1920s to "expose" inequities, "denounce" injustice, "awaken," "organize," and "revitalize" public opinion.[11] But if reform ideas remained valid, and if social and economic inequities such as poverty, unemployment, and tax-dodging continued to flout our democratic heritage, why criticize postwar progressives for clinging tenaciously or even inflexibly to beliefs developed over more than a generation? Significantly, in *The Great Campaigns*, Graham shifts the focus of his argument away from the alleged inadequacies of prewar progressivism to a less deprecatory, more sympathetic recognition of the burdens, tedium, and sacrifice inherent in reform work. Postwar progressives, Graham concludes, were the victims of disappointment rather than bewilderment.

Part of the difficulty in attempting an analysis of postwar progressivism rests, as Paul W. Glad has noted, in the temptation of searching for ideological unity.[12] It simply did not exist. Such unity may have been necessary for political success, and reformers in the twenties clearly lacked sufficient agreement both among themselves and with potential allies (such as organized labor and agrarian groups) either to organize an effective third party or gain control of a major one. But the survival of liberalism depended just as much upon the energy and persistence with which progressives confronted the issues and events of the postwar years. Earlier goals of bringing government closer to the people, shaping a classless society, restoring free competition, and occupying the middle ground between capital and labor were no longer viable or, in some cases, desirable.[13] Of course, there were some reformers who refused to change, and they listened to and were heard by no one but themselves. A number of progressives remained active after the war, however, and willingly confronted the old and new concerns of these years: farm relief, industrial democracy, free speech, disarmament, and social insurance.

This book is about many of those "survivors." It is an analysis of the publicists, lobbyists, and directors of reform organizations—of the *technicians* of postwar liberalism, and of their organizational structure and political attitudes. It is also a study of progressive failure. Few successes emerged from postwar liberalism. There are few accomplishments to chronicle, and even Pyrrhic victories seem to have eluded progressives' grasp. This is a history of struggle and defeat, of endlessly optimistic beginnings, and of constantly disappointing results. It is a painful reminder of activists' mistakes, arrogance, and pride. This is not a book for or about the faint of heart but a begrudging acknowledgment of liberals' energy, persistence, and faith.

From 1913 to 1933 one of the genuine voices of domestic reform emanated from a variety of farmer, labor, and liberal organizations which have left a rich legacy of associational activity. These groups were ephemeral, yet each drew support from an unusually homogeneous composition of reformers, many of whom moved easily from one organization to another. This remarkable flurry of organizational activity is suggestive of the "organize or perish" choice which many reformers felt themselves facing. It also testifies to their willingness to confront the myriad problems of the postwar society. But organizational activity does not mean that progressives were organized. Active, yes; but the results of their activities were so ambiguous that one must question their commitment to the ideal of organization itself. Their real enemies were not Republican conservatives or major party liberals. They could handle them well enough. Their central weakness lay in their extraordinary insularity and parochialism. They were suspicious of any organization that spread beyond their own narrow circle. Thus, while they paid lip service to the importance of building coalitions and alliances, they always demanded total control and withdrew when power had to be shared. Their own attempts at organization frequently sent them spinning off into small, competing groups.

Lest we proceed too far, let me offer readers an explanation concerning the use of certain words. *Progressive* and *liberal* are two of the most confusing terms for a historian to define, and many people will be dismayed by the decision to use them interchangeably. Throughout this book, progressivism and liberalism are used to suggest a concern for positive government intervention and a sensitivity for reform. Though conscious of the pitfalls of such vague and imprecise definitions, I am not ready to discard them because we have little with which to replace them. I also have avoided drawing a chronological line at the New Deal and attributing all predepression reform activity to *progressives* and all post-stock-market crash efforts to *liberals*. Contemporaries between 1913 and 1933 used the terms interchangeably, and I believe the words have acquired an unwarranted distinctiveness that owes more to the historical profession's historiographic wars than to any ideological differences. For purposes of convenience and differentiation, I have capitalized *Progressive* when referring to the Bull Moose movement between 1912 and 1916 and to the 1924 La Follette-Wheeler campaign.

The phrase "independent progressive" also deserves an explanation because it serves as the principal organizing mechanism for this analysis. In a political sense, it denotes a group of activists who operated within the progressive mainstream but clearly were on the periphery of the two-party system. Though favorably disposed toward the expansion of state involvement, most, though not all, remained suspicious of such growth and cherished their self-proclaimed role as guardians of the public interest. Only a handful sustained their commitment over an entire generation, and even if all were gathered together, they would still fit comfortably in a large living room. They often have been called "second-line" progressives, reflecting their position a step or two below the leadership, and some historians are wont to characterize their activities as representing a neglected or understudied aspect of early twentieth-century politics. I believe they deserve a position in the progressives' front line because they were the driving force behind political liberalism between the two Roosevelts.

I am sensitive to the danger in exaggerating the cohesiveness and continuity among independent progressives during these years. At the same time, I do not wish to overemphasize the episodic, disjointed nature of their activities. Obviously, progressive ideas did not remain static nor did reformers remain the same. I believe that the various groups examined in this book—the radicals within the Bull Moose party and the pacifists and labor leaders who pursued third-party action throughout the 1920s—do constitute parts of a larger independent progressive phenomenon whose common elements link Theodore Roosevelt's radical critics of 1913 with third-party activists twenty years later. They were the founders and mainstays of organizations that have been dismissed as the *progressive* footnote in too many accounts of American politics prior to the Great Depression.

I have chosen 1913 for the beginning of this study because the defeat of the Bull Moose party at the end of 1912 had a liberating effect on those progressives whose personal commitment to Theodore Roosevelt was secondary to a desire for fundamental economic change. Reformers such as Frederic C. Howe, Amos R. E. Pinchot, and George L. Record wanted their party to fight for the municipal ownership of public utilities, a modified version of the single tax that would exempt local buildings from taxation, government ownership of railroads and natural resources, and an antitrust program that would restore competitive capitalism. Their futile attempt to win TR's endorsement ended any lingering party ties and allowed these men and others to pursue their goals, though not totally unfettered by charges of political disloyalty. The second chapter examines the growth of this alternative radical program between 1913 and 1916 and analyzes the ideological and institutional constraints which impeded the radical Progressive program.

By 1915 many socially concerned Bull Moosers and Wilsonians had joined a coalition of peace activists, social workers, and social gospelers in opposition to militarism, preparedness, and conscription. These fighters for "peace and justice" blamed the war in Europe on economic exploitation and linked the cause of democracy to the cause of labor. The suffering, poverty, and unemployment which reformers saw all around compelled them to demand an end to secret diplomacy and the strictest possible policy of American neutrality. After the United States entered the conflict, reformers sought to take the profit out of war through the stringent use of income and inheritance taxes.[14] Chapter three examines the political and economic context of liberal-labor relations prior to the First World War, and chapter four traces the efforts of two groups—the American Union Against Militarism and the American Committee on War Finance—to achieve progressives' wartime goals.

The experiments in wartime mobilization, particularly the limited nationalization of the railroads, did suggest some hope for the future. Progressives looked optimistically for signs of political and economic democracy during the postwar "reconstruction." The fifth chapter deals with the efforts of the Committee of Forty-Eight, a disparate collection of liberals whose membership included both patrician reformers and social radicals, to forge a coalition with farmer-labor elements in 1920. Mutual respect between these groups came grudgingly, however, and it was not until 1922 that a new alliance was formed, this time with the railroad brotherhoods in ascendancy. Chapter six follows the development of the liberal-labor alliance, the Conference for Progressive Political Action, as it moved somewhat ambivalently toward Robert M. La Follette's 1924 independent presidential candidacy. A good deal of political expertise for that campaign emanated from a number of liberal lobbying groups and from the often-unsolicited efforts of independent progressives to influence campaign strategy.

Chapter seven, "The Wilderness Years," provides a detailed look at the post–La Follette era, a time of liberal uncertainty, drift, and self-imposed independence. Dismissed by organized labor, which had grown weary of liberal posturing and pretense, progressives returned to the issue-oriented, cross-class, and mass-based appeal which had inspired their movement in the first decade of the twentieth century. Between 1925 and 1928 liberal activists exposed the utility industry's stranglehold over the American economy, continued their calls for government ownership of railroads and natural resources, reiterated their vocal support for labor's right to organize and bargain collectively, and awakened the public to the continuation of dollar diplomacy in Latin America. This chapter also traces the experience of independent progressives in Alfred E. Smith's 1928 campaign.

Disturbed by Herbert Hoover's election and their own continued exclusion from political influence, independent progressives looked to a new third-party vehicle, the League for Independent Political Action, to lead a national realignment. League leaders, led by such intellectual giants as philosopher John Dewey and economist Paul H. Douglas, were eager to launch a new liberal third party based upon the social democratic ideals of the British Labour Party. In their search for the ideal society, however, such leaders displayed an unusually naive understanding of worker needs and an inability or unwillingness to communicate with the working class. Labor progressives, seeking reform within the union movement, displayed an equally crippling failure to cooperate with their liberal colleagues. A genuine liberal-labor alliance, which had seemed attainable on several previous occasions, proved strangely elusive well into the 1920s. Chapter eight offers a chronicle of independent political action during the early years of the Great Depression and examines progressives' relationship to Franklin D. Roosevelt and the early New Deal.

Independent progressivism remained a factor during the postwar era, but survival is not the same as success. The organizational mania which characterized progressives' activities during these years has left us boxes and boxes of manuscripts, endless pieces of letterhead stationery, and hundreds of essays and editorials in liberal journals. But all of this meticulously collected and preserved documentation only reinforces the impression that progressives were few in number, organizationally inept, and politically impotent. Were this a study of liberal triumphs, it would be a very short one. It is, instead, an examination of political activists, single-minded people who kept struggling, fighting, and organizing for what they believed.

The reformer, as Arthur M. Schlesinger, Sr., once observed, "is a disturber of the peace. He trespasses on forbidden ground and commits assault and battery on human complacency." Reformers are often obnoxious, dogmatic, and irritatingly self-righteous. Temperamentally rude, inflexibly stubborn, always claiming to be our social conscience, such people make virtue repulsive.[15] We may both love and hate them, but they will not let us ignore them.

NOTES

1. William Hard, "What is Progressivism?" *Nation* 118 (Jan. 9, Feb. 13, Mar. 26, Apr. 9, 1924), 27–28; 160–162; 342; 394.

2. J. Stanley Lemons, "The Sheppard-Towner Act: Progressivism in the 1920s," *Journal of American History* 55 (Mar. 1969), 776–786, and *idem., The Woman Citizen: Social Feminism in the 1920s* (Urbana: Univ. of Illinois Press, 1973).

3. Allen F. Davis, "Welfare, Reform and World War I," *American Quarterly* 19 (Fall 1967), 516–523.

4. Irving Bernstein, *The Lean Years: A History of the American Worker, 1920–1933* (Boston: Houghton Mifflin, 1960); Allen M. Wakstein, "The Origins of the Open Shop Movement, 1919–1920," *Journal of American History* 51 (Dec. 1964), 460–475.

5. Frederic C. Howe, *The Confessions of a Reformer* (New York: Charles Scribner's Sons, 1925), 222–224.

6. "Where are the Pre-War Radicals?" *Survey* 55 (Feb. 1, 1926), 556–566; (Apr. 1, 1926), 33–34.

7. Arthur S. Link, "What Happened to the Progressive Movement in the

1920s?" *American Historical Review* 64 (July 1959), 833–851; Charles B. Forcey, *The Crossroads of Liberalism: Croly, Weyl, Lippmann, and the Progressive Era, 1900–1925* (New York: Oxford Univ. Press, 1961); Richard Hofstadter, *The Age of Reform: From Bryan to F.D.R.* (New York: Random House, 1955); Clarke Chambers, *Seedtime of Reform: American Social Service and Social Action, 1918–1933* (Minneapolis: Univ. of Minnesota Press, 1963); Herbert F. Margulies, "Recent Opinion on the Decline of the Progressive Movement," *Mid-America* 45 (Oct. 1963), 250–268.

    8. Richard Lowitt, *George W. Norris: The Persistence of a Progressive, 1913–1933* (Urbana: Univ. of Illinois Press, 1971); LeRoy Ashby, *The Spearless Leader: Senator Borah and the Progressive Movement in the 1920s* (Urbana: Univ. of Illinois Press, 1972); Robert H. Zieger, *Republicans and Labor, 1919–1929* (Lexington: Univ. of Kentucky Press, 1969); Burl Noggle, *Into the Twenties: The United States from Armistice to Normalcy* (Urbana: Univ. of Illinois Press, 1974); Stanley Shapiro, "The Twilight of Reform: Advanced Progressives after the Armistice," *Historian* 33 (May 1971), 349–364; *idem.*, "The Passage of Power: Labor and the New Social Order," *Proceedings of the American Philosophical Society* 120 (Dec. 1976), 464–474; Kenneth Campbell MacKay, *The Progressive Movement of 1924* (New York: Columbia Univ. Press, 1947); Howard Zinn, *La Guardia in Congress* (Ithaca, N.Y.: Cornell Univ. Press, 1959); Michael Wreszin, *Oswald Garrison Villard: Pacifist at War* (Bloomington: Indiana Univ. Press, 1965).

    9. Otis L. Graham, Jr., *An Encore for Reform: The Old Progressives and the New Deal* (New York: Oxford Univ. Press, 1967), 62–63.

    10. Otis L. Graham, Jr., *The Great Campaigns: Reform and War in America, 1900–1928* (Englewood Cliffs, N.J.: Prentice-Hall, 1971), 114.

    11. *Ibid.*, 118–119. David M. Kennedy's *Over Here: The First World War and American Society* (New York: Oxford Univ. Press, 1980), 294–295, suggests that wartime disillusionment has been exaggerated.

    12. Paul W. Glad, "Progressives and the Business Culture of the 1920s," *Journal of American History* 53 (June 1966), 88.

    13. Ashby, *The Spearless Leader*, 64–65.

    14. Charles Chatfield, *For Peace and Justice: Pacifism in America, 1914–1941* (Knoxville: Univ. of Tennessee Press, 1971); Blanche Wiesen Cook, "Democracy in Wartime: Antimilitarism in England and the United States, 1914–1918," in Charles Chatfield, ed., *Peace Movements in America* (New York: Schocken Books, 1973), 39–56; C. Roland Marchand, *The American Peace Movement and Social Reform, 1898–1918* (Princeton: Princeton Univ. Press, 1972); Donald Johnson, *The Challenge to American Freedoms: World War I and the Rise of the American Civil Liberties Union* (Lexington: Univ. of Kentucky Press, 1963); and Charles DeBenedetti, *Origins of the Modern American Peace Movement, 1915–1929* (Millwood, N.Y.: KTO Press, 1978).

    15. Arthur M. Schlesinger, Sr., *The American as Reformer* (New York: Atheneum ed., 1968), 66–67.

II

Amos R. E. Pinchot and George L. Record: The Radical Progressive Alternative, 1912–1916

"The political situation is disgustingly mixed up," a disconsolate progressive wrote home in February 1912.[1] Much confusion stemmed from the growing rivalry between the followers of Robert M. La Follette and Theodore Roosevelt as each man eyed the Republican presidential nomination. Only a year earlier the Wisconsin senator had joined other reformers in creating the National Progressive Republican League as the first step in denying renomination to President William Howard Taft. In the intervening eleven months, La Follette, the only announced progressive Republican candidate, campaigned tirelessly across the country, usually against great odds and without significant public, moral, or financial support. The mere visibility of his candidacy, however, enabled him to benefit by comparison with Taft, whose policies on the tariff, congressional reform, and conservation had alienated a growing number of Republican voters.[2]

Former president Roosevelt's refusal to take himself out of the race or publicly declare his intentions added to the uncertainty. "If the Colonel adheres to his present policy of keeping quiet," one politician remarked, "the result will be that a lot of people will declare for him. . . . It will divide the Progressive vote, and [he] will go to the convention with every appearance of being a candidate, but with such a beggarly array of delegates as will make him ridiculous."[3] Many observers did not believe that TR would allow himself to drift into such an untenable position. La Follette's supporters feared that Roosevelt's availability, even as an unannounced candidate, would "take the wind out of the Senator's sails and leave him stranded"; nor were they confident that TR would stay in the race once La Follette was eliminated. They believed that many of the Colonel's supporters were not progressives but reactionaries and that TR was "playing both ends against the middle. . . . It is the worst situation I have ever seen," California progressive William Kent wrote his state's governor, Hiram W. Johnson.[4] "If ever a man played a mean dog-in-the-manger game, Roosevelt is doing it at the present time. He . . . is one of those great big, inhuman freaks, that occur from time to time in the world's history, and not a blundering human being that most of us are."[5]

Ironically, it was TR's larger than life image as the symbol of national progressivism that made him so attractive to many early La Follette supporters. "We went into this game," New York reformer Amos R. E. Pinchot observed, "with two definite objects in view—to prevent the nomination of a reactionary and to keep the Progressives . . . together during and beyond the national Presidential campaign of 1912. . . . We have got to meet a bad situation." La Follette, Pinchot acknowledged, was a "real progressive and man whom we all honor and desire to support. Roosevelt is a less real progressive, a man whom we all honor for his past services . . . but whose recent course has disappointed many of us. . . . La Follette cannot become the President in 1912. Roosevelt has a chance."[6] In the end, Roosevelt's availability, his enormous attractiveness as a symbolic progressive candidate, and the regional limitations of La Follette's appeal led many reformers like Pinchot to substitute political expedience for sentiment. The haste with which the realignment occurred, however, was so indecent and in such poor taste as to evoke the sordid image of deserting a still warm corpse.

Most accounts of the senator's apparent nervous breakdown before the Periodical Publishers' Association in Philadelphia on February 2, 1912, emphasize La Follette's haggard appearance, preoccupation with his daughter's impending surgery, and the rambling, incoherent, and repetitive delivery of his remarks. But as James Weinstein has noted, the publishers probably found the senator's radical attack on the tariff, patent laws, and monopolies equally alarming, and such notions may have struck his followers as politically reckless. Moreover, as William H. Harbaugh has suggested, the Philadelphia dinner merely served as a pretext for effecting a showdown on La Follette's candidacy.[7] "There are none of your real supporters," William Kent reluctantly wrote the senator, "who do not believe that the bottom has absolutely fallen out of your candidacy. . . . It seems to me that the best thing is to permit the union of progressive forces to stick together around Roosevelt, if they so elect."[8]

La Follette also heard from another early supporter, New Jersey progressive George L. Record. If anyone deserved to have mixed emotions in encouraging the senator's withdrawal, Record was the man. For over two years he had deluged La Follette with ideas and possible platform planks of the most radical nature. An advocate of the single tax and direct democracy, Record urged the senator to support government ownership of railroads and natural resources, complete public access to patents, direct attacks on special privilege, and the elimination of tariffs. He assured La Follette that his program was a "simple and workable" formula that would restore equal competition, insure full employment, and "secure to every man the exact proportion of annual wealth which he helped to produce by his mind, his labor, or his capital. . . . It is," he concluded, "a complete answer to socialism, and entirely in accord with our American character."[9]

From both a personal and ideological perspective, Record's views were consistently closer to those of La Follette than TR; nowhere was this more evident than in the senator's Philadelphia speech, which closely follows Record's original draft submitted eight months earlier. Yet the possibility of a Roosevelt-led victory apparently took precedence over friendship and agreement on fundamental issues. "It seems to me," Record gently wrote La Follette, "that you should now take the rest which you have so richly earned and leave the burden of this fight to be carried on by the rest of us." After further soothing the senator's ego and perhaps assuaging his own guilt as well, Record concluded that progressivism "has taken such a hold on the American people that *no man* can destroy it and *no man* can materially hinder its progress."[10] Of course, the real fear in the minds of men such as Kent, Pinchot, Johnson, and others was that one man—La Follette—could destroy the movement unless he withdrew and released his supporters.[11]

That release, excluding one misunderstanding, was never forthcoming. The special quality of martyrdom which comes from betrayal by one's friends sustained La Follette in his decision to continue a nominal candidacy. Certain of the "righteousness of his course," the senator chose vindication through history. "For the present," he wrote William Kent, "I must endure the pain and mortification attending upon the loss of political followers and even personal friends. But out of my trials I have been taught the lesson of fortitude and patience."[12] This was not the course of action desired by his friends, and Kent sadly concluded that the senator was "taking the wrong road to martyrdom."[13]

A similar assessment might have been made of TR's followers who bolted the GOP to start a third-party movement in August 1912. Some of the distinguished settlement house and social gospel reformers who attended the Bull Moose convention undoubtedly were caught up in the evangelistic fervor, camp meeting camaraderie, and crusading atmosphere that surrounded the Progressive party's birth. For others, however, the contagious euphoria that came from singing "The Battle Hymn of the Republic" and "Onward Christian Soldiers" did not survive the trip home. Some reformers had difficulty joining hands with the party's "money men"—conservative publishing tycoon Frank Munsey and J. P. Morgan partner George W. Perkins—and it must have been a chastening experience for all to realize that the Bull Moosers lacked any type of local, state, or national organization.

During the 1912 campaign there was a tendency among some journalists and voters alike to view the two progressive candidates, Roosevelt and Woodrow Wilson, his Democratic opponent, in remarkably similar terms and to argue that the differences between them were comparable to those between Tweedledum and Tweedledee. Of course, each man strongly dissented from this pronouncement. Their differences may indeed have narrowed as each moved closer to the political center in the campaign's concluding weeks, but the ideological distance between them remained great. Following the Republican convention, Roosevelt supporter Amos Pinchot declared that "the eternal and vital issue was whether the people . . . or the . . . great financial interests . . . shall hold the power of government."[14] That issue, as Pinchot probably realized, already had been partially resolved by the direction of the American economy since the 1880s; moreover, its moral overtone concealed a significant debate over the proper role of the state.

Roosevelt, as a result of his own experience while president and partly as a consequence of the influence of Munsey, Perkins, and journalist Herbert Croly, contended that concentrated economic power was inevitable and that competition was not always beneficial. He proposed a permanent system of government controls and planning to insure a more equitable and humane society for all groups. This "New Nationalism" differed markedly from the "New Freedom" espoused by Wilson and his closest adviser, Boston lawyer and onetime La Follette booster Louis D. Brandeis. They emphasized the gross inefficiency of trusts and monopoly and proposed the temporary intervention of government to eliminate special privilege and restore free competition.[15]

Naturally, there were varying degrees of loyalty and enthusiasm with which Roosevelt's and Wilson's followers espoused the party line. "As you know," George L. Record wrote TR, "I hold extremely radical notions, but I am always anxious in formulating our platform declarations . . . to put forward only such demands as there is a reasonable hope of accomplishing in the near future."[16] Though appointed to the Bull Moose party's educational arm, the Progressive Service, and named director of its Popular Government department, Record never gained access to the party's elite circle of decision-makers. Roosevelt did not trust the man he considered an "ultra-progressive," who "could be used and admired, but not followed, except with extreme caution."[17] The fate of the Bull Moosers was not, as Record realized, to stand at Armageddon and do battle for the Lord, but to work for TR's more earthly ambitions. Roosevelt respected his colleague's commitment, intelligence, and sincerity but not his loyalty to either the party or its leader. Though himself guilty of the most notorious kind of party irregularity, TR could not understand

Record's peculiar disregard of institutional ties or his willingness to sacrifice party loyalty for ideological concerns. Roosevelt also believed that "some of [Record's] plans are so wild that he tends to alienate men from the movement."[18] Those plans were also completely at odds with the New Nationalism. Record urged TR openly to attack the trusts, proposed temporary governmental intervention to destroy special privilege, and drew attention to the evil of concentrated wealth. No wonder Roosevelt ignored him—Record sounded just like Wilson!

"The reason I am for the Progressive party," observed Amos Pinchot, "is that [it] is an economic rather than a political force in this country."[19] No doubt, Pinchot believed these sentiments and acted on them in his own unsuccessful race for Congress as a Progressive candidate. His new party was, after all, ahead of the competition in advocacy of child labor reform, old age pensions, minimum wage legislation, factory safety inspection, workmen's compensation, and the eight-hour day. But, as one of Pinchot's socialist critics tellingly observed, such reforms, which aimed at ameliorating economic conditions as well as those emphasizing direct democracy, were mere palliatives. Industrial justice would never be achieved unless the causes of those conditions were eliminated. "The Progressive Party," noted an unimpressed socialist, "will never give the working class industrial or economic justice . . . since it is not willing to do away with the system of production and distribution which makes economic injustice possible and necessary."[20] The fact that many Progressives paid lip service to the rhetoric of social change without seriously considering its consequences underlined the inherent contradiction of their program. Repeated political reversals never led them to evaluate the real cause of their ineffectiveness. Such internal cohesion may have been personally reassuring but was politically disastrous.

The more radical Progressives such as Pinchot, Record, political scientist Charles E. Merriam of the University of Chicago, and Charles V. McCarthy of the Wisconsin Legislative Reference Library believed their party faced disintegration unless a definite and coherent set of demands was formulated. This feeling was especially evident following Woodrow Wilson's election, and the issue most central to the radicals' concerns was the regulation of big business. One man, George W. Perkins, the "dough" man of the Bull Moose campaign, and a member of the Board of Directors of U.S. Steel and of International Harvester, stood squarely in the path of economic reform and meaningful social change.

A strongly worded plank favoring equal competition and strict enforcement of the Sherman Antitrust Act had emerged from committee during the Progressive convention, as had a variation emphasizing the inevitability of economic concentration and the desirability of regulation by federal commission. For reasons still unclear, though some Progressives blamed Perkins's blue pencil, only a compromise plank without reference to the Sherman Antitrust Act reached the public's attention during the campaign.[21] The radicals or "ultra-progressives," as TR called them, bombarded the former president with demands that Perkins be removed as chairman of the National Executive Committee, that the "missing" antitrust clause be reinstated (which it was), and that the party reaffirm its unshakable and fundamental commitment "to destroy privilege and fight an oppressive industrial system."[22]

Roosevelt, whose faith in Perkins remained unshaken, staunchly defended his friend's "great organizing power" and financial generosity. He dismissed the controversy over the missing plank as an "utterly unimportant" detail which, even if included, would not have materially affected the outcome.[23] Rather, the Colonel attributed the party's defeat in part to the "ultra-progressives" whose extreme positions alienated moderate voters. Though clearly more comfortable with middle-of-the-road Bull Moosers, Roosevelt continued to pay lip service to the idea of a "radical" party. It was apparent, however, that the word had widely divergent meanings for TR and his Progressive critics. "In my judgment," he wrote Charles E. Merriam, it was "our clear duty to start a new permanent progressive party, a liberal party, a radical party—and therefore in the long run the only conservative party."[24] "We have no excuse," Roosevelt wrote Amos Pinchot, "for existing excepting as the radical party; but I want to keep it as the party of sane and tempered radicalism."[25]

In the immediate aftermath of the 1912 election the radical Progressives led by Pinchot and Record set out to capture control of their party from Munsey and Perkins, hopeful that TR would be a neutral arbiter. "I have seen enough of this movement," George L. Record wrote Merriam, "to believe that men like you and me, [Raymond] Robins and [Amos] Pinchot, can actually control [it] . . . if we go about it in a businesslike way." He suggested creating "a little insider coterie" who would formulate a program around a modified single tax, banking reform, and government ownership of railroads. Though aware that Perkins's role as a party spokesman was damaging, Record's instinct was "to keep everybody together" at least until after the radicals had a chance to gain control of the platform.[26] In the meantime, as he bluntly advised Roosevelt, the incidents involving Perkins and the platform underscored "a fact which exists and must continue to exist . . . that there will be two wings of the Progressive Party, the radical and the conservative."[27]

This ideological struggle concealed an equally troublesome conflict between the party's educators and organizers. The division, as John Gable notes in *The Bull Moose Years*, grew in seriousness as the party's finances and survival were imperiled. The debate, ostensibly a question pitting ultimate goals against immediate gains, was at heart a fight over the party's future direction.[28] Many radical Progressives, though committed to fundamental economic change, were not unmindful of the political imperatives of winning elections. Ideally, they would seek to formulate a far-reaching program of social change, sell it to the voters, and then implement their theories once in office. The New York City mayoralty election, scheduled for the fall of 1913, seemed to offer the best opportunity to chart the future.

The metropolitan New York faction of the radical Progressive nucleus included Pinchot, Record, and former Cleveland reformer Frederic C. Howe. A broader group of ideological sympathizers who periodically joined in support encompassed social gospeler John Haynes Holmes, watch manufacturer and single taxer Charles H. Ingersoll, political activist Benjamin C. Marsh, and New York City social work leader John A. Kingsbury. It was clearly a two-man movement, however, with Record and Pinchot providing most of the leadership and ideas. Their program, as it evolved during 1913, called for municipal ownership of public utilities, the exemption of buildings and personal property from taxation, government ownership of the railroads and natural resources, municipal home rule, and the destruction of "unnatural" or artificial combinations.

Few radicals anticipated an easy or rapid acceptance of their program. Though deeply committed to a realignment within the Progressive party, these men were not visionaries but opportunists seeking to take advantage of indecisiveness within the Bull Moose movement. Their advocacy of proposals then considered politically unacceptable was not representative of their intransigence or indicative of a willingness to polarize their party. "I do not want you to go away feeling that . . . some of . . . us have taken an extreme position," Amos Pinchot wrote Jane Addams, "and particularly that we do not understand the importance of the social and industrial program of the . . . party."[29] Men such as Pinchot and Record were diligent students of contemporary society. They understood that a decade of social reform had failed to remove the growing injustices in American life, and they believed the key to Progressive success rested with the elimination of economic inequality.[30] Anything less would leave Progressives vulnerable to charges of soft-peddling economic democracy and lead to the failure of the party. "We have been fighting sham battles . . . so long," Pinchot observed, "that it would be a comfort to get back to something real."[31]

As Progressives prepared for the 1913 elections, the radical nucleus, led by Pinchot and Record, aimed their propaganda campaign squarely at Roosevelt. From the beginning, the relationship between the radicals and the Colonel strained belief. On the one hand, there was TR, the conservative, patrician reformer, spokesman for a party with a divided conscience yet himself personally committed to seeking an accommodation with industrial capitalism; on the other hand, there was a small splinter group of radicals whose desire for fundamental economic change theoretically would turn the clock back a quarter-century. Neither side trusted the other nor denied their mutual suspicion, yet each in some arcane way needed the other. The radicals needed Roosevelt's glamour and popular appeal to legitimize their program among the party faithful, while TR, to a lesser extent, needed the radicals' acceptance of him as a genuine progressive.

The program to which Pinchot and Record hoped to tie Roosevelt called for the municipal ownership of utilities, home rule, a modified single tax, and, eventually, public ownership of natural resources. Such proposals probably placed these Bull Moosers on the outer edge of mainstream reform, but they were not socialists and would have gagged at that label. In fact, outside the confines of the Progressive party, few would have called them radicals. They believed in the restoration of free competition and the destruction of monopoly and special privilege, but their faith in an equitable capitalist system never faltered.

Roosevelt's career, as his biographer William H. Harbaugh suggests, was distinguished by occasional periods of compulsive, audacious, and bold behavior, while at other times he found it expedient to equivocate and temporize.[32] In the aftermath of the 1912 campaign, however, he displayed an unsettling tendency to combine both forms of behavior simultaneously with the result that confusion reigned within the party. This became evident early in 1913 as TR responded to platform proposals suggested by George L. Record. "The possible planks that you quote seem to me to be thoroughly sound," Roosevelt wrote Record. The Colonel endorsed municipal home rule, even going so far as to approve a modified version of the single tax and the municipal ownership of public utilities. But he cautioned his Progressive colleague that his letter was not for publication.[33]

Always the propagandist, Record ignored Roosevelt's hedging and kept hammering away at the inadequacy of the current Progressive program. "Wilson," he told TR, "will hold the center of the stage for eight years, if only surface questions are to be the subject of politics." The only way to defeat the president, Record argued, would be "to put forward gradually but surely a fundamental program."[34] The 1912 platform was "too indefinite" and "too scattered" to form the basis for a permanent organization. Record's solution lay in the "land question," which he predicted was "about to spring into a political issue . . . all over the U.S."[35] Roosevelt's willingness to endorse, or at least consider, such proposals depended upon confining their discussion to the local level. "I would fight tooth and nail anything," he wrote Record, "that could be tortured into a statement that we are for the single tax in State or Nation, because it would unify the entire farm vote against us." Timidity, TR assured Record, was not the source of his caution but rather uncertainty concerning the single tax's actual benefit for "poor people." But he added, "I am absolutely with you that we must stand for fundamental reforms in the interests of the mass of working people, and under no circumstances for mugwump measures merely in the interests of the taxpayers."[36]

The 1913 New York City mayoralty race offered an accessible test case for the implementation of radical Progressive ideas. Concurrently but not coincidentally, a small number of reformers began testing public opinion concerning a modified version of the single tax. In May two groups, the New York City Congestion Committee and an unnamed "businessman's" organization, enlisted support for a referendum that would reduce the municipal tax rate on buildings to one-half the tax on land. The membership of these two groups was notable for the number of radical Progressives whose names were linked to both organizations: Benjamin C. Marsh, executive director of the Committee on Congestion of Population, was a member of both groups; he was joined on the Congestion Committee by John Haynes Holmes of the Church of the Messiah and Frederic C. Howe, then director of the People's Institute, a community-action group that sponsored a public forum at Cooper Union and other educational activities. The businessmen's organization included its nominal chairman, Amos Pinchot, single-tax advocate Charles H. Ingersoll, and several local merchants. Frederic C. Howe struck the keynote for both groups: "We talk about bankruptcy and lack of city credit and yet we give away each year at least $100 million in the speculative increase of land values which the growth of the community creates. . . . New York," he concluded, "could pay a large part of its present budget out of land speculation profits alone if it only taxed land and exempted buildings."[37]

Although the press reported that several thousand New Yorkers signed the tax-exemption petitions, the movement barely got off the ground. The single tax not only represented a radical challenge, but symbolized that mysterious netherworld of economics, a discipline which seemed beyond the comprehension of most citizens. Moving swiftly to nip this campaign in its early development, the *New York Times* editorialized that "no general tax can affect values due to specific considerations." Perhaps more importantly, the editors warned that the city could not afford a reduction in tax revenue and that any increase would be felt most severely by renters. In a gratuitous slap in the face, the *Times* added that "nobody is under compulsion to pay rent in New York."[38]

It is likely, in view of the New York Progressives' disposition toward a fusion campaign for the mayoralty, that party leaders decided to deemphasize controversial issues. By July, Progressive moderates were pressuring their more radical colleagues to tone down their demands for the sake of party harmony. The time was not yet "right" for discussion of either municipal ownership of public utilities or the single tax. "At some future time public sentiment may be ready, but just now," according to the party line, "it is absolutely essential that all honest men should get together irrespective of their views . . . to save the city." One embittered radical, utility expert Delos F. Wilcox, observed that the effect of such collegial advice was to stifle political agitation so that the time would "never be ripe for municipal ownership or the single tax unless we [radicals] help to ripen it."[39]

Even sympathetic Bull Moosers such as Chester H. Rowell, a Progressive National Committee member from California and editor-publisher of the *Fresno Republican*, were ambivalent toward the radical program. Rowell was especially sensitive to the situation in New York City. The object of any fusion campaign, he realized, was the defeat of Tammany Hall. Such efforts usually were mounted by gentlemen reformers who "have no other objection to Tammany [than] . . . their fastidious repugnance to its vulgarity and bad taste." Compared with the machine's empathy and identification with the workers, such "kid-glove and silk-stocking reformers" were no match. "But if you go to the people with a proposition which will decrease rents and make light, heat, water, and transportation cheaper and better, and which will socially appeal to their class sense of resentment against exploitation," Rowell told Amos Pinchot, "you can ultimately get their support." Though this is exactly what the radical program envisioned, Rowell doubted whether any city had a class of men "intellectually outside . . . bourgeois limitations and financially independent" enough to prevent economic change from degenerating into revolution.[40]

Putting Rowell's fears aside, New York's radical Progressives were much more concerned that the fusion candidate should stand for a few important issues. They feared that the platform agreed to by the Citizens' Municipal Committee, a temporary coalition of various reform groups, might become a "silly," "talky" encyclopedic work. Radicals such as Pinchot wanted to specify a few issues and then ask the candidates whether they "would play ball or not."[41] Indeed, the Progressives let it be known that their party would not support a traditional "good-government" crusade. "The fight must be on issues far more vital than the old slogan of 'milk-diet' reform, 'we're good and they're bad, so vote for us.' "[42]

Those sentiments did not survive the nomination of independent Democrat John Purroy Mitchel as fusion candidate. "I have seen," Harold L. Ickes observed, "that Mitchel has been selected . . . on a platform that is *against* Tammany but *for* nothing in particular." Of course, that was not entirely true. Amos Pinchot might have written his Chicago colleague that the fusionists supported free lunches for children, "patent garbage cans," and if one looked carefully in the platform, he was sure there were probably directions on how to build a birch bark canoe.[43] "I wish," Ickes wrote, that "the fusionists could have stood for municipal ownership of public utilities. On such an issue one could afford to lose while on a merely anti-Tammany issue one cannot afford to win."[44]

Ickes's point proved most perceptive and his fears well grounded. Radical Progressives were deeply disappointed but perhaps not completely surprised either by the choice of candidate or the liberal tent which passed for a platform. "You once told me," Amos Pinchot wrote William Kent, "that the first lesson we all must learn was to eat dirt. I have eaten enough dirt in New York to make a good-sized vegetable garden."[45] Pinchot did not believe that Mitchel's election would have any measurable impact upon the people or upon the utility magnates and financiers who controlled the city. "When his reform administration is over," Pinchot predicted, the "people will be as poor as ever. They will pay just as much for transportation, gas, and electric light, probably more." In fact, like Ickes, Pinchot could see better days ahead if the Tammany candidate, Judge Edward E. McCall, was elected and then discredited. Mitchel was a good man but too preoccupied with efficiency, accounting, and budgetary problems, and too ambitious to risk offending New York's power brokers.[46]

Mitchel's election did little to dissuade Pinchot from his original conviction. In fact, he was more convinced than ever that monopoly could not be regulated by governmental commissions at any level. Natural monopolies relating to water power, electricity, and transportation should be owned and operated by the government. Artificial or private monopolies, he believed, should be destroyed; the key to economic democracy lay in recognizing that monopoly could not be regulated in the public interest.[47]

The hollow Progressive victory in the New York City fusion election symbolized a genuine lack of progress nationally for the Bull Moose movement. One year after the momentous stand at Armageddon, the glamour and excitement began to fade. Roosevelt started spending longer periods of time out of the country, and even his optimistic predictions could not disguise the party's visible organizational and financial deficiencies, which grew worse with each passing day. George W. Perkins and his radical critics continued their struggle throughout 1913, and though they tried to avoid public recriminations, their differences shortly became public knowledge. Forthcoming congressional elections in 1914 promised neither victory nor vindication, even though some of the party's brightest stars were scheduled to run. Progressive leaders discussed amalgamation, a subject most summarily dismissed only a year earlier.

The threats of fusion and amalgamation stirred the most anxiety among radical Progressives like Amos Pinchot and George L. Record, who lacked a viable alternative. Sensing, perhaps, that they might never again enjoy such ready access to potential power, the radicals launched another in a long line of "last efforts" to redirect their party's focus toward fundamental economic change. "It is obvious," Record wrote TR, "that we can never build up a party as a mere faction of the Republican party, and we can never attract the Democrats as long as one of their great fundamental principles is in adherence to the protective . . . tariff."[48] Roosevelt, beginning his final campaign as a Bull Mooser, though cordial as always, no longer was willing to debate the merits of radical proposals. He dismissed the single tax and municipal ownership of utilities and reaffirmed his commitment to government regulation as "the only sane view."[49] In many ways TR portrayed the debate within the Progressive party as a struggle between the opposite poles of sanity and lunacy. The future direction of his thinking had been evident back in March 1913 when he compared the avant-garde works of the Cubists, Futurists, and Near-Impressionists at the famous Sixty-Ninth Regiment Armory modern art exhibition to the "lunatic fringe" of the progressive movement.[50]

Throughout the summer and fall of 1913, Pinchot and Record futilely attempted to delay the inevitable amalgamation of the Progressives and Republicans by calling upon Roosevelt to renounce any interest in the GOP's 1916 presidential nomination.[51] Realistically, it was preposterous and impractical, as TR noted, to make such a categorical denial concerning a hypothetical matter so far in advance. The radicals, of course, were not interested in fairness or practicality for anyone but themselves. "I see TR is carefully firming things up," Amos Pinchot wrote his brother, Gifford, "so as to be the candidate of the Republican and Progressive parties." Amos, who was then moving toward his own political Armageddon, was concerned that the Colonel's statements were unfairly distorting his group's program. "He must know . . . that we do not intend to break up business or return to smaller units of production. . . . By the time he gets back [from South America], he will have framed us up as a bunch of maniacs trying to tear down every factory larger than a corner grocery." And, Pinchot acknowledged, "he is putting this over, too, for people do not understand the difference between fighting monopoly and fighting business on a large scale."[52]

Was there really a difference? Undoubtedly, the radicals were convinced, but these true believers needed to educate a much broader spectrum of the public, many of whom had grown weary of calls for the "destruction of privilege" and the "triumph of social justice." Radical Progressives like Pinchot and Record needed a new cause, one that would set them apart from opponents both within and outside their party. That issue required a personal, more concrete dimension, preferably with clearly defined villains, a readily understandable solution, and a dynamic new advocate. But try as they might to infuse the abolition of private monopoly with dramatic intensity, the radicals still found themselves attacking such abstract, impersonal institutions as the "money trust," the utilities, and railroads.[53] These were not issues that galvanized public opinion, nor were they likely to produce voter recognition for new Progressive leaders.

Once TR removed himself as a possible convert to the radical cause, Pinchot and Record hoped that Amos's brother, Gifford, former chief forester during the Roosevelt and Taft years, might use his 1914 candidacy for the U.S. Senate from Pennsylvania as a forum for the radical program. Both men tried to reassure the elder Pinchot that a campaign dedicated to the destruction of private monopoly would not be burdened with "technical explanations" or the "single tax of the long haired variety" but would reveal the vital links between the trusts and state political bosses, such as Pennsylvania's Boies Penrose.[54] Unfortunately, mixing family and politics proved an embarrassment for both brothers. Though Gifford considered himself "plenty radical for the present purpose," he was more cautious and conservative than his brother and, unlike Amos, personally devoted to Roosevelt.[55] Rather than jeopardize Gifford's chances, which were heavily dependent upon TR's personal appearances in his behalf, Record and Amos Pinchot backed away from using the Pennsylvania campaign as a sounding board for government ownership. "Frankly," Amos wrote Gifford, "I am not at all sure that a radical campaign . . . is wise . . . and perhaps this (fighting the big fight) can be done better by electing somebody first and putting out a program later."[56] But the younger Pinchot remained convinced that the only way to make Roosevelt choose the radical course was to force a fundamental difference of opinion on the Progressive party. "If something like this doesn't happen," he wrote California Progressive Francis J. Heney, "the Colonel will . . . drift back among the safe and sane, and all of us who believe in fundamentals will be left on a sandbar, where we will rot, join the Democrats, or become some kind of political osteopaths."[57]

Repeated Progressive party defeats during 1913 and 1914 revealed the wide discrepancy that existed between public acceptance of a Roosevelt-led party and voter responsiveness to such advanced economic proposals as the single tax and municipal ownership. Though the combined vote of Roosevelt, Wilson, and Eugene V. Debs in the 1912 election had apparently legitimized collectivist approaches on some aspects of public policy, the two years following the campaign demonstrated the political danger of any appeal which strayed from the status quo. Socialism did not emerge as a powerful political force nor did Progressive voters seem prepared to move further left.[58] The party's repeated disappointments at the polls reinforced Roosevelt's mistrust of the radicals' approach. No one within the party doubted that this suspicion was mutual, but few anticipated the extent of the bitterness or the lengths to which the radicals might go to seek recourse. Few radicals were more passionately committed to a new direction for the Progressive party than Amos Pinchot. A convert to the antimonopoly creed espoused by his friend Record, Pinchot emerged from the 1912 election as a tenacious, disciplined advocate of atomistic or competitive capitalism.[59] By the spring of 1914, Pinchot was at the edge of open revolt with his party. "I have done all I could to make the [Progressive] leaders . . . feel that the independence of the party from trust influence was really worth fighting for." But, as he told an old friend, newspaperman Gilson Gardner, there was only "one play left" and that was to contact the party's national committee enclosing his recommendations and warn that unless action was taken he would go public with his allegations. "I am heartily sick of it," he confessed. "It is rather pitiful business."[60] Still, as he told his brother, "declaring war against private monopoly . . . is the one great issue of the time."[61]

Pinchot's letter to Chairman Joseph M. Dixon and members of the Progressive National Committee combined an indictment of George W. Perkins with a muckraking exposé of U.S. Steel's antilabor activities and a call to action in the fight against industrial monopoly. The attack on Perkins was a caustic denunciation of the executive committee chairman's probusiness sympathies, from his vigorous opposition to the Sherman Antitrust Act during the 1912 campaign to his use of the party's organ, the *Progressive Bulletin*, to defend the trusts and glorify his own role as a business statesman. Pinchot condemned the hypocrisy of standing forth as an advocate of "social and industrial justice" while allowing party affairs to be manipulated by a genuine apologist of monopoly. "Our party," he concluded, cannot attempt "to be all things to all men. We must take sides in the struggle between democracy and privilege—and we must make it clear as sunlight which side we have taken."[62]

The response to Pinchot's broadside, which was later leaked to the press, made it clear that many Progressives, while sympathetic with his arguments, were nonetheless deeply upset by the public airing of a family squabble. Few, however, would have used the term "family" to describe relations within the party. Significantly, the rival factions of educators and organizers did not maintain any consensus on this matter. Instead, a wide range of individual responses surfaced ranging from a few unqualified endorsements of Pinchot's position to those Progressives, such as Senator Albert J. Beveridge of Indiana, who dismissed the letter as "utterly stupid" and treasonous.[63]

Typically, TR's response was equally plain. While on route to Spain in early June, he wired a note of total support to George W. Perkins. Arriving home at the end of the month, he declared that if Perkins was driven from the party, "they will have to read me out, too."[64] Throughout the remainder of 1914, and especially following the Progressives' horrendous electoral results, Roosevelt took an increasingly harder line toward his party's radicals. "It is my deliberate judgment," he wrote Kansas Progressive William Allen White, "that the party in the East would have gone out of existence if it had not been for Perkins, and most assuredly . . . if the people . . . got any idea that we were standing for men like Amos Pinchot and [George L.] Record as against Perkins."[65] In a letter to Hiram W. Johnson, one of the very few Progressives elected or returned to office, Roosevelt had Pinchot and Record in mind when he described the party's "wild-eyed fanatics" who were "apt to betray the men with whom they work in crisis, assuring themselves that they are doing it for the glory of the Lord." Roosevelt accused Pinchot of tarnishing the party's image by associating with radical labor leaders such as William D. "Big Bill" Haywood of the Industrial Workers of the World "and men of that stamp who openly champion dynamiting, anarchy, and murder."[66]

Through it all, Amos Pinchot managed to maintain his sense of humor. Responding to an editorial in *Collier's Weekly* supporting his brother's Senate campaign, he thanked editor Mark Sullivan "even if your method . . . is to try to mitigate [Gifford's] misfortune in having a 'cubist' brother like me." And though he gently needled Sullivan about *Collier's* increasingly moderate ("square") direction and as "a publication of only two dimensions—length and thickness," he thanked him for supporting Gifford's election and offered to consign the rest of his "frazzled reputation to still lower depths" to aid his brother's cause.[67]

The invective, hostility, and condemnation heaped upon Pinchot in the aftermath of the Perkins affair may have had a positive side in sharply defining differences within Progressive ranks. There is some question, however, over the effectiveness of Pinchot's challenge. George E. Mowry contends that Pinchot's letter catalyzed "latent hostility" to Perkins who "never again was . . . fully trusted by a large group in the party."[68] Helene M. Hooker, editor of Pinchot's *History of the Progressive Party*, concludes that Pinchot was the real loser, that he totally misread the reaction of his colleagues, and that in the end he, rather than Perkins, was forced out of the party. Division within the party was evident from the time of the 1912 convention, and Pinchot's departure was inevitable given his preference for the antimonopoly program of the New Freedom rather than the New Nationalism's dependence upon government regulation of the trusts. The Perkins affair did make it easier for all the parties to go their separate ways: Perkins and Roosevelt would gradually make their tortuous way back to the GOP, while the radicals like Pinchot and Record moved closer to the Wilson administration.

The radicals still found it exceedingly difficult to leave a party which genuinely did not want them. Even though TR had dismissed him as a party traitor, George L. Record intrepidly resumed his correspondence

with the Colonel. Incredibly, yet not unexpectedly, the New Jersey reformer presumptuously offered his own views on the 1914 New York
gubernatorial question. The Progressive party was badly divided over
the fusion question. Nationally, Roosevelt counseled against amalgamation with either party unless the Republicans or Democrats endorsed
the 1912 Bull Moose platform of social and industrial democracy. But in
New York, TR recommended fusion around an antimachine, good-government campaign. Record, like many Bull Moosers, considered anti-
bossism much too inadequate a basis upon which to run a campaign.
Mere "honesty," he wrote TR, will not destroy the boss system. "My
main suggestion is that in as dramatic and effective a way as possible
. . . you . . . push to the front as the main issue, the adoption of a genuine
primary law, as the instrument by which the 'boss system' is to be
destroyed."[69]

Though significant differences remained between them, Record agreed
with Roosevelt that "the thing to do is to smite the enemy and not pass
resolutions," particularly when party principles "don't amount to anything anyway."[70] He saw no reason to pledge the party to a meaningless
platform or to oppose the nomination of a progressive Republican. It
would have been far different if the party stood for something of importance such as municipal ownership or the single tax, but that was
not the case in 1914. Record sensed his party's rapidly declining influence. "One thing you ought to keep clearly in mind," he wrote Amos
Pinchot: "The Progressive party is dead. . . . There is very little for us to
do this year except not to be caught scuttling the ship, and keep as close
to TR as possible so that after the election we can push our ideas to the
front." He encouraged his colleagues to support the direct primary as
the key campaign issue in New York State. Such a step would "keep
us where we can have influence with Roosevelt, instead of getting him
completely disgusted with us as a lot of impractical fanatics."[71]

Record was especially sensitive to TR's charge that he had betrayed
the party in New Jersey and had joined the Democrats. President Wilson
was, after all, an old and friendly rival, and the two men had worked
closely during Wilson's early days as governor. Record confessed that
he approved of certain administration measures but hastened to assure
Roosevelt that "they were in no sense a solution of our industrial problems."[72] Still, Record had no qualms in sharing his advice with both
reform leaders. Writing to the president early in May 1914, he warned
Wilson to expect an outpouring of public outrage following the expected
passage of a treaty indemnifying Colombia for the seizure of Panama
during the Roosevelt administration. He also praised the president's
handling of the tariff, currency, and Mexican situations: "You are so
unquestionably right, that nothing but bad times can prevent discussion
of these issues resulting in an endorsement of your position."[73] Not

surprisingly, Record did not call TR's attention to his correspondence with another old New Jersey friend, Wilson's personal secretary, Joseph P. Tumulty, especially since the subject concerned the Democratic party's chances in New York State. Typically uninhibited over crossing party lines, Record offered Tumulty the same advice he had given TR. Instead of seeking the elimination of Republican boss William Barnes through advocacy of direct primary legislation, Record recommended using the same strategy against Tammany's Charles F. Murphy.[74]

Intentional deception, however, was never a significant part of Record's relationship with Roosevelt. Long before the fall elections, he predicted to the Colonel that the party would not survive its "pitiful showing." "If this proves to be the fact, then we must all go somewhere to continue our fight." But where? Record urged a series of postelection conferences and pledged that he would not leave the party until after a thorough discussion of the alternatives.[75] In the meantime, he intended to stay as close to TR as possible, hoping, as he told Pinchot, either to make the Colonel "become the real leader of the genuine radicals" or force him "out of the game."[76]

Amos Pinchot viewed the party's failure as reflecting the "futility of superficial reform." It was not defeat itself that upset him but rather the party's neglect in providing the public with something they "could really believe in and care about." He had no doubts that a platform calling for the single tax, municipal ownership of utilities, and nationalization of the railroads would have produced the same miserable results, but at least Progressives "would have had something left to continue fighting for."[77]

Neither Pinchot nor Record had any illusions about the party's future, nor were they oblivious to their strained relations with Roosevelt. However, they must have been surprised by the unusually bitter response evoked by their calls for a more radical party. Even before the postmortems at the party's December 1914 meeting, TR's correspondence bristled with personal attacks aimed squarely at the two radical Progressives. Writing to Edwin A. Van Valkenburg, editor of the Philadelphia *North American*, Roosevelt dismissed Pinchot as an ex-Progressive whose "preposterous attitude" was unworthy of recognition. Both he and Record, "the appointee of a Democratic Governor," should be "publicly and emphatically" ignored and their connection with the party severed.[78] Less than a week later TR again vented his anger, this time at Pinchot alone, whom he disparagingly called a "parlor socialist" lacking "enough capacity for coherent thought to make him a Socialist." Once more Roosevelt dismissed his radical critic as "utterly impotent" and a "treacherous friend" who must not be allowed within the party ever again.[79] Roosevelt was convinced that the enormity of the party's electoral disaster stemmed from an inability to attract the support of

solid, small businessmen and other "good citizens" who had been alienated by "unbalanced radicals" and "men of wild theories."[80]

Roosevelt's nonattendance at the Progressives' December meeting was
revealing. It reflected his postelection pessimism but also suggested an
attempt at disassociation. Though on record as favoring a restatement
of the party's 1912 principles, TR did not seek to force such views on
the Chicago meeting's participants. He practically ignored the social-
welfare aspects of the New Nationalism and stressed the interrelation-
ship of the protective tariff and prosperity.[81] Though the Progressive
National Committee disclaimed any intention of disbanding, rumors of
wholesale defections were rampant.

No one was more prescient in predicting the denouement of the Progressive party than George L. Record. Unfortunately, his assessment of
the radicals' relations with Roosevelt also proved correct. The party was
dead; TR had been forced out of the game but not before expressing his
complete disgust for the movement's "impractical fanatics." Perhaps
because there were no real winners in this battle, one can understand
Record's willingness to try yet again to convert Roosevelt to the radical
position. What is surprising is that Roosevelt renewed their unusual cat-
and-mouse relationship. Though TR came to despise Amos Pinchot,
Record remained on cordial, even friendly terms with the Colonel, their
relationship devoid of animosity or recrimination. Unlike Pinchot, with
whom he shared a common political outlook, Record exercised greater
patience, displayed more deference, and proceeded much more cautiously in dealing with men such as Roosevelt, La Follette, and Wilson.
He cultivated the political elite, knew when to soothe egos, ignored or
overlooked personal attacks, and always was eager for the next battle.

Their widely divergent backgrounds may offer some insight into each
man's distinctive behavior. Record grew up in rural Maine in circumstances which precluded a carefree childhood. Odd jobs helped him
earn his way through Bates College, and a brief stint as a legal steno-
grapher in New York City paid the rent while he studied law. In 1887,
the twenty-eight-year-old Record was admitted to the New Jersey bar
and established a law practice in Jersey City. Originally a Democrat, he
grew weary of battling the party's extremely provincial Irish-Catholic
machine in Hudson County. In 1896, Record did an about-face and
turned Republican, ostensibly out of disgust with William Jennings
Bryan's free silver campaign, but probably because the GOP offered the
prospect of more rapid political advancement for a Yankee Protestant.
His "overnight" success actually took fourteen years, during which time
he built up a law practice, served on the local school board, worked as
a counsel for the state riparian commission, and paid his political dues
by volunteering to run for state senate from an overwhelmingly Democratic district. His reward was appointment as Jersey City corporation

counsel under the city's new, young Republican mayor, Mark M. Fagan. From 1902 to 1908, these two men attracted national attention and joined the ranks of urban reformers across America in the fight for the equal taxation of railroad property and the regulation of public utilities. The struggle to eliminate corporate tax-dodging and special privilege led Fagan and Record to join other progressive Republicans across New Jersey in the "New Idea" movement, which lobbied for home rule, tax reform, and, ultimately, the municipal operation and ownership of public utilities. Though Fagan was defeated in his bid for a fourth term, Record continued as a major reform ideologue, characteristically ignoring party lines. He played a critical role in Woodrow Wilson's election as governor in 1910, helped draft two significant pieces of legislation for the Democratic administration, but continued to stay active within progressive Republican circles. In 1911 he participated in the formation of the National Progressive Republican League and began his mercurial relationship with La Follette and Roosevelt.[82]

Amos Richards Eno Pinchot emerged from quite different circumstances. Born into a family of substantial wealth and pedigree, Pinchot was raised in the fashionable neighborhood across from Manhattan's Gramercy Park. He spent his summers vacationing in Europe or at the family's homes in Connecticut and Pennsylvania. He was educated at Saint George's School in Newport, Rhode Island, and family tradition dictated his enrollment at Yale, from which he was graduated in 1897 at the age of twenty-four. Law studies at Columbia University were interrupted by an impetuous enlistment during the Spanish-American War. Finishing his legal training at New York Law School, Pinchot was admitted to the bar in 1900, but it took only a year as a deputy assistant district attorney for him to realize that law was not satisfying enough for his life's work.

Socially, the cultivated young attorney belonged to the best clubs. He volunteered his time, money, and name to a variety of good causes but barely scratched the surface of his intellect and felt very much the dilettante following in the wake of his famous brother Gifford's rising political prominence. Ironically, his brother's involvement in the Ballinger-Pinchot affair, a controversy over conservation policy and cause célèbre during the Taft administration, changed all that, and the younger Pinchot acquired an eye-opening political education and an insider's intimacy with some of the nation's most prominent and powerful intellectuals and politicians. Though he would ultimately attack his own privileged class for its exploitive manipulation of the masses, Pinchot's approach to reform was deeply influenced by his patrician background. Pinchot possessed an aristocrat's certainty of the correctness of his actions, and his familiarity with the power elite occasionally made him contemptuous of those who disagreed with his opinions. But where

Record resorted to flattery and cajolery, the tools of the outsider, Pinchot's disappointment over the failure to convert his own kind elicited an insider's angry ridicule.[83]

In private Record often used language as emotionally charged as Pinchot's. Many politicians found the New Jersey reformer's personality annoyingly dogmatic, unyielding, and occasionally unbearable. But he usually was under control, especially around those whom he wished to influence. Record might call TR "crazy" and "nonsensical" but never to his face or to anyone who might reveal such opinions.[84] In December 1914, Roosevelt finally rejected Record's proposal that he lead the Progressives back into the Republican party "to make a fight for more radical policies than we have yet touched." Yet the Colonel acknowledged his radical critic "was most kind and friendly in all he had to say about me personally and has been so throughout."[85] Pinchot, on the other hand, seemed recklessly eager to destroy whatever remained of his friendship with TR, as if he were trying to prove that his own personal commitment to progressivism was the equal of Roosevelt's.

The lingering death of the Progressive party after 1914 led the two radicals, almost by default, to move closer to the Wilson administration. Having failed to capture control of the Bull Moose party, Pinchot and Record really had nowhere else to turn. Though both men supported the New Freedom's emphasis on the restoration of free competition and were admirers of the president, serious problems accompanied their political detour. They were not Democrats, and, in spite of Record's unique relationship with Wilson, their suggestions and advice would always be suspect. As outsiders they would not have access to the party's policymakers, nor would they be welcome inside Democratic circles. A problem of more serious long-term concern was also taking shape. The belief in direct democracy and a more equitable distribution of wealth and power, two ideals which had been the linchpin of reform, were slowly becoming obsolete. Promises to eliminate the causes of privilege—monopoly and unfair business practices—would gradually be replaced by a more sophisticated emphasis upon efficiency and government regulation. Recognizing that monopolies were unlikely to disappear, the Wilson administration discarded the New Freedom's antitrust direction and substituted the New Nationalism's belief in scientific expertise to reduce the waste that accompanied social injustice.

In 1915, however, few of these trends were well defined. Both Pinchot and Record still had hopes that the recently created Federal Trade Commission (1914), which combined features of Roosevelt's and Wilson's philosophies, might actually remove the causes of monopoly and restore equality of opportunity. Their interest in the FTC deepened when the White House leaked word that the president anticipated nominating Record to a vacancy on the commission. For a few short weeks in February it seemed that these two Bull Moose renegades might yet find a home for their ideas—ironically inside the federal bureaucracy. Amos Pinchot alerted friends across the country to contact any senator who would fight for Record's nomination: "I would rather see him on that Commission than even Brandeis." Pinchot told an old friend that "if Record isn't kept out of the job by the railroads, it will mean that government ownership and the whole radical program . . . will be materially advanced."[86] That chance never presented itself. Record's name was not sent to the Senate for confirmation, and there is doubt whether Wilson intended to submit the appointment. It is unclear whether the president was testing the political waters with a trial balloon or merely paying Record a compliment by acknowledging his consideration for the vacancy.[87] Two other possible reasons suggest themselves: Wilson intended to make the appointment but was surprised by the strength of conservative opposition, or he saw the specter of Record on the commission as guaranteeing the nomination of another candidate once he appeared to be backing down on so radical a choice.[88]

The FTC episode symbolized Pinchot's and Record's powerlessness in dealing with the Wilson administration. Both men were incapable of influencing events in which they were either participants or interested observers. They wrote letters, attended meetings, and lobbied friends on Capitol Hill, but in the end they were victims of circumstances beyond their control. It was as if there was a public level of discussion to which Pinchot and Record responded and another level beyond their reach where the real decisions were made. They might occasionally achieve notoriety but rarely succeeded in translating such publicity into political influence. Having given up a secure but narrow base of operations in a dying political party, the Bull Moose radicals temporarily settled for a token position on the outer limits of an established party. Their new position was less satisfying and equally frustrating, but it was the only game in town.

An indefatigable spirit and seemingly inexhaustible energy supply sustained the radical Progressives into the spring of 1915. Concerned that the frequency of attacks upon Wilson's antitrust program might endanger the president's chances for reelection, Pinchot passed some advice along to William Kent, an old friend from the La Follette campaign and now a Democratic congressman from California. The president, Pinchot suggested, should make people understand that his program was not designed to take U.S. Steel back to the blacksmith stage or to turn railroads into stagecoaches. "If he would only show that he is fighting monopoly . . . and nothing else, no one could attack him."[89] Wilson's failure to convince the people that his antitrust program would not mean "war on . . . business" allowed his enemies to exaggerate administration goals. The president, Pinchot warned Frank Cobb of the

New York World, has been "marked for slaughter." His only solution lay in distinguishing antimonopoly from anticombination and in supporting government ownership of transportation as the best means to insure efficient, competitive industry.[90]

Time and again, Record and Pinchot returned to government ownership as being indispensable for the restoration of equal competition. All available funds, Pinchot told progressive publishing tycoon E. W. Scripps, should be spent in educating the public and especially organized labor to the evils of industrial monopoly. By the fall of 1915, however, a disappointed Pinchot conceded that the Wilson administration had failed to teach the people the differences between democracy and privilege. "Today, any man that talks against privilege is considered more an ass than he was when Wilson came into office."[91] Perhaps the task was more than one man could handle; even Pinchot in a lighter moment pleaded facetiously that he, too, was only a human being, "even if [he] was for a short time a slender pillar of the progressive party."[92]

Such disappointments were minor setbacks whose pain was eased by compassionate but equally driven colleagues. Frederic C. Howe, one of the original La Follette supporters, a partner of Pinchot's in the abortive New York City single-tax movement, and Commissioner of Immigration for the Port of New York under Wilson, raised the radical standard early in the new year. In a vague yet typically ambitious letter, Howe proposed that a meeting of "radical-minded persons" draft a national progressive program for the consideration of reformers across the nation.[93] It is characteristic of the radical Progressives' experiences that even if such a gathering had occurred, it would have emphasized ideas rather than organization.

Though professing interest in Howe's ideas, Pinchot's sole political concern early in 1916 lay in insuring Wilson's reelection, preferably following the president's rededication to the importance of competitive capitalism. "I sincerely hope," he wrote Wilson, "that you will make us all understand that political democracy alone does not mean democracy, that economic power is the great power of the world, and while this is in the hands of a few people . . . there will be no real democracy."[94]

The radical Progressives could only hope that the president would come around to their way of thinking; there was no other alternative. After the Republicans selected Supreme Court Justice Charles Evans Hughes and TR declined the Progressive party's nomination, Wilson became the reformers' only hope for achieving economic democracy and maintaining American peace in a world being torn apart by war. Though many ex-Bull Moosers, such as Gifford Pinchot, Harold L. Ickes, and Raymond Robins, followed Roosevelt back into the GOP, a number of others, among them Ben Lindsey, Edward P. Costigan, and Francis J. Heney, supported the president. Their reasons touched both domestic and diplomatic concerns, but they also shared a deep, abiding resentment toward TR, whom they held responsible for manipulating, deceiving, and finally deserting them at the 1916 Bull Moose convention. No one was more caustic or biting in ridiculing the Colonel than Amos Pinchot. During the campaign, he served as vice-president of the "Wilson-[Samuel] Seabury League" in New York City and did extensive work for the "Wilson Volunteers," a group of independents, Democrats, and friends of the president who barnstormed New York State by automobile.[95] Some of those who joined this effort, such as Frederic C. Howe, Rabbi Stephen Wise, and Norman Hapgood, were men who placed progressive priorities ahead of party loyalty. They moved within the same reform circles, shared a common concern for the rights of working people, and recognized the fundamental importance of economic democracy.

The Wilson volunteers spent much of their time attacking TR, lamenting the failure of the Progressive party to side with the people against the "interests," and portraying the Republicans as the "war party" of "dollar patriotism," the tool of privilege, and "the friend of the people's enemies." "There is one great issue in the campaign," Pinchot told the voters. It was not that Wilson had "kept us out of war," nor was it the "danger of changing horses" in midstream, nor even the prospect that a Republican victory would mean an aggressive, militaristic foreign policy. "The great issue is whether the country shall be governed by the people or the exploiters of the people."[96] As one might have expected, the ex-Bull Moose radical reserved his harshest and most intemperate criticism for Roosevelt.

It would be difficult to find two men who detested each other more than TR and Pinchot. Their mutual capacity for sarcasm, defamation, abuse, and outright cruelty was unmatched. Four years of petty bickering, backbiting, and deception culminated in a campaign which did credit to neither man. Pinchot, the more vocal of the two, appeared to engage in a single-minded personal campaign to vilify Roosevelt, while Woodrow Wilson's reelection became a secondary consideration. "With the rest of the Progressives," Pinchot recalled, "I went into battle singing hymns and announcing that I would stand at Armageddon and battle for the Lord. And when we said the Lord, we meant social justice for the people of America—we did not have in mind Wall Street or the G.O.P."[97] As the campaign entered its late stages, Pinchot unrelentingly ridiculed the former president as "the bell hop of Wall Street" and mocked TR's commitment to military preparedness by calling him "Colonel-Sit-by-the-Fire" and "The Only Patriotic American."[98] Pinchot was fond of portraying Roosevelt as a hot-air balloon, the captive of "undesirable citizens who pull him down to earth or let him blow around up in the air, according to the needs of the time." In later years an older and more forgiving Pinchot would portray TR in a much kinder light, but in the heat of the 1916 campaign there was no sympathy. "No one ought to pity the Colonel," Pinchot declared. "He is now just where he has wanted to be all along—back in the stronghold of respectable, benevolent plutocracy. Nothing could be more desirable for the oyster man, he is now resting comfortably with a full belly."[99] Roosevelt's unequivocal response was equally cruel: "When I spoke of the Progressive Party as having a lunatic fringe," he wrote Pinchot, "I specifically had you in mind. On the supposition that you are of entire sound mind, I should be obliged to say that you are absolutely dishonorable and untruthful. I prefer to accept the former alternative."[100]

The 1916 election finally freed the radical Progressives from TR's disapproving gaze, but they never escaped the "lunatic" label he attached to them. Appropriately, the main achievements of both the Progressive party and its radical critics tended to be negative and self-destructive. In analyzing the cause of Progressive failure more than twenty years later, Amos Pinchot would blame his own "lunatic fringe" for assuming that Roosevelt "belonged to the left wing" and would start on a "long-pull program that might . . . bring a radical party into power."[101] The radicals must also share the responsibility for destroying a movement that they helped create. They were an odd mixture of contradictions: unyielding yet practical, willing to cross once-sacred party lines, yet innately conservative in their desire for a more competitive economic system.

The activities which TR's radical Progressive critics pursued between 1912 and 1916 established a pattern which lasted for the next twenty years. They never wavered in their commitment to such fundamental issues as nationalization of the railroads, destruction of monopoly, and elimination of economic inequality. Yet they were never able to mobilize the voting constituency necessary to translate their reformist sentiments into concrete achievements. In part their political ineffectiveness reflected a fundamental paradox of independent progressive thought and outlook. Positive government intervention required the limited abandonment of individual freedom and a willingness to place the national interest above self-interest. While Progressives trusted themselves to make such a sacrifice, they arrogantly identified their needs with the nation's and dismissed others' demands as parochial and self-serving.[102]

Yet it would be a mistake to dismiss these independent Progressives as overly dogmatic theoreticians inflexibly tied to narrow concerns, for they were not insensitive or oblivious to the world around them. Though wary of succumbing to the blandishments of such national leaders as Roosevelt and Wilson, men like George L. Record and Amos Pinchot constantly sought access to political power. But because their concerns and strategy already had forced them outside the two-party system, their future credibility required constant efforts at organization and co-alition-building. In this area they would prove to be abysmal failures. It is ironic that these independent Progressives, who were both prominent citizens and major party pariahs, would spend the better part of the next two decades struggling to regain the respectability which their views and political affiliations denied them. As they moved involuntarily beyond the structured confines of the post-Bull Moose years, independent Progressives encountered a broader constituency whose own needs would force a significant modification in ideas and tactics. No one, especially not the once-radical Progressives, could predict whether such adjustments, if made, would lead to political survival and advancement or to stagnation and impotence.

NOTES

1. William Kent to Adaline Dutton Kent, Feb. 1, 1912, William Kent Papers, Yale Univ., hereinafter cited as Kent Papers.

2. This development is discussed in the following important works: David P. Thelen, *Robert M. La Follette and the Insurgent Spirit* (Boston: Little, Brown, 1976); George E. Mowry, *Theodore Roosevelt and the Birth of Modern America, 1900–1912* (New York: Harper & Row, 1958); the same author's earlier study, *Theodore Roosevelt and the Progressive Movement* (Madison: Univ. of Wisconsin Press, 1946).

3. George L. Record to Walter L. Houser, La Follette's campaign manager, Jan. 8, 1912, La Follette Family Papers, Library of Congress, hereinafter cited as La Follette Papers.

4. William Kent to Hiram W. Johnson, Jan. 31, 1912, Kent Papers.

5. William Kent to Adaline D. Kent, Feb. 1, 1912, *ibid.*

6. Amos R. E. Pinchot to William B. Colver, Feb. 12, 1912, box 11, Amos Pinchot Papers, Library of Congress, hereinafter cited as Amos Pinchot Papers.

7. Robert M. La Follette, *La Follette's Autobiography* (Madison: Univ. of Wisconsin Press, 1963), 322–342; James Weinstein, *The Corporate Ideal in the Liberal State, 1900–1918* (Boston: Beacon Press, 1968), 157–159; William H. Harbaugh, *Power and Responsibility: The Life and Times of Theodore Roosevelt* (New York: Farrar, Straus and Cudahy, 1961), 418–419.

8. William Kent to Robert M. La Follette, Feb. 12, 1912, box 11, Amos Pinchot Papers.

9. George L. Record, "A Complete Program," typescript in La Follette Papers.

10. George L. Record to Robert M. La Follette, Feb. 17, 1912, *ibid.* (italics mine).

11. Amos R. E. Pinchot to Gilson Gardner, Washington correspondent (Scripps Newspaper Chain), Newspaper Enterprise Association, Feb. 7, 1912, box 11, Amos Pinchot Papers.

12. Robert M. La Follette to William Kent, Feb. 15, 1912, Kent Papers.

13. William Kent to Hiram W. Johnson, Feb. 16, 1912, *ibid.*

14. Amos R. E. Pinchot to Raymond St. John, secretary, Republican Club,

29th Assembly District, NYC, June 29, 1912, box 12, Amos Pinchot Papers. John Milton Cooper, Jr., discusses the differences between the New Nationalism and New Freedom in *The Warrior and the Priest: Woodrow Wilson and Theodore Roosevelt* (Cambridge: Harvard Univ. Press, 1983), 206–221.

15. Ellis W. Hawley, *The New Deal and the Problem of Monopoly: A Study in Economic Ambivalence* (Princeton: Princeton Univ. Press, 1966), 7–9.

16. George L. Record to Theodore Roosevelt, June 3, 1912, reel #2, Theodore Roosevelt Papers, Library of Congress, hereinafter cited as TR Papers.

17. TR to Henry Cabot Lodge, Dec. 13, 1911, in Elting E. Morison, ed., *The Letters of Theodore Roosevelt*, 8 vols. (Cambridge: Harvard Univ. Press, 1951–1954), VII: 456; TR to Gifford Pinchot, Dec. 12, 1911, *ibid.*, 455–456.

18. TR to Gifford Pinchot, *ibid.*

19. Amos R. E. Pinchot to Bishop James Steptoe Johnston, Sept. 10, 1912, box 12, Amos Pinchot Papers.

20. Frederick Kerby (secretary to Gilson Gardner) to Amos R. E. Pinchot, Oct. 17, 1912, box 12, *ibid.*

21. See John A. Gable, *The Bull Moose Years: Theodore Roosevelt and The Progressive Party* (Port Washington, N.Y.: Kennikat Press, 1978), 99–105.

22. Amos R. E. Pinchot to TR, Dec. 3, 1912, cited in "Amos R. E. Pinchot," *History of the Progressive Party, 1912–1916*, ed., Helene M. Hooker (New York: New York Univ. Press, 1958), 184–191.

23. TR to Charles E. Merriam, Nov. 23, 1912, box 22, Charles E. Merriam Papers, University of Chicago, hereinafter cited as Merriam Papers; Charles E. Merriam to George L. Record, Nov. 26, 1912, box 21, *ibid.*; and Harold L. Ickes to Amos R. E. Pinchot, Dec. 2, 1912, box 13, Amos Pinchot Papers.

24. TR to Charles E. Merriam, Nov. 23, 1912, Merriam Papers.

25. TR to Amos R. E. Pinchot, Dec. 31, 1912, cited in Pinchot, *History of the Progressive Party*, 211–212.

26. George L. Record to Charles E. Merriam, Dec. 2, 1912, box 21, Merriam Papers.

27. George L. Record to TR, Dec. 16, 1912, TR Papers.

28. Gable, *The Bull Moose Years*, 184–188.

29. Amos R. E. Pinchot to Jane Addams, Feb. 17, 1913, box 14, Amos Pinchot Papers.

30. Speeches of George L. Record and Amos R. E. Pinchot, reported in the *Newark Evening News*, Feb. 13, 1913, box 14, Amos Pinchot Papers.

31. Amos R. E. Pinchot to Jane Addams, Feb. 17, 1913; Amos R. E. Pinchot to Clarence P. Dodge, *Colorado Springs Gazette*, Feb. 21, 1913, box 14, *ibid.*

32. Harbaugh, *Power and Responsibility*, 421.

33. TR to George L. Record, Mar. 15, 1913, TR Papers.

34. George L. Record to TR, Apr. 30, 1913, *ibid.*

35. *Ibid.*

36. TR to George L. Record, May 5, 1913, *Letters*, VII: 725–727.

37. *New York Times*, May 11, 1913, II, 6:1; May 30, 1913, 6:6.

38. *Ibid.*, June 4, 1913, 10:4.

39. Delos F. Wilcox to Amos R. E. Pinchot, July 17, 1913, box 15, Amos Pinchot Papers.

40. Chester H. Rowell to Amos R. E. Pinchot, July 19, 1913, *ibid.*

41. Amos R. E. Pinchot to Francis W. "Billy" Bird, New York County Progressive party chairman, July 22, 1913, *ibid.*

42. *New York Evening Post*, Apr. 25, 1913, 1; quoted in Augustus Cerillo, Jr., "The Reform of Municipal Government in New York City; From Seth Low to John Purroy Mitchel," *New-York Historical Society Quarterly* 57 (Jan. 1973), 68.

43. Harold L. Ickes to Amos R. E. Pinchot, Aug. 8, 1913, box 15, Amos Pinchot Papers; Amos R. E. Pinchot to Francis W. Bird, July 22, 1913, *ibid.*; Amos R. E. Pinchot to Edmund Osborne, a New Jersey radical Progressive, July 22, 1913, and Delos F. Wilcox to Amos R. E. Pinchot, Aug. 1, 1913, box 15, *ibid.*

44. Harold L. Ickes to Amos R. E. Pinchot, Aug. 8, 1913, *ibid.*

45. Amos R. E. Pinchot to William Kent, July 22, 1913, *ibid.*

46. Amos R. E. Pinchot to Rev. William S. Rainsford, Oct. 23, 1913, *ibid.*

47. Amos R. E. Pinchot to Prof. Alfred Hayes, Cornell University, Dec. 5, 1913; Amos R. E. Pinchot to Gifford Pinchot, Dec. 9, 1913, *ibid.*

48. George L. Record to TR, Aug. 28, 1913, TR Papers.

49. TR to George L. Record, Sept. 2, 1913, *Letters*, VII: 746.

50. Harbaugh, *Power and Responsibility*, 459.

51. TR to Victor Murdock, Sept. 30, 1913; TR to William A. White, Oct. 8, 1913, *Letters*, VII: 750–753.

52. Amos R. E. Pinchot to Gifford Pinchot, Nov. 26, 1913, box 15, Amos Pinchot Papers.

53. Amos R. E. Pinchot to Gilson Gardner, Dec. 9, 1913, *ibid.*

54. Amos R. E. Pinchot to Gifford Pinchot, *ibid.*; George L. Record to Gifford Pinchot, Jan. 17, 19, 21, 27, 28, 1914, box 180, Gifford Pinchot Papers, Library of Congress.

55. Gifford Pinchot to George L. Record, Aug. 2, 1913, box 167, Gifford Pinchot Papers; quoted in Rex O. Mooney, "Amos Pinchot and Atomistic Capitalism: A Study in Reform Ideas" (Ph.D. diss., Louisiana State Univ., 1973), 34.

56. Amos R. E. Pinchot to Gifford Pinchot, Feb. 3, 1914, box 16, Amos Pinchot Papers.

57. Amos R. E. Pinchot to Francis J. Heney, Jan. 20, 1914, *ibid.*

58. Nick Salvatore, *Eugene V. Debs: Citizen and Socialist* (Urbana: Univ. of Illinois Press, 1982), 264–267, notes the precipitous decline in Socialist party membership between 1912 and 1915. Kenneth McNaught, "American Progressives and the Great Society," *Journal of American History* 53:3 (Dec. 1966), 504–520, discusses the party's problems after 1912.

59. Mooney, "Amos Pinchot and Atomistic Capitalism," 143–146.

60. Amos R. E. Pinchot to Gilson Gardner, Apr. 24, 1914, box 16, Amos Pinchot Papers.

61. Amos R. E. Pinchot to Gifford Pinchot, Apr. 28, 1914, *ibid.*

62. Amos R. E. Pinchot to Joseph M. Dixon, May 23, 1914, quoted in Pinchot, *History of the Progressive Party*, 248–263

63. Gable, *The Bull Moose Years*, 190; Helene M. Hooker, ed., "Biographical Introduction" to Pinchot's *History*, 55.

64. *New York Evening Post*, June 25, 1914; *New York World*, June 26, 1914; quoted in Gable, *The Bull Moose Years*, 191; TR to George W. Perkins, June 2, 1914, *Letters*, VII: 764–765.

65. TR to William A. White, July 6, 1914, *ibid.*, 773.

66. TR to Hiram W. Johnson, July 30, 1914, *ibid.*, 784–790.

67. Amos R. E. Pinchot to Mark Sullivan, July 23, 1914, box 17, Amos Pinchot Papers.

68. Mowry, *Theodore Roosevelt and the Progressive Movement*, 299; Hooker, ed., *History of the Progressive Party*, 58.

69. George L. Record to TR, Aug. 3, 1914, box 17, Amos Pinchot Papers. Roosevelt's response, Aug. 5, 1914, "I think those are fine suggestions. . . . I am really obliged to you," can be found in *ibid.*

70. Gable, *The Bull Moose Years*, 198–199; George L. Record to Amos R. E. Pinchot, Aug. 6, 1914, box 17, Amos Pinchot Papers.

71. George L. Record to Amos R. E. Pinchot, Aug. 6, 20, 1914, *ibid.*

72. George L. Record to TR, Aug. 12, 1914, box 17, Amos Pinchot Papers.

73. George L. Record to Woodrow Wilson, May 7, 1914, Woodrow Wilson Papers, Library of Congress, hereinafter cited as Wilson Papers.

74. George L. Record to Joseph P. Tumulty, June 22, 1914, Joseph P. Tumulty Papers, Library of Congress.

75. George L. Record to TR, Aug. 12, 1914, box 17, Amos Pinchot Papers.

76. George L. Record to Amos R. E. Pinchot, Aug. 20, 1914, *ibid.*

77. Amos R. E. Pinchot to E. W. Scripps, Nov. 11, 1914, box 18, *ibid.*

78. TR to Edwin A. Van Valkenburg, Nov. 23, 1914, *Letters*, VIII: 848–849.

79. TR to Henry Frederick Cochems, Progressive National Committeeman from Wisconsin, Nov. 28, 1914, *ibid.*, VIII: 850.

80. TR to Meyer Lissner, Dec. 11, 1914, *ibid.*, VIII: 863–864.

81. Mowry, *Theodore Roosevelt and the Progressive Movement*, 300.

82. Those interested in George L. Record's career will want to consult the following works: Ransom E. Noble, Jr., *New Jersey Progressivism Before Wilson* (Princeton: Princeton Univ. Press, 1946); the same author's "Henry George and the Progressive Movement," *American Journal of Economics and Sociology* 8 (Apr. 1949), 259–269; "George L. Record's Struggle for Economic Democracy," *ibid.*, 10 (Oct. 1950), 70–83; and Eugene M. Tobin, *George L. Record and the Progressive Spirit* (Trenton: New Jersey Historical Commission, 1979), 5–38.

83. There is no single biographical study of Amos R. E. Pinchot, although Helene M. Hooker's biographical introduction to Pinchot's *History of the Progressive Party* is extremely insightful and well written. So, too, is her (Helene [Hooker] Brewer's) sketch of Pinchot in the *Dictionary of American Biography, Supplement Three, 1941–1945* (New York: Charles Scribner's Sons, 1973), 603–605. His career can be studied especially during the postwar years and 1920s by examining Paul W. Glad, "Progressives and the Business Culture of the 1920s," *Journal of American History* 53 (June 1966), 75–89; Stanley Shapiro, "The Twilight of Reform: Advanced Progressives after the Armistice," *Historian* 33 (May 1971), 349–364; and Otis L. Graham, Jr., *An Encore for Reform: The Old Progressives and the New Deal* (New York: Oxford Univ. Press, 1967). An interesting dissertation dealing with his career is Rex O. Mooney, "Amos Pinchot and Atomistic Capitalism: A Study in Reform Ideas," (Ph.D. diss., Louisiana State Univ., 1973).

84. George L. Record to Amos R. E. Pinchot, n.d. (probably Aug., 1915), box 23, Amos Pinchot Papers.

85. TR to Chester H. Rowell, Dec. 17, 1914, *Letters*, VIII: 866–867; TR to Victor Murdock, Kansas congressman and chairman of the Progressive National Com-

mittee, Feb. 19, 1914, *ibid.*, 893; and TR to George L. Record, Dec. 12, 1914, TR Papers.

86. Amos R. E. Pinchot to Frederick Kerby, Feb. 14, 1915; and letters from Pinchot to William Kent, Harry A. Slattery, George Rublee, and John Hannan, Feb. 4, 1915, and to Gilson Gardner, Feb. 5, 1915, box 19, Amos Pinchot Papers.

87. George L. Record to Ray Stannard Baker, Apr. 12, 1926, Ray Stannard Baker Papers, Library of Congress, hereinafter cited as Baker Papers.

88. Woodrow Wilson to George L. Record, Feb. 25, 1915, Wilson Papers.

89. Amos R. E. Pinchot to William Kent, Apr. 12, 1915, box 20, Amos Pinchot Papers.

90. Amos R. E. Pinchot to Frank I. Cobb, Apr. 22, 1915, *ibid.*

91. Amos R. E. Pinchot to E. W. Scripps, June 9, 1915, box 21; and another letter to Scripps, Nov. 3, 1915, box 22, Amos Pinchot Papers.

92. Amos R. E. Pinchot to Edmund B. Osborne, Dec. 3, 1915, box 23, *ibid.*, Amos Pinchot Papers.

93. Frederic C. Howe to Amos R. E. Pinchot, Jan. 11, 1916, box 25, *ibid.*

94. Amos R. E. Pinchot to Woodrow Wilson, Jan. 27, 1916, *ibid.*

95. Pinchot, *History of the Progressive Party*, 68–69.

96. "Statement by Amos Pinchot," n.d. (Fall 1916), box 25, Amos Pinchot Papers.

97. *Ibid.*

98. Pinchot, *History of the Progressive Party*, 69.

99. Amos R. E. Pinchot to William Kent, July 6, 1916, box 25, Amos Pinchot Papers.

100. TR to Amos R. E. Pinchot, Nov. 3, 1916, *Letters*, VIII: 1122.

101. Pinchot, *History of the Progressive Party*, 181.

102. Cooper, Jr., *The Warrior and the Priest*, 215–218.

III

Liberal-Labor Relations before the War

The years from 1914 to 1916 were notable for much more than the demise of the Progressive party. Preparedness advocates and their pacifist opponents vigorously competed for public attention, but most Americans seemed more concerned with the rising incidence of labor violence and lawlessness at home than with events in Europe. All across the nation, workers and employers engaged in pitched battles, exchanged mutual threats, and contributed to a tension-filled atmosphere in which neutrality ceased to have meaning.

From labor's standpoint, the problems were unambiguous: an increasingly unequal distribution of wealth had left between one-third and one-fourth of those families engaged in industrial labor barely above the subsistence level. The separation of management from ownership made industrial work impersonal, rendered the individual worker powerless against the corporation, and necessitated unionization and collective bargaining. Yet employers harassed union workers, insisted on yellow-dog contracts, hired strikebreakers and industrial spies, and received judicial and legislative support from the public sector. Management, on the other hand, pointed fearfully at the increased amount of labor radicalism, property destruction, and violence.

Concern over these developments, as well as a fundamental anxiety over America's future, prompted a variety of groups to pressure the Taft administration into establishing a federal investigatory commission. The most prominent of the lobbyists was the awkwardly but appropriately named Committee on Industrial Relations to Secure the Appointment of a Federal Commission on Industrial Relations. Its letterhead read like a who's who of progressivism and contained the names of settlement leaders such as Jane Addams, Lillian Wald, and Mary K. Simkhovitch; leading social gospelers including Washington Gladden, Rabbi Stephen

S. Wise, John Haynes Holmes, and Father John A. Ryan; social activists
such as Paul Kellogg, John A. Kingsbury, Edward T. Devine, John Collier, Louis D. Brandeis, and Florence Kelley; and prominent academics
including Irving Fisher, Ernst Freund, Edward Ross, and Edwin R. A.
Seligman. "The time has come," Committee Chairman Edward T. Devine wrote, "for a new approach to the problems underlying industrial
conflicts and for the elimination of such of their causes as are prevent-
able."[1] Citing the recent publicity accorded overcapitalization, watered
stock, and centralization of financial power, issues which were soon to
be investigated by the Pujo Committee, these progressives asked that
"the light of truth be thrown also on industrial relations." In August
1912, Congress responded with the creation of the U.S. Commission on
Industrial Relations (CIR) and authorized it to "seek to discover the
underlying causes of dissatisfaction in the industrial situation and report
its conclusions."[2]

Bitter wrangling over the membership of the nine-member commission delayed its actual inauguration until the fall of 1913 under the aegis
of the Wilson administration. But well before the CIR began nationwide
hearings under the direction of its chairman, Kansas City labor lawyer
Frank P. Walsh, many reformers had come to realize that class harmony
was a nonexistent, self-serving myth. Such sentiments were widely shared
by a number of prominent liberals, many of them veterans of the ill-
fated Bull Moose party. They worried that all the gains made in im-
proving working conditions over the past decade would be forgotten as
public attention was distracted by labor violence and unrest.[3] They genuinely empathized with the aspirations of individual workers, though
some retained an anachronistic belief in a classless society. They gathered at fashionable liberal meeting places, joined hands with workers
at strike battlegrounds, lent money to labor defense funds, drafted and
redrafted impassioned letters to the editor, and looked for underlying
causes of worker unrest that would link their evolving political ideology
to meaningful economic and social change.[4]

But beneath their rhetoric was an inner conflict stemming perhaps
from self-doubt, but more likely occasioned by criticism from members
of their own class. "You blame me for spreading dissatisfaction among
laboring people," Amos Pinchot wrote an old friend. "Frankly, I want
to spread dissatisfaction with present economic conditions . . . I think
that the besetting social sin of Americans is an easy tolerance of injustice
suffered by somebody else, and a willingness on the part of the rich
people like ourselves to say to the poor: 'think how much worse it has
been and how much worse it might be.' You and I and all intelligent
people . . . know that mere political democracy does not result in real
democracy at all. Economic power is the real power in the world."[5]

The emphasis upon economic democracy and the attempt to link social injustice to private monopoly drew progressives such as Pinchot, Frederic C. Howe, Norman Hapgood, and Benjamin C. Marsh into distinctly working-class, occasionally socialist circles. The causes which these men espoused—textile and coal strikers at Paterson, New Jersey, and Ludlow, Colorado; the establishment of labor defense funds; local governmental programs for relief of the unemployed; legal and financial support for provocative socialist magazines; government ownership of transportation and natural resources; and spirited endorsement of collective bargaining, industrial democracy, and civil liberties—all reflected a coherent political philosophy which had its roots in the radical faction of the Bull Moose party. Yet, such progressives always seemed to share much more in common with their conservative opponents than with anarchist and revolutionary elements on the political left. Most were neither saints nor socialists. Many questioned the need for class-oriented legislation; others remained suspicious of labor unions.[6] Though clearly aware of gross inequities in the distribution of wealth and power, most did not support a redistribution to eliminate those inequities. Some were motivated out of fear that worker unrest represented a highly volatile element which had to be pacified.

We need make no excuses for their class bias or occasional lapses into paternalistic attitudes. They were the first generation who faced the consequences of unrestrained urban-industrial growth and the first group of progressives to seek a working relationship with the more militant elements of the labor movement. Their initial attempts at creating a liberal-labor coalition were farcical—replete with charges of distrust, suspicion, and misrepresentation. Financial support made them essential to labor, but mutual respect came grudgingly as both sides tried to break down the barriers of class and ideology. Lasting partnerships are not built upon sympathy, money, or lost causes, but relationships often begin that way. Progressives and labor radicals did not always succeed in overcoming their justifiable suspicions, but the experiences derived from the years 1914 to 1916 would form the basis for the continuation of liberal-labor cooperation during and after the war.

In November 1913, Max Eastman, editor of the "intellectually irreverent" socialist journal the *Masses*, was indicted along with cartoonist Art Young for libeling the Associated Press (AP).[7] Specifically, Eastman accused the AP of holding an antilabor bias and of suppressing fact while publishing lies and slander. Young's accompanying cartoon was equally intemperate; it portrayed the AP as a sewer into which were poured lies and class hatred. As he had since the magazine's beginnings, Amos Pinchot helped keep the *Masses* afloat through loans and generous personal contributions. He obtained the services of attorney Gilbert E. Roe, a confidant of Senator La Follette, and chaired a labor defense committee whose well-heeled contributors included E. W. Scripps, Samuel Untermyer, Mabel Dodge, and Rose Pastor Stokes. Pinchot also helped organize a "Free Press Protest Meeting" at Cooper Union which featured addresses by John Haynes Holmes, muckraker Lincoln Steffens, feminist Charlotte Perkins Gilman, and socialist author William E. Walling.[8]

The AP suit never materialized, and after two years the libel action was dropped.[9] Since the *Masses* was in and out of trouble during this period—for blasphemy, anticlericalism, eroticism, and eventually allegedly seditious statements—this one incident is devoid of any profound historical import, except for Pinchot's role. He criticized the AP in much the same way he attacked U.S. Steel and International Harvester. The AP was a monopoly whose unscrupulous control over the distribution of information perverted the truth and produced bitterness and violence. "I am not a socialist myself," Pinchot cautiously reassured potential contributors to the *Masses* defense fund, but "I do not believe in sending socialists to prison for speaking the truth."[10]

Still, the free speech issue was a rather tenuous peg upon which to base a defense, especially when as ardent a civil libertarian as Oswald Garrison Villard, of the *New York Post*, was so deeply offended by Art Young's cartoon that he offered to testify in the AP's behalf.[11] Thus, a strict antimonopoly approach was both safer and ideologically more consistent with Pinchot's political development since 1912. "The A.P.," he reminded the editors of the *New York Times*, "is a monopoly controlling the distribution of a vital necessity, . . . the price at which [it] shall be sold; and it goes still farther than other trusts in monopolistic power, for it exercises an absolute discrimination as to whom its product shall be sold to."[12]

The problem with an antimonopoly approach lay in overcoming public apathy toward impersonal, distant institutions. The radical Progressives' failure to capture control of their party between 1913 and 1915 stemmed in part from an absence of public support for their program of government ownership. But if attacks upon such symbols of corporate arrogance as the steel trust failed to generate grass-roots protest, a campaign directed against the AP, an institution even more removed from the lives of most Americans, would be much less successful. An issue, cause, or crisis was needed, preferably one which crossed class lines, demonstrated that private monopoly contributed to social injustice, and justified governmental action to alleviate the distress and correct the abuse.

During the winter of 1914–15, cutbacks in American foreign trade, precipitated by the war in Europe, produced massive unemployment across urban America. Nowhere was the deprivation, misery, and fear for the future more acute than in New York City, where hundreds of thousands of men, women, and children were cold, hungry, angry, and out of work. Mayor John P. Mitchel, the victorious fusion candidate of 1913 and an advocate of efficiency, economy, and honesty in government, placed his faith in the business community. Two of the nation's corporate leaders, Elbert H. Gary, chairman of the board of U.S. Steel, and George W. Perkins, a director of both U.S. Steel and International Harvester, were appointed chairmen of two municipal commissions on the causes of unemployment and the cost of living. Though the Gary Committee approved proposals for emergency public works projects and appealed to local businessmen to maintain wages, avoid layoffs, and manufacture a surplus reserve, cooperation was not forthcoming. Even the creation of municipal workshops, where men and women rolled bandages and repaired shoes and furniture, barely scratched the surface of the problem. To the committee's credit, it dismissed a number of outlandish schemes for redistributing the unemployed ranging from a back-to-the-land proposal to outright banishment. Its final recommendations, however, bristled with strong social control implications and a repugnant degree of patronizing.[13]

Nothing was more inevitable under these circumstances than Amos Pinchot's emergence as a critic of the Gary Committee's handling of the unemployment crisis. The situation not only involved a dilemma of major human concern ready-made for mobilizing public outrage, but its protagonists included Pinchot's favorite whipping boys, each of whom represented two of the most powerful corporations in America. Portraying Gary and Perkins as "two of America's most distinguished exploiters," Pinchot contended that their appointment "has made it absolutely sure that the commission will not report on the causes of unemployment but will . . . focus public attention on giving some of the poor devils (mighty few) a place to lie down and half enough food until summer comes and they can go on the road." Naturally, Pinchot identified monopoly as the villain. The cause of the massive unemployment, he wrote Mrs. George Bernard Shaw, "is that the source of energy and the raw materials in this country are all cornered."[14] The community, Pinchot lectured Mayor Mitchel, owes every man who is willing the opportunity to work. "This is not a debatable proposition; it is not a question of charity or policy. It is a matter of sheer fundamental justice."[15]

Pinchot's "reward" for such civic concern was appointment to the New York Unemployment Commission and chairmanship of the Publicity and Press Committee. Together with his committee colleagues—old cronies Benjamin C. Marsh, Frederic C. Howe, John Haynes Holmes, and *New Republic* editor Walter Lippmann—Pinchot flooded the local press with requests designed to pressure the foot-dragging Mitchel administration to initiate municipal public works projects. But it was to no avail. As Pinchot had predicted, the administration had become a model of "intelligent, enlightened, Christian non-interference with the big grafters." Though the mayor was an able administrator and "honest in a petty way," his policies had merely "respectabilized [sic] privilege and put the city government . . . into the hands of the Rockefeller dynasty." The whole fusion effort and the city government's woeful response to the unemployment crisis left progressives bitterly disappointed. "The spectacle of Mitchel holding down the mayoralty respectably and creditably does not enthuse me," Pinchot observed. "I think there ought to be a law against men holding down jobs . . . unless they stand for something real." Unfortunately, he concluded, Mitchel was probably "a man of just the limited vision that city politics demands."[16]

Pinchot's role in New York City's unemployment crisis contains no hidden meanings. At a time when his political activities stressed the singular importance of government ownership as the best means of restoring competition, he followed a parallel, often intersecting course of identifying artificial or private monopoly as the main cause of social injustice. Though men such as Pinchot, Howe, and Marsh never doubted the potential influence of government ownership of the railroads and natural resources to reconstruct American society, they could not depend upon the blind faith of others to lead the way. They had to transform an apparently sterile, impersonal economic proposal like government ownership into a dramatic yet realistic solution with mass appeal. That goal necessitated speaking out on major issues, particularly those affecting the working class, and demonstrating the sincerity of that commitment by traveling to places like Paterson to protest the denial of free speech and due process to members of the Industrial Workers of the World (IWW) or to the Colorado coalfields in the aftermath of the Ludlow Massacre.

Pinchot first arrived in Paterson in late May 1913, accompanied by colleagues from the People's Institute including its director Frederic C. Howe and investigator John Collier. They had come for a firsthand look at strike conditions in "silk city," a euphemism for the much-troubled industrial community along the banks of the Passaic River. The strike, which had begun in late February and would collapse in failure by July, had been precipitated by an increasingly familiar set of circumstances: mill owners radically altered work and safety standards by installing an automatic four-loom weaving system in place of the more traditional two-loom operation; wages remained substandard for the mass of unskilled Italian, Jewish, and Polish immigrants who had to withstand ten-hour days and insufferable working conditions that included required kickbacks to company foremen, inaccurate measurement of worker productivity, and differential wage scales within the same shop.[17] Subsequent intervention by the feared IWW added tension to an already volatile situation. Inflammatory rhetoric by Wobbly leaders Bill Haywood, Patrick Quinlan, Elizabeth Gurley Flynn, and Carlo Tresca produced equally irresponsible behavior by Paterson officials. City leaders abused their authority and responded with an utterly inhumane, inflexible, and repressive brand of justice that sanctioned the suppression of free speech and the wholesale arrest of thousands.

Fortunately, an overwhelming number of these arrests and convictions were overturned in higher courts. Still, the inexorable force of the institutional process ensnared men who pushed authorities to the limits of the law and then suffered the consequences of certain built-in inequities. Wobbly leader Patrick Quinlan was one of the system's unfortunate victims. A number of indictments had been returned against other Wobblies including Haywood, Flynn, and Tresca, but their cases ended either in deadlocked juries and dismissal, retrial and acquittal, or reversal on appeal. Alone among those who began this legal odyssey, Quinlan did not escape. His arrest occurred the first day of the industry-wide strike, and he was indicted by a totally unrepresentative grand jury for violating an antirioting statute.[18] His trials (the first ended in a hung jury) were laden with emotionalism and bigotry. The government's case was based overwhelmingly upon circumstantial evidence, much of it harmful and prejudicial. The prosecutor emphasized Quinlan's Wobbly ties, called him an "educated agitator of the most dangerous type," and warned the jury that failure to convict would be tantamount to rendering Passaic County helpless and declaring martial law.[19]

Quinlan's conviction produced the expected range of widely divergent reactions. Elizabeth Gurley Flynn labeled the decision a "class verdict" and another example of "Jersey justice." The *Paterson Call*, an antiunion paper which had denounced the first deadlocked jury as a disgrace to the community, smugly acknowledged that Quinlan was probably found guilty on "general principles." But the progressive Republican *Newark Evening News* observed that the prosecutor's plea to the jury was "as anarchistic as any of the utterances credited to the leaders of the strike."[20]

In January 1915, Quinlan reached the end of the appellate process. Most of those indicted during the strike had been acquitted or had their cases dismissed; some guilty verdicts were overturned as a result of Quinlan's experience. For in the aftermath of public protest following his conviction, the state supreme court permitted "foreign juries" selected outside Paterson to sit in subsequent trials. On February 26, 1915, two years and a day after his arrest, Quinlan was sentenced to a term of from two to seven years in Trenton State Prison.[21] All told he would spend twenty-one months in the penitentiary, a victim of guilt by association with a revolutionary labor movement that challenged the basic principles of a capitalist society.[22] It may well be, as William Preston, Jr., has suggested, that the punishment of these prewar radicals predestined the widespread repression of the Red Scare.[23]

It was the political nature of Quinlan's crime, of course, which sustained the interest of the liberal community. His confinement, long after other Wobblies had indictments against them dismissed, outraged reformers who seized upon this perceived miscarriage of justice to denounce the suppression of free speech. In a public letter to Quinlan in which he enclosed a check for $500 to help with legal expenses, Amos Pinchot denounced the "official anarchy" sanctioned by Paterson officials. "The bitterness of the people against industrial oppression and their desire for a living wage and . . . an opportunity for better conditions . . . is so vital . . . that methods such as . . . are being used in Paterson . . . are too fraught with danger . . . to be tolerated . . . without protest."[24]

Ewing Galloway, editor of the *Literary Digest*, visited Paterson about this same time and observed that "if the addresses of Quinlan . . . and the other leaders were felonies, Patrick Henry should have been hanged for his 'Give-me-liberty' speech and Colonel Roosevelt ought to be serving a life term in Sing Sing for his denunciations of political grafters and predatory corporations."[25] The Quinlan case also enabled commentators to attack broader social and economic inequities. "The Paterson affair is only an example of what is going on through the whole country," Pinchot told a sympathetic audience. "The wealth and power in the community is all passing into the control of a few men, and none of our great political leaders dares to act in any but a narrow, prescribed manner. . . . We must face the tremendous problems of the unequal division of wealth, for preparedness in that direction is far more vital . . . than getting ready for a war that is not coming."[26] Throughout the Paterson strike a fear of recurring violence was always near the surface. Reformers like Pinchot believed that repeated instances of judicial abuse would irrevocably polarize future relations between labor and management. If such flagrant abuses were allowed to go unchallenged, the workers would lose all confidence in the judicial system, and the resultant feeling of helplessness would be "a powerful incentive to violence."[27]

Patrick Quinlan was an unfortunate victim of the judicial process, but his case also served as a catharsis for disenchanted progressives and provided a needed forum for labor militants. Quinlan and his Wobbly associates needed the financial support and sense of legitimacy the liberal community could furnish. Reformers, in turn, enjoyed the sense of fulfillment, camaraderie, and singleness of purpose participation in such events as the IWW's Madison Square Garden Pageant in June 1913 provided.[28] Certainly, for some progressives the Paterson episode was nothing more than an exciting interlude in their lives, a place to go "slumming" on Sunday afternoons to watch the strikers sing "The International." But for others the events which occurred in that grimy, industrial, hate-filled city forced them to open their eyes and minds to help explain the feelings in their hearts which first had drawn them to Paterson.

Early in 1915, Pinchot appeared before the United States Commission on Industrial Relations (CIR) as an expert witness on labor-management conflict. His testimony represented a thoughtful exposition of his developing approach to social injustice and economic inequality. Were he himself a member of the working class, Pinchot declared, he would devote his energy toward strengthening his union and "forcing its recognition upon his employer." Only through collective bargaining could the "benevolent absolutism" of industrial capitalism be broken. But collective bargaining and union recognition alone would not end industrial violence, which he attributed to a monopolistic system that limited production and curtailed competition and created large-scale unemployment. His solution, as one might have expected, lay in government ownership of railroads and natural resources. Industrial competition depended upon insuring equal access to transportation and raw materials, which were the basis of industry. He did not recommend any larger role for government beyond this limited intervention. Here again, Pinchot's proposals fit squarely within the radical Progressives' critique of American society. As a final suggestion for the peaceful settlement of future industrial disputes, he emphasized the importance of an impartial press. He singled out the AP for its biased coverage of coal strikes in West Virginia and Colorado which left strikers totally alienated, without hope, and prone to violence.[29]

Across the continent from New York City, far from the sedate environs of the CIR hearings but in a setting not totally dissimilar from the brutality of the Paterson strike, another industrial nightmare was unfolding. Predictably, the events of April 20, 1914, in the tent city of Ludlow, Colorado, caught most Americans completely by surprise. Far beyond the scrutiny of the public eye, the Colorado Fuel and Iron Company (CFI), a Rockefeller-controlled enterprise, had created its own hell on earth. Conditions in its company towns were inhumane and intolerable; housing was uninhabitable and sanitation nonexistent. Miners were paid meager wages in scrip redeemable only at high-priced company stores. A complete absence of intellectual, religious, and educational freedom and the oppressiveness of social control recalled the worst aspects of feudalism during the Middle Ages. In September 1913, over 10,000 miners and their families walked out of these mining camps in support of the United Mine Workers' demands for an eight-hour day, union recognition, wage increases, enforcement of safety standards, and the abolition of company scrip. Labor and management soon assumed the roles of belligerents, and Colorado became an armed camp replete with machine guns and trench warfare. Company gunmen and special deputies hired by state authorities, but paid by the CFI, engaged in guerrilla war while strikers, armed with shotguns and small arms ammunition, hastily constructed a defense perimeter. Brutality, violence, death, looting, and arson became a way of life which culminated in the massacre at Ludlow when National Guardsmen burned the tent colony to the ground, killing two women and eleven children in the process.[30]

Throughout the summer and fall of 1914, Amos Pinchot kept a close eye on events in Colorado. Deeply concerned about the CFI's economic stranglehold over the state, he was equally committed to helping an old Bull Moose friend, Edward P. Costigan, who was running for governor as an anti-Rockefeller candidate. But neither $1,000 of Pinchot's money nor his extensive efforts at fund-raising were enough to prevent Costigan's defeat.[31] Though disappointed, Pinchot remained convinced that economic democracy was the only solution for the nation's ills. At a New York City rally in July he joined a number of reformers including New York Civil Service Commissioner Henry Moskowitz, anti-Tammany Democrat Dudley Field Malone, John Moody (editor of *Moody's Magazine*), Walter Weyl (then in the process of preparing the *New Republic*'s first issue), and the brilliant, socially conscious journalist John Reed in supporting government ownership of the Colorado coal mines as the best means of ending that state's industrial strife.[32]

Six months after his appearance before the Commission on Industrial Relations, Pinchot traveled to Denver in behalf of John Lawson, a national organizer for the United Mine Workers who had been indicted for murder and conspiracy in the repressive aftermath of the Ludlow Massacre. Addressing a labor meeting on July 31, 1915, Pinchot told the crowd that the great question facing the country was not whether Lawson and others were to spend their natural lives in or out of jail. "It is bigger than that—larger than the fortunes of any man. The question is whether the public shall spend its natural life in the condition of political and economic freedom . . . or become subject to a commercial absolutism which . . . would mean the end of American democracy." The violence in Colorado and throughout the country, in New Jersey, Michigan, and West Virginia, reflected the "irreconcilable conflict" between freedom and industrial absolutism. The "law and order" issue, he told his listeners, was a ready-made weapon with which management could bludgeon strikers into submission—usually with public approval. The huge surplus work force and the nationwide railroad network making strikebreakers available to management also meant that "labor can no longer win by strikes alone. . . . Labor gets killed more, pitied less, and framed up by the courts generally [but] it no longer wins in strikes, peaceful or bloody."

One hundred years ago, Pinchot reminded the crowd, chattel slavery enslaved men's bodies; today "we enslave them by possession or control of the things men must have in order to live—the soil, natural resources, the mines, the minerals, and the transportation system." This industrial slavery was responsible for the "slave pens" of Lawrence and the "degradations" of the western mining and southern lumber towns. Pinchot challenged labor to fight for government ownership of essential resources. "It means its own emancipation." Of all the institutions in American life labor was the "main hope of democracy." Reformers, Pinchot observed, never reached below the surface of a problem, and they wasted energy needlessly. Political parties were essentially selfish bodies preoccupied with winning elections. The churches, like reformers, paid lip service to social amelioration but ultimately sustained the special privileges of the rich. "But the labor group," he told his predominantly working-class audience, "stands out as the one organized body that is ready to make great sacrifices for a simple and righteous aspiration."[33]

When considering most political speeches, one must never lose sight of the audience for whom it was intended. Pinchot probably would have acknowledged that he had laid it on a bit heavy. Even the disclaimer that he was not "an apostle of labor's cause" and that he had come to Denver as an impartial citizen was merely a rhetorical flourish designed to lend legitimacy and nonpartisanship to his prolabor remarks. Viewed in the context of other events, however, Pinchot's visits to Paterson and Denver and his testimony before the CIR reflected the Wilson administration's accelerating preelection concerns with social justice. The president's support for national child-labor reform, federal workmen's compensation, an eight-hour day for railroad workers; his appointment of the "people's lawyer," Louis D. Brandeis to the Supreme Court; and other measures all were intended to keep progressive Democrats in his corner and attract the support of ex-Bull Moosers as well. But, as James Weinstein has observed, such activities also sapped the strength of the Socialist party and lent credence to the notion that radical intellectuals and militant labor leaders could work together to shape public policy.[34]

Amos Pinchot would become a leading exponent of that notion. By the fall of 1915, his sensitivity to labor needs had begun to fuse with his antimonopoly beliefs. As industrial and economic democracy became inseparable goals in his mind, the idea of a liberal-labor political coalition began to take shape. An important step in the evolution of his thought grew as a result of his participation on the Committee on Industrial Relations, a private lobbying group organized to provide the widest possible publicity for the U.S. Commission on Industrial Relations' official recommendations. Those proposals were less than enthusiastically endorsed by all of the commission's nonlabor members, and the CIR's expiration was marked by the same internecine debate as had characterized its creation three years earlier.

Divisions within the commission prompted three separate reports: a staff report, written by Basil M. Manly and endorsed by chairman Frank P. Walsh and labor commissioners John Lennon, James O'Connell, and

Austin B. Garretson; the "Commons" report drafted by the commission's "public" representatives, labor economist John R. Commons and prominent Democrat and social worker Florence Harriman; and a third or "Employers" report written by a Bull Moose businessman, Harris Weinstock of California.[35]

These differences first became public in January 1915, when Walsh dismissed Charles V. McCarthy, the commission's director of research and founder of Wisconsin's Legislative Reference Library. The two men disagreed over the comparative benefits of research and publicity. McCarthy, an associate of Commons and Robert M. La Follette, and a disciple of the "Wisconsin idea"—emphasizing impartial research, bill drafting, and a thorough investigation of industrial conditions—believed that the research compiled by his brilliant young staff should be the commission's major contribution. "The more I see of the work of the Commission," he wrote one of his experts, "the greater is my belief that the fundamental thing to be considered is not the condition of labor as it is now or the causes of industrial unrest as they are now but what the trend is. . . . We must project our minds twenty-five or fifty years in the future and ask . . . whether the different things which are before our eyes today . . . will lead to a better American citizenship."[36]

Walsh, on the other hand, faced with a reduced federal appropriation, believed that political confrontation, publicity, and agitation were the keys to eliminating the worst of industrial abuse. He was a consummate politician, decisively prolabor in his sympathies, and much closer to the radical left than most of his prewar progressive contemporaries. Like most successful public figures, Walsh had the killer instinct, and he went for the jugular in this dispute. He intimidated and bullied McCarthy much as he had hostile witnesses who appeared before the commission. He "exposed" McCarthy's friendship and apparent close working relationship with John D. Rockefeller, Jr., an old college classmate at Brown University, who was one of the principals in the commission's Colorado investigation. Walsh was so eager to hold Rockefeller morally accountable for the Ludlow Massacre that he smeared McCarthy, implying that his research director was playing both sides of the fence. Few observers seemed willing to accept McCarthy's argument that he had simply tried to discourage Rockefeller from sponsoring a competing inquiry into industrial unrest, and that as a middle-aged government employee struggling to stay out of debt his friendship with one of America's richest men had not brought him financial security or monetary reward. Walsh's attacks upon McCarthy and Rockefeller revealed his hatred for arbitrary economic power and suspicion of industrially subsidized research by such philanthropic institutions as the Rockefeller Foundation, which had begun its own investigation into labor unrest.[37]

McCarthy's dismissal did not end division within the CIR, but, unfortunately, it did overshadow the minority reports. The Commons-Harriman plan, in particular, deserved serious consideration. It emphasized the need for enforceable legislation that would earn public confidence. Professor Commons's bill-drafting experiences on the Wisconsin Industrial Commission, especially in the areas of unemployment and workmen's compensation legislation, convinced him of the adversarial positions occupied by labor and capital. But like many of his progressive contemporaries, Commons was optimistic that an accommodation could be reached. Drawing upon developments in Wisconsin, he emphasized the need for expanded labor-management industrial commissions at the state and federal levels. These agencies would coordinate employer-worker agreements and assist in administering basic legislation. A nonpartisan federal advisory council made up of the Secretaries of Commerce and Labor would oversee the development and implementation of codes of behavior. At state levels, advisory boards would be composed of employer and union representatives. Collective bargaining and voluntary mediation, rather than political action or compulsory arbitration, would be the key to industrial stability and progress. The emphasis was on investigation, disclosure, public education, and corrective legislation, all of which were classic progressive remedies.

There was much in the Commons report to commend it to working people. Labor's right to organize, strike, and boycott was recognized. Minimum wage laws would protect the earning power of women and children. Eight-hour days would be required for all continuous industries. Federal and state employment offices would serve the needs of the unemployed. Detective agencies were to be regulated in their use of armed guards and strikebreakers. Limits were to be imposed on corporate political contributions. Unions engaged in labor disputes would be protected from criminal liability stemming from injunctions alleging conspiracy or unlawful combination. The emphasis throughout was upon cooperative, impartial, administrative, and voluntary adjudication of differences. The Commons report attacked no one, offered no immediate panaceas, and was "wise but unexciting."[38]

Few observers paid much attention to the Commons proposals following publication of the Manly or Major report, written by Basil M. Manly, McCarthy's successor as director of research. This was not surprising in view of the unprecedented recommendations to emerge from this labor-supported staff document and the fact that it appeared first in the commission's final report. Quickly accepted as the majority report though supported by a minority of the commissioners, its tone was exceedingly strident, partisan, accusatory, and dramatic. Where the Commons report studiously avoided laying blame, Manly's report did so enthusiastically and pointedly. The miscreants included the federal government for tolerating an unequal distribution of wealth, paternalistic and dictatorial employers, the general public for withholding support of union organization, and the national press for biased reporting. "Political freedom," Manly wrote, "can only exist where there is industrial freedom; political democracy only where there is industrial democracy." The report attributed industrial unrest to an increasingly unequal distribution of wealth and income, a rising unemployment rate which left workers jobless at least 20 percent of the year, the absence of even the most elementary constitutional guarantees, and, finally, the denial of the right to organize and bargain collectively.[39]

What set the Manly report apart from earlier state and federal investigations was the scope of its analysis, its willingness to cast blame freely, its unprecedented prolabor sentiments, and its recommendations, which were as advanced as anything then under serious discussion in socialist, labor, and radical progressive circles. The report made abundantly clear the sources of industrial violence. It indicted an economic system in which one-third of the workers lived in abject poverty, between one-half and two-thirds lived below the subsistence level, up to one-third of male factory and mine operatives earned less than $10 per week, from two-thirds to three-fourths took home less than $15, and the same percentage of women workers earned less than $8 per week. The report compared these wage scales to infant mortality rates and concluded that "the babies of the poor die at least three times the rate of the fairly well-to-do."[40] Conditions were just as dismal and hopeless for agricultural laborers. As farm tenancy increased, so, too, did landlord exploitation. The report concluded that as a group sharecroppers and tenant farmers were "badly housed, ill nourished, and uneducated." In order to eliminate these inequities, Manly recommended a sharply graded inheritance tax whose revenue would be used for education, social services, and state and local public works programs. All inheritances would be limited to $1,000,000.[41]

The Manly report blamed unemployment upon two factors: the unequal distribution of income, which contributed to an absence of consumer purchasing power and thus periodic layoffs, and monopolization of land and natural resources, which eliminated competition, curtailed employment, and made farming prohibitive for all but the wealthy. Manly's solutions reflected some ideas popularized by the radical Progressives, including government ownership of the land and natural resources and a modified single tax exempting all improvements from taxation that would force idle land into use. Other recommendations proposed creation of a national employment service that would act as an information clearinghouse for the unemployed with responsibility for developing an unemployment insurance system, and, lastly, establishment of a special board that would prepare contingency plans for extensive public works programs to be implemented during periods of depression and the winter months.[42]

High atop the grievance list of American workers was the conviction that "courts discriminate against the poor," that sections of the Constitution had been perverted so that property rights rather than human rights received federal protection, and that laws designed to protect workers' rights had been ignored. Manly's report decried the worker's vulnerability to loan sharks and fraudulent employment agents and powerlessness to prevent employers from docking pay and levying exorbitant fines. It criticized public officials for suspending constitutional guarantees during strikes and for sanctioning false arrests, excessive bail, sweeping injunctions, and martial law while excluding workers from petit and grand juries. The Manly report urged Congress to enact two constitutional amendments: the first to reaffirm the guarantees provided in the Bill of Rights, and the second, a somewhat ill-conceived proposal, to prohibit the judiciary from declaring legislative acts invalid. Other recommendations included broadening the list of prospective jurors to approximate the population at large, interstate regulation of private detective agencies, and congressional legislation banning the shipment of men or weapons across interstate lines for use in strikes.[43]

Finally, the Manly report bluntly held workers responsible for their own suffering, exploitation, and oppression because they had been "blind to their collective strength and deaf to the cries of their fellows." Freedom, democracy, and fair treatment could be obtained only through organization. "Until the workers themselves realize their responsibility and utilize to the full their collective power, no action, whether governmental or altruistic, can work any genuine and lasting improvement." The report strongly endorsed labor's right to organize and bargain collectively and proposed a constitutional amendment or legislation to guarantee those rights. It also recommended enactment of a statute authorizing the Federal Trade Commission to prohibit such unfair employer practices as excessive work hours, unsafe or unsanitary conditions, low wages, and the refusal to bargain collectively. The key remained an enthusiastic call for worker organization. Manly encouraged labor to view collective power as both an economic force that could obtain higher wages, shorter hours, and better conditions, and as a political force that would "unshackle" labor from the constraints imposed by the courts, government, and employers.[44]

The Final Report of the Commission on Industrial Relations, representing eleven volumes of testimony and over 250 pages of recommendations, had a limited immediate impact. Graham Adams, Jr., the commission's biographer, notes CIR influence in several pieces of legislation supported by the Wilson administration during 1915 and 1916 including the Keating-Owen National Child Labor Act, the Adamson Eight-Hour Day Act for railroad workers, and the La Follette Seamen's Act. Both Adams and James Weinstein point to World War I as a major factor in turning public attention away from domestic reform. "Few immediate reforms came from the Commission hearings or recommendations," writes Weinstein, "because preparedness and then American entrance into the World War followed quickly upon the end of the Commission's work."[45] "In one sense," observes Adams, "World War I prevented further possible reforms on the home front. Both the government and the public turned away from peacetime domestic problems."[46]

There is no question that the war in Europe pushed consideration of the CIR's recommendations off the front page. But the war cannot be blamed for the tepid public reaction to twenty-two months of investigation, hundreds of hours of well-publicized hearings, and thousands of pages of testimony. The CIR's proposals were ignored, when they were not dismissed, precisely because most progressives found the Manly report disruptive, biased, and ill-balanced. Quite simply, it scared them. "Never before has any agency of the federal government," observed *Survey*, "issued a pronouncement that so breathed the spirit and the bitter resentment of organized labor. . . . It sets forth . . . the essential claims and the indignant protest of a class that feels itself consistently and habitually the victim of oppression." But where were the facts? "Inquiry and publicity are indispensable," noted the *Nation*, but the whole problem was too vast and too delicate to be solved by "half-baked, uncritical, and even grotesque" recommendations. What the report lacks, noted the *New Republic*, "is that massing of evidence, that organized picture, which would give it a body and a life." Dismissing the Manly report as "thin and verbal," the editors characterized its conclusions as "uncritical denunciation" and "a skeleton of evils" rather than a proportional survey of the life in which such wrongs occur.[47]

By contrast, progressives fell all over themselves in embracing the "careful thinking" and "conscientiously thoughtful proposals" of the Commons report. Where the Manly report was unbalanced, strident, and merely accusatory, the former's recommendations were "cooperative," "impartial," "reasonable," "advisory," and "representative." There was a faintly negative side to progressives' praise when the *New Republic* noted that the Commons plan was not spectacular. "It predicts no sudden, beneficent transformation. . . . It is significant, even revolutionary, and yet humdrum." But its revolutionary nature, as the editors quickly added, lay in its call for proper methods of legislation, interpretation, and administration to make labor laws more enforceable. The *Nation* concluded that though the entire history of the CIR had been a "fiasco," the Commons report would receive serious consideration long after other "maunderings" had been cast aside.[48]

The progressive establishment's reactions to the Manly and Commons reports illustrate emerging differences within the liberal community. Most progressives continued to identify themselves with organized labor. Their sympathy for the oppressed was partly sentimental and romantic, but also represented a commitment to eliminate injustice and to provide equality of opportunity through temporary government action. Their solutions were the tried and true remedies of earlier campaigns—institutional change, legislative reform, and public education. Most progressives advocated the mechanics of collective bargaining and believed that a benevolent, wise, and scientific bureaucracy would solve the problem of industrial unrest. The idea that labor might resort to political action was distasteful to most liberals because it implied special needs that could not be reconciled with the public interest. The further possibility that industrial conflict was caused by maladjustments which could not be cured or removed by administrative reform was too pessimistic a conclusion for most progressives to accept. But that was precisely the motivation behind the Manly report. "What is needed," Manly angrily wrote the *New Republic*, "is not technique but understanding; not an intellectual method but an awakened social consciousness and sympathy."[49]

Basil M. Manly's report reached the public only after the commission's official expiration. It did so without the benefit of any educational or publicity campaign. Early in November 1915, Frank P. Walsh, Manly, the CIR's labor commissioners, and representatives of the railroad brotherhoods, United Mine Workers of America, and Women's Trade Union League joined reformers Frederic C. Howe and Amos Pinchot in creating a private support group. Missing from the letterhead of this new "Committee on Industrial Relations" were the names of all those settlement leaders, social gospel activists, social reformers, and academics who had lobbied for the creation of a federal commission three years earlier. Deeply offended by the Manly report's accusatory style and the radical tone of its recommendations, these men and women wanted no part of a committee which advocated fundamental and radical reforms, even if they were for the welfare of the nation. Not surprisingly, organized labor responded quite differently. Editors and union leaders warmly embraced the Manly report's prolabor sentiments and helped finance its wide-scale publication and dissemination. Moreover, the inclusion of conservative leaders from the railroad brotherhoods on the same committee with more militant colleagues from the Chicago Federation of Labor suggested a unanimity of support distinctly absent among progressives.[50]

The new Committee on Industrial Relations had a liberal patina but was clearly controlled by organized labor. Acting unofficially as a national lobbyist, the committee kept labor issues before Congress by recommending friendly witnesses and by suggesting potentially fruitful lines of inquiry to sympathetic congressmen. In addition to publicizing labor concerns, the committee optimistically planned an intensive educational campaign in support of collective bargaining, including a forum service which would provide speakers for interested groups, a lecture series on the Chautauqua circuit, and even a number of motion pictures based upon the lives of labor leaders. The committee also was active in drafting legislation for possible enactment at state and federal levels. Many of the bills proposed by director Basil M. Manly, such as a trades dispute act protecting the right of workers to organize, a measure forbidding courts from invalidating legislation, and a democratic jury bill, all had been included in the Manly report. Other recommendations included proposals that would insure constitutional guarantees during martial law, protect the right of peaceful picketing, encourage school-teachers to unionize, and guarantee public employees a decent minimum wage.[51]

None of this activity seems to have had much impact on Congress. Labor's modest muscle-flexing did not impress its traditional enemies, but it did risk the further alienation of the liberal community. At the same time, progressives who had been affronted by labor's championing of the Manly report faced a much more frightening prospect of watching their country prepare for war. Unlike industrial relations, which remained a divisive issue between liberal and labor leaders, preparedness raised more elemental questions that allowed both sides temporarily to submerge their differences.

Rather than an issue which diverted public attention from domestic concerns, the preparedness controversy precipitated a nationwide debate in which war and reform held center stage. The Committee on Industrial Relations avoided formal association with pacifist or antiwar themes but did concern itself with some ethical and economic issues. It recommended that all military supplies, munitions, and equipment be manufactured in government-owned or operated plants. "There must be no profit," Manly wrote, "in the killing of men." The committee was equally sensitive to the danger of an emerging military caste in the United States. It suggested that the militia and national guard systems be organized on a democratic basis "with equal opportunity for wage earners and those without means to obtain commissions on a merit basis." Such forces, the committee contended, must confine their activities to national defense and "must never be used against workmen on strike." The most significant recommendation of the committee in light of future events concerned the financing of the war. The committee urged Congress to obtain additional revenue through income and inheritance taxes rather than resorting to "heavier taxes upon the necessities and comforts of the workers, such as sugar, tea, coffee, tobacco, and the like, nor by bond issues which are a continuing burden upon the producers."[52]

The conflict over preparedness and war was inextricably linked in most progressives' minds with the struggle against special privilege and economic concentration. Progressives contended that preparedness would redirect reform energies away from the desperate problems of mass poverty, unemployment, class hatred, and industrial violence. Militarism would destroy democracy. Gains already made would be jeopardized, while insurmountable barriers would block future reform. The men and women who gathered in the various antipreparedness and antiwar societies in 1915 and 1916 shared common experiences as social workers, government ownership advocates, defenders of labor rights, and veterans of the Bull Moose and New Freedom movements. Many had assisted strikers at Lawrence and Paterson; some had lobbied for labor legislation while others had fought for the creation of the CIR.

It is clear, however, that most progressives were more comfortable espousing workers' rights than contemplating a strong union movement. Liberals remained patronizing, arrogant, and condescending in their attitudes toward organized labor. Accustomed to exercising influence within the system, they were temperamentally unsuited to challenge the established structure. Because they valued constancy and consistency, progressives saw no need to compartmentalize their lives or beliefs. This holistic and symbiotic view of the world was emotionally comforting but politically naive. It left no room for ambiguity. Progressives rejected the possibility of an atomistic, segmented society but also refused to participate with any group who did not accept their views. Thus, progressives would come to see the struggle for labor rights as inseparable from *their* related fights for open diplomacy, preservation of civil liberties, and a "pay-as-you-go" program of war finance. But the mutual cooperation necessary for the success of such efforts required a liberal-labor coalition. Most progressives were incapable of accepting the notion of a partnership between equals.

NOTES

1. Allen F. Davis, "The Campaign for the Industrial Relations Commission, 1911–1913," *Mid-America* 45 (Oct. 1963), 211–228. See also the form letter, Feb. 8, 1912, box 239, W. Jett Lauck Papers, University of Virginia, hereinafter cited as Lauck Papers.

2. Graham Adams, Jr., *Age of Industrial Violence, 1910–1915: The Activities and Findings of the United States Commission on Industrial Relations* (New York: Columbia Univ. Press, 1966), 40–41. See also Vincent P. Carosso, "The Wall Street

Money Trust from Pujo through Medina," *Business History Review* 47 (Winter 1973), 421–437.

3. Davis, "The Campaign for the Industrial Relations Commission," 214. John F. McClymer's *War and Welfare: Social Engineering in America, 1890–1925* (Westport, Conn.: Greenwood Press, 1980), 12–49, documents the progressive penchant for investigation.

4. See Frederic C. Howe to Amos R. E. Pinchot, May 26, 1913, box 14, Amos Pinchot Papers and Upton Sinclair to Amos R. E. Pinchot, May 31, 1913, *ibid.*

5. Amos R. E. Pinchot to William H. Ingersoll, Mar. 14, 1916, box 25, *ibid.*

6. See Roy Lubove, "Frederic C. Howe and the Quest for Community in America," *Historian* 39 (Feb. 1977), 270–291; and Stanley Shapiro, "The Twilight of Reform: Advanced Progressives After the Armistice, *ibid.*, 33 (May 1971), 349–364. See also Lafayette G. Harter, Jr., *John R. Commons: His Assault on Laissez-Faire* (Corvallis: Oregon State Univ. Press, 1962), 132–133.

7. William L. O'Neill, *The Last Romantic: A Life of Max Eastman* (New York: Oxford Univ. Press, 1978), 41. Leslie Fishbein, *Rebels in Bohemia: The Radicals of "The Masses", 1911–1917* (Chapel Hill: Univ. of North Carolina Press, 1982), 20, discusses Pinchot's role in this affair.

8. Amos R. E. Pinchot to Mrs. Morris W. Kellogg, Dec. 29, 1913, box 15, Pinchot Papers "Letter to the Editor," Feb. 27, 1914, box 111, *ibid.*; and "Announcement of Free Press Protest Meeting," *ibid.* The patrons' list included a sprinkling of New York's most prominent social workers, journalists, and activist intellectuals: Charles and Mary Beard, Allan Benson, John Dewey, Morris Hillquit, Norman and Hutchins Hapgood, Florence Kelley, Frances Perkins, John Spargo, Walter Weyl, and Walter Lippmann.

9. Helene M. Hooker, ed., "Amos R. E. Pinchot," *History of the Progressive Party 1912–1916* (New York: New York Univ. Press, 1958), 66–67.

10. Amos R. E. Pinchot to Mrs. Morris W. Kellogg, Dec. 29, 1913, box 15, Amos Pinchot Papers.

11. Oswald G. Villard to Marie Jenney Howe (Mrs. Frederic C. Howe), Feb. 21, 1914, box 16, *ibid.*

12. Amos R. E. Pinchot, "Letter to the Editor," Mar. 7, 1914, *ibid.*, follows the *New York Times* coverage of the Cooper Union protest meeting.

13. Donald A. Ritchie, "The Gary Committee: Businessmen, Progressives, and Unemployment in New York City, 1914–1915," *New-York Historical Society Quarterly* 57 (Oct. 1973), 327–347.

14. Amos R. E. Pinchot to Mrs. George Bernard Shaw, Jan. 6, 1915, box 19, Amos Pinchot Papers.

15. Amos R. E. Pinchot to John P. Mitchel, public letter, Jan. 12, 1915, *ibid.*

16. Amos R. E. Pinchot to Rabbi Stephen S. Wise, Nov. 22, 1916, box 25, *ibid.*, Amos R. E. Pinchot to Alexander J. McKelway, Feb. 2, 1916, box 34, *ibid.*, and Amos R. E. Pinchot to Ernest Harvier, June 23, 1917, box 30, *ibid.* Two articles by Augustus Cerillo, Jr., are also helpful on this issue: "The Reform of Municipal Government in New York City: From Seth Low to John Purroy Mitchel," *New-York Historical Society Quarterly* 57 (Jan. 1973), 51–71, and "The Impact of Reform Ideology: Early Twentieth-Century Municipal Government in New York City," in Michael H. Ebner and Eugene M. Tobin, eds., *The Age of Urban Reform: New*

Perspectives on the Progressive Era (Port Washington, N.Y.: Kennikat Press, 1977), 68–85.

17. The 1913 Paterson silk strike is the subject of an ever-proliferating body of literature. For a beginning one might start with: Melvyn Dubofsky, *We Shall Be All: A History of the Industrial Workers of the World* (New York: Quadrangle, 1969), 263–290; Graham Adams, Jr., *Age of Industrial Violence*, 75–100; Philip S. Foner, *History of the Labor Movement in the United States*, Vol. IV: *The Industrial Workers of the World, 1905–1917* (New York: International Publishers, 1965), 352–372; Joyce L. Kornbluh, ed., *Rebel Voices: An I.W.W. Anthology* (Ann Arbor: Univ. of Michigan Press, 1964), 197–226; Robert H. Zieger, "Robin Hood in the Silk City: The IWW and the Paterson Strike of 1913," *Proceedings of the New Jersey Historical Society* 84 (1966), 182–195. Portions of this chapter dealing with Paterson are taken from my essay, "Direct Action and Conscience: The 1913 Paterson Strike as Example of the Relationship Between Labor Radicals and Liberals," *Labor History* 20 (Winter 1979), 73–88. A recent essay worth close attention is Steve Golin, "Defeat Becomes Disaster: The Paterson Strike of 1913 and the Decline of the IWW," *Labor History* 24 (Spring 1983), 223–248.

18. The statute under which a number of Wobblies were indicted was a criminal anarchy law passed following Pres. William McKinley's assassination; see *Laws of New Jersey*, 1902, Ch. 33, Sect. 1.

19. See *Newark Evening News*, May 8, 9, 1913; *New York Times*, May 10, 1913, 7:2.

20. The quotation from the *Paterson Call* was reprinted in a *Newark Evening News* editorial, May 15, 1913. Elizabeth Gurley Flynn discusses "Jersey justice" in *The Rebel Girl: An Autobiography, My First Life, 1906–1926* (New York: International Publishers, 1973), 160.

21. See *State of New Jersey, Defendant in Error, v. Patrick Quinlan, Plaintiff in Error*, 86 N.J.L. 120 (Sup. Ct., 1914), and 87 N.J.L. 333 (Ct. E & A, 1914). The question of an impartial jury selection process is discussed in "Editorial Notes," *New Jersey Law Journal* 37 (Apr. 1914), n.p.; *Final Report and Testimony Submitted to Congress by the Commission on Industrial Relations* (CIR), Vol. III, Senate Document No. 415, 64th Congress, 1st Session (Washington, D.C., 1916), 2536–2539. The selection of grand juries at the time of the Paterson strike was the responsibility of the county sheriff, who arbitrarily selected citizens eligible for service.

22. *New York Times*, June 6, 1914, 4:3; Feb. 27, 1915, 6:5; June 20, 1915, II, 9:8; Dec. 28, 1915, 4:6; Feb. 3, 1917, 20:3; and Patrick Quinlan, "The Trenton Penitentiary," *New Republic* 9 (Jan. 23, 1917), 292–295.

23. William Preston, Jr., *Aliens and Dissenters: Federal Suppression of Radicals, 1903–1933* (Cambridge: Harvard Univ. Press, 1963), 55–62.

24. Amos R. E. Pinchot to Patrick Quinlan, May 23, 1913, box 14, Pinchot Papers.

25. Ewing Galloway to Amos R. E. Pinchot, May 27, 1913, *ibid.*

26. *New York Times*, Dec. 13, 1915, 22:1.

27. Amos R. E. Pinchot to Treadwell Cleveland, government editor, *Newark Evening News*, Feb. 5, 1915, box 19, *ibid.*

28. For a description of the pageant see Dubofsky, *We Shall Be All*, 279ff; Foner, *The Industrial Workers of the World*, 264–267.

29. *Final Report and Testimony*, Commission on Industrial Relations, Vol. IX, 8041–8052.

30. James Weinstein, *The Corporate Ideal in the Liberal State 1900–1918* (Boston: Beacon Press, 1968), 191–194; Adams, *Age of Industrial Violence*, 146–161. See also George S. McGovern and Leonard F. Guttridge, *The Great Coalfield War* (Boston: Houghton Mifflin Co., 1972), 210–231.

31. See Amos R. E. Pinchot to Edward P. Costigan, Sept. 25, 1914; and his fund-raising attempts in letters to Franklin K. Lane, secretary of the interior, Sept. 11, 1914, and to E. W. Scripps, Sept. 11, 1914, box 14, Amos Pinchot Papers.

32. Amos R. E. Pinchot, form letter, July 15, 1914, box 17, announcing rally, "Speech of Amos Pinchot at a Mass Meeting Held at Webster Hall, New York City, Friday evening, July 17, 1914, to Discuss the Colorado Strike," box 95, Amos Pinchot Papers.

33. Amos R. E. Pinchot, "Labor and the Future," address before the Justice League at the Lawson Protest Meeting, Denver, July 31, 1915, box 206, Amos Pinchot Papers; see also undated newspaper clippings pertaining to Pinchot's activities in Colorado, box 112, *ibid.*

34. Weinstein, *The Corporate Ideal in the Liberal State*, 213.

35. *Final Report and Testimony*, U.S. Commission on Industrial Relations, Vol. I, 231–248, covers the "Employers" report; the Commons-Harriman report covers pages 171–230. A one-volume edition can be found in the *Final Report of the Commission on Industrial Relations* (Washington, D.C., 1915). The Manly report can be found on pages 1–252, the Commons-Harriman report on 307–404, and the "Employers" report on 407–439.

36. Mark Perlman, *Labor Union Theories in America: Background and Development* (Evanston, Ill.: Row, Peterson and Co., 1958), 284–286, lists the brilliant nucleus which McCarthy gathered around him; many would go on to active careers during the war and into the 1920s in a variety of liberal-labor causes: Basil M. Manly, who would replace McCarthy as research director (and later succeed Frank P. Walsh as co-chairman of the War Labor Board), was initially brought in as an expert on the industrial problems of organized labor; Crystal Eastman, feminist, lawyer, contributor to the *Masses* and co-publisher of its successor, the *Liberator*, specialist on industrial relations and the courts, served as an investigator on the *Pittsburgh Survey* and later was an active force in the American Union Against Militarism and Woman's Peace Party; W. Jett Lauck, the CIR's managing expert, economist, later secretary of the War Labor Board conference board, would be an active participant in labor investigations during the 1920s; labor experts Selig Perlman, Paul Brissenden, and David Saposs would all be major figures in the postwar progressive labor movement. The quotation is in a letter from Charles V. McCarthy to W. Jett Lauck, Sept. 8, 1914, box 239, Lauck Papers.

37. Adams, *Age of Industrial Violence*, 204–214; Weinstein, *The Corporate Ideal in the Liberal State*, 198–200; and Harter, *John R. Commons*, 139. Walsh's attack on McCarthy's integrity appears unwarranted in light of a letter from McCarthy to W. Jett Lauck, August 20, 1914, requesting an investigation into the Rockefeller Foundation's relationship to "industrial enterprises" owned by the Rockefeller Corporation, box 239, Lauck Papers.

38. Adams, *Age of Industrial Violence*, 225; John R. Commons, *Myself* (New York: Macmillan, 1934), 173–175; *Final Report and Testimony* (CIR), I, 171–230. See also Milton Derber, "The Idea of Industrial Democracy in America, 1898–1915," *Labor History* 7 (Fall 1966), 262–265. The quotation is from the *New Republic*, "Industrial Conflict," 4 (Aug. 28, 1915), 91.

39. Summary of the Manly report of the Commission on Industrial Relations, prepared and distributed by the Committee on Industrial Relations, box 110, Amos Pinchot Papers.

40. *Final Report and Testimony*, I, 22–23.

41. *Ibid.*, 25, 29–35.

42. *Ibid.*, 35–38.

43. *Ibid.*, 38–61.

44. *Ibid.*, 61–68.

45. Weinstein, *The Corporate Ideal*, 213.

46. Adams, *Age of Industrial Violence*, 222.

47. John A. Fitch, "Probing the Causes of Industrial Unrest," *Survey* 35 (Dec. 18, 1915), 317–319, 320–323; *Nation*, "The Fiasco of the Industrial Commission," 101 (Aug. 26, 1915), 251; *New Republic*, "Industrial Conflict," 4 (Aug. 28, 1915), 89–92.

48. *Survey*, "The Commons Report," 35 (Jan. 1, 1916), 395–400, 401–406; *New Republic*, "The Commons Report," 4 (Aug. 28, 1915), 91; *Nation*, "This Week," 101 (Sept. 2, 1915), 277.

49. Basil M. Manly, "Letter to the Editor," *New Republic*, 4 (Sept. 18, 1915), 183–184.

50. *Survey*, "A Follow-Up Committee on Industrial Relations," 35 (Nov. 6, 1915), 155–156.

51. Report of Basil M. Manly for Committee on Industrial Relations Meeting, Dec. 11, 1915, box 110, Amos Pinchot Papers.

52. *Ibid.*, and *Survey*, "A Follow-Up Committee," 156.

IV

The Road from
Henry Street to
Wall Street

Peace is the problem of democracy. Peace is the first great cause of labor.... Permanent lasting peace will only come with an end of war.... Labor . . . is at war with war.[1]

Gradually, almost inexorably, the war in Europe intruded itself into America's consciousness. Heated internal debates during 1916–1917 educated the public to the potential advantages and dangers inherent in preparedness, militarism, and conscription. As the war came physically and psychologically nearer, and as the Wilson administration edged closer to intervention, popular attitudes hardened toward those who urged neutrality and counseled against military preparedness. Those reformers who refused to allow their progressive sentiments to degenerate into an unreasoning nationalism and maintained their prewar commitment to industrial and economic democracy were the objects of hatred, suspicion, and ridicule.[2] These social workers, social gospel ministers, activist intellectuals, publicists, and pacifists drew upon the shared experiences of a decade's involvement in prewar struggles for economic and political democracy. Admittedly, they never had been a totally unified or coherent group; frequent disagreements had been common even during the golden years of prewar reform. Yet most of these men and women shared an underlying faith in the value of organization, a lesson learned after unsuccessful individual struggles against entrenched political bosses, recalcitrant public utilities, and indifferent state legislators. They had yet to demonstrate, however, the ability or inclination to organize beyond their own narrow circle.

As war approached, nonresistants, antiwar liberals, and all those in between refused to be silenced by the rising chorus for preparedness and conscription. Courageously, perhaps quixotically, they joined in a massive educational campaign to warn their fellow citizens against the horrors of modern warfare and the dangers to free speech and civil liberties at home. When the battle against intervention was lost, they regrouped. Many prowar progressives drifted away, but others remained to denounce privilege, exploitation, and unjustified profit. These reformers challenged the American people and their leaders to adopt an international perspective that would put democracy and peace ahead of nationalism; dignity and justice before profit. Their activities have been chronicled with meticulous care and represent an important chapter in the history of American liberalism.[3]

It is the movement's survivors who hold center stage in this analysis, particularly activists like Amos Pinchot, whose opposition to preparedness and war led him into the American Union Against Militarism, then to fight for a pay-as-you-go program in the American Committee on War Finance, and finally at war's end to the conclusion that the survival of liberalism lay intertwined with the future of labor. Pinchot is the focus of this chapter, rather than some of his more celebrated contemporaries (Jane Addams, Oswald G. Villard, Scott Nearing) because I believe him to be most representative of those prewar progressives who aspired to reach beyond their class but failed. Like many liberal patricians of his generation, Pinchot never permitted himself to make a clean break. He thus joined other antiwar liberals who seemed unable or uninterested in moving beyond their comfortable surroundings to engage anyone but themselves.

Shortly after the outbreak of war in Europe, a group of social-justice progressives gathered at New York City's Henry Street Settlement to assess the conflict's potential impact upon American society in general and reform in particular. These men and women, including Jane Addams, Frederic C. Howe, Lillian Wald, John Haynes Holmes, Oswald G. Villard, Crystal Eastman, and Rabbi Stephen S. Wise, were veterans of numerous campaigns for child labor reform, free speech, labor's right to organize, and a dozen other concerns accumulated from a decade's confrontation with urban-industrial America. They were not ideologues. Some aspired to varying degrees of pacifism; others possessed a more general, unarticulated horror of war. For the Henry Street group the conflict in Europe was another legacy of social injustice. Like poverty, infant mortality, and child labor, it was the result of the strong exploiting the weak. Though some progressives would support both preparedness and American involvement in the war, the Henry Street group's antimilitarism was not primarily pacifist in origin; it was rooted, instead, in an unwillingness to tolerate any form of societal inequity.

Few among them dared contemplate the war's possibilities for positive social change. Rather, their overwhelming fear concerned the war's potential destructiveness on reforms achieved after years of work and sacrifice. Their antimilitarist attitudes had not required sleight of hand, verbal gymnastics, or sudden conversion. They saw a direct correlation between political and economic democracy at home and abroad. "Present-day wars," Frederic C. Howe observed, "are primarily the result of the conflict of powerful economic interests. . . . Surplus wealth seeking privileges in foreign lands is the proximate cause of [this] war just as wealth seeking monopoly profits is the cause of the civil conflicts that have involved our cities and States."[4]

In March 1915, eighteen members of the Henry Street group signed a declaration of principles which appeared in *Survey*. Their statement, optimistically entitled "Toward the Peace That Shall Last," was a collective protest against the "retardation" of progress and reactionary "throwback" which they claimed had occurred within six months of their first meeting. With the misery, hunger, fear, and deprivation of the past winter still vivid in their minds, reformers held the war makers responsible for the nationwide unemployment which had crippled urban America and particularly New York City. The belligerents were held accountable for the financial depression which impeded needed emergency relief and for the absence of humanitarian concern which had contributed to "hot anger and civil strife." But beyond this long-suffering litany of injustices, the reformers paradoxically struck a provincial and universal note: "We have a right to speak," they declared, "by our consciousness that every instinct and motive and ideal at work in this war . . . has had some counterpart in our national history and our current life. . . . We can speak as fellow-victims of this great oppression."[5]

After some false starts, the Henry Street group reorganized into a more formal organization in November 1915 following President Wilson's public conversion to preparedness and call for a strengthened army and national guard.[6] This was just the beginning. Its evolution would encompass eighteen critical months of debate over the issues of militarism and preparedness. During this time, its composition, name, and concerns underwent substantial change, finally emerging in April 1916 as the American Union Against Militarism (AUAM). In the fall of 1915, however, the AUAM was just another unknown, struggling organization with an unwieldy, imprecise name—the "Anti-Militarism Committee"—attempting to capture public attention and find its sense of direction. During this developmental stage, committee leaders found comfort and continuity from their shared experiences in recent struggles. One of the most important common denominators proved to be the earlier association of committee members Crystal Eastman and Frederic C. Howe with the U.S. Commission on Industrial Relations.[7] If the group's early press releases and policy statements are any indication, Howe's and Eastman's influence was responsible for the Anti-Militarism Committee's endorsement of CIR recommendations. Closely paralleling Basil M. Manly's proposals for the Committee on Industrial Relations, pacifists and antiwar liberals urged that all expenditures for military preparedness be financed by income and inheritance taxes rather than "consumption" taxes on tobacco, sugar, coffee, and gasoline. The antimilitarists also echoed Manly's argument that the profit motive could be eliminated by manufacturing armaments in government factories.[8]

But preparedness advocates would not be denied. Lobbyists from the Army, Navy, National Security, and American Defense leagues descended upon Congress with proposals for an expanded national guard, regular army, and government-funded summer training camps. They were better financed than their opponents and possessed the affirmative side of an argument whose stature grew following the sinking of the *Lusitania*, the frequency with which German atrocity stories appeared in the American press, and President Wilson's gradual conversion to the preparedness cause. Still, the antimilitarists remained undaunted and expanded their own activities to counter their adversaries' moves. In January 1916, these antiwar liberals opened a Washington office, broadened their leadership base, and instituted a name change to dispel any confusion as to their major purpose.

The new "Anti-Preparedness Committee" could now boast a Washington lobbyist and a letterhead with leaders who finally reached beyond the borders of New York City including Jane Addams (Chicago), Elizabeth Glendower Evans (Boston), and Zona Gale (Portage, Wisconsin). But these were surface changes. Committee meetings continued to be held weekly in New York, and it mattered little to supporters or critics whether the committee attacked militarism in general or naval and military expansion in particular. One constant, which had not changed since the group's first discussions at Henry Street House, remained an unwillingness to separate militarism from the progressive struggle against social injustice. An announcement of the committee's new name and membership protested "against the effort to divert public funds, needed in constructive programs for national health and well-being, into the manufacture of engines of death. . . . We are against all the various 'preparedness' programs," the committee declared, "because they are extravagant, unnecessary, and contrary to all that is best in our national traditions."[9] But the argument that the country faced no danger from invasion grew less convincing after the *Lusitania* incident, nor did Wilson's eight-day, seven-city speaking tour in behalf of preparedness legislation, in late January 1916, dispel liberal doubts about his administration's pronounced drift toward militarism.[10]

The president's actions did prompt another organizational change within the Henry Street group: a significantly expanded Washington-based AUAM emerged in April with Lillian Wald and Paul Kellogg as chairman and vice-chairman; Crystal Eastman, fresh from her work with the Woman's Peace Party as executive secretary; and an executive committee with a host of new faces including Amos Pinchot, Cincinnati activist Herbert S. Bigelow, Pennsylvania State Federation of Labor president James H. Maurer, radical economist Scott Nearing, and Brooklyn surgeon James Warbasse. The surge of enthusiasm and excitement which came from new blood and new money found expression in the creation of an antiwar news service which the AUAM provided labor, grange, and farm weeklies. A much more celebrated aspect of the union's growth was its "truth about Preparedness campaign" in response to Woodrow Wilson's challenge for a national preparedness debate. The union organized well-attended mass meetings in eleven cities over a ten-day period in its own "swing around the circle." Its speakers opposed any increases in the military budget, warned against the menace of preparedness and conscription, and portrayed the debate as a struggle between militarism and democracy. Though the delight of satirists, perhaps because the union's speakers were accompanied by a gigantic papier-mâché dinosaur boorishly named "Jingo," the episode's real importance lay in its publicity value and the doors it opened to the White House.[11]

Early in May 1916, a group of AUAM leaders met with President Wilson. Though skeptical of his administration's drift toward preparedness, reformers such as Lillian Wald, Rabbi Stephen S. Wise, and Amos Pinchot still retained an almost childlike faith in the president's judgment. His actions since January had demonstrated a continued commitment to social reform. The Democratic Congress had approved his appointment of progressive activist Louis D. Brandeis to the Supreme Court and was well on its way toward approving a federal child labor act and a collection of other welfare legislation that included workmen's compensation reform, an eight-hour day for railroad workers, safety regulations for seamen, and an expanded loan program for family farmers. Moreover, many of these antiwar progressives had campaigned actively for Wilson in 1912 and would do so again. He was "their" president, a progressive like them, and if there were differences they would be kept within the "family."[12]

Mindful of the constraints under which Wilson operated, union leaders tried during their meeting to be as accommodating as possible without sacrificing their own independence. They told the president that the AUAM was not opposed to "sane and reasonable 'preparedness,' " nor did it advocate "peace at any price." Disclaiming any belief in "radical pacifism," they nonetheless attacked the "so-called 'preparedness' movement" as an "unnecessary ... and dangerous expression of class and national aggression."[13]

Amos Pinchot, who soon would represent a more radical wing within the union, reminded the president that militaristic attitudes encouraged economic imperialism. Pointing to the recent organization of the American International Corporation, he warned that a conglomerate of its size, power, and ambition would be a powerful influence for aggressive nationalism. The growth of such multinational corporations reflected conscious attempts to "find new worlds to conquer" while imposing upon the rest of civilization "the same system of exploitation they have so successfully brought to perfection here."[14]

The ongoing deterioration in Mexican-American relations, following Pancho Villa's murderous raid on Columbus, New Mexico, in early March 1916, increased Pinchot's suspicion of "sinister" and "unscrupulous" business interests who urged intervention or annexation to safeguard their billion-dollar investments. The de facto regime of Venustiano Carranza was not without its faults, as Pinchot observed, but the Mexican people, he believed, were battling a problem common to their northern neighbors. "They believe that as long as the natural resources of Mexico are in the hand of a few powerful individuals and great companies there will never be any real freedom, any democracy that is worth anything to the common man." Economic exploitation and "aggressive commercial aggrandizement," Pinchot concluded, were as dangerous to peace as conscription and preparedness.[15]

The AUAM's primary argument, however, remained moral rather than economic. Union leaders warned of the dangers of preparedness propaganda and the untoward consequences of universal military training. "Once we were a fearless people," Rabbi Stephen S. Wise told an antipreparedness rally at Carnegie Hall in early April, "are we to become a contemptible, fearful people?" "When I learn that the price we must pay for the security of our republic is the abandonment of every ideal that makes the republic," observed John Haynes Holmes, "I for one refuse to pay the price." In response, President Wilson was sympathetic, philosophical, and polite. Though sensitive to his fellow progressives' fears and genuinely opposed to the spread of militarism, the president emphasized present-day realities. He told union representatives that they were living in a time of "madness" and "insanity." "All the world is seeing red," he observed, "and in the last analysis the peace of society is obtained . . . by the ultimate application of force."[16] This was not the message peace advocates had hoped to receive. Wilson's remarks left his listeners benumbed and alone. He had tried to soothe their feelings but ended up rubbing their noses in militaristic bombast. Though probably unintentionally, the president had dismissed any connection between war and the destruction of reform by echoing conventional preparedness rhetoric about the traditional role played by citizen soldiers in wartime. Such sentiments already were well on the way toward transforming the cherished progressive concept of "service" into mandatory military service. "Under the seemingly reasonable term of 'preparedness,' " observed Lillian Wald, "militarism . . . has attempted to substitute the absolutism of military control for wholesome, sane preparedness, for the service of a citizen."[17] Like many members of the Henry Street group, Wald understood that military duty, like taxation, had become equated with a citizen's public responsibility.

Wilson's honest if blunt candor reflected a fact of political life. His administration could easily bear the loss of AUAM support. It would have been regrettable but politically expedient. In fact, as the president probably realized, the union's support was inevitable once the alternatives were considered. The candidacies of Charles E. Hughes and Roosevelt only aroused feelings of negative horror among peace advocates. The Bull Moose party, once the bright hope of many reformers, tragically led the remaining faithful toward unquestioned support for preparedness and compulsory military training. Though the president's "peace" candidacy received strong endorsement from the antiwar community, in reality groups such as the AUAM had nowhere else to turn. Moreover, the struggle against preparedness largely had been lost by the end of 1916. The union's future success would depend upon mobilizing an aroused public opinion behind the preservation of peace, as it succeeded in doing in June 1916 when war with Mexico was averted partly as a result of the AUAM's publicity campaign. It was apparent to the men and women of the union that though they no longer could innocently trust Wilson's judgment, he remained the most important hope of the antiwar movement.[18] Just as the radical Progressives, convinced of TR's good intentions, had followed him to Armageddon, many now found themselves ineluctably approaching a far more final battle.

Following the president's narrow reelection in November and the breaking off of diplomatic relations with Germany in February 1917, the antiwar movement underwent a marked change in mood and strategy. Where in June 1916, AUAM editorial director Charles Hallinan had joked about the need for a "Handbook for Pacifists" being written quickly, in December, the union's executive secretary, Crystal Eastman, broadened the AUAM appeal to include "every exhausted anti-militarist, every lover of democracy, every radical, every man who objects to having the taxes wasted, every trade-unionist, [and] every ordinary citizen who dislikes . . . the war trust."[19] That same sense of panic and grasping after straws seemed to have inspired the hope behind "armed neutrality." Seizing upon this stratagem as the best means of defending neutral rights, a handful of antiwar intellectuals, led by Amos Pinchot, Max Eastman, and Randolph Bourne, organized the Committee for Democratic Control to give the armed neutrality proposal the widest possible publicity through petitions to Congress, pamphlets, and public forums.[20] There was something unseemly, however, about antiwar liberals marching shoulder-to-shoulder with outspoken proponents of intervention.

Pacifists hoped that armed neutrality would avert the need for compulsory military training, while their critics-momentarily-turned-colleagues envisioned the arming of merchant vessels as the first step toward war. This partnership proved to be of brief duration; even before the declaration of war against Germany in early April, antiwar liberals and interventionists returned to their accustomed adversary relationship.

The AUAM's struggles paralleled on a much smaller scale a debate then underway in Congress. The armed-ship bill, after winning approval in the House, never reached the Senate floor for a vote. Four midwestern senators, led by Robert M. La Follette, conducted a weekend-long filibuster that ended only when Congress adjourned on March 4 prior to Wilson's second inauguration. The president denounced this paralysis of the Senate by "a little group of willful men" who "have rendered the great Government of the United States helpless and contemptible." But, as Arthur S. Link has noted, the La Follette group had acted out of genuine patriotism in refusing the president permission to engage in undeclared war.[21] The media, choosing to ignore that side of the argument, viciously lashed out at La Follette and his colleagues. Cartoonists had a field day satirically and cruelly portraying these senators in German uniforms decorated with the Iron Cross. Editorial writers castigated them as traitors, cowards, and weaklings, and college students hung them in effigy.[22]

Amos Pinchot was one of the few public figures to defend La Follette, but his own activities with the AUAM and the Committee for Democratic Control already had set him apart from respectable public opinion. One joke then making the rounds of official Washington had "A" saying to "B":

"I wish Roosevelt were President."
"Why?"
"Because if he were, he would order Gifford to shoot Amos and Gifford would do it."[23]

On Monday, March 5, the day of Wilson's second inauguration, Pinchot commiserated with his longtime progressive colleague from Wisconsin. He applauded La Follette's "great personal sacrifice" and courage to withstand "pressure such as few public men have the strength to resist." Armed neutrality, Pinchot admitted, probably would lead America into war—"a new and immeasurable disaster to humanity." But the tragedy was all the more appalling because "the dying multitudes" and "the millions of wretched human beings waiting in sorrow at home do not know what they are fighting and waiting for. . . . God knows," he concluded, "our commercial profits in the war have taken from us all right to preach."[24]

As the increasingly melancholy nature of Pinchot's prose suggests, preaching was one right he was not about to surrender. Though he continued to emphasize the connections between war and domestic issues, his invective lacked the moderation necessary to build bridges among natural allies. His attacks were substantively powerful but politically reckless. Thus, he denounced conscription as "a great commercial policy . . . that the exploiters are forging for their own protection at home and in the interest of . . . financial imperialism abroad," but he did so in a public letter to American Federation of Labor President Samuel Gompers, an advisory committee member to the Council of National Defense. Gompers was not a downtrodden Wobbly seeking financial and moral support but a pillar of the establishment who had kept labor squarely in the center of mainstream opinion while "more radical, less realistic groups" were left by the wayside. The AFL president had no sympathy for "traitors" or "dissenters" like Pinchot who blamed the war on economic imperialism or on Wall Street's desire for a meek, obedient, and disciplined labor movement that would transform American "citizens" into American "subjects."[25] It is not surprising that both men found themselves on the opposite sides of the preparedness question. What is interesting, however, is how little progressives really understood about organized labor. There seems no other explanation, save extraordinary political naiveté, to justify the casualness with which antiwar liberals dismissed the most powerful elements within the union movement.

Pinchot's calculated public attack on Wall Street drew severe criticism from the establishment press. "There is an organization calling itself the AUAM," the *Philadelphia Inquirer* observed. "It is composed of a handful of half-baked Americans of the Amos Pinchot variety—peace-at-any-price persons who would rather see men and women murdered on the high seas than lift a hand to defend them." In these days, the editors concluded, "American citizens are either for the U.S. or against it. There is no half way course."[26]

These were not choices which allowed the antiwar movement control over its destiny. With American intervention imminent, peace advocates chose neither to man the barricades in a futile attempt to prevent war nor to retreat into total silence in abdication to the militarists. A small group of radical antiwar militants returned to an issue that had been germinating for almost two years. They demanded that the costs of war be borne by those most capable of shouldering the burden. "Democracy has a right to insist," Frederic C. Howe observed, "that preparedness is not merely a demand for private profit; that an increased navy is not designed as an agency for the promotion of overseas finance, and that militarism shall not be the grave of the things we hold most dear." Why is it, he asked, that the same classes who attacked the Wilson administration for the inadequacy of its defense program are the very ones who now refuse to pay their just share of the taxes? One of the few weaknesses in preparedness arguments always had been that the most enthusiastic congressional advocates of defense spending were equally unrestrained in demanding that the war be financed by loans, bond drives, indirect taxes, and higher tariffs rather than by income and inheritance taxation. "If twentieth-century wars are economic in . . . origin," as Howe and his radical colleagues believed, "they [could] only be ended by the elimination of the causes which make for war." In *Why War*, Howe's analysis of the European situation, published in 1916, he called for an attack on the privileges, profits, and immunities enjoyed by the ruling classes. Seeking to identify all classes with the antiwar movement, he set forth a program to safeguard the future peace of the world. Such precautions included the democratization of foreign affairs by eliminating secret diplomacy and stripping foreign investors of their privileges and the financial classes of their profits. Howe's proposals envisioned the replacement of the private munitions industry by government-owned plants, creation of a citizen army, and an uncompromisable rule that all sacrifice must be universal.[27] Written in the radical Progressive idiom, *Why War* found a sympathetic audience among those activists unwilling to sever domestic concerns from foreign policy.

Within the antiwar community Howe's ideas were especially attractive to the more radical members of the AUAM who believed war encouraged privilege and monopoly while it destroyed economic democracy. A small group of militants led by Amos Pinchot established the American Committee on War Finance (ACWF) on March 30, 1917. On April 1, the day before Wilson's war message to Congress, newspapers across the nation carried full-page advertisements:

We hope and work for peace, but if war comes . . . rich and poor must be ready to make patriotic sacrifices. But the poor man will make the greatest sacrifice. He will do the bulk of the fighting. . . . The least that can be done by . . . those people of means who do not go to the front is to bear their share of the nation's burdens by the free and prompt offering of their wealth to the nation's cause.

The committee proposed a sliding war tax beginning at 2 percent on all incomes over $2,000, increasing to a point where no one would be allowed more than $100,000 in net income and a specific profit margin ranging from 3 1/2 percent for manufacturers to 6 percent for food wholesalers and retailers. Failure to comply with these guidelines would constitute a felony punishable by fine and imprisonment. Echoing sentiments that recalled Basil M. Manly's report for the Committee on Industrial Relations and the first meetings of the Henry Street group, the ACWF demanded that the war be financed on a pay-as-you-go basis. "The war must be paid as it proceeds, in dollars as in lives. There must be no crushing bonded debt to be paid in taxes by the men who have done the fighting and their children. Let's make this a cash war, a pay-as-you-enter war."[28]

There was something reassuring, admirable, "progressive," and familiar about the committee's struggle for a democratically financed war. After almost two years of trying and failing to curb preparedness sentiment amidst cries of treason and disloyalty, intervention forced antiwar liberals to return to a more solid ground attacking palpable injustice. Even the new accusations hurled against them—"confiscator" and "anarchist"—were comfortably old and tolerable. Less than a year earlier Congress had passed a "landmark" revenue act which shifted the tax burden from the middle and lower classes onto the shoulders of the more well-to-do through new taxes on estates, excess profits, and munitions, along with higher surtaxes on income and inheritances. With the president squarely on the sidelines during this debate, progressives in and out of Congress played influential roles in mobilizing public opinion behind tax reform. One group in particular, the Association for an Equitable Federal Income Tax, deserves special mention. Like so many progressive organizations, it was a temporary coalition created for the purpose of securing passage of a specific piece of legislation. But beyond that, its membership—Frederic C. Howe, Benjamin C. Marsh, Amos Pinchot, and George L. Record—was drawn from an unusually homogeneous group of men, most of whom had participated in radical Bull Moose circles and in related efforts such as the 1913 New York City mayoralty campaign and the more recent activities involving the AUAM.[29]

Unlike the AUAM, which was identified with radical pacifism and often smeared as un-American, the ACWF tried to draw support from a broader social and ideological spectrum. But it, too, found the going difficult even among likely supporters. Prowar Socialist Algie M. Simons faulted the ACWF for failing to emphasize either industrial democracy or the eight-hour day.[30] Progressive publisher E. W. Scripps was reluctant to lend the financial or editorial support of his newspaper chain to the ACWF. "Last issue of *Times*," he wired Pinchot, "annalist [sic] appears sympathetic to our ideas [but] states that former pacifists are rightly subject to suspicion when they now appear as advocates of pay as you go." Scripps's hesitation was echoed in the reluctance of several newspapers to sell the committee advertising space fearing, as did the *New York Times*, that it might discourage enlistment "if the poor got the idea that the rich were not doing their share." Pinchot hurriedly reassured Scripps that pacifism played no role in the ACWF program. "We are not embarrassing but supporting the administration."[31] Plans were also underway to form a more conservative committee composed of men such as Boston merchant-reformer Edward A. Filene and various mem-

bers of the U.S. Chamber of Commerce "and [to] go forward on a platform not calling for confiscation of incomes . . . but for . . . financing the
war by an income tax."[32] Still, any venture which solicited the support
of capitalists, socialists, and single taxers was bound to have organizational and ideological problems. "Personally I believe the war to be so
uncalled for, so wicked and so certain to bring disaster," single-taxer
Daniel Kiefer wrote Pinchot, "that I would rather give myself to opposing
it, or some of its undemocratic results like conscription or universal
service, than to securing means to carry it on."[33]

The debate over war finance reunited many prewar progressives,
sometimes in uneasy and unacknowledged alliance, such as the coupling
of Roosevelt and La Follette on the same side of a pay-as-you-go revenue
policy. Following a Labor Day address in which he proposed "a heavily—a very heavily graduated tax on the excess profits due to war conditions . . . ," TR still felt compelled to disassociate himself from his fellow
progressive. "You do not need to be told the contempt I have for La
Follette and his associates," the Colonel reassured Senator Frank B.
Kellogg. "I am . . . attacking openly and as strongly as I know how, La
Follette and the I.W.W. and the party Socialists and all of the rest of
that gang. But I most emphatically hope that none of us shall . . . be
responsible for enormous profits being made out of the war. . . . As re-
gards La Follette, anything he proposes I look upon with deepest distrust
but of course neither you nor I would be willing to let this distrust warp
our judgement if we found that for some doubtless bad reason he happened on some point to advocate something good."[34]

The real struggle over war taxation was fought in the committees,
cloakrooms, and halls of Congress as special interests pleaded their
cases. "Washington today," observed Amos Pinchot, "is swarming with
lobbyists who have been sent there by rich men and rich corporations
to fight against the income tax and the excess profits tax. These vicarious
patriots . . . have made the discovery that the American flag . . . can be a
life-saving money saving substitute for genuine patriotism."[35] The ACWF,
as Pinchot's rhetoric might indicate, was very much a part of this debate.
Its Washington representative, Alexander J. McKelway, onetime executive secretary of the National Child Labor Committee, worked closely
with congressional insurgents such as House Majority Leader Claude
Kitchin and La Follette and traveled throughout the country soliciting
support from state legislators. Pinchot conducted an extensive letter-
writing campaign within liberal, labor, and radical circles to drum up
enthusiasm for significantly higher income and excess profits taxes. It
was evident that Congress would never adopt such a policy unless "great
pressure [was] brought to bear from the people."[36] On May 15, 1917,
Pinchot testified before the Senate Finance Committee as the spokesman
of the ACWF's plan for higher income, inheritance, and excess profits

taxes. Rising to defend the rights of consumers and the working class, he reminded the committee of the increasing unequal distribution of wealth, the high cost of living, and the sacrifices made by those who would do the fighting, work in the factories, and raise the food. "They are the people," he told the senators, "that this bill should consider."[37] On this and other occasions Pinchot kept returning to the ACWF's strongest argument—"that conscription of men [could] not be defended if unaccompanied by conscription of incomes." If the war effort was to be "a great social enterprise," as the Wilson administration urged, then the government's war financing must not give preference to property rights at the expense of human life. "For some," Pinchot observed, "the duty is to fight; for others to furnish money. . . . The man who goes to the front cannot be paid back the life or the limb he may lose. The man who stays at home should contribute his just share . . . without expectation of repayment." A situation which would force a returning veteran and his family to bear the burden of paying for the war's cost would be a "crying injustice." "If conscription of men is right," he concluded, "conscription of income is the more so."[38]

The response to Pinchot's appearance was mixed. Nine days after his testimony the House of Representatives passed a $1.8 billion revenue bill providing that two-thirds of that amount should come from "drastic increases in income taxes, surtaxes, and war profits taxes."[39] Pinchot's friends and critics soon let their feelings be known. Albert Todd, president of the Public Ownership League, an organization composed of leftward-leaning progressives and socialists, praised Pinchot's "valuable and patriotic service" but had little hope for any real success. "The fact that . . . those who advocate public ownership and social justice have . . . not been invited into the councils of Government confirms the view that the Government is largely controlled by those who wish to make private profit out of the war." Todd did believe, however, that if the profits were cut off, the war would end more quickly.[40] Pinchot's detractors also had a field day critiquing his performance. "You have been nothing but a pro-German obstructionist all through the controversy," wrote New York congressman Edmund Platt. "If you were a little closer to those whom you refer to as the 'common people' . . . you would know that they were more prosperous, and never more willing to stand their share of the expenses of a war." Platt accused Pinchot of interfering with business development. "It is pretty near time," he insultingly concluded, "that you settled down to do something useful. Go hire yourself out to a farmer and get down to the soil and see if you can't dig some sensible ideas into your head."[41]

This negative image of Pinchot's role was reinforced by the appearance of Douglas Fairbanks's film *In Again, Out Again*. The heart of the plot, as described by Pinchot's ACWF colleague Owen R. Lovejoy, was the

confrontation between the heroic Teddy Rutherford (Fairbanks) and a
pacifist named "Pinchit," who proves to be a villainous German spy
responsible for the destruction of several industrial plants. "Teddy R.
is, of course, the alluring militarist and puts it all over Pinchit who is
revealed as a pro-German villain instead of the mild pacifist he pretended
to be."[42] Pinchot's characteristic response was to imagine his brother
Gifford's feelings having the family name associated with German plots;
yet he refused to be silenced by such intimidation.[43] Instead, he went
on the offensive, attacking the "small group of rich people . . . and great
corporations working in secret . . . to keep down war taxes on their incomes." He accused "some very wealthy and respectable citizens" of
dodging sacrifice, suffering, and moral responsiblity. "I repeat," Pinchot
declared, "that every man or woman with surplus wealth, who stands
unready to give such surplus to the country in war time, and who works
openly or secretly against a heavy income tax . . . is a valuable ally of the
Kaiser and a fully qualified candidate for the Iron Cross."[44]

A more concerned Pinchot did reveal the burden of unpopularity in
a thoughtful letter to an old colleague then in Britain. "The horrible
thing about this whole war time," he wrote Norman Hapgood, "is that
it takes out of human nature the one most beautiful and adorable quality—
that of being happy. . . . It seems to me too horrible the way a curtain
of gloom has descended over the world. Most people even in normal
times are unable to be as good, as kind or as happy as they naturally
want to be. Now we have got to be everything we hate . . . We don't
really realize we are in it yet; but that will come later on, too vividly, I
fear, when our young boys go down to the post office . . . and find . . .
what their families will consider a death warrant."[45]

Such moments of introspection and pessimism became more pronounced as the battle for a pay-as-you-go revenue bill shifted from the
House to the Senate. Though the public heard much about the progressive group led by La Follette, George W. Norris, William E. Borah,
and Hiram W. Johnson who demanded an end to the "blood money"
made by war profiteers, the ACWF concentrated its efforts on converting
the nonbelievers and fence-sitters.[46] Senator Furnifold M. Simmons, the
Wilsonian Finance Committee chairman and an opponent of higher income and excess profits taxes, was Pinchot's special project. The ACWF
deluged the North Carolina Democrat with a package of ten-by-fourteen
cardboard exhibits containing resolutions in support of conscripting large
incomes signed by various farm, labor, civic, religious, and professional
organizations. Pinchot reassured Simmons that Congress could double
the amount of money requested by the administration if it would "cut
out the . . . unjustified proposed taxes on the necessaries of life and on
the simple comforts and amusements of poor people, and impose taxes
comparable to those in Great Britain on incomes and excess profits."

Most Americans did not hate the rich, but Pinchot warned that "all the flag-waving in the world will not persuade the average man that his more fortunate neighbor is a patriot, if he either makes money out of the war or tries to save his money during it."[47]

The Senate version of the revenue bill established a graduated profits tax of approximately 31 percent, the figure desired by the Wilson administration but far from the progressives' goal of 80 percent then in effect in Britain. Though not displeased, Pinchot made one final bid to win the House-Senate Conference Committee over to the higher war profits levy. In a boldly outrageous, offensive stroke, guaranteed to generate national publicity, he accused the Council of National Defense (CND) of being the "main offenders in the unpatriotic business of discrediting the war by commercializing it." He provided names of CND members holding positions as officers or directors of corporations profiting from war-related contracts. Pinchot urged Congress to demand full financial disclosure by all CND personnel, especially a statement of all purchases or sales of stocks with companies which might potentially receive government contracts. America could not conduct a war to "make the world safe for democracy and . . . plutocracy at the same time. If the war is to serve God, it cannot serve Mammon." "Money means power," Pinchot acknowledged, and as the war accelerated the concentration of wealth into fewer and fewer hands, the people faced a future with "the two undesirable alternatives of bondage and revolution staring them in the face."[48]

Pinchot's letter to the conference committee once again brought out the critics, friendly and otherwise. Some of the more exasperated letters came from old family friends, who resented the rumors denigrating his character but found them difficult to ignore. "You feel that [it] is indefensible, worse—ungentlemanly—of me to have attacked people personally," Pinchot wrote one disappointed correspondent. "Perhaps I do not know what being a gentleman is, but I do not think it consists in shouting for the war and then making money out of it." His own family had divested its holdings in "war profiteering stocks," moved out of its Park Avenue home into a smaller apartment, closed down its summer house, and spent much of its own money toward achieving "permanent peace and the end of German militarism." Pinchot dismissed his criticism of the Council of National Defense as "extremely gentle" and quite distinct from the objectionable newspaper condemnations of such antiwar leaders as Jane Addams, John Haynes Holmes, and Scott Nearing. He admitted his opposition to the war before American intervention but affirmed his commitment to seeing it through so long as "it should not be used to rob the people upon whom it has been forced."[49]

The Revenue Act which President Wilson signed into law on October 3, 1917, reflected progressive efforts to force the burden of war taxation upon wealthy individuals and corporations. Back in June, while the bill was still under consideration by the Senate, an apparently satisfied Pinchot admitted that though the measure fell short of insurgent hopes, "it [was] an opening wedge . . . and much more radical . . . than anybody had dreamed of."[50] But in October his feelings had changed. Perhaps the reason stems, as one scholar suggests, from the widespread dissatisfaction with the Revenue Act, a measure which seemingly pleased no one. Few of the working-class Americans who ostensibly benefited from the bill believed that Congress had curbed war profiteering. Businessmen resented shouldering the brunt of the taxation while being held accountable for exploiting the public, and progressives considered the act unsound, "a mere makeshift with . . . publicity value."[51] Still, the ACWF had made some gains: four million Americans had signed petitions in support of conscripting wealth; Congress approved higher rates of taxation than it might otherwise have without ACWF efforts; the public was made aware of the profitability of war; and even the U.S. Chamber of Commerce subsequently adopted a position similar to the ACWF's on war taxation.[52]

But if privilege had been exposed, it had not been fought, only "nagged." "How can we get the public to realize," Pinchot asked, "that there is only one way to protect themselves? How can we get men interested in fighting exploitation . . . at its source?"[53] His solution, inevitably, lay with government ownership, for his commitment to that goal had remained unchanged since the Bull Moose days and now, with the federal operation of the railroads, seemed a step closer to fulfillment. Yet even more pressing concerns forced men like Pinchot and other public ownership advocates to postpone the struggle for economic democracy until the postwar period.[54] In truth, the nature of the war's internal impact often prompted reformers to jump from one issue to another. Progressives rarely initiated such changes; rather they reacted to them. This was the case with the treatment of conscientious objectors (COs) as well as the whole question of civil liberties in wartime.

Even before the ACWF used its last piece of letterhead stationery, most antiwar progressives already had shifted their attention from property rights to human rights. The AUAM's initial commitment to protecting the rights of COs had grown out of its struggle against militarism, preparedness, and conscription. Few members differentiated assistance to COs and potential draftees from their organization's other antiwar activities. In fact, during the ACWF's lobbying campaign, Pinchot, Herbert Croly, and others tried "to prevent some of the more savage infringements against [the] rights and liberties of [such] uninfluential people." Most congressmen, however, feared broadening the conscientious objector classification beyond members of those recognized denominations which forbade fighting. "They also seem to be afraid,"

Pinchot only half-jokingly wrote an English friend, "that if you leave a little loophole, everybody will try to crawl through at once, so that there would be more people killed by the jam than by the war."[55]

The union advised COs to register for the draft and then state their personal objections against participation. "Obedience to law, to the utmost limit of conscience," an AUAM press release patriotically declared, "is the basis of good citizenship." "It seems to me," Pinchot wrote Scott Nearing, "it is better to go to jail for not fighting than not registering." He dismissed the idea of testing the constitutionality of the conscription act by observing that "when it comes down to the courts, the proverb that necessity knows no law is especially true."[56]

The union's attractiveness to radicals such as Nearing, its dependence upon the leftist leadership provided by Roger N. Baldwin, Norman Thomas, and Crystal Eastman, and almost total absorption with the CO issue alarmed its more moderate members. Lillian Wald and Paul Kellogg, founders of the original Henry Street group, along with David Starr Jordan, Oswald G. Villard, A. A. Berle, H. R. Mussey, and others, feared that such radical associations might endanger friendly relations with the Wilson administration, distort public estimation of union goals, and minimize the organization's influence among nonpacifist liberals.[57] These concerns paralleled the creation of the People's Council of America for Democracy and Peace, a radical organization with strong socialist and militant trade-union ties, which emerged late in May 1917. Drawing heavily upon the more radical elements in the antiwar movement, the People's Council advocated repeal of the draft, constitutional protection for all citizens, work stoppages to protest the war, an "early and democratic peace by negotiation" based upon the terms of "no annexation, no indemnities" (announced by the new socialist government in Russia), and creation of an international organization to prevent future wars.[58]

Though a number of prominent liberals, including several AUAM leaders, briefly flirted with the council, it quickly fell victim to charges of being un-American, pro-German, and Bolshevik in sentiment.[59] The People's Council's impact rested less in its own achievements, which were negligible, and more in the near-hysterical reactions its proposals elicited from opponents. Ironically, much of the council's program mirrored AUAM attitudes and Woodrow Wilson's later Fourteen Points, but a controversial and unpopular stigma of "peace-at-any-price" destroyed the organization's credibility.[60] Perhaps more importantly, the public outrage evoked by the council contributed to an atmosphere of guilt by association, which severely hampered the entire antiwar movement. Its principal casualty proved to be the AUAM, whose leaders, now increasingly divided, had difficulty maintaining the fragile compromise between the two groups Crystal Eastman once called "revolutionaries" and the "nonresistants." On October 1, 1917, this long-smoldering debate over the union's future direction resulted in the separation of the Bureau of Conscientious Objectors from the parent society and its reorganization as the National Civil Liberties Bureau.[61]

Only five months earlier Eastman had written hopefully about holding everyone together and avoiding a breakup. "Why cross the bridge till we come to it?" she asked. Once it was evident that the union could not effectively espouse antimilitarism and civil liberties and still hold hands with the Wilson administration, a dissolution was inevitable. And like any family separation, it was painful. For author Zona Gale, living hundreds of miles away from New York in Portage, Wisconsin, the debate was but another variation of a familiar dilemma: whether to work for the righting of immediate wrongs (as suggested by civil liberties advocates) or remove the cause of those wrongs (as desired by union moderates). "If there is division," she wrote Crystal Eastman, "I do not . . . care what is done about the name, or which side bears it." She did, however, agree with those who considered division more dangerous than the violation of civil rights. "The whole fight for 'rights' is not the one to which I can give my highest enthusiasm," she observed. "I know that 'rights' . . . means liberties." But were such rights our most precious possessions? "I confess," she concluded, "I do not know."[62]

Others within the AUAM were, by comparison to Zona Gale, less confused, more radical, and realistic. Even conservatives such as Lillian Wald and Paul Kellogg, perhaps because they were much closer to events than their Wisconsin colleague, had pinpointed the crucial problem. "In the last few months," Wald wrote Eastman, "the American Union Against Militarism . . . has been largely the Civil Liberties Bureau." And Kellogg's fear, stated as early as June 1917, had been that the union would become "so hopelessly identified in the public with 'anti-war' agitation as to make it impossible . . . to lead the liberal sentiment for peace."[63] The AUAM's more radical members had been making similar predictions for different reasons. "To abandon our work for civil liberties," James H. Maurer declared, "would prove fatal to our organization . . . and there would remain a very faint excuse for our existence." Norman Thomas echoed the sentiments of many when he suggested "that an active Civil Liberties Bureau would find it extremely difficult to keep out of the ground staked off for the AUAM," and the latter would find it equally troublesome to eliminate militarism without touching the question of civil liberties. "Even the name, American Union Against Militarism," Thomas concluded, "cannot be separated against its past and made to stand for something different at this particular juncture."[64]

The apparent solution was to change the parent body's name, and in November 1917, the AUAM became the American Union for a Democratic Peace (AUDP). Amos Pinchot was named chairman, and Crystal Eastman, who tried so desperately to hold the old group together, remained as secretary. The executive committee contained a familiar mix of moderate and radical opinion and included: Max Eastman, Zona Gale, David S. Jordan, Oswald G. Villard, Norman Thomas, and James H. Maurer.[65] "Our new name," Crystal Eastman declared, "means no change in the fundamental beliefs or in the objects of the Union. It does mean a change of emphasis." These veterans of the preparedness and conscription campaigns suddenly acquired a whole new "look" with the motto: "Free peoples, free markets, free seas, world union for disarmament." The new direction toward a "democratic and enduring peace," based upon the promotion and discussion of war aims, reflected a strategic decision to disassociate the union from earlier charges of disloyalty, distinguish its goals from its predecessor and the National Civil Liberties Bureau, and reestablish credibility with prowar liberals and the Wilson administration. But there still was a moderate leftist tone to union rhetoric. Like the German and Russian Socialists and the British Labour Party, these American progressives denounced any peace settlement that hinted at imperialistic ends. They called upon the president to fulfill his pledge of seeking a peace based upon the right of free people to self-government, security, and economic equality.[66]

"I think I am putting it mildly," Pinchot wrote Wilson, "that the American public will never be interested in the redistribution [of borders] according to nationality; that it has no wish to see England own more of Africa than she now possesses; and I do not think the average American cares whether the Turk is driven out of Europe or not. All of these things do not appear ... germane to the general proposition of making the world safe for democracy." He predicted that if the president would formulate a policy of war aims "similar to those of the Russian Council of Soldiers and Workmen, the people will be solidly behind the war."[67] In letter after letter, Pinchot pleaded with sympathetic liberals inside the administration to recognize that "dynastic forces" might seize the moment to "put over a policy of industrial aggression hardly less dangerous to democracy than Prussia's." Though his faith in Wilson remained strong, he lamented the administration's callous treatment of the liberal community and the president's reluctance to mobilize public opinion. "When will the time come," he asked Assistant Secretary of Labor Louis F. Post, "that the President [will] begin to talk and help the public realize the great possibilities and the equally great dangers of the situation?"[68]

The problem, as Pinchot candidly told George Creel, chairman of the Committee on Public Information, was that everyone supporting the president's peace program was being branded a Bolshevik, pacifist, or pro-German sympathizer. "For God's sake, George," he implored, "can't Wilson and the administration see what they are up against ... ? Do you suppose that all the money in Wall Street can ever persuade labor, the farmers, the Irish-Americans, the German-Americans, the Jews, the foreigners within our gates, that such a war is a war for permanent peace . . . ?" The president's "war-for-democracy" policy was sound, but should he acquiesce to the press, Wall Street, and the "annexationists," the nation would "rise up and curse Wilson's name and the names of all who have been implicated in . . . [the] betrayal of America."[69] Almost two decades would pass before a notorious investigation by the Senate's Nye Committee lent some credence to this prophecy. But in the fall of 1917, most of the accusations and opprobrium emanating from professional, even well-meaning patriots was directed against men such as Pinchot and those Roosevelt delighted in calling "restless, mischievous creatures." "Amos Pinchot must be a good deal of a maniac," Roosevelt wrote George W. Perkins. "Of course, he is a skunk, too; but only a lunatic skunk could talk as he has been recently."[70]

Less than a month after the AUAM's reorganization, it became apparent that neither the change of name nor policy had arrested the union's rapidly diminishing influence or its disintegration into "a small and dwindling group of pacifists."[71] Having led the fight against militarism, the union could not overcome its public image as an unpatriotic, even un-American organization. "We are in the unfortunate position," an AUAM leader later observed, "of having fought 'preparedness' and that it is manifestly due to us—this ironically—that our boys are going up against the 'Huns' armed with popguns."[72] Perhaps these progressives also were exceptionally naive in expecting public support for a "democratic peace" without anticipating suspicion of the motives behind such proposals. Like their *New Republic* colleagues—Walter Weyl, Herbert Croly, and Walter Lippmann—union leaders lived in their own "fool's paradise," believing that liberals could influence the administration's wartime policy.[73] But we should not be surprised by such behavior. On at least two earlier occasions, many of these same progressives had demonstrated a similar credulity in following Roosevelt back in 1912 and Wilson during the fight over preparedness.

There were other problems, notably a lack of unanimity, which contributed to the union's demise. Amos Pinchot might have supported the war effort in hope of currying favor with the administration and war liberals, but others, especially Crystal Eastman, could not. For almost three years this courageous, determined, and intelligent leader had been the union's heart, soul, and conscience. Now her own conscience prevented her from endorsing the vigorous prosecution of the war. "War offends my common sense and my regard for human life too much," she wrote Oswald G. Villard. "Even if I admit that good may come out of it, I could not encourage other people to die for a cause I am not ready to die for myself." She concluded that "the only great movement against war must be in the radical movement."[74]

While Crystal Eastman contemplated cooperating with her brother Max on a new radical journal, which eventually became the *Liberator*, Pinchot was also moving left in his pursuit of economic democracy. In the fall of 1917 he actively campaigned in behalf of Morris Hillquit's Socialist candidacy for the mayoralty of New York City. He believed Hillquit's demands for the restoration of civil liberties and an early democratic peace would best serve the nation, but he also wanted to draw a Socialist vote large enough to offset "imperialist" war aims emanating from the Anglo-American press.[75] In the meantime Pinchot's once-enthusiastic support for President Wilson gradually disintegrated over the issues of censorship and a dictated peace settlement.

The president's refusal to curb Postmaster General Albert Burleson's use of mailing privileges to suppress leftist publications left Pinchot deeply troubled. The trial of three personal friends, Max Eastman, Art Young, and John Reed of the *Masses*, for violating the Espionage Act added to his growing loss of respect for the administration. "It is hard for me to write impartially about the . . . trial," he told the president. "The attempt . . . to convict innocent men . . . as a part of the routine of carrying on a war for justice—is definitely horrible. They are being put on trial . . . on an indictment unsustained by evidence, and . . . in [an] atmosphere of fear and hysteria." Though the two trials of the *Masses'* editors ended in hung juries, Pinchot wondered whether the country would ever "drag itself out of this slough of hyprocrisy."[76]

Still, Pinchot remained hopeful that publication of the once-secret treaties committing our European allies to punitive indemnities and territorial aggrandizement would enable the president to discredit such aims and attain an equitable, democratic settlement. To his old friend George L. Record, Pinchot observed that Wilson was "now offered the same chance that Roosevelt was—to lead the radical forces. If he does not accept it, he is a goner," and the country would fall victim to a reactionary coalition of government and business interests.[77] As a remedy, Pinchot proposed a postwar settlement based upon the announced program of the British Labour Party—no indemnities and no annexations.[78] In fact, Pinchot urged American liberals to stake out a similar position predicated upon a close working relationship with organized labor. Just a few months earlier he had predicted to George Creel that the labor movement was destined to become a "great cohesive force which will soon make demands . . . rather than suggestions to the government . . . and in this group, not even the American Federation of Labor . . . will stand behind the policy of war for annexation."[79]

It is hard to believe, however, that antiwar liberals had much credibility within labor circles. Aside from unsupported claims of friendship and the self-proclaimed title as champions of organized labor, antiwar progressives had minimal direct experience working with union leaders and had given no indication of understanding the basis for such a partnership. Neither the AUAM nor any of its confusingly renamed offshoots, such as the American Union for a Democratic Peace or the Committee for Democratic Control, had ever reached out to the union movement. The one antiwar organization which did, the People's Council for Democracy and Peace, already had denounced the AFL and Samuel Gompers for selling the labor movement out to capitalism. For its troubles, the People's Council was dismissed as pro-German, obstructionist, and ultimately un-American. Determined to convince both the Wilson administration and the public of labor's loyalty, Gompers hastily created the American Alliance for Labor and Democracy (AALD) to check left-wing agitation and labor pacifism. While the struggle between the AALD and the People's Council was fought in the press and within Socialist party ranks, the issue was never in doubt. Enjoying unlimited government support as a subsidiary of the Committee on Public Information, the AALD wrapped itself in the flag and the free-enterprise system. Middle-class liberals and radicals might debate the merits of democratic socialism and industrial democracy, but America's skilled workers were enjoying higher wages, overtime pay, and government protection for the right to organize and bargain collectively.[80] Moreover, once the Wilson administration officially entered the struggle for public opinion, democracy, nationalism, and Americanism all seemed to fuse together; similarly, all criticism and opposition became synonymous with disloyalty.

The AUAM played a minimal role in the critical period after the United States entered the war. In part, it succumbed to the overwhelmingly patriotic atmosphere shaped by the Committee on Public Information. In other ways it was a victim of earlier success. "In the past," executive director Charles T. Hallinan observed in April 1918, "we have had an influence in Washington all out of proportion to our numerical strength; today that influence seems almost entirely gone."[81] The AUAM, like so many antiwar liberal organizations, always possessed a semblance of structure but little strength. It enjoyed name recognition but no real influence. Its leaders could generate debate but rarely win an argument. They were too polished and pedigreed to earn working-class support yet too respectable to threaten the establishment.

One is left with the unsettling feeling that much of the antiwar progressives' "style" may have come at the expense of substance. To their credit, many approached the Armistice disappointed by the existence of secret treaties and ready to repudiate Wilsonian rhetoric. The real test of liberalism, many believed, had yet to be faced. The League of Nations struck some as a purely symbolic gesture. "To stand for political democracy in these days," one progressive wrote Woodrow Wilson in March 1919, "is like standing for the Ten Commandments—it is a worthy thing to do, but there is nothing heroic or great about it. . . . The issue of political democracy has passed. The issue is now one of industrial or economic democracy."[82] This line, like many progressive observations, is memorable because the prose seems crisp and imaginative. We should not be surprised that the progressives could coin a phrase; many, after all, spent their lives as publicists. Progressives had always displayed a unique capacity to speak for others, particularly organized labor. But the ability to turn a phrase is quite distinct from accepting its implications. It was evident to many in the postwar years that the future would depend upon resolving the unanswered problems posed by economic and industrial democracy. Progressives had given no indication in the past of an ability to do more than speak the lines. How a liberal-labor coalition might be formed, how equal such a partnership would be, and how much of a role each side would play remained unclear but not unpredictable. After a decade's worth of experience, organized labor had every reason to be suspicious of progressives bearing gifts.

NOTES

1. Frederic C. Howe, *Why War* (New York: Charles Scribner's Sons, 1916), 340.

2. Charles Forcey, *The Crossroads of Liberalism: Croly, Weyl, Lippmann, and the Progressive Era* (New York: Oxford Univ. Press, 1961), 247–248.

3. It will be obvious to readers familiar with the history of American pacifism that this chapter leans very heavily upon an unusually influential number of works. I am indebted to the following scholars: Charles Chatfield, *For Peace and Justice: Pacifism in America, 1914–1941* (Knoxville: Univ. of Tennessee Press, 1971); C. Roland Marchand, *The American Peace Movement and Social Reform, 1898–1918* (Princeton: Princeton Univ. Press, 1972); Blanche Wiesen Cook, "Democracy in Wartime: Anti-Militarism in England and the United States, 1914–1918," in Charles Chatfield, ed., *Peace Movements in America* (New York: Schocken Books, 1973), 39–56; *idem.*, "Woodrow Wilson and the Anti-Militarists, 1914–1917, (Ph.D. diss., The Johns Hopkins Univ., 1970); Donald Johnson, *The Challenge to American Freedoms: World War I and The Rise of the American Civil Liberties Union* (Lexington: The Univ. Press of Kentucky, 1963); and Frank L. Grubbs, Jr., *The Struggle for Labor Loyalty: Gompers, the A.F. of L. and the Pacifists, 1917–1920* (Durham, N.C.: Duke Univ. Press, 1968).

4. Howe, *Why War*, viii.

5. "Towards the Peace That Shall Last," *Survey* II, 32 (Mar. 6, 1915), in Document Group 4, box 1, American Union Against Militarism Papers, Swarthmore College Peace Collection, hereinafter cited as AUAM Papers.

6. John Gary Clifford, *The Citizen Soldiers: The Plattsburg Training Camp Movement, 1913–1920* (Lexington: The Univ. Press of Kentucky, 1972), 118–123.

7. Crystal Eastman's remarkable and sadly short-lived career as a radical activist, feminist, and antimilitarist began with an undergraduate degree from Vassar, a master's in sociology from Columbia, and a law degree from New York University. She followed her concern for working people and labor rights

to Pittsburgh, where she participated in the famous *Survey* of that city's industrial conditions. In 1909 she helped organize the New York City branch of the American Association for Labor Legislation. Subsequent interests led her to found the Woman's Peace Party for New York, the Congressional Union for Women's Suffrage, and to act as an expert in collective bargaining for the U.S. Commission on Industrial Relations. See Blanche Wiesen Cook, ed., *Toward the Great Change: Crystal and Max Eastman and Feminism, Antimilitarism, and Revolution* (New York: Garland Publishing, Inc., 1976) and *idem.*, *Crystal Eastman on Women and Revolution* (New York: Oxford Univ. Press, 1978). Frederic Howe, like Crystal Eastman, had impeccable academic credentials (from Johns Hopkins), but he also put his training to work in Cleveland as an adviser to reform mayor Tom L. Johnson and member of the city council and state senate. At the time of the AUAM's developmental stage, Howe was the U.S. Commissioner of Immigration at Ellis Island in New York. For a closer look at his career see Robert H. Bremner, "Honest Man's Story: Frederic C. Howe," *American Journal of Economics and Sociology* 9 (July 1949), 413–414, 419–422, and Roy Lubove, "Frederic C. Howe and the Quest for Community in America," *Historian* 39 (Feb. 1977), 270–291. Readers also will want to consult Landon Warner's insightful sketch in the *Dictionary of American Biography* (New York: Charles Scribner's Sons, 1958), 326–328. Howe's provocative autobiography is essential reading: *The Confessions of a Reformer* (New York: Charles Scribner's Sons, 1925).

8. Minutes, Organizational meeting, Nov. 29, 1915, Doc. Group 4, box 1, AUAM Papers.

9. "Anti-Preparedness Committee," statement, undated, box 90, Amos Pinchot Papers; News Release, Jan. 10, 1916, AUAM Papers, DG 4, box 1, and pamphlet, *ibid*.

10. Arthur S. Link, *Wilson: Confusions and Crises, 1915–1916* (Princeton: Princeton Univ. Press, 1964), 46–50. See also David M. Kennedy, *Over Here: The First World War and American Society* (New York: Oxford Univ. Press, 1980), 31–34.

11. "The Latest Publicity Feature of the Anti-'Preparedness' Committee," *Survey* 36 (Apr. 1, 1916), 37; "An Animal of Extinction," *ibid.* 36 (May 6, 1916), 165; Lillian Wald to Woodrow Wilson, Apr. 21, 1916, Series 4, box 377, File 1935, Wilson Papers; also Marchand, *The American Peace Movement and Social Reform*, 242, and Chatfield, *For Peace and Justice*, 23.

12. Link, *Wilson: Confusions and Crises*, 325–326.

13. News Release, AUAM, May 6, 1916, DG 4, box 1, AUAM Papers.

14. James Kerney, *The Political Education of Woodrow Wilson* (New York: Century, 1926), 363–364, and Amos R. E. Pinchot to Rabbi Stephen S. Wise, Apr. 26, 1916, box 25, Amos Pinchot Papers.

15. "We Can Have Peace If We Want It: An Open Letter About Mexico," *New York Times*, June 30, 1916.

16. James Kerney, *The Political Education of Woodrow Wilson*, 363–365; see also "Swinging Around the Circle Against Militarism," *Survey*, 36 (Apr. 22, 1916), 95–96.

17. John Gable, *The Bull Moose Years: Theodore Roosevelt and the Progressive Party* (Port Washington, N.Y.: Kennikat Press, 1978), 240–241; Clifford, *The Citizen Soldiers*, 37, and Michael D. Pearlman, *To Make Democracy Safe for America: Pa-*

tricians and Preparedness in the Progressive Era (Champaign: Univ. of Illinois Press, 1984).

18. Link, *Confusions and Crises*, 303–318; on the failure to amend the "Hayden Joker," a provision in the Army Reorganization Act that called for a draft in case of war, see letters from Amos R. E. Pinchot to Woodrow Wilson, Aug. 9, 1916; Woodrow Wilson to Amos R. E. Pinchot, Aug. 11, 1916, box 24, Amos Pinchot Papers, also a telegram signed by twenty-five members of the AUAM, Feb. 1, 1917, box 30, *ibid.*, and "A Federal Conscription Act?" *Survey* 36 (Sept. 16, 1916), 596–597.

19. Charles T. Hallinan, "The New Army Law," *Survey 36 (June 17, 1916), 309, and ibid.* 37 (Dec. 16, 1916), 308.

20. Link, *Wilson: Campaigns for Progressivism and Peace, 1916–1917* (Princeton: Princeton Univ. Press, 1965), 306–307; *New York Times*, Mar. 4, 1917, I, 10; "Armed Neutrality," *Public* 20 (Feb. 16, 1917), 154; "1917—American Rights—1798," *New Republic* 10 (Feb. 17, 1917), 82; Charles Downer Hazen, "Democratic Control of History," *ibid.*, 10 (Feb. 24, 1917), 105; and Amos R. E. Pinchot, "In Defense of Armed Neutrality," *ibid.*, 10 (Mar. 10, 1917), 163–164.

21. Link, *Campaigns for Progressivism and Peace*, 362. La Follette's supporters included A. J. Gronna (North Dakota), George W. Norris (Nebraska), and Albert Cummins (Iowa). All told, eleven senators refused to sign a Republican-initiated statement that demanded an end to the filibuster.

22. Link, *Campaigns for Progressivism and Peace*, 365.

23. Alexander J. McKelway, secretary, National Child Labor Committee, to Amos R. E. Pinchot, Feb. 21, 1917, box 28, Amos Pinchot Papers.

24. Amos R. E. Pinchot to Robert M. La Follette, Mar. 5, 1917, box 29, *ibid.*

25. Harold C. Livesay, *Samuel Gompers and Organized Labor in America* (Boston: Little Brown, 1978), 173–176; also see Amos R. E. Pinchot to Samuel Gompers, Mar. 10, 1917, box 30, Amos Pinchot Papers, and *New York Times*, Mar. 13, 1917, 4.

26. *Philadelphia Inquirer*, Mar. 12, 1917, copy in box 30, Amos Pinchot Papers.

27. Howe, *Why War*, 326–327, 341, 360.

28. *New York Times*, Apr. 1, 1917, in box 31, Amos Pinchot Papers.

29. Link, *Campaigns for Progressivism and Peace*, 61–65; see also the Association for an Equitable Income Tax, form letter, July 26, 1916, box 25, *ibid.*

30. Algie M. Simons to Amos R. E. Pinchot, Apr. 2, 1917, box 31, *ibid.*

31. E. W. Scripps, telegram, to Amos R. E. Pinchot, Apr. 10, 1917; Amos R. E. Pinchot to E. W. Scripps, Apr. 12, 1917, and Apr. 18, 1917, boxes 27 and 32, *ibid.*

32. Amos R. E. Pinchot to E. W. Scripps, Apr. 18, 1917, box 29, *ibid.*; Amos R. E. Pinchot to Henry Ford, Apr. 11, 1917, box 34. Basil Manly had proposed the idea of asking a select group of well-to-do businessmen to testify before the House Finance Committee renouncing their wealth; see Amos R. E. Pinchot to Daniel Kiefer, Apr. 19, 1917, box 34, *ibid.*

33. Link, *Campaigns for Progressivism and Peace*, 61–62; Daniel Kiefer to Amos R. E. Pinchot, Apr. 21, 1917, box 34, *ibid.*

34. TR to Hiram W. Johnson, Aug. 28, 1917, *Letters of Theodore Roosevelt*, Elting E. Morison, ed., VIII (Cambridge: Harvard Univ. Press, 1954), 1228, and TR to Sen. Frank B. Kellogg, Sept. 8, 1917, *Ibid.*, 1237–1238.

35. Amos R. E. Pinchot, "Statement on behalf of the League for Democratic Control," May 11, 1917, box 196, Amos Pinchot Papers.

36. C. William Ramseyer (Rep., Iowa) to Amos R. E. Pinchot, May 2, 1917, box 32, *ibid*. Amos R. E. Pinchot to Upton Sinclair, May 8, 1917, Upton Sinclair Papers, Lilly Library, Indiana University. The ACWF received extensive labor support from such unions as the Pennsylvania State Federation of Labor, United Brotherhood of Carpenters and Joiners, International Brotherhood of Electrical Workers, Amalgamated Clothing Workers, United Mine Workers, Brotherhood of Locomotive Engineers, Order of Railway Conductors, and such farm groups as the Pennsylvania State Grange, the Farmers National Committee on War Finance, and the Nonpartisan League; see box 207, Amos Pinchot Papers.

37. Statement of Amos R. E. Pinchot before Senate Finance Committee, May 15, 1917, box 196, *ibid*.

38. Amos R. E. Pinchot, "Who Shall Pay for the War?" box 196, *ibid*., Amos R. E. Pinchot to Sen. John B. Kendrick (Dem., Wyoming), May 25, 1917, box 29, *ibid*.

39. Seward W. Livermore, *Woodrow Wilson and the War Congress, 1916–1918* (Seattle: Univ. of Washington Press, rev. ed., 1968), 58–59; Kennedy, *Over Here*, 107–110.

40. Albert Todd to Amos R. E. Pinchot, May 17, 1917, box 32, Amos Pinchot Papers. The Public Ownership League listed Jane Addams and Frederic C. Howe as vice-presidents, Carl Thompson as secretary, Charles H. Ingersoll as treasurer, and Amos Pinchot and Milwaukee's Socialist congressman Victor Berger on the executive committee.

41. Edmund Platt (Rep., New York) to Amos R. E. Pinchot, May 13, 1917, box 29, *ibid*.

42. Owen R. Lovejoy to Amos R. E. Pinchot, May 17, 1917, box 29, *ibid*.; and Alistair Cooke, *Douglas Fairbanks: The Making of a Screen Character* (New York: Museum of Modern Art, 1960), 17.

43. Amos R. E. Pinchot to Owen R. Lovejoy, May 18, 1917, box 29, Amos Pinchot Papers; letters to Amos R. E. Pinchot from ACWF Washington representative, Alexander J. McKelway, especially one dated July 30, 1917, box 29, clearly point up the negative impact Pinchot's pacifist beliefs were having upon the ACWF program. See also Amos R. E. Pinchot to Alexander Kerensky, July 25, 1917, in which the American progressive has praise for the March Revolution in Russia, *ibid*.

44. Amos R. E. Pinchot, "The Kaiser's Iron Cross," *Humanitarian* 2:14 (June 1917), 7–8.

45. Amos R. E. Pinchot to Norman Hapgood, May 17, 1917, box 29, Amos Pinchot Papers.

46. Livermore, *Wilson and the War Congress*, 59.

47. Amos R. E. Pinchot to Sen. Furnifold M. Simmons, June 8, 1917, box 33, Amos Pinchot Papers. David P. Thelen discusses the senator's lack of support for a pay-as-you-go finance bill in *Robert M. La Follette and the Insurgent Spirit* (Boston: Little, Brown, 1976), 138.

48. Amos R. E. Pinchot, "War Profits and Patriotism," Letter to Conference Committee of Senate and House of Representatives, Sept. 18, 1917, box 196, Amos Pinchot Papers; also published in complete or abridged form in the *Ma-*

chinists Monthly Journal 19:10 (Oct. 1917), 860–862; *Brotherhood of Locomotive Firemen and Enginemen's Magazine* 63:7 (Oct. 1, 1917), 1; and *Public* 20:107 (Sept. 28, 1917), 931–934.

49. Amos R. E. Pinchot to Rev. William S. Rainsford, Sept. 29, 1917, box 31, Amos Pinchot Papers.

50. Amos R. E. Pinchot to Rev. John E. Landner, June 17, 1917, box 29, *ibid.*

51. Livermore, *Wilson and the War Congress*, 61.

52. Chamber of Commerce of the United States of America, Referendum No. 25 on the Report of the Special Committee on Financing War, Aug. 13, 1918, box 204, Amos Pinchot Papers. The U.S. Chamber of Commerce did not wish to see wartime taxation continued. Its report called for high income and excess profits taxes but broke with the ACWF by supporting heavy taxation on such consumer commodities as tea, coffee, tobacco, beer, and gasoline.

53. Amos R. E. Pinchot to Charles H. Ingersoll, Oct. 3, 1917, box 24, *ibid.*

54. Testimony to the fact that such issues were raised can be found in Edward W. Bemis, "From Regulation to Public Ownership," *Real Democracy* 3:1 (Jan. 2, 1918), box 196, *ibid.*

55. Amos R. E. Pinchot to J. Howard Whitehouse, M.P., May 7, 1917, box 29, *ibid.*

56. Amos R. E. Pinchot, statement, May 23, 1917, box 90, *ibid.*; Amos R. E. Pinchot to Scott Nearing, May 11, 1917, box 33; and Scott Nearing to Amos R. E. Pinchot, May 6, 1917, box 27, *ibid.* Scott Nearing, who would soon emerge as a leading figure in the People's Council of America for Democracy and Peace, was a Socialist party publicist, a radical pacifist, and a former economist at both the universities of Pennsylvania and Toledo where his political beliefs had been unwelcome. See Stephen J. Whitfield, *Scott Nearing: Apostle of American Radicalism* (New York: Columbia Univ. Press, 1974).

57. Crystal Eastman, memorandum to AUAM executive committee, June 14, 1917, DG 4, box 1, AUAM Papers, contains Crystal Eastman's view of the Wald-Kellogg letters.

58. Donald Johnson, *The Challenge to American Freedoms*, 19–25.

59. Gilbert C. Fite and Horace Peterson, *Opponents of War, 1917–1918* (Madison: The Univ. of Wisconsin Press, 1957), 78–80; Morris Hillquit, one of the early leaders of the People's Council, describes his experience in *Loose Leaves from a Busy Life* (New York: Macmillan Co., 1934), 172ff; James H. Maurer, an AUAM leader with council ties, explains his view in *It Can Be Done* (New York: The Rand School Press, 1938), 223. Other union leaders who had early contact with the People's Council included Mary Ware Dennett, Emily G. Balch, David S. Jordan, Gilbert E. Roe, Florence Kelley, and John Haynes Holmes. See Amos R. E. Pinchot to John D. Works, former U.S. senator from California, July 10, 1917, box 27; Amos R. E. Pinchot to Woodrow Wilson, July 25, 1917, supporting the war aims of the Socialist government in Russia, *ibid.*, Amos Pinchot Papers.

60. Whitfield, *Scott Nearing*, 74–97.

61. Roger N. Baldwin, Reminiscences, Oral History Research Office, Columbia University, 55 (COHC).

62. Zona Gale to Crystal Eastman, Sept. 27, 1917, DG 4, box 1, AUAM Papers.

63. Eastman, memorandum, June 14, 1917, *ibid.*

64. James H. Maurer to Crystal Eastman, Sept. 26, 1917, and Norman Thomas to Crystal Eastman, Sept. 27, 1917, *ibid.*

65. Other members of the new American Union for a Democratic Peace's executive committee included Emily G. Balch, A. A. Berle, Herbert S. Bigelow, Frank Bohn, William F. Cochran, John Lovejoy Elliott, Owen R. Lovejoy, H. R. Mussey, Frederick Lynch, Alexander Trachtenberg, and L. Hollingsworth Wood. Press release, AUAM, Nov. 12, 1917, DG 4, box 1, *ibid.*

66. *Ibid.*

67. Amos R. E. Pinchot to Woodrow Wilson, July 25, 1917, box 27, Amos Pinchot Papers.

68. Amos R. E. Pinchot to Louis F. Post, Oct. 2, 1917, box 34, *ibid.*

69. Amos R. E. Pinchot to George Creel, Nov. 14, 1917, box 34, *ibid.* Creel may not have been a sympathetic listener; see Stephen Vaughn, *Holding Fast the Inner Lines: Democracy, Nationalism, and the Committee on Public Information* (Chapel Hill: Univ. of North Carolina Press, 1980), 218–219, and David M. Kennedy, *Over Here*, 45–92.

70. Roosevelt to George W. Perkins, Nov. 6, 1917, George W. Perkins Papers, Columbia Univ.; Roosevelt to Theodore Roosevelt, Jr., Nov. 29, 1917, *Letters*, VIII, 1260.

71. Crystal Eastman to Oswald G. Villard, Nov. 16, 1917, DG 4, box 3, AUAM Papers.

72. Charles T. Hallinan to AUAM Executive Committee, Apr. 15, 1918, DG 4, box 1, *ibid.*

73. Forcey, *The Crossroads of Liberalism*, 274–289; Christopher Lasch, *The New Radicalism in America, 1889–1963: The Intellectual as a Social Type* (New York: Knopf, 1966), 181–224; Ronald Steel, *Walter Lippmann and the American Century* (Boston: Little, Brown and Co., 1980), 101–115, 155–170.

74. Crystal Eastman to Oswald G. Villard, Nov. 16, 1917, DG 4, box 3, AUAM Papers; Roger N. Baldwin's description of his colleague can be found in his Reminiscences, 55 (COHC).

75. Hillquit, *Loose Leaves*, 180–219; James Weinstein, *The Decline of Socialism in America, 1912–1925* (New York: Monthly Review Press, 1967), 149–154; *New York Times*, Nov. 1, 1917, 1. New York voters did not elect Hillquit, but the size of his vote helped defeat the incumbent, John P. Mitchel, the fusion choice back in 1913. See the *New York Times*, Nov. 7, 1917, 1.

76. Amos R. E. Pinchot to Woodrow Wilson, May 24, 1918, box 37, Amos Pinchot Papers; Amos R. E. Pinchot to Owen R. Lovejoy, June 19, 1918, *ibid.* Background correspondence on this issue can be found in Amos R. E. Pinchot, John Reed, and Max Eastman to Woodrow Wilson, July 14, 1917, box 29, *ibid.*, Woodrow Wilson to Amos R. E. Pinchot, July 17, 1917, *ibid.* Pinchot served as the treasurer of the "Liberty Defense Union," whose executive committee also included Max Eastman, Elizabeth Gurley Flynn, Norman Thomas, Louis P. Lochner, Roger N. Baldwin, and Scott Nearing; see Louis P. Lochner to Amos R. E. Pinchot, July 3, 1918, box 37, Amos Pinchot Papers, and William L. O'Neill, *The Last Romantic: A Life of Max Eastman* (New York: Oxford Univ. Press, 1978), 75–80. See also Leslie Fishbein, *Rebels in Bohemia: The Radicals of "The Masses," 1911–1917* (Chapel Hill: Univ. of North Carolina Press, 1982), 24–26, 28–29.

77. Amos R. E. Pinchot to George L. Record, Dec. 2, 1918, box 37, *ibid.*, Amos

R. E. Pinchot to William B. Colver, chairman of the Federal Trade Commission, Aug. 28, 1918, box 36, *ibid*.

78. Amos R. E. Pinchot to Col. Edward M. House, Jan. 28, 1918, box 37, *ibid*. For the emergence of the British Labour Party and its impact in the United States, see Stanley Shapiro, "The Passage of Power: Labor and the New Social Order," *Proceedings of the American Philosophical Society* 120:6 (Dec. 1976), 464–474.

79. Amos R. E. Pinchot to George Creel, Nov. 14, 1917, box 34, Pinchot Papers.

80. Frank L. Grubbs, Jr., *The Struggle for Labor Loyalty*, 69–79, and Ronald Radosh, *American Labor and United States Foreign Policy* (New York: Random House, 1969), 58–71.

81. Charles T. Hallinan to AUAM Executive Committee, Apr. 15, 1918, DG 4, box 1, AUAM Papers; Executive Committee Minutes, Jan. 20, 1922, *ibid.*, box 3. Fittingly, when the time came for the union's last rites, the group once called the "brains of the pacifist movement" decreed that its library be donated to Haverford College with the hope that future generations would find the AUAM's legacy more enduring than had contemporaries.

82. James Kerney, *The Political Education of Woodrow Wilson*, 439, and Amos R. E. Pinchot, "Amos Pinchot Calls for a Separate Peace," *World Tomorrow* 2 (June 1919), 172.

V

Liberals and the Postwar Reconstruction, 1919–1920

The immediate postwar years represent a significant and formative period in the growth of American liberalism. The events, proposals, and developments of this time were, however, neither novel, unexpected, nor enduring. This is not to dismiss the optimism, enthusiasm, and creativity which pervaded this reconstruction era. Nor are these generalizations intended to diminish the significance of liberal-labor calls for "industrial democracy," nationalization of natural resources and transportation, or creation of a new political alignment. These were important and essential issues which established the agenda and set the tone for liberal-labor relations until the Great Depression.

But there are other questions which reach beyond strategy and programs to touch the core of the immediate postwar liberal experience. At the heart of that core is failure: failure to recognize the distance which separated liberal rhetoric from practice; failure to acknowledge labor's right to a position of equality in any political or economic alliance; failure in the ability to rise above class prejudice; and, perhaps most contemptible, the absence of integrity and the liberals' propensity for self-indulgence and unquestioning acceptance of their own propaganda.

This failure is all the more disturbing when compared with superficially comparable British developments. There, a successful wartime movement of pacifists, socialists, and liberals coalesced into the British Labour Party (BLP). The latter's emergence as a powerful economic and political force served as a model for American progressives, yet our own experience pointed to a less successful, more destructive, and hypocritical side of postwar liberalism. Because Anglo-American liberal and labor relations seemed to parallel one another so closely, their subsequent divergence clearly shows American liberals at a disadvantage. In both countries a majority of each nation's liberal and labor leaders quickly threw their weight behind the successful prosecution of the war. By embracing the national interest the respective labor establishments—the Trades Union Congress and the American Federation of Labor—finally acquired the sense of legitimacy, status, and prestige each had sought for so long.

Yet, on both sides of the Atlantic, alternative courses of action did emerge. In Britain, opposition to conscription, territorial aggrandizement, and profiteering, and calls for disarmament helped shape an internationalist, pacifist, antiwar movement led by the Union of Democratic Control (UDC). Like its American counterparts, the UDC, especially after the Russian Revolution and publication of the secret treaties, supported open diplomacy, democratic control of foreign policy, and an international association for peace. Opposition to compulsory military training led many UDC members to found the "No-Conscription Fellowship," just as the AUAM would be instrumental in creating the Bureau of Conscientious Objectors as the forerunner of the American Civil Liberties Union. Equally important in terms of the future was the UDC's role in bridging the ideological gap separating Liberal Party pacifists from the socialists of the Independent Labour Party.[1]

Yet, even this step pales in significance with the parliamentary Labour Party's official adoption of a socialist program in its June 1918 manifesto, *Labour and the New Social Order*. This remarkable document held the government responsible for insuring a decent standard of living for every citizen. A "national minimum" would guarantee full employment, factory safety, public health care, and adequate housing and education. The new social order would begin with "common ownership of the means of production" and "democratic control of industry," particularly in the areas of transportation, communications, and utilities. Tax reform, based upon wartime experiments with excess profits and steeply graduated income taxes, would stimulate a "revolution in national finance," provide for a more equitable distribution of money and power, and allow for the apportionment of surplus wealth to educational, social, and artistic programs. Here, as in most of the Labour Party's program, however, the emphasis was not on wild-eyed, revolutionary social change or even "worker democracy," but rather on a "pure-and-simple" sanitized version of democratic state socialism.[2] But that was exactly what made the Labour Party so attractive to disaffected Liberals. Rather than embrace a doctrine they long had found repugnant, most Liberals converted in spite of the Labour Party's identification with socialism.[3] *Labour and the New Social Order* may have seemed to herald the cooperative commonwealth, but, in reality, party officials deliberately curbed the influence of affiliated socialist societies while increasing the power of the trade unions.[4] Perhaps that was the price of success, for in 1918 the

Labour Party drew 20 percent of the vote and established itself as one of Britain's two major parties.[5]

Ironically, the American left failed to see beyond the rhetorical glitter. Our own wartime mobilization, with its limited nationalization of the railroads and means of communication, seemed to suggest a collectivistic trend toward greater public ownership and government regulation in the postwar years. Progressives faced "reconstruction" with boundless enthusiasm and hope for the possibilities of meaningful national realignment. International developments, particularly news of the Russian Revolution and emergence of the BLP, reinforced the sense of impending social and economic change at home. Organizations across the country with disparate political persuasions convened special "reconstruction" conferences to plan for the immediate postwar era.[6] There was much discussion but little agreement as special interests lobbied over the future of federal regulation of the railroads, labor's right to bargain collectively, the restoration of free speech, the changing roles of American women, the farmer's place in reconstruction, the fate of the League of Nations, and the government's responsibility for public housing, vocational rehabilitation, and unemployment relief. An untold number of speeches were given, words written and published, and banquets hosted with little to show for the effort save confusion, boredom, and indigestion. " 'Reconstruction' has of late been so tiresomely reiterated, not to say violently abused," reported one group in February 1919, "that it has become . . . a word of aversion. . . . Yet the majority of us still find ourselves bewildered and helpless."[7]

In some quarters, however, certainty carried the day. The U.S. Chamber of Commerce confidently dismissed government ownership of the railroads, called for moderation in taxation, and demanded a revision of the Sherman Antitrust Act. At the opposite end of the ideological spectrum, the National Catholic War Council's "Bishops' Program of Social Reconstruction" endorsed the vigorous enforcement of antitrust laws, government competition with unrestrained monopolies, and establishment of cooperative stores. Government would be held responsible and a worker's industry financially accountable for providing insurance protection against unemployment, ill health, invalidism, and old age. The program envisioned creation of a decent minimum wage, continuation of the U.S. Employment Service, local governmental financing of public housing, and the elimination of class divisions in education by providing freedom of choice in curricular decisions.

Even this remarkable program, largely the work of longtime social gospel activist Father John A. Ryan, had its blind spots. In an effort to avert massive postwar unemployment, the "Bishops' Program" proposed a back-to-the land movement, underwritten by government loans and supported by the Interior Department, that would place returning "colonies" of servicemen "upon some part of the millions . . . of acres of arid, swamp, and cut-over timber lands, in order to prepare them for cultivation." Equally ambiguous in its potential benefits was a projected solution for the problems facing "women war workers." To its credit the Catholic War Council stipulated that women deserved equal pay for equal work. But a more accurate reflection of contemporary mores was the plan's support for the rapid removal of women from occupations "harmful to health or morals . . . and other activities for which conditions of life and their physique render them unfit."[8]

Inevitably, the British Labour Party emerged as a major topic of discussion among liberals and labor leaders. Political liberals, professional reformers, government planners, and labor unionists openly discussed the merits of guild or state socialism, industrial democracy, and direct political action. "Whoever is running the Labour Party . . . is a big man," George L. Record wrote Oswald G. Villard. After reading a summary of the BLP's postwar aims, the New Jersey progressive was eager to call "a series of meetings of the really intelligent radicals of the country . . . to get ready some fundamental program."[9] His colleague, Amos Pinchot, felt "the best thing to say would be: 'We, representing the labor and farm interests, and the people of America generally, hereby endorse the program of the BLP.' "[10] Record even considered the possibility of running a "radical" Republican such as Hiram W. Johnson or William E. Borah in the 1920 GOP primaries and then linking up with various farmer-labor organizations such as the Nonpartisan League, local labor parties, and prowar socialists. Such optimistic rhetoric led to the creation of a short-lived "National Party" during the 1918 congressional elections, and its existence was testimony to both liberal ambition and credulity. Its abortive development also suggested how unaware progressives were of the enormous difficulties involved in establishing a "lib-lab" party in America.[11]

Publication of *Labour and the New Social Order* stimulated a babel of discussion in the United States. Though numerous liberal, labor, and farm journals studiously debated its many proposals, most attention, naturally, was drawn to the demand for worker control.[12] At a reconstruction conference sponsored by the National Popular Government League in January 1919, Assistant Secretary of Labor Louis F. Post addressed the question of democracy in industry. A veteran single-taxer, reform publicist, and onetime editor of the radical-liberal journal called the *Public*, Post had maintained close ties to both the progressive and labor communities. In his speech he acknowledged the existence of industrial cooperation but contended that industrial democracy would never be attained as long as workers had to bargain with men who controlled the environment. "The real power in industry," Post told his audience, "is control of natural resources. . . . Neither industrial nor political democracy can exist unless every man has equal opportunity—an equal standing in the government and on the earth." While Post seemed to be edging closer to nationalization as a means of securing industrial democracy, another conference participant, Arthur E. Holder, a former AFL legislative assistant, expressed a more traditional faith in the classic progressive solution of public education. He recommended utilization of public forums and educational campaigns until "the great masses of the people will become the governing class and democracy will become an accomplished fact. And that finally means," Holder noted, "the power of self-employment—real industrial democracy."[13]

Holder and Post assumed they were discussing the same issue, but their solutions reveal how far apart they actually were. Phrases such as "democratic control" and "industrial democracy" were the buzz words of the reconstruction years, the mere mention of which evoked images of the political left. Such phrases were effective in drawing liberal, labor, and farmer groups together but tragically misleading once the symbols gave way to substantive discussion. Nowhere was this more clearly demonstrated than in the relationship between two organizations which emerged in 1919, the liberal Committee of Forty-Eight and the National Labor Party, an outgrowth of the militant Chicago Federation of Labor.

Many liberals who helped create the Committee of Forty-Eight were veterans of both the prewar fight for worker (as distinct from union) rights and the wartime struggle to preserve civil liberties. Uniformity, however, was not one of the group's strengths. The organization represented a strange amalgam of patrician reformers and social radicals, each of whom tolerated the other, belonged to the same social clubs, spent holidays together, and wrote for the same prestigious journals. The 48ers were a disparate group with fundamental differences, as was to be expected from a coalition of former Wilsonians and Bull Moosers, single-taxers and efficiency experts, academics and political activists. Still, the 48ers shared a basic resentment at the Wilson administration's tolerance of wartime hysteria, suppression of civil liberties, and abandonment of liberal goals.

The committee's membership contained such shapers of liberal public opinion as editors Oswald G. Villard of the *Nation*, Walter Weyl and Herbert Croly of the *New Republic*, and Albert Jay Nock of the *Freeman*. Among its intellectual elite were such pillars of the eastern liberal establishment as philosopher Horace Kallen; social activist John Haynes Holmes; literary critic and soon-to-be-expatriot Harold Stearns; former Commissioner of Immigration Frederic C. Howe; social work leader Mary K. Simkhovitch; historian Will Durant; journalists Lincoln Colcord, Gilson Gardner, and William Hard; attorney Gilbert E. Roe; and civil liberties advocate Arthur Garfield Hays. The real decision-making power rested, however, with a small coterie of experienced but perennially unsuccessful political separatists: J. A. H. Hopkins, a onetime treasurer of the Progressive party in New Jersey and a moving force behind the ill-fated National party; Amos Pinchot and George L. Record, veterans of the Bull Moose and other campaigns; and Allen McCurdy, a New York publicist.[14]

Preliminary work during the spring and summer of 1919 formalized the committee's organizational structure, placed full-page advertisements in liberal journals announcing a call to a national progressive convention, and queried potential recruits on such issues as formation of a new political party, restoration of civil liberties, abolition of secret diplomacy, nationalization of the railroads, equal rights for women, immigration restriction, and the enforcement of antilynching laws.[15] The results of the referendum revealed the deep-seated fissures which lay just below the surface of 48er optimism. Committee supporters were unable to agree on the degree of government ownership, nationalization of industry, or the controlling element in any new third party.

The division among the rank and file mirrored significant differences within the leadership. Though many future 48ers had infused their post-Armistice writing with calls for industrial and collectivist democracy, others remained suspicious of labor and were committed to an open, voluntaristic, classless society. This libertarian and competitive faction, represented by men such as Pinchot and Record, believed that reform could best be achieved through a diminution of class divisions and the elimination of monopoly and special privilege. Government ownership was a last resort only to be implemented when private initiative failed. Though the ex-Wilsonians and Bull Moosers who composed this group represented an influential segment, their view was by no means the only view or the majority one. A more advanced group of postwar liberals, led by men such as Frederic C. Howe and Dudley F. Malone, advocated a more far-reaching program modeled after that of the British Labour Party calling for guild socialism, industrial democracy, and extensive nationalization.[16] Were it not for the fact that most progressives fell somewhere in between these positions and that both groups sought salvation through a third party, the Committee of Forty-Eight could not have survived its differences.

The most advanced 48ers were willing to embrace the cause of labor and to submerge themselves into a national labor party that would espouse genuine industrial democracy. The potential for such a movement was evident with the appearance of militant local labor parties in Bridgeport, Connecticut, and New York City. Each grew out of trade union dissatisfaction with the Wilson administration's abdication of domestic policy and disenchantment with the AFL's conservative opposition to a separate labor party.[17] The centerpiece for this slowly germinating national labor movement was the Chicago Federation of Labor (CFL), under the dynamic leadership of its president John Fitzpatrick, long a leader of radical worker insurgency with strong ties to the socialist movement. Other labor officials, such as James H. Maurer of the Pennsylvania State Federation of Labor, William H. Johnston of the International Association of Machinists, Max Hayes of the International Typographical Union, and Benjamin Stolberg of the International Ladies' Garment Workers Union, all moved easily between militant labor unions and socialist circles.[18]

Less than a week after the Armistice, the CFL published its counterpoint to President Wilson's Fourteen Points and an American version of the BLP's *Labour and the New Social Order*. The statement was drafted by Basil M. Manly, onetime director of research for the U.S. Commission on Industrial Relations and Frank P. Walsh's successor as co-chairman of the War Labor Board. "Labor's Fourteen Points" called for the right to organize and bargain collectively; an eight-hour day; federal life, health, and accident insurance; equal rights for all; nationalization of resources; and democratic control of industry. Other proposals made the government responsible for a decent minimum wage, full employment, and an end to profiteering. The CFL supported a graduated income tax, as well as assessments upon inheritances and excess profits. Point number ten urged public ownership of utilities while the fourteenth point emphasized internationalism: "It recommended a league of the workers of all nations pledged and organized to enforce the destruction of autocracy, militarism, and economic imperialism throughout the world."[19]

This militant manifesto, the bible of the CFL, quickly became the symbol of the radical labor movement and the impetus behind organization of the National Labor Party in August 1919. The success of any liberal-labor reconstruction effort depended upon the new Labor Party's willingness and ability to attract financial and moral support beyond its limited circle. Laborites needed to reach out for the assistance of the middle-class reformers in the Committee of Forty-Eight and the Public Ownership League, agrarian radicals in the Nonpartisan League, and the rank-and-file members in the Socialist party.[20] At their national convention in Chicago in November 1919, Labor Party leaders made every effort to temper a class-conscious rhetoric with a platform broad enough to encompass as many discontented groups as possible. The result, as the *New Republic* observed, was an unimpressive platform of thirty-two incoherent planks representing more of a tribute to interest politics than to social vision.[21] Though the Labor Party's official voice, the *New Majority*, bravely fantasized about the new "dawn in store for the workers," the actual climate at the end of 1919 was exceedingly repressive.[22] Equally evident were the party's internal problems. Denounced by Samuel Gompers and the AFL as an agent of "red-eyed radicalism," the militant laborites became pariahs to the general public.[23] The much-hoped-for coalition of farmers and laborers came apart over the farmer's recurring inability to choose an identity as either a businessman or agrarian worker. The initial enthusiasm displayed by the Nonpartisan League gradually diminished as its leaders grew concerned over the party's lack of public acceptance. Though serious, these defections would prove minor when compared with the Labor Party's inability to overcome the mutual suspicion it shared with the Committee of Forty-Eight.

Ever since the appearance of Labor's Fourteen Points, conservative elements within the committee feared becoming an appendage to a class-conscious labor party. "If we . . . do not offer leadership based upon a radical program adapted to American conditions," George L. Record wrote a colleague, "then new men, presumably produced by the Labor or Farming group, will come upon the scene and take the leadership." Anticipating the nomination and election of a Republican reactionary "of the type of Warren Harding," Record encouraged progressive Republicans to fight for the proposals espoused by the Nonpartisan League and Illinois labor party. "My own personal notion," he added, "is that in due time . . . a new party will come forward with this general platform. . . . It is high time that we should now start a movement which is first of all fundamentally right, and which is tied up to ideas and not to men."[24]

No issue during reconstruction was of more fundamental importance or better captured the emerging political and economic divisions in postwar America than the future of federal railroad regulation. The debate among railroad managers, shippers, labor unions, and government officials symbolized many of the most important developments in government-business-labor relations over the past two decades. At stake was control of the country's transportation system as well as a whole series of questions whose answers would directly shape attitudes toward public ownership, industrial democracy, profit-sharing, and the need for more efficiency and standardization in railroad management. The railroad question presented legislators with a variety of policy options, each one enthusiastically endorsed by the special interest most directly involved. Though the Wilson administration characteristically relinquished leadership in this area to Congress, the government's position was reflected in the views of Treasury Secretary William Gibbs McAdoo, director-general of the railroads during the war. He argued for five more years of federal control, but this request met with little success in Congress. Railroad management also supported federal regulation (including a no-strike clause) but drew back from Senator Albert Cummins's plan for government-imposed rail consolidation with its attendant redistribution of corporate earnings.

The new ingredients in these negotiations were the railway labor brotherhoods, immeasurably strengthened by their wartime ties to the Wilson administration, now eager to flex their muscles in behalf of public ownership and the anticipated higher wages that would result from nationalization. Uniting behind the plan devised by their general counsel Glenn Plumb, the unions proposed creation of a federally owned corporation that would sell bonds and purchase and operate the lines under the direction of a fifteen-member board of directors appointed by the president. These individuals were to be drawn from management, government, and labor, thus providing workers with a real opportunity for industrial democracy. Theoretically, such employee involvement would encourage worker efficiency, which would lead to lower prices on railroad-shipped goods; a snowball effect would then stimulate purchasing power, creating more jobs and allowing for employee profit-sharing.[25]

A Plumb Plan League (PPL) was established; chapters were organized around the country; and the most committed of the railway brotherhoods underwrote the costs of a weekly newspaper, *Labor*, to publicize the plan and educate the public. Financial and moral support came from advocates of public ownership and efficiency, such as the Public Ownership League of America (POL); from agrarian protest groups seeking reduced freight rates, such as the Nonpartisan League (NPL) and the Farmers' National Council (FNC); and from reform activists linked to these groups, such as Amos Pinchot (POL), Frederic C. Howe (PPL), and Benjamin C. Marsh (FNC). These veterans of many prewar social and political crusades were now convinced that public ownership was a necessary first step toward the possible nationalization of all transportation, communications, and natural resources.[26]

With the fate of the railroads still in doubt, and on the eve of a wave of nationwide strikes, the intrepid liberals in the Committee of Forty-Eight issued an optimistic call for a national conference to meet in St. Louis in early December 1919: "It is a time of grave peril and great hope. . . . We must . . . strike off the shackles from the minds and muscles of men and women so that all who toil with hand or brain shall be . . . free to work and live as freemen."[27] Preconference platform discussions were infused with this type of romantic proletarian rhetoric. The drafting committee debated tentative planks that would make the government responsible for unemployment, old age, accident, and health insurance; provide for progressive income and inheritance taxes that would redistribute the wealth; prohibit land from being held out of use for speculative or monopolistic purposes; demand the democratization of foreign policy; and require a national referendum for a declaration of war except in case of invasion. Other issues under consideration included proposals for universal disarmament, opposition to compulsory military training, changes in the patent laws to insure equality of opportunity, immigration restriction, and the abolition of injunctions in labor disputes.[28]

Many of these proposals had rich, historical legacies, some dating back to the days of the Bull Moose movement; others clearly reflect the prewar experiences of the U.S. Commission on Industrial Relations, the wartime struggles of the AUAM and American Committee on War Finance, all the way up to the creation of the British Labour Party and the postwar reconstruction conferences. The final 48er platform, however, proved to be decidedly less radical than the preliminary deliberations. Several reasons account for this about-face. Between the September "call to action" and the December convention public attitudes toward meaningful social change underwent an abrupt transformation.[29] The great steel, coal, Boston police, and Seattle general strikes, blamed on Bolshevik agitation and labor radicalism; the rising high cost of living and lagging productivity attributed to union greed; and the rash of bombings and cultural and racial tensions left many Americans eager for stability and convinced that the enemy lay within. "Politically," Oswald G. Villard wrote Emily G. Balch, "the situation is perfectly disgusting and tends to make every liberal more and more of a revolutionist as time goes on." But the editor of the *Nation* could not ignore the persistence of "great bitterness against those who opposed the war. . . . It is the universal opinion that anybody who differs from the prevailing point of view should be shot."[30]

External events undoubtedly influenced the outcome of 48er deliberations. But the platform's distinctive three-point, "postcard program"—restoration of civil liberties, public ownership of raw materials, and nationalization of transportation and related facilities—also bore the unmistakable stamp of Amos Pinchot and George L. Record, two of the 48ers most committed to a prewar vision of free competition and a classless society. For years they had argued for a simple, fundamental economic program contending that society's ills could not be cured by political tinkering. Like many 48ers, these third-party veterans had lost faith in a two-party system controlled by the same economic forces. "It has been an unhappy accident of our national life," one reformer noted, "that has produced but one major party: the Republican-Democratic party of order and stability." In a hauntingly familiar phrase that captured a perennial liberal lament, Allen McCurdy observed: "Once we were thrilled by the idea of a square deal; but now we want a new deal. Then the demand was for a third party; now the demand is for a second party. What some Americans really want is to discuss issues."[31]

For Pinchot and Record monopoly remained the overriding issue in 1919 just as it had been since 1912. It permitted the ongoing exploitation of consumers, the oppression of labor, and denial of civil liberties and collective bargaining; monopoly eliminated needed competition and produced unconscionable profits while workers labored for substandard wages. These 48ers called upon government to take over and operate the railroads, oil pipelines, public utilities, and warehouse facilities; and to lease natural resources such as coal, iron ore, oil, lumber, water power, and other raw materials on a nonpreferential competitive basis. Since this was the same program Record and Pinchot had been seeking for over a decade, certain ingredients were added to make it more attractive to potential allies in the labor movement. Chief among them was a blanket statement in behalf of labor's right to organize and bargain collectively and a more ambiguous endorsement of the workers' right to "share in the management of industry."[32] That expression of faith prompted Labor Party representative Duncan MacDonald, president of the Illinois Federation of Labor, to propose a "triple alliance" of farmers, laborers, and the railway brotherhoods united together for a common purpose. Other 48er proposals paid deference to the needs of potential supporters, large and small: though unnamed, women and blacks were promised equal economic, political, and legal rights, and single-taxers were recognized with a statement prohibiting the holding of land out of use for speculative or monopolistic purposes.[33]

In spite of this impressive organizational activity, hindsight makes it difficult to understand how the 48ers and laborites could have taken themselves so seriously. The Labor Party lacked a single leader of national prominence or even a nationwide organization. As for the Committee of Forty-Eight, it possessed unimpeachable liberal credentials at a time when liberalism was unfashionable. It had access to the intellectual elite, but how many Americans read or even were familiar with the *New Republic*, the *Nation*, *Survey*, or the *Public*? The 48ers possessed respectability within mainstream politics, yet their key leaders were viewed as political mavericks, having operated outside the two-party system for more than a decade. During the difficult period of the Red Scare, the more conservative press either killed the 48ers with derision or identified them as "enemies of the republic" and "Communist wolves in liberal sheepskins." The 48ers' December 1919 convention in St. Louis typified their difficulties. First, a court injunction was needed merely to force their hotel to serve as the conference site; then the Justice Department placed the hotel under surveillance and recorded the proceedings. Finally, and most humiliating, the press focused attention upon the inevitable cavalcade of eccentrics who paraded forth: "health enthusiasts" and "nudists"; "fundamentalists" and "scientists"; "back-to-nature and forward-to-technology orators. . . . One delegate proposed the building of an Arcadian highway around the world with little houses, each with its own garden, dotting the road, as a path to international understanding and as a method to end war."[34]

Still, for a time, optimism prevailed among third-party advocates. This was partly the result of confidence in their own strength and partly a reflection of alleged widespread dissatisfaction with the two major parties, each of whom seemed to be preparing for 1920 as if nothing had happened to the world since 1914. Preliminary negotiations between representatives of the Committee of Forty-Eight and the Labor Party indicated genuine interest in a unified political coalition.[35] Though differences remained—notably conflicting views toward the efficacy of class legislation and industrial democracy—shared grievances, principally disgust at the imminent passage of the Esch-Cummins Transportation Act, temporarily obscured their disagreements.[36]

Meanwhile, other more pressing concerns troubled both groups: Would the powerful railroad brotherhoods become active participants in a third-party effort? Would such involvement be dependent upon lib-lab support for the Plumb Plan? What complications might arise from a coalition of the AFL and liberal Democrats? These questions helped fuel a constantly changing rumor mill. One among many which created consternation within 48er circles had the Democrats offering the vice-presidential nomination to Warren S. Stone, president of the Brotherhood of Locomotive Engineers, in order to preclude any third-party action by the railway unions. Few 48ers had any illusions about winning Samuel Gompers over to their side, especially after he dismissed them as "professors . . . writers and sermonizers."[37] Most expected him to "swing every ounce of his energy toward lining up labor with the Democratic party." Many held him accountable for undermining the effectiveness of the Plumb Plan League, though it was an indication of division within the committee that some members like Pinchot and Record agreed with Gompers in detesting the socialistic elements in Plumb's proposal. Even more disturbing to these 48ers was news that plans were under way for a new, expanded Plumb Plan for all basic industries.[38] Such a proposal, George L. Record predicted, would place Plumb far ahead of accepted political propriety; it would divide lib-lab forces, dissipate the energy needed for promoting a constructive economic program, and allow socialists to use Plumb's name and influence to promote their own goals.[39]

Forty-Eighter leaders like J. A. H. Hopkins, George L. Record, and Amos Pinchot never doubted themselves to be the most important element in any third-party effort. Everyone who counted in their world— readers of the *Nation* and the *New Republic*—shared the same assumptions. Liberals, after all, were the ones taking the risks, supplying the essential organizational and intellectual talent, and serving as the nation's conscience. No one denied it was an inopportune time to start a new party—"as inopportune as say any other time has been or will be." But the alternative, as Pinchot observed, was to set aside "all but a cynical . . . interest in events . . . and [wait] for the apple to rot and fall instead of the more exciting business of clubbing the tree." The 48ers would bring a new party into the world and would have great fun doing so. They would not merely curb the worst abuses of the privileged classes but intended to eliminate the sources of that power by removing transportation and natural resources from private control. They did not foresee any obstacles to fusion with the Labor Party. "They are pretty sensible," Pinchot somewhat condescendingly noted. "They see that a purely class movement has no future. . . . Nobody wants to put labor in power, just as nobody is particularly interested in having [industry] run by and for the employees." Pinchot's arrogance was matched only by his total misreading of the situation: "The question appears to be," he concluded, "whether the war has started anything that is new enough and large enough to demand expression through an agency that does not exist."[40] Evidently, neither class consciousness, industrial democracy, nor the creation of a separate labor party met those criteria.

The 48er's supreme self-confidence could not survive on promises and protest. An organization had to be staffed, a national base of support secured, and agreements reached with like-minded but competing progressive groups. The committee's leaders were much like political candidates: each found the transition from campaigning to organizing or governing tedious, time-consuming, and less gratifying than anticipated. Past experience had not prepared the 48ers. Though many had participated in either the Bull Moose or Wilsonian movements, and most were veterans of causes too numerous to mention, very few had expertise in building a broadly based national party. These eastern, urbane Protestants were comfortable as publicists, lobbyists, and organizers, but rarely had they ventured beyond their tightly knit geographical and social boundaries. Based primarily in New York City, they already possessed the intellectual (or perhaps the New Yorker's) view of an America consisting of two coasts linked (in 1920) by a series of one-lane country roads. The 48ers were dedicated, conscientious, and extremely hardworking individuals who enjoyed both the limelight and behind-the-scenes politicking. They were not, however, prepared either by disposition or background for the routine demands of organizational work: knocking on doors, licking envelopes, compiling mailing lists, or soliciting signatures. They were patricians accustomed to deference, willing—almost eager—to accept criticism from powerful (equal) adversaries; yet they seemed emotionally incapable of paying more than lip service to the needs of those less equal except in a benevolent but plainly patronizing fashion.

In March 1920 some of these deficiencies became obvious as the 48ers' self-confidence began to be tested. Each passing week brought a new problem. It was not always a momentous crisis but usually a matter necessitating the application of some ordinary solution: How should fund-raising receipts be divided between state and national headquarters? Who should pay the expenses of state organizers? How much authority should the executive committee exercise? What efforts should be made to cooperate with other liberal and radical groups? A detailed look into the 48ers' handling of one vexing problem—the racial question—offers some revealing insights into the committee's tightrope-walking act.[41]

The 48ers' platform contained an unqualified endorsement of equal rights regardless of race, color, or sex. But race riots in East St. Louis and Chicago, Illinois, in 1917 and 1919, continued lynchings in the South, and the rapid growth of the black population in the Middle West and Northeast presented northern liberals with a problem below the Mason-Dixon line. "We know that the color question in the South is a delicate subject," J. A. H. Hopkins observed in a triumph of understatement. The 48ers' executive chairman hoped his North Carolina counterpart, Wade B. Leonard, would appreciate the equal delicacy of the national committee's situation. "We cannot take one position in the North and another in the South." However, Hopkins temporized, the practical application of racial equality was a state prerogative. He reiterated that the 48ers had no intention of building up "a colored party in the South. . . . We are not presuming to dictate to our white friends . . . what local restrictions or qualifications they should apply." Up North, he noted, it was a much different situation. Three million normally black Republican voters were in rebellion after years of having been "cheated, deceived, and ignored." Of course, Hopkins reassured his southern colleague, "the colored voters in the North are a more educated race . . . and are actuated by precisely the same aspirations and motives as we are ourselves."[42]

Hopkins probably handled this problem as well as could have been expected. The 48ers did not "take to cover" but did use what their Maryland state chairman, Mercer Green Johnston, called a "liberal amount of horse-sense." Southerners like Johnston, son of an Episcopal bishop and an ordained (but nonpracticing) minister with strong ties to the social gospel and free speech movements, argued that the 48ers "ought to find a large natural following in the South . . . if we keep our movement economic-end first and foremost."[43] The 48ers did not find much support in the South. The inclusion of their controversial equal rights proposal and a practically nonexistent organization undoubtedly were contributing factors. But so, too, was the committee's general ignorance and insensitivity to southern mores. In June, with the 48er and Labor Party conventions fast approaching, northern liberals gave serious consideration to renaming their movement the "Lincoln Party," without realizing that Lincoln's was not a name "to woo [southern] voters with."[44]

As spring changed into summer, the 48ers faced two pressing problems: the first concerned growing doubts about effecting a coalition with the Labor Party; and the second, related to the first, revolved around a presidential candidate who might yet unite disparate liberal, labor, and agrarian elements. The closer these groups came to amalgamation, the more intense was their mutual animosity and suspicion. "The question is being asked with increasing insistence," Amos Pinchot wrote in *Reconstruction*, "whether in this [vital] time . . . the country will be dominated by popular or privileged class thought." The hidden irony in Pinchot's observation was that he objected to any kind of class consciousness, whether from the governing or the working classes.[45] Pinchot and George L. Record, as the most active theoreticians among the 48ers, found themselves singled out as libertarians and individualists. Their "socialistically inclined friends" accused them of "staging the last stand of individualism in a world destined to communistic organization," while capitalistic critics portrayed them as the "forerunner of Marxian socialism." In a two-part essay in the *Freeman*, Pinchot defended the individualistic ethos as preferable to "minority control of opportunity," which was bound to produce a violent movement toward communism. In such a society the government, he argued, would not only run the railroads but "tell us how and when to brush our teeth. . . . Man is a libertarian animal," Pinchot concluded. "It is only because the privileged class has taken from him this power of choice and . . . struck at his earning power and physical comfort, that he turns his eyes to the unwelcome concept of an over-socialized world, in which, though the State may be his master, it will be a master of his own making."[46]

"Will you be out . . . at the Labor Party conference?" Pinchot apprehensively wrote his friend, labor leader James H. Maurer. "It looks to me as if there would be a number of hotheads who want a class party."[47] "This is where we have trouble with labor, for labor still wants to think as labor and function as labor, though it should be clear enough that there is no place for a class party in a country constituted as ours." Pinchot remained committed to a broad cooperative coalition of dissident elements united behind the abolition of privilege and the opening up of natural resources to free competitive production. The 1920 campaign would serve as a means of educating the public on key issues. "We do not intend to bait little hooks for every group, but form a party and put out a program which will not be for any class."[48] The problem was that the Labor Party refused to surrender its class-conscious approach, while the 48er leadership seemed wedded to a nineteenth-century notion of free competition tempered only by a call for limited nationalization of natural resources.[49] The Labor Party would not compromise its independence, its platform, or its name. Coalition with liberals and other disaffected groups was welcome but on labor's terms. The 48ers were invited by *New Majority* editor Robert M. Buck, himself a renegade Bull Mooser, to join labor in a subordinate capacity as propagandists among "white collar folk."[50] Liberals' money was always helpful; liberal names on a third-party masthead was desirable; liberal editorial and intellectual support was gratifying, but labor considered none of these things essential.

One interesting sidelight to the often-turbulent relations between the 48ers and laborites is that their respective rank and file seemed to get along quite well. Mercer G. Johnston, the 48er state chairman in Maryland, displayed a much greater sensitivity to the psychological and political needs of labor, socialist, and agrarian groups than the committee's national leaders. "It has occurred to me," he wrote Toscan Bennett, a retired attorney and Labor Party founder, "that . . . instead of fighting like bigots, [we ought] to practice as much comity towards each other as possible."[51] And, to a Baltimore neighbor, Johnston warmly praised the Socialist party's 1920 platform: it "contains little . . . I could not swallow with relish"; the party's candidates "would be as acceptable to me as any our group might agree upon."[52] But Johnston hoped his Socialist friend would realize that in a political climate which attacked the 48ers as communists, the Socialist party had little chance for success. Indeed, "with a socialist ticket in the field, and Labor divided against itself, and the farmer asleep in the barn, the outlook in Maryland [was] not cheerful."[53]

The only possibility for fusion among dissident elements on the left depended upon attracting a candidate of national stature around whom both 48ers and laborites would willingly sacrifice their growing animosity. Between March and June 1920, a number of names were tossed around, some seriously, others in mere speculation. Herbert Hoover, as many scholars have noted, was a particular favorite of postwar reformers. Interestingly, the onetime Food Relief administrator's appeal extended even to moderately left-wing circles. E. W. Scripps, the cantankerous, occasionally radical newspaper publisher, admitted a desperate longing for something or someone worthwhile. After toying with the idea of supporting Henry Ford or William Randolph Hearst, the Californian decided Hoover would be the best choice. "I believe [he] will be as indifferent to the mob of snobs as he is to the mob of my friends," Scripps confided to Amos Pinchot. In part, this fascination with Hoover reflected a lack of confidence in the other frequently mentioned candidates—Warren G. Harding, Calvin Coolidge, Hiram W. Johnson, Leonard Wood, Frank Lowden, William G. McAdoo, and A. Mitchell Palmer. "If he is an egotist and of course he is," Scripps observed, "it is only because of his low opinion of others, and not because of his opinion of himself."[54] Pro-Hoover sentiment, however, was far from unanimous. Senator Hiram W. Johnson called his California rival an "intellectual crook" whose "sinister crookedness" pervaded his "serpentine political activities." Another Hoover booster, however, prowar Socialist John Spargo, organizer of the Social Democratic League, felt that a Hoover-led independent movement would gather its own momentum and become a radical force in any third-party campaign.[55]

Those closer to the Committee of Forty-Eight were less infatuated with a Hoover candidacy. Pinchot, for example, initially hoped that a third party led by labor lawyer Frank P. Walsh or Nonpartisan League advocate and North Dakota Governor Lynn Frazier might poll four or five million votes and prepare the electorate for a serious bid four years later. J. A. H. Hopkins, 48er national chairman, was sympathetic to Walsh's nomination since his candidacy would insure the Labor Party's enthusiastic support. But Walsh's Catholicism and reputation for radicalism were grounds for concern. As for Frazier, his renomination for governor made it unlikely that he would sacrifice his real power in North Dakota for the frustrations of a purely educational campaign. When both of these men indicated no immediate interest, attention shifted to Robert M. La Follette.[56]

The Wisconsin senator, one of the most loved and despised men of his time, already was stimulating friends and critics to new heights of partisanship. His nomination "would be the supreme folly Liberalism could commit," observed Mercer G. Johnston. "Personally, I could not stomach him—simply could not! And if I could not with all the social aspirations I share with him, what hope would there be of getting the tens of millions of Americans who stand far to the right of me even so much as to look in our direction." Johnston's opinion reflected a deep-seated, almost irrational antipathy for the senator's antiwar activities. Prowar liberals who had been involved in the fighting would not forgive those who continued to dissent after American intervention. From a more practical standpoint, Johnston argued that La Follette's radical reputation was too large a burden for a new party to bear. "I am perfectly willing . . . to fail with the right man . . . but with La Follette we would either have to win or be damned forever; and to win . . . would require a political miracle of the kind that hardly happens once in a thousand years."[57]

Other postwar liberals also had doubts about the senator, but few denied that he alone could bridge the gap dividing progressives and laborites. La Follette seemed to have a foot in both camps. Many veteran progressive Republicans admired him for his insurgent attacks upon corporate arrogance and his support of direct democracy and consumer rights. Men like Pinchot and Record had first entered national politics as the senator's supporters in 1910 before unceremoniously deserting him for Roosevelt. During the war, La Follette was one of very few public officials to acknowledge the work of pacifist and civil libertarian groups and to put his career on the line for the principles espoused by the AUAM and the American Committee on War Finance. But neither guilt nor sentiment affected the 48ers' position; La Follette was their last hope.

Following the Republican convention, when it became clear that the senator might be interested in a third-party candidacy, an intense out-pouring of progressive flattery and persuasion was directed his way. "I know that you are above the cheap ambition in wishing to figure in history," one 48er wrote La Follette, "except [as] you can render a service which entitled you to such a place." "In talking to you about such things," cajoled another liberal, "I feel like a sign painter giving Leon-ardo advice."[58] But the charm and feigned solemnity did not mean that politicians like Pinchot and Record would meekly surrender their prin-ciples to a glamorous national candidate. They would convert La Follette or go their own way. The alternatives—compromise, identification as the senator's personal political vehicle, or absorption by a more powerful Labor Party—were not acceptable. There either would be a third party with the senator standing on the 48ers' platform or an independent movement without the liberals, at least without their more conservative and committed leaders. Convinced that they had been betrayed by both Roosevelt and Wilson, veteran progressives pledged to resist temptation a third time.

Preliminary meetings between 48ers Pinchot and Record with Robert M. La Follette, Jr., and the senator's law partner, Gilbert E. Roe, prompted two lengthy letters to the Wisconsin patriarch. The 48ers desperately wanted to separate the senator from his "Wisconsin platform," an eight-een-plank testimonial to a variety of pre- and postwar societal ills, rang-ing from nationalization of the railroads to repeal of the Espionage and Sedition acts. Pinchot and Record did not disagree with the substance of these proposals but feared that a large number of issues would scatter energies and confuse the public. In words and phrases that must have evoked La Follette's memories of his abortive 1912 candidacy, Record asked the senator to insure that the abolition of privilege would be the "paramount issue"; private ownership of the railroads would be elim-inated; patents would be made available to the public on a more equitable basis; and the principal natural resources of coal, iron, copper, timber, oil, and water power would be owned by the government and possibly leased for private operation. The only stumbling block to this twentieth-century utopia, according to the 48ers, was a faction within the Labor Party that did not see "the big issue at all." Expediency might require the insertion of other planks into the platform, such as support for free speech, opposition to the use of injunctions in labor cases, and the right of workers to strike and bargain collectively. But Pinchot and Record tried to convince the senator that "every additional idea . . . divides our forces" and offers critics "the opportunity of picking upon what they consider our weakest point of attack." Though this reasoning may not have been entirely self-serving, the two 48ers used it to justify excluding the Labor Party's central concern—the democratic control of industry—from the 48er platform.[59]

The La Follette of 1912 or maybe even 1917 might have agreed that the elimination of corporate abuses was more important than meeting the specific needs of particular interest groups. But the wartime collectivization in industry and agriculture and the rising militancy of farmers and workers changed all that. Whether or not the shift in progressive thought from "consumer-taxpayer insurgency" to "job-oriented" militancy was as decisive and clear-cut as David P. Thelen contends, no one can doubt that an increasingly class-conscious farmer-labor movement represented the most powerful opposition to politics as usual in 1920.[60] Robert M. La Follette wanted to be part of this new movement. He was far from being a political innocent and possessed a healthy ego and more than a passing interest in a third-party nomination. Mindful of the problems posed by an independent candidacy, the senator realized that though farmers and laborers were dissatisfied with the economy, they were divided over the proper solutions to pursue. Some sought political relief through the old parties; others demanded a new organization; while still others expressed support for the pressure tactics of the Nonpartisan League and the American Federation of Labor. "Aside from these two groups," the senator confided, "there is no class, no large body from which the rank and file of a new party can be recruited." La Follette respected the Committee of Forty-Eight for raising "the voice of protest" but concluded that its members had no following among workers or farmers.

Though his correspondence is deceiving in this regard, the senator does not appear to have undergone elaborate or agonizing soul-searching concerning the nomination. His decision, as he told the laborites and 48ers, would be determined by the similarities (and agreement) between the two conventions' programs and his own "Wisconsin platform." Convinced that only a new party could achieve meaningful economic change, La Follette urged an issue-oriented organization with strong class appeal among farmers and laborers. Yet his own inclination was to see himself as the only legitimate standard bearer of a third party movement. "There is only one leader with a national following," he observed, "who would stand upon [such a] platform." That candidate will be "maligned, traduced, and lampooned . . . but win or lose . . . [he] . . . will win a higher place in the history of the country than has been achieved by anyone since the foundation of the government."[61] If La Follette suffered from a lack of confidence, any such doubts would have been assuaged by columnist William Hard's firsthand impressions from the liberal-labor convention sites in Chicago. The veteran progressive journalist noted the 48er and laborite differences over such questions as the " 'democratic control' of nationalized industry" but detected over-whelming support for the senator's candidacy. "You are worthy of it, and the moment is worthy of you. . . . The road ahead is a terrible one," Hard concluded, "but to have travelled it will be the best souvenir one could take along out of this age and the best memorial one could leave."[62]

Hard was not an impartial observer. His letters to the senator are filled with admiration for the Labor Party. Its delegates are "sparks out of a fire," and John Fitzpatrick's opening speech was "like water coming from a spring—unstudied, . . . absolutely natural, and irresistible." It was not a "passing revolt" against the two old parties but a movement of the future—"a permanent war" led by producers in industry, transpor-tation, and agriculture.[63] Like other veterans of prewar progressivism, Hard's only previous third-party experience dated back to Theodore Roosevelt's 1912 bid. The Bull Moosers, he believed, had focused upon political reform, philanthropy, and personality. The new labor move-ment, however, was interested in economic change, in "power for the 'workers' " rather than "sympathy for the 'oppressed.' "[64]

Labor Party leaders, however, were less than sanguine about the 48ers and La Follette, particularly after marathon conference sessions at the convention and at the senator's Wisconsin home failed to produce agree-ment on a platform or even a party name. No one would compromise. The laborites refused to sacrifice their class vision to a white-collar move-ment; they would not relinquish their demand for greater control over industry, nor were they prepared to allow La Follette to co-opt their party. The conservative libertarian element of the 48ers led by Pinchot, Record, and McCurdy ("coupon-clipping intellectuals," "plutocratic phi-lanthropists," and "slick lawyers," according to the laborites), clung desperately to a limited program of government ownership of natural monopolies, restoration of free competition, and opposition to special class legislation.[65] As for the senator, he announced that he would accept a third-party nomination only upon the basis of the "Wisconsin plat-form." The results were anticlimactic: the rank-and-file 48ers ("honest, well-meaning mushheads," according to Pinchot and Record) ignored their leaders, merged with the laborites to form the Farmer-Labor Party, and proceeded to rush headlong into historical oblivion behind the can-didacy of Parley Parker Christensen, a radical Utah lawyer who had managed to antagonize few of the delegates as chairman of the joint conventions.[66]

The five months prior to the election were filled with recriminations rather than reconciliation. Depending upon one's vantage point, re-sponsibility for this debacle was widely distributed but rarely acknowl-edged. Not surprisingly, the rank and file of both the Committee of Forty-Eight and the Labor Party absolved themselves and blamed their own and each other's leaders.[67] In letters and published articles, the

Pinchot-Record faction denounced the Farmer-Labor Party's class-conscious socialism. These "conservative individualists" maintained that widespread nationalization of industry, as proposed in the new party's platform, was "bad economics." The government should intervene, they contended, only in industries dominated by artificial monopolies. Pinchot was particularly upset by the controversy surrounding the proposal for "democratic control" of industry and by critics who questioned his own class bias. Hadn't he paid his dues—on the picket lines at Paterson and Ludlow, by his generous contributions to various labor defense funds, through his fight for a pay-as-you-go program of war taxation, and in his testimony before the U.S. Commission on Industrial Relations? His commitment to industrial democracy may not have been as advanced as that of the laborites, but Pinchot believed that labor had to recognize the necessity of "playing a bigger game . . . and of frankly joining . . . with the rest of the public . . . in freeing all the exploited classes together."[68] Such ideals once may have been noble and realistic; in 1920 they were neither. They ignored the rise of class tension, worker militancy, political action, and the impact of wartime gains upon the labor movement.

Part of the shock experienced by many liberal leaders in the aftermath of the Chicago fiasco was the realization that though they believed the Labor Party needed them, the laborites did not. Within the Committee of Forty-Eight there also was genuine hostility directed toward the "Eastern" or "New York" group whose undemocratic decisions allegedly were made "out of sight and hearing." "I simply cannot believe in the thoroughness of the democracy of anybody," Mercer G. Johnston observed, "who thinks that all that is necessary . . . to make the U.S. Steel Corporation 'good' is to deprive it of its present advantage of $2 per ton of steel ore."[69] Johnston, a solidly middle-class progressive with working-class sympathies, reflected the internal resentment within the committee in a letter to his father. "How deep and wide the breach in our social fabric must already be when such sons of privilege as Amos Pinchot . . . who go into such a movement . . . draw back . . . towards the side of privilege when they come cheek-by-jowl with the dead-in-earnest multitude now awakening to a sense of its wrongs!"[70] Socialists like Allan L. Benson, the party's 1916 presidential candidate, were even less sympathetic. In accepting an article by Johnston for publication in his journal, *Reconstruction*, Benson added his own disdain for liberal elites such as those who dominated the 48ers. "The best thing that can be said of some . . . is that they are politicians; the best that can be said of others is that they are well-meaning gentlemen whose wealth has prevented them from having the slightest knowledge of life—and the best that can be said of others is that, believing themselves to be democrats, they are, in fact hopeless snobs."[71]

Progressives like Mercer G. Johnston and his Baltimore colleague Elisabeth Gilman worried about the "thin-skinned" democracy of the 48er leaders and the latter's betrayal of labor's trust. "They will say, and I feel, with reason," Gilman wrote J. A. H. Hopkins, "that the Intellectuals were not straightforward, and for the future, Labor will steer clear of such entangling alliances. . . . My hope," she concluded prophetically, but certainly without reason, "is that sometime in . . . the future we may have a party, a confederation like the British Labour Party, where our joint forces, even if not identical, will work together harmoniously for the good and the regeneration of our country."[72]

In spite of its impressive name, the Farmer-Labor Party was not to be the vehicle for that salvation. As its principal biographer notes, no significant agrarian organization—not the Nonpartisan League which sympathized with its goals nor the progressive Farmers' National Council which considered it too class conscious—lent the new party any support. Though clearly working class in orientation, the Farmer-Labor Party received only minimal assistance from organized labor and none from the United Mine Workers, the railway brotherhoods, or the AFL.[73] Unlike its Bull Moose predecessor, the Farmer-Labor Party lacked every ingredient essential for success: it possessed neither enthusiasm, money, nor a dynamic leader. It was on the ballot in twenty states, but in only half of those were local candidates running as Farmer-Laborites. Like the 48ers a year earlier, it was endorsed by both the *New Republic* and the *Nation* with similarly negligible results. Interested observers drew diametrically opposite lessons from the Farmer-Labor Party's inadequacies. Agrarian spokesmen, put off by the party's working-class emphasis, looked hopefully to the major parties for relief. The railway brotherhoods, then involved in their first tentative steps toward a nonpartisan independent congressional campaign, steered clear of this apparent disaster. Samuel Gompers and the American Federation of Labor, resentful of the Labor Party's original threat to its supremacy, unofficially supported the Democratic ticket as the least undesirable choice. Socialists, though critical of the new party's toned-down socialism, anticipated amalgamation in the future, while leftward-leaning progressives argued that a protest vote for Eugene V. Debs would be more meaningful than one for Parley P. Christensen.[74]

Though the Farmer-Labor Party ticket and platform may not have been the "joke" George L. Record said it was, it clearly was "a negligible quantity politically." So too, unfortunately, was the Committee of Forty-Eight. Badly embarrassed by the laborites who took advantage of their political naiveté, men such as Record, Hopkins, Pinchot, and McCurdy were eager to save face and maintain their self-respect within the progressive community. The lesson these much maligned survivors took away from the Chicago conventions was that the "same tremendous need for a new party" still existed. They believed another convention should be called with the declared intention of nominating Senator La Follette upon a platform of his own choosing.[75] The new "Liberal Party," which had been created by some sixty 48ers in the postconvention confusion, might serve as the institutional framework for such a campaign. Had the 48ers alone been behind such activity La Follette and his advisers would have dismissed the idea, but that was not the case. Lynn Haines, a much-respected political observer and editor-publisher of the *Searchlight on Congress*, hurriedly wrote the senator shortly after the Chicago convention, "What I . . . want to express is the feeling that you must in some way bring yourself to take the nomination. The need is so desperate, and the opportunity so promising that I simply cannot give up your candidacy at this time." Like other progressives Haines was repelled by the two major party candidates; he also did not harbor illusions about a third party's chances in 1920. Yet the *Searchlight*'s analysis of Warren G. Harding's senatorial record produced "an indictment against which no candidate can possibly stand. All my contacts," Haines told La Follette, "convince me that he will be the biggest joke ever entered in a campaign." As for James M. Cox, the Democratic nominee, Haines concluded that the weight of Wilsonism plus public knowledge that "his nomination came out of the very underworld of politics" doomed his chances. But even if there were no chance this year, Haines urged the senator to run in preparation for a serious effort in 1924. Once again there was flattery and the appeal for sacrifice: "You are the only possible man of the hour," Haines wrote. "You know . . . that the nation is full of leaders who have capacity and character but they are unknown, and always will be . . . unless such a fight as only you can lead is made." For Haines the worst possible consequence of La Follette not running would be the continuation of sharp class distinctions in politics. "You, and you only, are . . . well enough entrenched in the confidence of all classes to . . . give shape to a party which will put all in one class."[76]

Evidence concerning the senator's receptivity to the whole question of class is contradictory at best. David P. Thelen's work demonstrates that La Follette's struggle against the Esch-Cummins Transportation Act moved him into closer contact with the railway labor brotherhoods and farm groups, and, hence, toward a producer and class-oriented political direction. Yet the "Wisconsin platform" made no reference to industrial democracy and had more in common with the 48ers' St. Louis program than with the Labor Party's celebrated Fourteen Points.[77] The senator's spokesmen also contributed to the confusion. One of those, Dudley F. Malone, represented the collectivist faction within the Committee of Forty-Eight and was one of the few well-known progressives to join the Farmer-Labor movement. Another, the senator's law partner Gilbert E. Roe, counseled against a third-party bid while planning a 1924 campaign that would undertake "the destruction of 'capitalism' as we know it."[78] The inconsistencies emanating from the La Follette camp were, one suspects, reflections of the senator's dual image. As Thelen contends, "La Follette was more often identified as a fighter than he was with postwar ideologies."[79] Fighters occasionally win, ideologues usually do not.

Late in July the senator's advisers, preoccupied with the presidential bug, still had not ruled out a third-party candidacy. Basil M. Manly, then director of the Scripps Economic Bureau, supported a strategy suggested by respected Washington lobbyist Harry A. Slattery. In this scenario twenty prominent Americans representing farm, labor, and liberal groups would issue a call urging independent citizens to nominate La Follette by petition. In circumventing the convention process Manly and Slattery hoped to avoid the embarrassment that had befallen those in Chicago and at the same time insure that the campaign would be entirely under the senator's control. Organizations sympathetic to La Follette's views would lead the petition drive with the Hearst newspaper syndicate providing national exposure. The campaign would seek the endorsement of organizations such as the Nonpartisan League, the American Federation of Labor, and the railway brotherhoods, which had remained cool to the Farmer-Labor Party and the idea of a permanent third party. Yet, paradoxically, the Manly-Slattery plan anticipated creation of a "substantial party movement" if successful at the polls.[80]

On July 25, less than ten days after the Chicago conventions, a group of disaffected 48ers gathered at the La Follette family farm. Led by George L. Record, Amos Pinchot, and Allen McCurdy (and subsequently joined by J. A. H. Hopkins), they had come to Madison for one last attempt at convincing the senator to run as a third-party candidate. Upon arriving they discovered that La Follette's advisers—Basil M. Manly, Robert M. La Follette, Jr., and veteran Wisconsin politico, Charles Crownhart—already were involved in evaluating the available options. Typically, Record took the initiative. He urged that a new convention be called to nominate the senator upon a previously agreed platform; all proposed changes or opposition would be "steam-rollered." Record objected to the strategy of nominating by petition and argued in favor of a permanent third party. "An independent candidate," he noted, "never succeeds . . . nobody pays any attention to him because it is a campaign that has no future."[81] But such a course, as Manly and others argued, would require La Follette to make all the sacrifices. Moreover, Record's calls for the senator's nomination on a rubber-stamped platform rammed home by an elite coterie of insiders had an air of unreality about it; at best it offered an ironic commentary on the uses of power by the politically powerless. The senator's advisers concluded that the Committee of Forty-Eight and its offshoot, the Liberal Party, were uncontrollable "individualists" who represented a political liability for any future campaign. Such sentiments were echoed by Mercer G. Johnston, now an ex–48er and formerly one of La Follette's worst critics. He urged the senator to steer clear of these "self-styled 'responsible leaders' " who had "played fast and loose with the laborites." "It would be a colossal blunder for you to be sponsored by the discredited 'rump' of the Committee of Forty-Eight. . . . I feel sure," he concluded, "you have little or no idea of being the butt of this joke."[82]

Though La Follette was not about to enter such a campaign, the possibility of a completely independent presidential candidacy remained inviting.[83] Gilbert E. Roe explained the immediate problems and their foreseeable consequences. First, there was the difficulty of getting on the ballot in enough states merely to insure a respectable protest vote. Second, a third-party candidacy would bring the senator into conflict with friends in agriculture and labor who either were committed to the Farmer-Labor Party or were devoting their energy toward supporting independent campaigns in behalf of all progressive candidates. The alternatives were few. Roe advised La Follette to lend his support to all sympathetic groups. "They will fail. With their failure will come recognition . . . that a third party is their only salvation . . . and with the full realization of that knowledge, will come a willingness to compromise." Roe's advice, therefore, was to prepare for 1924 through a series of state and local nonpartisan educational campaigns that might lead to "a strong sound sentiment for a new radical but constructive party."[84]

Advice from Basil M. Manly lent support to this strategy. Though once committed to the idea of an independent candidacy, Manly now did an about face. Rather than attempt to create a new party, he recommended building up a congressional "Battalion of Death" that would fight the people's fight "against the combined servants of privilege in the two old parties."[85] The key elements in this plan depended upon the willingness of the railway brotherhoods and progressive farm organizations to cooperate with each other and political insurgents. Progressives like La Follette were heartened, therefore, by news of the Brotherhood of Locomotive Engineers' financial commitment to save the Bank of North Dakota, an institution with ties to the Nonpartisan League and the state's radical agrarian governor Lynn Frazier. The importance of this act lay less in the decision to transfer union funds to assure farmers adequate credit than in the cooperation such an act required and the future implications of such action.

Where all of this left more traditional and conservative progressives, such as those in the Committee of Forty-Eight, remained unclear. Reading their correspondence one senses an unwillingness to accept defeat, for to do so implied recognition of political impotence and, worse, ineptness of their program. An almost desperate quality characterized their activities as they prepared for one final grasp at the presidential ring in the late summer of 1920. For years a few of these men had exercised a disproportionate amount of influence; now, once again isolated and discredited, baffled by their peers' indifference, mortified by labor's class-consciousness, their political survival demanded either steadfast loyalty to principle or an expedient retreat to more defensible positions. Characteristically, they flapped their arms about, contemplated the inconceivable, and did little but wait for events over which they had no control to overtake them.

"How would it be," Gilson Gardner asked Amos Pinchot, "for our Forty-Eighters to go ahead and put [Parley P.] Christensen on the ballot as Liberal candidate with George [L.] Record as Vice-President...?" Anticipating the Farmer-Labor Party's financial and organizational problems, Gardner believed Christensen's vote could be used to secure a ballot position for the Liberal Party in 1924. "I know you will object that Christensen knows little or nothing about the [48ers'] St. Louis platform. That makes no difference, George could sit down with him and show him in an hour. Besides George would talk platform and let Christensen talk the other stuff. Why might this not be a way out?"[86] Gardner's suggestion, though quickly forgotten, speaks to one of the 48ers' glaring weaknesses. Its leaders concurrently managed to display an inordinate amount of political naiveté and ruthlessness. Dismissing the Farmer-Labor Party's platform as inconsequential and assuming the third-party's willingness to step aside for the greater glory of eastern liberals testifies to the 48ers' consummate conceit.

By late August not even the most optimistic 48er held any illusion of starting a new party or of drafting La Follette into an independent movement. Freed from the constraints imposed by success, this handful of liberals resumed their unacknowledged role as critics and political prognosticators. George L. Record, in particular, eagerly looked forward to an overwhelming Republican triumph that would discredit the Farmer-Labor Party and leave the Democrats "little hope of coming back for the next eight years. Many . . . will then be ready to join us who are not free to do so; in addition . . . the real labor men . . . will then see that we are right and will then be ready to cooperate with us."[87] When the election brought the Harding landslide and Christensen's embarrassingly small protest vote, Record hardly could restrain his joy in writing La Follette. But this letter, like so many others he had written the senator since 1910, contained the same message and many familiar phrases: "Now that the election is over"; "It seems to me that we should"; "if we could get together a new group of men." La Follette could have closed his eyes and imagined himself back in Madison eight years earlier reading another letter after the abortive Bull Moose campaign; better yet, he might simply have checked his files because Record's program remained unchanged: nothing was to be gained from organizing a new movement around temporary issues. Government ownership of the railroads and major natural resources provided the only means of eliminating privilege. No lands should be held out of use for speculative purposes. Patent laws should be liberalized to prevent corporate monopolization. Except for minor variations to accommodate changes in public attitudes, this letter echoed the sentiments of Record's first memorandum to La Follette nine years earlier. Now, in the aftermath of the Republican triumph, he called upon the senator to lay the foundation of "a great new party. . . . It is my judgement that by doing so you can render the greatest possible service to the people, which I know is your one object in life."[88] There was no response.

In the immediate postwar years the American people experienced the divisiveness and hysteria of the Red Scare, the unfulfilled hopes and optimism of a short-lived "reconstruction," and the emergence of a class-conscious labor movement. The most remarkable aspect of this tumultuous period was the conventional result of its culminating event, Warren G. Harding's election in 1920. What did it mean for the future of progressivism? There were a number of conflicting signals and no lack of interpretations or "lessons" to be learned. For the 48ers it was clear that they had failed to create a liberal-labor coalition. "We have had our day in court for this year," Record observed.[89] "The case is not perhaps hopeless," another liberal noted, "and we have at least learned the very useful lesson that oil and water will not mix. We cannot merge the class-conscious, radical labor group with the white-collar middle class people, who will not admit that they are labor."[90]

The tragedy, of course, is that unlike oil and water, liberal-labor politics do mix. Class and ideology were formidable barriers, but as events would show, they were unacceptable excuses for the failure in Chicago. Mutual respect came grudgingly and sometimes not at all as both groups tried to maintain their collective identities while adapting to the associational and interest-oriented politics of the 1920s. Occasionally, an organization did appear whose leadership, methods, and goals aimed directly for a fusion of farmer, labor, and liberal forces. The All American Farmer-Labor Cooperative Commission, created in 1920 and supported by the railway labor brotherhoods, offered such a glimpse into the future. The commission promoted cooperative stores, published and distributed bulletins, and maintained a press and information service. Its executive secretary, veteran reformer Frederic C. Howe, had moved far beyond the Committee of Forty-Eight in his search for a partnership of "hand and brain." The commission's organizers—Duncan MacDonald of the Illinois Federation of Labor, Sidney Hillman of the Amalgamated Clothing Workers, George P. Hampton of the Farmers' National Council, and Warren S. Stone of the Brotherhood of Locomotive Engineers—represented a small number of national leaders whose organizations were interested in shaping public policy and were willing to finance "cooperative efforts of producers and consumers."[91]

But for every organization like the All American Farmer-Labor Cooperative Commission which stood on the threshold of progress, one still could find reminders of narrower, more selfish movements such as the Committee of Forty-Eight. Even those members like George L. Record and Amos Pinchot who resigned did so for the wrong reasons. Unwilling to accept any modifications in their demand for the abolition of privilege, the two progressives regarded their colleagues as economic incompetents and denounced the committee's drift toward socialism. Most 48ers regarded the schism as a confrontation between conservatives and liberals, but neither Pinchot nor Record acknowledged the conservative label. They continued to see themselves as "constructive radicals," dismissing their onetime associates as well-meaning but intellectually vacuous romantics.[92] "I know that you and George . . . think that the rest of us are blind on one side," an exasperated J. A. H. Hopkins wrote Pinchot. "Perhaps you think we are blind on both sides. But . . . has it ever occurred to you that you and George may be blind on one side also."[93] It never did.

NOTES

1. J. H. Stewart Reid, *The Origins of the British Labour Party* (Minneapolis: Univ. of Minnesota Press, 1955); G. D. H. Cole, *History of the Labour Party from 1914* (London: Routledge & K. Paul, 1948); Philip Poirier, *The Advent of the British Labour Party* (New York: Columbia Univ. Press, 1958); and Henry Pelling, *The Origins of the Labour Party* (London: Macmillan & Co., Ltd., 1954).

2. Carl F. Brand, *The British Labour Party: A Short History* (Stanford, Ca.: Hoover Institution Press, 1974); and Catherine Ann Cline, *Recruits to Labour: The British Labour Party* (Syracuse, N.Y.: Syracuse Univ. Press, 1963).

3. Catherine Ann Cline, *Recruits to Labour*, 128–129. See also Arthur Marwick, *The Deluge: British Society and the First World War* (New York: Norton, 1970), 239–240.

4. Stanley Shapiro, "The Passage of Power: Labor and the New Social Order," *Proceedings of the American Philosophical Society* 120:6 (Dec. 1976), 466–467.

5. Cole, *History of the Labour Party*, 84–101.

6. Burl Noggle, *Into the Twenties: The United States from Armistice to Normalcy* (Urbana: Univ. of Illinois Press, 1974), 31–45; David M. Kennedy captures the fervor of "reconstruction" in *Over Here: The First World War and American Society* (New York: Oxford Univ. Press, 1980), 245–295. For the AFL's program see *Report of the Proceedings of the Thirty-Ninth Annual Convention of the A.F. of L.* (Washington, D.C., 1919), 70–80.

7. Reconstruction Pamphlets, No. 1, "Social Reconstruction: A General Review of the Problems and Survey of Remedies," The Committee on Special War

Activities, National Catholic War Council, Feb. 13, 1919, box 112, Amos Pinchot Papers.

8. Burl Noggle discusses the "Bishops' Program" in *Into the Twenties*, 73–75. The quotation is from the National Catholic War Council's pamphlet on "Social Reconstruction."

9. George L. Record to Oswald G. Villard, Jan. 24, 1918, box 36, Amos Pinchot Papers.

10. Amos R. E. Pinchot to George L. Record, Jan. 26, 1918, *ibid.*

11. George L. Record to Amos R. E. Pinchot, Feb. 7, 1918, box 35, *ibid.* See John Spargo, "The New National Party," *National Municipal Review* 7:3 (May 1918), 284–287; "The New 'National' Party," *Nation* 106 (Mar. 14, 1918), 284–285; and *New York Times*, Mar. 9, 1918.

12. The single best source for liberal-labor response to the BLP manifesto is Stanley Shapiro's excellent dissertation, "Hand and Brain: The Farmer-Labor Party of 1920," (Ph.D. diss., Univ. of California, Berkeley, 1967), especially Ch. Two: "In the Reconstruction Mood: The Liberals," 39–68. Representative samples of contemporary views include: *Public* 21 (May 4, 1918), 556; *Collier's* 63 (Apr. 26, 1919), 16, and *New Republic* 14 (Feb. 16, 1918), 2.

13. Louis F. Post, "Democracy in Industry," and Arthur E. Holder, "The People Must Organize," *Reconstruction Conference*, National Popular Government League, Jan. 9–11, 1919, box 69, Judson King Papers, Library of Congress (hereinafter cited as King Papers).

14. The Committee of Forty-Eight was so named in order to suggest its nationwide representation across America: in point of fact, however, it was dominated by a handful of New York liberals. See J. A. H. Hopkins to Amos R. E. Pinchot, Feb. 13, Feb. 15, and Mar. 1, 1919, box 39, Amos Pinchot Papers.

15. "Revolution or Reconstruction? A Call to Americans," *Survey* 41 (Mar. 22, 1919); "A New Political Alignment," *Nation* 108 (Mar. 29, 1919), 460–461. For responses to the "Call," see the autobiographies of two 48er leaders: Will Durant, *Transition, A Sentimental Story of One Mind and One Era* (New York: Simon and Schuster, 1927), 298, and Arthur G. Hays, *City Lawyer, The Autobiography of a Law Practice* (New York: Simon and Schuster, 1942), 253–254. For a look at the questionnaire sent to signers of the "Call," see box 67, Mercer G. Johnston Papers, Library of Congress, hereinafter cited as Johnston Papers.

16. *New York Times*, Aug. 18, 1919, 7; Shapiro, "Hand and Brain," 60–66; *idem.*, "The Twilight of Reform: Advanced Progressives after the Armistice," *Historian* 33:3 (May 1971), 361–363. See Milton Derber, "The Idea of Industrial Democracy in America, 1915–1935," *Labor History* 8:1 (Winter 1967), 3–29.

17. Shapiro, "Hand and Brain," 75–76; 84–86; and 97–100.

18. *Ibid.*, 69–104.

19. Nathan Fine, *Labor and Farmer Parties in the United States, 1828–1928* (New York: Rand School of Social Science, 1928), 378–379.

20. Shapiro, "Hand and Brain," discusses the problems inherent in cooperating with the Socialist party, 163–167.

21. "Enter the Labor Party," *New Republic* 21 (Dec. 10, 1919), 54; *ibid.*, (Dec. 31, 1919), 134.

22. *New Majority* 2 (Nov. 29, 1919), 1; the citation is from Shapiro, "Hand and Brain," 173.

23. Shapiro, "Hand and Brain," 125; and Harold C. Livesay, *Samuel Gompers and Organized Labor in America* (Boston: Little, Brown & Co., 1978), 180, talks abour "tar[ring] the upstarts with the red brush."

24. George L. Record to Amos R. E. Pinchot, Apr. 21 and June 18, 1919, box 39, Amos Pinchot Papers. Record desired meetings with the editors of both the *Nation* and the *New Republic*.

25. K. Austin Kerr, *American Railroad Politics 1914–1920: Rates, Wages and Efficiency* (Pittsburgh: Univ. of Pittsburgh Press, 1968), 66–83; and David A. Shannon, *Between the Wars, 1919–1941* (2nd ed., Boston: Houghton Mifflin Co., 1979), 23–25.

26. The Public Ownership League of America held a conference in Chicago during November attended by almost a thousand delegates; see its "Tentative Program," Sept. 9–12, 1919, box 39, Amos Pinchot Papers.

27. "A Call to Action," Committee of Forty-Eight, box 67, Johnston Papers.

28. Oswald G. Villard, chairman, Drafting Committee, to Amos R. E. Pinchot, Oct. 23, 1919, box 39, Amos Pinchot Papers.

29. Amos R. E. Pinchot, "The Coal Strike," *La Follette's Magazine* 11:2 (Nov. 1919), 167, optimistically predicted that the public would not tolerate the suppression of the striking miners.

30. Oswald G. Villard to Emily G. Balch, Nov. 4, 1919, Oswald G. Villard Papers, Houghton Library, Harvard University, hereinafter cited as Villard Papers.

31. Allen McCurdy, "Wanted—A Ballot Box," Pamphlet No. 1, published by the Committee of Forty-Eight, reprinted with permission from the *Nation* 110 (July 5, 1919), box 67, Johnston Papers.

32. "Facts," Committee of Forty-Eight, 1:4 (Dec. 12, 1919), 1, box 84, Amos Pinchot Papers.

33. *New York Times*, Dec. 22, 1919, 5.

34. Shapiro, "Hand and Brain," 177–178, and Hays, *City Lawyer*, 252–254.

35. J. A. H. Hopkins to Committee of Forty-Eight Executive Committee, Feb. 19, 1920, box 45, Johnston Papers.

36. The Esch-Cummins Transportation Act with its combination of public and private regulation pleased very few groups. It rejected the Plumb Plan's call for nationalization or any significant degree of governmental regulation. David P. Thelen, *Robert M. La Follette and the Insurgent Spirit* (Boston: Little, Brown & Co., 1976), 158–159, has argued that the measure gave the railroads everything they had been seeking since the 1890s: legalized pools, guaranteed minimum prices, and exemption from antitrust action. See also Kerr, *American Railroad Politics*, 204–227, and Kennedy, *Over Here*, 256–258.

37. Shapiro, "Hand and Brain," 182–183. See the *American Federationist* 26 (Apr. 1919), 518–519.

38. Lincoln Colcord to George L. Record, Dec. 26, 1919, box 39, Amos Pinchot Papers.

39. George L. Record to Lincoln Colcord; George L. Record to Amos R. E. Pinchot; and Lincoln Colcord to Warren S. Stone, Dec. 29, 1919, *ibid*.

40. Amos R. E. Pinchot to E. W. Scripps, Feb. 17, 1920, box 41, Amos Pinchot Papers.

41. On the question of "revenue-sharing" between the national and state 48er committees, see: A. W. Ricker, assistant treasurer, Executive Committee, to

Elisabeth Gilman, Mar. 23, 1920; Mercer G. Johnston to J. A. H. Hopkins, Mar. 24, 1920; A. W. Ricker to Mercer G. Johnston, Mar. 25, 1920, and J. A. H. Hopkins to Mercer G. Johnston, Apr. 7, 1920, box 45, Johnston Papers. In the end, the split in funds was to be 75 percent to the states and 25 percent of the gross to the national committee. The question of authority, and especially of the national committee's dominance, evoked a number of negative comments, most notably from the Wisconsin state committee: see Arthur J. Sweet to National Executive Committee, Feb. 18, 1920 and Arthur J. Sweet to Mercer G. Johnston, June 30, 1920, box 45, Johnston Papers.

42. J. A. H. Hopkins to Wade B. Leonard, Mar. 8, 1920, *ibid.*

43. Mercer G. Johnston to J. A. H. Hopkins, Mar. 10, 1920, *ibid.* For a revealing look into Johnston's social conscience, see a letter to his father, Bishop James S. Johnston, Mar. 31, 1920, box 23, *ibid.*

44. Committee of Forty-Eight, Executive Committee Minutes, May 27, 1920, box 84, Amos Pinchot Papers; Robert A. Pope to Mercer G. Johnston, June 15, 1920, and Mercer G. Johnston to J. A. H. Hopkins, June 17, 1920, box 45, Johnston Papers.

45. Amos R. E. Pinchot, "A Cross-Section of the American Mind," *Reconstruction* 2:4 (Apr. 1920), 169–171.

46. Amos R. E. Pinchot, "The Case for a Third Party: II, *Freeman* 1:17 (July 7, 1920), 394–396.

47. Amos R. E. Pinchot to James H. Maurer, Mar. 23, 1920, box 41, Amos Pinchot Papers.

48. Amos R. E. Pinchot to Francis J. Heney, Apr. 26, 1920, box 40, *ibid.*

49. Amos R. E. Pinchot, "The Bogey of Bolshevism," *Current Opinion* (May 1920); *idem.*, "Mr. Pinchot Cites the Wrongs That the 48ers Would Right," *Reconstruction* 2:2 (Feb. 1920), 51–56.

50. Shapiro, "Hand and Brain," 189; *New Majority* 3 (June 19, 1920), 4; *ibid.*, 4 (June 26, 1920), 4:4 (July 3, 1920), 4; see also Rex O. Mooney, "Amos Pinchot and Atomistic Capitalism: A Study in Reform Ideas," (Ph.D. diss., Louisiana State Univ., 1973), 91–92; and Nathan Fine, *Labor and Farmer Parties in the U.S.*, 384–385.

51. Mercer G. Johnston to Toscan Bennett, May 7, 1920, box 45, Johnston Papers.

52. Mercer G. Johnston to S. L. V. Young, June 10, 1920, *ibid.*

53. Mercer G. Johnston to Arthur G. Wray, mayor of York, Neb., June 14, 1920, *ibid.*

54. E. W. Scripps to Amos R. E. Pinchot, Mar. 29, 1920, box 41, Amos Pinchot Papers.

55. Hiram W. Johnson to Carlos K. McClatchy (*Fresno Bee*), Nov. 9, 1920, Part III, box 3, and Hiram W. Johnson to Meyer Lissner, Jan. 24, 1920, Part VI, box 2, Hiram W. Johnson Papers, Bancroft Library, Univ. of California, Berkeley, hereinafter cited as Johnson Papers; John Spargo to Mercer G. Johnston, Apr. 1, 1920, box 45, Johnston Papers.

56. J. A. H. Hopkins to Mercer G. Johnston, May 18, 1920, box 45, Johnston Papers; Hopkins to Frank Walsh, June 15, 1920, box 34, Frank Walsh Papers, New York Public Library.

57. Mercer G. Johnston to J. A. H. Hopkins, Mar. 12, 1920, box 45, Johnston Papers.

58. George L. Record to Robert M. La Follette, June 25, 1920, box 86, series B, La Follette Papers, Library of Congress, hereinafter cited as La Follette Papers; and Amos R. E. Pinchot to Robert M. La Follette, June 25, 1920, box 41, Pinchot Papers.

59. Amos R. E. Pinchot to Robert La Follette, *ibid.*, and George L. Record to Robert M. La Follette, June 25, 1920, box 86, series B, La Follette Papers.

60. David P. Thelen, *The New Citizenship: The Origins of Progressivism in Wisconsin, 1885–1900* (Columbia: Univ. of Missouri Press, 1972) and *idem.*, *Robert M. La Follette and the Insurgent Spirit* emphasize the changing nature of progressivism from consumer to producer concerns.

61. Robert M. La Follette to Bill (Hard?), June 28, 1920, box 180, series B, La Follette Papers.

62. William Hard to Robert M. La Follette, July 9, 1920, box 85, *ibid.*

63. William Hard to Robert M. La Follette, July 11, 1920, *ibid.*

64. William Hard, "Seeking More Power for Those Who Work," *Chicago Daily News*, July 10–13, 1920, box 85, *ibid.*

65. Amos R. E. Pinchot, "The New Party," July 15, 1920, *New York Evening Post*, box 84, Amos Pinchot Papers; *New York Times*, July 19, 1920, 1; Gilson Gardner to R. P. Scripps, July 19, 1920, box 40, Amos Pinchot Papers; and Fine, *Labor and Farmer Parties in the U.S.*, 393.

66. Memorandum of a conversation with Robert M. La Follette, prepared by Gilbert E. Roe and Robert M. La Follette, Jr., undated, probably July 10–11, 1920, box 180, series B, La Follette Papers; J. A. H. Hopkins to "My Fellow Members of the Committee of 48," July 1920, box 45, Johnston Papers; and Shapiro, "Hand and Brain," 194–208.

67. Dudley F. Malone, "The Birth of the Third Party," *Freeman* (July 28, 1920), 467–468, in box 86, series B, La Follette Papers; see also the statement written by Malone and Swineburne Hale, Aug. 13, 1920, box 45, Johnston Papers.

68. Amos R. E. Pinchot, "Personal Statement," July 16, 1920, box 180, La Follette Papers; and "Statement of Amos Pinchot," undated, box 86, Amos Pinchot Papers.

69. Mercer G. Johnston to J. A. H. Hopkins, July 28, 1920, box 45, Johnston Papers; and Mercer G. Johnston to Rev. Olympia Brown, Aug. 13, 1920, *ibid.*

70. Mercer G. Johnston to Bishop James S. Johnston, July 30, 1920, box 23, *ibid.*

71. Allan L. Benson to Mercer G. Johnston, Aug. 25, 1920, box 45, *ibid.*

72. Elisabeth Gilman to J. A. H. Hopkins, July 29, 1920, *ibid.*, and J. A. H. Hopkins to Mercer G. Johnston, Aug. 4, 1920, *ibid.*

73. Shapiro, "Hand and Brain," 208–215, and James H. Shideler, *Farm Crisis, 1919–1923* (Berkeley: Univ. of California Press, 1957), 32–33.

74. *New Republic* 23 (June 30, 1920), 139–140; 23 (July 28, 1920), 239–240; 24 (Sept. 22, 1920), 82; 24 (Oct. 22, 1920), 204; and 24 (Oct. 27, 1920), 204. *Nation* 111 (July 24, 1920), 88; 111 (Sept. 4, 1920), 260, and Charles P. Sweeney, "The Farmer-Labor Campaign," *ibid.* (Sept. 25, 1920), 344–345; Shapiro, "Hand and Brain," 208–215.

75. George L. Record to Robert M. La Follette, July 16, 1920, box 86, series

B, La Follette Papers; J. A. H. Hopkins to Robert M. La Follette, Jr., July 16, 1920, *ibid.*, and George L. Record to Amos R. E. Pinchot, July 20, 1920, box 40, Amos Pinchot Papers.

76. Lynn Haines to Robert M. La Follette, July 21, 1920, box 35, Lynn Haines Papers, Minnesota Historical Society, hereinafter cited as Haines Papers.

77. Thelen, *Robert M. La Follette and the Insurgent Spirit*, 158–165, and Shapiro, "Hand and Brain," 199–200.

78. Dudley F. Malone, "The Birth of the Third Party," *Freeman* (July 28, 1920), 467–468, in box 86, series B, La Follette Papers and Gilbert E. Roe to Robert M. La Follette, July 22, 1920, *ibid.*

79. Thelen, *Robert M. La Follette and the Insurgent Spirit*, 164.

80. Basil M. Manly to Lynn Haines, July 22, 1920, box 35, Haines Papers; Manly, "Memorandum of a Conference at Madison, Wisconsin, July 25–27, 1920," dated Aug. 2, 1920, box 86, series B, La Follette Papers.

81. George L. Record to Amos R. E. Pinchot, Aug. 25, 1920, box 40, Amos Pinchot Papers.

82. Mercer G. Johnston to Robert M. La Follette, Aug. 4, 1920, box 85, series B, La Follette Papers.

83. Basil M. Manly, "Memorandum," Aug. 2, 1920, box 86, series B; and Basil M. Manly to Gilbert E. Roe, July 28, 1920, box 112, *ibid.*

84. Gilbert E. Roe to Robert M. La Follette, July 22, 1920, box 86, and Basil M. Manly to Robert M. La Follette, Jr., Aug. 4, 1920, *ibid.*

85. Basil M. Manly to Robert M. La Follette, Jr., Aug. 6, 1920, box 86, *ibid.*

86. Gilson Gardner to Amos R. E. Pinchot, Aug. 11, 1920, box 41, Amos Pinchot Papers.

87. George L. Record to Amos R. E. Pinchot, Aug. 25, 1920, box 40, *ibid.*

88. George L. Record to Robert M. La Follette, Nov. 9, 1920, box 86, series B, La Follette Papers.

89. George L. Record to Amos R. E. Pinchot, Aug. 30, 1920, box 40, Amos Pinchot Papers.

90. Gilson Gardner to R. P. Scripps, July 19, 1920, *ibid.*

91. Frederic C. Howe to Robert M. La Follette, Oct. 15, 1920, box 86, series B, La Follette Papers.

92. Amos R. E. Pinchot to J. A. H. Hopkins, Nov. 26, 1920, box 40, Amos Pinchot Papers; J. A. H. Hopkins to George L. Record, Nov. 30, 1920, *ibid.*, George L. Record to J. A. H. Hopkins, Dec. 2, 1920, *ibid.*; A. W. Ricker to Allen McCurdy, Dec. 7, 1920, *ibid.*; A. W. Ricker to Allen McCurdy, Dec. 13, 1920, and A. W. Ricker to Arthur Wray, Dec. 14, 1920, *ibid.* See also Paul W. Glad, "Progressives and the Business Culture of the 1920s," *Journal of American History* 53:1 (June 1966), 83; and Burl Noggle, *Into the Twenties*, 185–186.

93. J. A. H. Hopkins to Amos R. E. Pinchot, Nov. 30, 1920, box 40, Amos Pinchot Papers.

VI

Independent Progressives, 1921–1924

It is the end of Progressivism . . . during our generation.
Hiram W. Johnson to Meyer Lissner, November 8, 1920

By September 1920, the inevitability of a conservative triumph in the November elections prompted a handful of Senate progressives to take a collective look at their political futures. The public might have been familiar with some of the participants—Robert L. Owen (Dem., Okla.), Joseph I. France (Rep., Md.), David I. Walsh (Dem., Mass.), and George W. Norris (Rep., Neb.)—and no doubt would have recognized Robert M. La Follette, the maverick Republican from Wisconsin. Less well known but no less important for the survival of progressivism was the inclusion of a number of prominent labor leaders and sympathizers such as Frank Walsh, the former chairman of the U.S. Commission on Industrial Relations and co-chairman of the War Labor Board; Edward Keating, a onetime congressman from Colorado, manager of the Plumb Plan League and editor of *Labor*, voice of the railroad brotherhoods; and Warren S. Stone, president of the Brotherhood of Locomotive Engineers. Their presence represented the belated recognition of labor's critical role in progressive politics, a role that was bound to increase as liberals sensed the practical value of the labor movement's financial and organizational strength.

These liberal and labor leaders agreed to seek support for an informational and publicity bureau "which would compile the data necessary for the fights which will have to be made."[1] In January 1921, with the full import of Warren G. Harding's landslide victory clear—a Republican majority of 172 votes in the House of Representatives and a 22-seat margin in the Senate—congressional progressives formally launched the People's Legislative Service (PLS). In combative, clearly partisan rhetoric reflecting a siege mentality, PLS director Basil M. Manly called for "practical methods of safeguarding the public interest and combating the political forces of reaction and special privilege during the next four years."[2] The PLS, a creation of Washington's liberal establishment, would provide progressive congressmen with technical support in bill drafting and research. The PLS might keep the public informed and help coordinate the activities of various groups, but these were not its major goals, nor did it presume to represent a national constituency.[3] Still, its appearance was symptomatic of progressive activity and paralleled developments among other special interest groups who also were groping their way toward a policy of constructive opposition to the new Republican administration.

No organization better typified contemporary liberal thinking than the People's Reconstruction League (PRL), the most aggressive and innovative lobbying group then formulating a progressive program. Organized early in 1921 by groups sympathetic to the goals of the PLS, the league represented a union of farmer, labor, and progressive groups committed to economic democracy. Funded by the railway unions, led by veteran lobbyist Benjamin C. Marsh, drawing its leaders from influential members of the Farmers' National Council and the International Association of Machinists, the PRL fought for public ownership of the railroads; public operation and development of natural resources; a progressive tax upon incomes, estates, excess profits, and land values; short-term rural credit; revision of the Federal Reserve System; creation of cooperative banks; regulation of the meat-packing industry; and an end to universal military training. The league billed these eclectic proposals as "a program of economic justice which will save the people on farms, in factories, in mines, offices, trade, and transportation six billion dollars a year." Budget-cutting and economizing were important league goals, and its populist-progressive attacks upon special privilege and monopoly always were balanced by conscious taxpayer appeals to both producers and consumers.[4] In that sense, even this most progressive of organizations accommodated its message of economic and social justice to the changing mores of a business culture.

There is a danger in attributing excessive influence to an organization like the PRL simply because it had a published program, a Washington address, and letterhead stationery. The league was very much a shoestring operation which its executive secretary, Benjamin C. Marsh, carried around in his hip pocket. Indeed, Marsh was the PRL just as he also represented the interests of the Farmers' National Council, his other principal employer. As a professional lobbyist for both groups, Marsh appeared before congressional committees testifying in behalf of federal regulation of the meat-packing industry, supporting George W. Norris's Farmers' Export Financing Corporation, attacking the Harding administration's Ship Subsidy Bill, and defending the Federal Trade Commission from critics. During the recession years of 1921–22, he also lobbied for presidential pressure on employers to maintain high levels of employment; supported a survey of needed public works, housing, and factory construction; called for federal loans to cities and counties for such programs; and proposed that the purchasing power of the "producing classes" be increased by imposing heavier taxation on the incomes and inheritances of the well-to-do.[5] The less glamorous side of his work, however, much of which was conducted out of a cubbyhole office in a soon-to-be condemned building, involved organizing state conferences on the league program, paying his own way to speaking engagements, sleeping in third-rate hotels, and hustling wealthy liberal friends for contributions.[6]

Men such as Marsh, Manly, and Mercer G. Johnston became the custodians, managers, and publicists of postwar liberalism. They handled day-to-day operations for progressive lobbies, kept tabs on liberal legislation, raised money for their organizations' mass mailings, and generally harassed both friends and enemies. One important element distinguished their activities from their progressive predecessors: they worked for organized labor. When union leaders offered advice on policy or legislation, these men listened and acted accordingly. Union presidents sat prominently on their boards of directors, and the labor movement's participation in liberal politics was openly acknowledged and solicited.

Labor's influential role in shaping liberal policy also reflected the absence of any overriding popular issue. This factor had important consequences for postwar progressivism. It limited the active participants in liberal causes to the highly committed and insured that well-organized and financially independent interest groups would dominate leadership positions. In this setting the railroad labor brotherhoods emerged as the single most dominant progressive force. Suddenly, but not coincidentally, a number of progressive lobbyists and tacticians rediscovered the importance of public ownership. Long a staple of reform thought dating back to the populists' calls for nationalization of the railroads, telephone, and telegraph systems in the .1880s and to the municipal ownership movement of the early twentieth century, government ownership placed the railroad brotherhoods in the forefront of postwar progressivism. Though lacking the emotional appeal necessary for a mass-based popular crusade such as prohibition or women's suffrage, government ownership had the advantage of casting a sufficiently large net encompassing advocates of nationalization, independent political action, industrial democracy, and antimonopoly who had little else in common. Liberal party leader J. A. H. Hopkins, for example, supported government ownership because its adoption would require creation of a new political party.

Conservative former 48ers such as Amos Pinchot and George L. Record endorsed it because implementation would mean the destruction of privilege. Leaders of the Public Ownership League such as Albert Todd and Carl Thompson advocated nationalization of the railroads as a first step toward achieving their goal of government ownership of all industry.[7] In the end, however, it was the railway brotherhoods who initiated the call to a Conference for Progressive Political Action (CPPA), invited the participants, set the agenda, underwrote the costs, and called the shots.

It was appropriate that William H. Johnston, president of the International Association of Machinists (IAM) and an executive committee member of both the PLS and the PRL, should have signed the call and keynoted the CPPA's first meeting in February 1922. Drawing upon over thirty years experience in labor's populist, progressive, and socialist wing, Johnston represented the antithesis to Samuel Gompers's "pure and simple unionism." He advocated industrial unions and independent political action when such ideas were considered heretical by the AFL. Membership on the War Labor Board had given him a favorable view of government intervention in the economy, and he helped found the Plumb Plan League to promote nationalization of the railroads. Johnston's personal interests, however, also reflected the needs of his union. Though one of the largest in the AFL, the machinists enjoyed no representation on the international's Executive Council. Unlike the federation, which reluctantly engaged in political action, the IAM successfully used the political process to fight for the eight-hour day. Postwar economic and political conditions—particularly the 1921–22 recession, rising unemployment, a hostile Railroad Labor Board (the tribunal governing wages, hours, and conditions), the likelihood of an antilabor Congress, and the Harding administration's enthusiastic support of company unions—impelled Johnston to join other railway brotherhoods, farm organizations, and independent progressives in seeking "common understanding to bind the workers together."[8]

In the timeless rhetoric of American reform, labor's call to action offered indignation—"all of the inherent rights of men . . . are being rapidly destroyed by the agents of privilege"—balanced by conservatively hopeful solutions—"there must be some fundamental economic principles that can be invoked to restore the opportunities of the nation to the people of the nation."[9] Restraint also was evident in the call's cautious allusion to political action. "This is not an attempt to form a new political party. It is an effort to make use of those constructive forces already in existence, and by cooperation bring about political unity." "Constructive," "cooperation," and "unity" were such soothing, reassuring words that they may have disguised what one contemporary called "the underlying desire to attain more say in the affairs of government and life for the producing classes."[10]

The call stimulated a good deal of speculation among nonunion progressives, some of it of the most mundane kind. Veteran reformer Mercer G. Johnston expressed practical concerns about the conference's importance. "Have you any inside dope?," he asked *Labor*'s Edward Keating. "If it is anything very special, I will try to go. But I have been thinking about going to the Farmer-Labor Party convention in May . . . and . . . could not very well go to both." But Johnston did go. Like many activists he was addicted to such meetings; it was an important part of his life, a vital element in his sense of identity and self-esteem. Professional and personal gratification alone, however, did not bring him to Chicago. Public ownership and democratic control of the railroads (and coal mines) did. "Nothing short of that," he told Keating, "is even going to get us started toward industrial peace." Another reason for Johnston's presence in Chicago speaks directly to the liberal-labor differences which had surfaced so dramatically in that city almost two years earlier. Unlike most of his colleagues in the Committee of Forty-Eight, particularly those in policymaking positions, Johnston had sided with the laborites in behalf of worker control and industrial democracy and had supported the Farmer-Labor Party during the campaign. Facing a similar situation, he could not dispel fears that the railway brotherhoods' commitment to economic and social justice did not extend beyond public ownership of the railroads. He went to the conference, therefore, to maintain a progressive presence and, if necessary, to "make our railroad and miner brethren cross their hearts . . . that they wouldn't lay down on the balance of the program when it came time to put more of it across."[11]

The 300 or so men and women who assembled at the Masonic Temple in Chicago on February 21, 1922, represented a cross section of a very ill-defined progressive movement. They enjoyed little in common except the motivation which brought them together and a catalogue of grievances which were more easily stated than solved. The Conference's "Declaration of Principles" singled out the villains and their crimes with such singular delight that one could almost hear the sound of hissing in the background. Even groups as divergent in their interests as single-taxers, socialists, Farmer-Labor party supporters, farm leaders, and union officials could not fail to condemn such symbols of injustice as the "money power," "tax-dodging capitalists," and "war profiteers" whose "greed," "corruption," and "betrayal" had created "new privileges and immunities for capital [while] trampling under foot the rights of man."[12]

Such cliché-ridden rhetoric provided good newspaper copy but offered no clue as to the kind of organization the CPPA might become or what policies it might pursue. A look at the composition of its National Committee of Fifteen suggested that policy and practice would be distinct from conference rhetoric and campaign hoopla. Chaired by William H. Johnston, the committee included four other representatives from the railroad brotherhoods while ten different organizations contributed the remaining members. Though Johnston exercised a major role in all decisions, the nuts-and-bolts mechanics of operating this amorphous organization benefited from the accumulated experience of four veteran liberal-labor lobbyists and tacticians: Benjamin C. Marsh (PRL and Farmers' National Council), Basil M. Manly (PLS), Edward Keating (*Labor*), and Frederic C. Howe (CPPA secretary).[13] These were practical and patient men, cool-headed and thorough, well versed in Capitol Hill idiosyncrasies, insiders who possessed familiarity with the Washington bureaucracy. In their hands the CPPA's rhetoric would be tempered by an eye for detail, respect for power, and an ability to compromise.

William H. Johnston's "Call to Action," the chairman's report to the CPPA Executive Committee on the results of the February conference, reflected two sides of the organization's personality. Speaking to the Socialists, Farmer-Laborites, and more radical progressives, he denounced the conspiracy of nonproducers—"bankers, business men, lawyers, and editors"—who paralyzed the nation's farmers and laborers, "[who] destroyed the purchasing power . . . and used political power to extort oppressive railroad rates and misuse the nation's credit." Then, wearing his hat as a representative of the more cautious railroad brotherhoods, Johnston argued that though the time was "ripe for progressive political action" patience was needed before launching a new party. He called for the creation of a "producers' bloc" of at least 100 friendly congressmen from both major parties but warned that "when action within the old parties is futile," independent organization was preferable to "wasting ballots on men who cannot be trusted." At best, the message was ambiguous; the CPPA seemed to be sending out conflicting signals to its disparate constituent groups: organize but do not be too independent. In fact, however, the CPPA leadership had decided to pursue an aggressive and flexible policy of nonpartisanship. Following the successful example of the Nonpartisan League, the CPPA's state and local chapters would support progressives in major party primaries, and where that failed independent candidates would be nominated in the general election.[14]

If no one left Chicago singing "Onward Christian Soldiers" or "Solidarity Forever," few could accuse the railroad brotherhoods of raising false hopes. Mercer G. Johnston had come to the conference predisposed toward its success; he returned home hopeful, if only partially satisfied. "The curse of the labor movement," he wrote Edward Keating, "still is the little-mindedness—the hard and narrow and exclusive sectarianism—of those in positions of leadership." Disappointed with some labor leaders' "Holier than thou stuff," he wondered when such men would "get cheek by jowl with every group that is ready to march against the common enemy."[15]

In the meantime, CPPA secretary Frederic C. Howe sat in his Washington office churning out propaganda in which progressive differences were ignored and the only distinctions that counted were between "the class that produces and the class that lives off those that produce. The producers," Howe added, "should vote together, and leave the exploiters to vote together." It remained unclear, however, what the functional basis for this producers' alliance would be; even the CPPA's stated objective—"to organize factory workers, farmers, radical, and progressive elements in every state for united political action on a permanent basis"—avoided specific commitment to a third party.[16]

Presidential politics and third-party action remained the chief topic of conversation among liberal and labor leaders. Because of its glamour and appeal, a third-party candidacy possessed the greatest potential for "lib-lab" cooperation. Paradoxically, it also represented a troublesome issue for unions accustomed to working with major party politicians and for liberal officeholders who risked their political future by straying from orthodoxy. Still, the alternatives were not attractive. Progressives might gloat over the end of the "Harding Honeymoon" with Congress but could scarcely take comfort in observing that "big business [was] not only in the saddle but . . . sitting on the neck of the horse [government]." We now have a Senate, Hiram W. Johnson wrote his sons, "more subservient, more servile, and more contemptibly sycophantic than the Senate has ever been during my residence here."[17] These observations made the absence of a viable third-party alternative all the more troubling. Some veterans of the 1920 campaign still hoped to create an American counterpart to the British Labour Party, but progressives lacked the issue or cause around which they could unite and submerge their differences and egos. The war was over and pacifism in disrepute; poverty, a genuine progressive concern in past years, got lost in the shuffle of widespread middle-class economic discontent; corruption still sold newspapers, but as the Harding scandals would soon show, public outrage gave way to a perverse curiosity in human frailty.

Inequality in the distribution of wealth and power spoke more directly to contemporary needs, but its solutions struck too close to home for many liberals. Progressivism was not dead; the war had not "killed" it, nor was the postwar disillusionment as pervasive as the anguished prose of American expatriots might suggest. Causes remained, as did those committed to them. There was much talk of it being "high time" for some "serious thought" on the part of "real honest-to-goodness liberals."[18] Since talking was what progressives still did best, one learned a great deal about their concerns by reading the liberal journals but comparatively less about organized labor's views, whose leaders guarded their opinions more closely and were less accustomed to airing them in public.

The issue of independent political action versus nonpartisanship continued to trouble those CPPA members who were less interested in issues than in starting a new party. Many progressives, of course, made no distinction, seeing the two as inseparable and mutually reinforcing. Others gravitated more toward the principles of a platform, believing that they should first educate the public and sympathetic politicians to their program before attaching or mortgaging their movement to an outsider. Thus, many progressives spent the summer of 1922 campaigning for friendly candidates and debating platform planks for use in the fall.

Two of the most persistent participants in these ideological battles were George L. Record and Amos Pinchot. These former 48ers, dedicated antimonopolists, third-party activists, and self-proclaimed individualists, were clearly to the right of most CPPA members. Lacking organizational support or influence, speaking primarily for themselves and a handful of friends, they nonetheless affected the policy debate by offering alternatives to a slowly emerging CPPA program. How two men so thoroughly repudiated by Labor Party leaders in 1920 could emerge two years later in another labor-dominated movement is partly explained by the love-hate relationship which had characterized liberal-labor relations since before the First World War. That relationship had undergone a major role reversal. The prewar partnership had been predicated upon the twin evils of inequality and fear. Labor was unequal and liberals were afraid of the violent consequences of continued oppression. Though progressives may not always have been embraced at strike scenes, liberals were welcomed at Lawrence and Ludlow because their physical presence signified a larger commitment. The involvement of men such as Amos Pinchot, Oswald G. Villard, Roger N. Baldwin, and Norman Thomas lent a sense of legitimacy to workers' struggles; it provided access to pocketbooks in Greenwich Village salons and opened an occasional billfold in a corporate boardroom. Liberal sponsorship usually guaranteed favorable coverage in magazines read by an influential and highly motivated public as well as sympathetic advocacy in the halls of Congress. Whether or not the peace of mind, camaraderie, and gratification liberals received from their involvement represented a fair exchange is not the point. By war's end reformers no longer were the dominant party in liberal-labor relations. Organized labor had emerged from the war with a new partner. Government intervention had created a labor movement that was stronger organizationally, financially, and politically than its prewar predecessor. The consequences of these changes were felt in 1919 when militant Labor Party leaders refused to assume their accustomed position at the feet of liberals in the Committee of Forty-Eight. Both sides' refusal to compromise doomed their chances in the 1920 election. Now, two years later, liberal and labor leaders prepared to forge a new political alliance, and once again Record and Pinchot entered the debate. Their program was remarkably similar to proposals they had introduced ten years earlier.

Both men had a realistic awareness of labor's strength and respect for the railway unions' potential political power, yet each vehemently opposed the idea of a separate labor party or a class movement. Recognizing labor's "solidarity of opinion" with regard to wages, hours, and conditions, they still maintained that workers were not an isolated group. "Labor works as labor, we admit," Pinchot observed. "But it lives, feels, thinks, and above all, votes as part of the public, as it demonstrated with peculiar clarity in the last election."[19] The solution to social injustice was not class legislation but a more equitable distribution of wealth. Though they punctuated their arguments with an occasional reference to the "producers of wealth," Pinchot and Record managed to reject every major proposal identified with the labor movement.[20]

It was a remarkable performance but one Pinchot and Record had grown accustomed to giving for over a decade. Neither man was an obstructionist, yet both were so totally committed to this peculiar view of the world that every attack, every defeat, strengthened their conviction in the absolute correctness of their position. Forty years of government regulation, they contended, had failed to control or limit monopolistic growth.

Pinchot and Record proposed to take control of the marketplace away from the trusts through government ownership of the railroads and government leasing of natural resources. The two antimonopolists concluded that the problem was not capitalism but privilege.[21] They proposed a series of conferences attended by socialists, single-taxers, independent progressives, the railway labor unions, La Follette supporters, and representatives of the Farmer-Labor movement. Fearful of repeating the experience of the 1920 Labor Party-Committee of Forty-Eight gatherings, Record and Pinchot emphasized the importance of formulating a program before the convention. They feared being overwhelmed by socialists and union leaders who would "use the same . . . stock phrases [and] emphasize the class consciousness which seeks to array the propertyless class against the class that has property." Such a program, they believed, would encounter widespread and deep-rooted prejudice (especially their own) and contain too many different ideas (in addition to their own) to permit an effective campaign. "If we cannot agree," they asked, "how can we hope that the great public can agree?"[22]

It is tempting to denigrate such men and dismiss them as armchair theorists who asked others to take the political risks and make the personal sacrifices. This would be unfair. Record and Pinchot frequently put their ideas to the test, notably in Record's flamboyant fifty-day tent campaign in the spring of 1922 to capture the New Jersey Republican senatorial nomination. No stranger to campaigning, Record's electoral aspirations dated back at least a quarter-century and included sundry unsuccessful bids for local, state, and national office. Widely praised by his admirers as an "able, bold, resourceful, powerful, and persuasive advocate . . . with an engaging, attractive personality," he was just as enthusiastically condemned by his foes as a hypocritical "soldier of fortune" whose election "would be about as safe and sensible [as sending] Lenine [*sic*] and Trotsky to the Senate."[23]

His opponent in the GOP primary was the incumbent, Joseph S. Frelinghuysen, one of President Harding's favorite poker and golfing companions, whose conservative, antilabor record made him a vulnerable target of the CPPA's campaign to elect more progressive candidates to office. Frelinghuysen had supported the Esch-Cummins Transportation Act returning the railroads to private ownership, given his unqualified endorsement to Treasury Secretary Andrew Mellon's regressive tax and revenue legislation, opposed passage of the soldier's bonus bill, and joined Old Guard colleagues in welcoming Truman H. Newberry to the Senate in spite of the charges of fraud and corruption surrounding the latter's victory over Henry Ford in the 1918 Michigan senatorial election.[24] Record, however, was himself an unusually vulnerable candidate. For all his experience, he carried too much political baggage and had endured so many defeats that his credibility was suspect. His was an easily recognizable name but not one to which the general voter normally paid much serious attention.[25] One might surmise from a Frelinghuysen staffer's observation of a Record tent meeting—"about 100 present, mostly long-haired men and short-haired women"—that he appealed to an avant-garde constituency or a small coterie of intellectuals and such may well have been the case.[26]

Amos Pinchot attended many of Record's rallies and wrote numerous letters in his behalf to such people as La Follette and Henry Ford. He captured the essence of his friend's campaign in a note to Frederic C. Howe. "Record is the one man I know who has always been uncompromising in his stand for a radical program. . . . George can neither be silenced nor seduced, and even if he does not get the nomination, his campaign will be enormously educational."[27] But how helpful to the cause of government ownership was an outspoken, fiercely independent, unreconstructed exponent of free competition? The contributions of such men to any political organization were formidable; they were adept at generating discussion and stimulating a healthy, vigorous debate. A group struggling for political recognition depended upon their enthusiasm, courage, and energy. Once policies were established, however, debate had to give way to consensus. Alternative positions were less welcome, for political criticism had lost its constructive role. Once respectability replaced survival as the group's primary consideration, wiser, more cautious heads prevailed, and the holders of independent opinions became an unnecessary liability. Leaders of the CPPA may well have breathed a sigh of relief upon learning of Record's defeat. Though their organization was still struggling for a permanent political identity and was not yet secure, it had gained respectability and recognition. Record's maverick public record, personal eccentricity, identification with losing causes, and obvious differences with the CPPA's labor leaders over industrial democracy and nationalization were all liabilities for a fledgling political coalition.

The 1922 congressional elections legitimized the CPPA's political ambitions, even if the results were not always attributable to its efforts. The Republican majority in the Senate was cut from 24 seats to 10, and in the House, where the Democrats gained 76 seats, the margin was cut to 20. La Follette was overwhelmingly reelected from Wisconsin and was joined by three new progressive senators: Henrik Shipstead, the Farmer-Labor party winner from Minnesota; Smith W. Brookhart, the "cowhide radical" Republican and La Follette protégé from Iowa; and Montana Democrat Burton K. Wheeler.[28] Still, as one scholar correctly reminds us, the results were not as catastrophic and staggering as some alleged; in spite of the normal setbacks anticipated by the majority party in off-year elections, the GOP still controlled both houses of Congress. Its enemies lacked unity, and the returns are more easily understood as a highly individualized response to peculiar local issues and conditions. On the other hand, progressives could take heart from the Harding administration's inept handling of the coal and rail strikes, its identification with "Newberryism," and public displeasure with the high protectionism and self-interest of the administration-backed Fordney-McCumber Tariff.[29]

Perhaps, in retrospect, it was clear that the election results did not signal a return to progressivism or a radical new direction in domestic politics. That was not as readily apparent, however, in the fall of 1922. In fact, most progressives were jubilant. Oswald G. Villard, editor of the *Nation*, was "elated" with the "magnificent beginning." Twelve of sixteen gubernatorial candidates supported by the CPPA, including Alfred E. Smith in New York and Gifford Pinchot in Pennsylvania, won election. Chairman William H. Johnston called the results "epoch making . . . surpassing every expectation" and attributed the victories "to the activities set in motion by the [CPPA's] Chicago conference."[30] Veteran Washington hand Harry A. Slattery considered the election "a swat at the reactionaries. . . . Imperial Washington," he crowed, "has on crape." He hoped progressives would "continue to hold 'that the battle is not for a day, etc.' "[31]

That advice was taken to heart by all sides. Two days after the election, President Harding issued a call for a special legislative session with hopes of pushing his administration's Ship Subsidy Bill and other measures through the lameduck Congress. Concurrently, Robert M. La Follette, basking in the personal glow of a 289,000 vote majority, with a progressive twinkle in his eye and presidential ambition on his mind, summoned the congressional faithful to a December 1 meeting in Washington for some political muscle-flexing by the new progressive voting bloc.[32] Hiram W. Johnson, a nonparticipant, resurrected TR's "lunatic fringe" phrase to dismiss the La Follette supporters as "all the crazy advocates of 'isms' ... in the country." He had little faith that anything even remotely constructive would emerge from this two-day progressive spectacle. Participants came to enjoy the postelection euphoria, see their colleagues, and be seen. Those who came for more serious purposes left disappointed. Little was accomplished beyond renewing commitments to such platitudes as eliminating special privilege, restoring government to the people, initiating electoral reform, and redistributing the wealth. Press coverage transformed this substantively trite affair into an event, but it amounted to little more than a progressive reunion and warm-up for the CPPA meeting ten days later in Cleveland.[33]

There were more sparks at the CPPA's second conference, but they came less from forward movement than from the brakes applied by the railroad brotherhoods. Some of the delegates, notably those from the Farmer-Labor Party led by Robert M. Buck and John Fitzpatrick and the militant socialists in the needle trades led by Sidney Hillman, seemed to think "that they had the political world by the tail and it was time to start a labor party."[34] This was not the majority sentiment, nor was the division strictly along ideological, occupational, or geographic lines. Nonpartisan leaguers from North Dakota favored the continuation of capturing primaries over the riskier gamble of third-party independence. Socialists like James Oneal and Morris Hillquit counseled patience. "Progress," Hillquit told the delegates, "is always made safely and slowly, step by step." Though the more radical Hillman argued that labor "had no future as a tail to either of the two old parties," the votes were simply not there for any resolution supporting creation of a third party.[35] Independent progressives who pinned their hopes to a CPPA-led third party disliked what they perceived as the labor brotherhoods' conservatism. But the former's unhappiness was also a reluctant recognition of their political dependence on organized labor.

The door for independent political action remained ajar, but the railroad unions' caution militated against precipitous developments. The CPPA's "hold-back boys," as one scholar calls them, clearly appreciated the tranquilizing effects of an uneventful convention. They consciously choreographed the meeting in their own backyard and paid lip service to a host of conventional progressive concerns such as tax and primary reform, infancy and maternity protection; and agricultural price supports; but their principal hope was to attract the broadest possible support for a presidential candidate to a campaign organized around government ownership.[36] One of the most likely candidates to lead such an effort, Robert M. La Follette, expressed general agreement with Frederic C. Howe's observation that "safe-guarding the public interest" now devolved chiefly upon labor groups.[37] How soon that responsibility would be met and by whom remained to be answered.

Much of the uncertainty stemmed from the quadrennial nature of American politics. Everyone seemed to be waiting for 1924; the off-year elections were over, and only the most zealous political activists had the tenacity and strength of conviction to keep going in what might be termed an "off-off year" such as 1923. Such people played a necessary and crucial role in the political process; they were nuisances to those with influence and to others who sought it. Their willingness to endure the drudgery and tedium of constant political work was matched only by the stubbornness with which they clung to their own unique program. But they were not eccentrics or quacks easily dismissed by their peers. They survived, in part, because of an incredible persistence but also because there was something appealing in their message.

"I write to renew the suggestion I made in Washington," George L. Record advised *Labor*'s Edward Keating, "that you arrange an early opportunity for Mr. Pinchot and me to . . . present to . . . your friends our idea of political action." That idea, as Keating knew from experience, revolved around "a direct attack on the great interests." It had little regard for recent CPPA declarations which "go to the root of no problem" and completely rejected all class legislation as "politically inexpedient even if economically sound." Should the CPPA fail to adopt a program with universal appeal, Record warned that it would "pass as the old Populists' movements floated into Congress upon waves of discontent [only to] have their day and disappear."[38] CPPA leaders undoubtedly wished that Record would disappear. In their eyes continued association would bring no advantage but only obstruction. Respectability and caution now took precedence over the value of internal dissent. Labor leaders struggling to reach consensus and acquire public respectability cut off debate with independent progressives like Record who had shown no willingness to accept either labor's views or the need for a comprehensive platform with broad popular appeal.

Recognizing their lack of credibility within labor circles, Record and Pinchot began assembling a "liberal group" to formulate "a concrete plan for political action, so that we can bring to an end the meaningless conferences and get the public interested in an understandable brief program to relieve conditions."[39] This group began weekly meetings at Pinchot's New York home during the winter of 1923 and met regularly throughout the spring. Its more active participants included Karl Bickel,

president of the United Press news service; Henry T. Hunt, former
mayor of Cincinnati and onetime member of the Railroad Labor Board;
Oswald G. Villard of the *Nation*; Robert Bruere, director of the Bureau
of Municipal Research (New York City); Gilson Gardner, of the Newspaper Enterprise Association and Scripps Editorial Board; Grenville S.
MacFarland, a Boston attorney who represented the Hearst interests;
veteran suffragist leader Abby Scott Baker; and Father John A. Ryan,
the liberal Catholic theologian. This study group spent much of the time
engaged in an economic analysis of contemporary problems. Though
they had their differences, sufficient agreement existed to emphasize
the evil of monopoly and the importance of government ownership as
their primary concerns. Many wished to see a third-party candidate
adopt their program in 1924 as part of a "real nationwide debate upon
an important question."[40] They had no expectation of winning on a
public ownership platform but hoped for a realignment that might make
victory possible in 1928. Though constantly reiterating the Pinchot-Record objections to socialism, these liberals had no wish to isolate themselves from either labor leaders or the working class. On the other hand,
they did not want a partnership but only an obedient following. "The
object of the intellectuals in politics," Grenville S. MacFarland smugly
observed, "is to be the general staff of the labor forces. Our task is to
furnish them with the facts, arguments and . . . all other data necessary
to give direction to their numbers."[41]

Pinchot and Record agreed that liberals should guide if not mix with
labor, but both really wanted influence among their own liberal leaders.
Record warned La Follette that the progressive movement would wander
indefinitely "in the political wilderness" unless its leaders offered something more concrete and effective than government regulation, which,
like the legislation creating it, was the captive of business influence.
"The Progressive movement," he told the senator, "is in a most discouraging state. . . . If nothing is done to crystallize sentiment around a
paramount issue, [progressives] will have their little day in public life,
with their various ineffective remedies, and then the public discourage-
ment will sink back into another period of hopeless reaction." Ignoring
several years' worth of meetings by various liberal organizations, Record
proposed yet another gathering of "the leading and influential Progressives." But the burden of responsibility was still La Follette's. "If men
like you . . . will not devote the time . . . to crystallizing . . . a common and
simple policy, then . . . we must drift along in the present unsatisfactory
condition for the indefinite future."[42] Though independent progressives
realistically needed the support of nationally prominent politicians, a
decade's disappointments with Roosevelt, Wilson, and La Follette em-
boldened reformers to be more assertive in their dealings with progressive leaders. This seemed especially true of men like Record, Pinchot,

and their colleagues, whose political activity stemmed from a particular ideological interest rather than from a personal devotion to an individual candidate. Yet even those often close-minded, occasionally self-righteous ideologues proved emotionally incapable of severing their ties to their movement's remaining national figures. They might have been insensitive and overbearing in their relations with representatives of organized labor, whom they did not respect, but they stopped far short of impertinence in dealing with their own progressive heroes. If compromises were to be made, independent progressives would grudgingly accede to the wishes of their liberal leaders but displayed much less flexibility in their relations with organized labor. For their part, leaders like La Follette bore the scars of their own disappointments and were cautious in dealing with traditional supporters. In the end both sides engaged in a good deal of friendly, verbal sparring, but neither side could do much without the other and practically nothing without the support of organized labor.

Stalemate within liberal circles during the summer of 1923 sent numbers of progressives scurrying off in different directions. One would be hard pressed to pinpoint the focus or direction of such efforts. In early July delegates of the Workers' (Communist) party, attending a "unity convention" of liberals and labor radicals in Chicago sponsored by John Fitzpatrick's Farmer-Labor party, transformed a weakened Farmer-Labor movement into a third party known as the Federated Farmer-Labor party.[43] Though the platform which emerged from this meeting was similar to current progressive proposals, liberals reacted suspiciously to a convention widely assumed to have been controlled by the Communists.[44] Some progressives were engaged in their own behind-the-scenes activities exhausting their energy and occasionally their credibility. Reformers' fascination with Henry Ford's presidential ambitions, in spite of his ignorance of many subjects and views on many others, qualified as one example of this manic behavior. So, too, would the Committee of Forty-Eight's premature endorsement of Senator William E. Borah as the progressives' "missing Moses."[45]

Most Americans had their attention diverted elsewhere that summer of 1923. Sports fans could look ahead to a subway series between the Giants and Yankees and a heavyweight championship fight between Jack Dempsey and Louis Firpo. Washington watchers readied in preparation for the first session of the Senate's Teapot Dome subcommittee hearings. In June, President Harding left on his ill-fated trip to Alaska, which ended with his death on August 2 and Calvin Coolidge's accession to the presidency.

For most progressives, however, the significant news that summer, other than the Harding-Coolidge transition, was the election to the Senate of the Minnesota Farmer-Labor party's Magnus Johnson. Commenting on this Minnesota dentist's tremendous victory over the major party candidates, the *Nation*'s editors euphorically observed that election day, "July 16, was a great day for those who long for a real third party in America, in which country and city producers may join hands to realize a fundamental economic program."[46] Johnson's triumph provided a big lift for those who saw his election as the portent of future success. "Things are gradually coming . . . around my way," a happy Mercer G. Johnston wrote his father; yet he wondered whether the current kinds of disorganized protest could be brought together in time for the 1924 election.[47] "We are at this time a good deal at sea as to what we ought to do," he wrote labor leader James Duncan, "and I am writing to you as a clear-headed and unafraid representative of labor in whose leadership I have confidence for such light and leading as you can furnish."[48] In the meantime, Johnston, always the twenty-four-hour-a-day activist, occupied himself with the Public Ownership League's "Super-Power" conference and efforts to secure amnesty for political prisoners, but such participation did little to allay his concerns about 1924, nor did these activities satisfy his political habit.[49]

The Teapot Dome revelations which came flooding out of Washington in late January and February 1924 soon gave a focus to the yearning for political news felt by Johnston and his fellow progressives. The discovery of old fashioned political corruption reaching the highest levels of government and business must have been enormously gratifying for reformers. Their letters were full of moral outrage, recriminations, and doubts about the nation's future, but one also finds an undeniable smugness and satisfaction in having been right all along.[50] The Harding scandals had the advantage of placing the progressives' traditional commitment to political democracy back in the limelight at the expense of more controversial but less glamorous issues like government ownership of the railroads. Naturally, it also was much easier promoting independent political action when both major parties were tainted by unethical behavior if not outright malfeasance. "I do not see how you can be in any doubt whatever," Oswald G. Villard wrote Robert M. La Follette, "as to your duty in view of what is coming out in the revelations of the Teapot Dome." Those revelations included charges which smeared former Treasury Secretary William G. McAdoo, the most prominent Democratic presidential aspirant and favorite of the railroad brotherhoods. Declaring that Americans were sick and tired of voting for "Tweedle-Dum and Tweedle-Dee," Villard urged La Follette to run so that millions of voters would have a genuine alternative. "The Democratic Administration turned over the government during the war to the Wall Street interests," he told the senator, "and the Harding Government went into partnership with those interests." At the least, Villard believed, an early announcement of La Follette's candidacy might discourage Coolidge and "compel the Republican Party to put someone else forward."[51]

But Calvin Coolidge deftly took control of his administration. He brilliantly disassociated himself from the scandals, appointed two major party representatives as special prosecutors, forced Attorney General Harry Daugherty from the cabinet, took credit for ending the bitter Pennsylvania coal strike, and benefited from a conservative counterattack which accused progressives of engaging in character assassination.[52] Some liberals became even less optimistic about the chances for a third-party candidacy. "We have no Ramsay MacDonald," observed Mercer G. Johnston, referring to Britain's Labour Party prime minister. "If we had, he would probably be in Atlanta prison, or like [Eugene V.] Debs, at large stripped naked of his citizenship." Convinced that neither of the major parties would nominate someone he could vote for with a good conscience, Johnston thought La Follette "probably the fittest man . . . to be our next president" but with little chance of winning. Still, the opportunity to "pile up as big a vote for him as possible . . . will be as good service as can be rendered the cause of democracy."[53]

Progressives like Mercer G. Johnston, as well as eastern intellectuals like Amos Pinchot and George L. Record, had few illusions about capturing the presidency but were interested in preparing the public for a more serious attempt in 1928. Thus, the Coolidge strategy of ignoring the scandals and the Democrats' willingness to follow suit, forced progressives back to an issue-oriented campaign—back to government ownership and back into the cautious embrace of the CPPA, whose February 1924 meeting endorsed a call for a national nominating convention on July 4 in Cleveland. "In a campaign of this kind," Pinchot noted, "how easy it would be to put on the defensive a man like . . . Mr. Coolidge . . . whose main preoccupation is to dodge real issues and who does not affirm the existence of any serious American problem. Above all, what fun it would be to see American politics, so long starved on husks, chaff, and hokum, once more sink its teeth in solid food."[54] There were no guarantees, however, that government ownership was a solid political issue. Politicians like La Follette, imbued with the prewar insurgent's hatred of monopoly and reinforced by progressive intellectuals, may no longer have reflected the sentiments of their farmer and labor constituents who longed for economic growth not free competition. That the Wisconsin senator was aware of this inconsistency was evident in his uncertainty about whether government ownership, trust-busting, or producer and consumer cooperatives was the best means to destroy economic concentration.[55]

Such uncertainty was noticeably absent from the thinking of Record's and Pinchot's liberal group who, while applauding La Follette's support for government ownership, wanted him "to present the . . . issue . . . as an attack upon the power of the privileged interests and a means of breaking up monopoly and reducing prices." Looking ahead to a much discussed and often postponed government ownership conference, Pinchot wrote Gilson Gardner that "this meeting is to be distinguished very carefully from a third-party movement." It would be a railroad conference strictly devoted to questions of improved transportation, rate education, and price fixing. Of course, Pinchot admitted, such discussions might generate specific platform planks on government ownership which might be "a proper platform for a political party, old or new."[56]

Springtime 1924 found progressives impaled on the horns of a dilemma. Men like Pinchot, Record, and J. A. H. Hopkins continued to advocate independent political action, but the only legitimate third-party vehicle, the Farmer-Labor movement, had gained a reputation as a Communist front. Hopkins had participated in the Minnesota Farmer-Labor Federation's St. Paul convention held the previous fall, and he enthusiastically supported its call for a united front. He initially appeared undismayed by Communist involvement or by the National Farmer-Labor party's condemnation of the CPPA as a "scab and dual organization."[57] Minnesota Farmer-Labor leader William Mahoney agreed that the Communist element was so small and sentiment for La Follette so strong that there was little chance of subversion.[58] The national nominating convention scheduled by the Farmer-Labor movement for May 30 (later postponed until June 17) already was committed to a platform calling for the abolition of special privilege, public ownership of railroads, government control of money and credit, nationalization of natural resources, and preservation of civil rights. "Now that our opportunity has come," Hopkins wrote Mahoney, "we cannot allow anyone to take any steps that will tend to divide the progressive forces."[59]

Four and a half months later, however, Hopkins did a complete about-face and engaged in the kind of tortured verbal gymnastics considered the hallmark of American Communists.[60] Announcing the Committee of Forty-Eight's withdrawal from the June 17 National Farmer-Labor–Progressive Convention, he now admitted a longtime suspicion of the Communists and declared his intention to support the decision of the CPPA's delegates to the July 4 Cleveland convention. The precipitating event in this 180-degree turnabout was a letter released by Robert M. La Follette in late May 1924 which denounced the Communists as "the mortal enemies of the Progressive movement and democratic ideals. . . . I believe," the senator wrote Wisconsin Attorney General Herman L. Ekern, "that all progressives should refuse to participate in any movement which makes common cause with any Communist organization."[61]

The Ekern letter went through several drafts and received attention worthy of a major policy statement. Why La Follette, the overwhelming choice of the Farmer-Labor movement, so decisively repudiated this important, albeit, controversial element in the progressive coalition tells us much about "Battling Bob" the politician. Communist endorsement would have meant the resurrection of Red Scare tactics, renewed attacks upon his highly unpopular antiwar position, and the alienation of his supporters within the labor movement. Given the Communists' much acclaimed ability to control outside organizations, there was the added danger that a La Follette candidacy might become a Communist "front."

These fears, however, were more than matched by the still unresolved matter of whether the senator should create a new third party or run a purely independent campaign. Like his conservative backers in the CPPA on whom he was financially and organizationally dependent, La Follette was anxious to run unaligned and unencumbered by any political affiliation. The railroad brotherhoods supported this position because it kept them within the framework of the two-party system and did not risk the long-term alienation of friendly politicians. The advantages of an independent candidacy for La Follette were threefold: it guaranteed needed CPPA support, allowed his followers to concentrate their efforts on the presidential campaign without the added burden of organizing a party from scratch, and avoided the possibility of jeopardizing the election of progressives from both major parties.[62]

Whether or not the senator would have received the Farmer-Labor movement's nomination, however, is problematical. In *American Communism and Soviet Russia*, Theodore Draper argues that eight days before the Ekern letter was released the Comintern secretly instructed American Communists in the Farmer-Labor party to make La Follette an offer he could not accept without sacrificing personal control of his campaign. Rejection of such conditions would free the Communists to nominate their own candidates. There is really no evidence to indicate that had the senator endorsed the June 17 Farmer-Labor convention or remained silent that his supporters would not have overwhelmed the Communist minority. The editors of the Milwaukee *Leader* believed that "had La Follette wanted the convention to be a success, had he wanted to overwhelm the Communists . . . had he wanted a strong and virile new party formed, all he had to do was urge his supporters to go to the convention in large numbers."[63] The results of the National Farmer-Labor–Progressive Convention are, at least, cause for further consideration. In spite of the fact that only 500 of the expected 5,000 delegates attended, 99 percent of whom were somewhat fancifully estimated to be Communists by the *Christian Science Monitor*, and in spite of their "amazing talent for parliamentary manipulation and organizational discipline," the Communists were unable to silence the delegates' strong La Follette sentiment. The end result was a compromise in which veteran labor leader and third-party advocate Duncan MacDonald accepted the convention's presidential nomination only after agreeing to withdraw in favor of La Follette following the CPPA's endorsement on July 4.[64]

In the June 7, 1924, issue of *Labor*, voice of the railroad brotherhoods and the CPPA, there is a cartoon captioned "Battling Bob's Double Wallop," showing the senator with arms outstretched, KO'ing the "old Guard" on his right and the Communists on his left. No doubt his liberal supporters enjoyed the image of their kind of progressivism representing a centrist approach. The political center, however, did not seem particularly interested in free speech. J. A. H. Hopkins, in a frenetic attempt to get right with La Follette, now declared that he would have excluded from the recent Farmer-Labor–Progressive Convention everyone "holding or advocating communistic views."[65]

While third-party liberals and independents sought to purify or purge progressive ranks, Amos Pinchot and George L. Record assumed their familiar roles behind the scenes suggesting, exhorting, and lecturing La Follette and his advisers on the direction the campaign should take. Only this time they found themselves in the unusual position of being invited to make suggestions. "I think we all agree," Pinchot wrote the senator, "that the big purpose of a third-party movement is to unite progressive forces in a carefully thought-out and intelligent attack upon the power of plutocracy." The overriding issue was not the tariff, prohibition, railroads, or farm policy, but a more practical question: "Shall the U.S. be controlled by its people or by the plutocracy?"[66] If the senator could show voters not only how they were controlled by a plutocracy but how power could be returned to the people, Pinchot grandiloquently predicted that he "will have performed the greatest service that any American has performed since Lincoln and perhaps since our country has existed."[67]

It is difficult to determine how much influence, if any, Pinchot and Record had on the senator's thinking. The Progressive platform's opening sentence—"The great issue before the American people today is the control of government by private monopoly"—suggests that after twelve years of unremitting advice the three men shared a common commitment rooted in antimonopoly and free competition. The platform's remaining thirteen points (thirteen too many for Record and Pinchot)—ranging from repeal of the Esch-Cummins Transportation Act and public ownership of water power to a congressional veto over judicial review—reflected long-standing progressive concerns and the candidate's personal predilections.[68] But the election was not destined to be a test of progressive ideas. La Follette might have wished to hammer away at economic issues, but the times, as at least one progressive realized, were "out of joint for that kind of constructive campaign."[69]

Still, the Republicans' nomination of Coolidge and the fratricidal Democratic bloodletting which produced John W. Davis's candidacy heartened progressives, who hoped that five million La Follette votes would show the need for a permanent liberal party.[70] Similar sentiments were echoed by Bull Moose veteran Harold L. Ickes in one of his famous "Dear Chief" letters to Senator Hiram W. Johnson of California. "I hope that [La Follette] will help to give the Republican Party the licking that it so richly deserves," wrote Ickes, and "that you will refuse to throw a life line to the precious crew that are today in full control of the republican [sic] boat. The sooner they sink the better it will be for the Republican party and for the country."[71] Having just concluded a bitterly unsuccessful six-month campaign for the Republican nomination, Johnson was in a much less optimistic frame of mind and not particularly charitable toward his progressive colleagues. "I have been amused," he responded, "at some of the definitions of Progressive adopted by those who have appropriated of late the label. I read in the *New Republic* that there are really only two Progressives, La Follette and Borah." The California senator found his Idaho colleague's inclusion surprising in view of Borah's support of Andrew Mellon's tax-reduction plan and opposition to a child-labor amendment. "With such contrary exponents of Progressivism . . . held out to us by our omniscient intellectuals," Johnson concluded, "the ordinary intellect may be pardoned by a bit of confusion."[72]

It was indicative of the 1924 campaign that freewheeling activists, who could wait patiently for the educational benefits of the La Follette movement to take hold, were more optimistic than progressive officeholders who faced reelection. Independents like Mercer G. Johnston and Amos Pinchot shared Hiram W. Johnson's concerns but were reassured in the knowledge that this progressive campaign was "no political sideshow." La Follette and his running mate, Democratic Senator Burton K. Wheeler of Montana, were taken seriously. Their ticket was not another "Parley P. Christensen-Max Hayes affair" evoking the seriocomic debacle of 1920. Few progressives, however, operated under any illusions about immediate success or their candidates' forward-looking vision. "The most I would say for them," observed Mercer G. Johnston, "is that they see far enough into the future for the purposes of this campaign, that they are honest, that their hearts are in the right place . . . and that . . . they are men one can at least travel forward hopefully with in the day of battle."[73]

Another compelling reason for progressive participation had a more practical side to it. The future of liberal-labor political cooperation required evidence of good faith. The time had come for progressives to pay their dues. Reflecting concerns that were no less prominent in 1924 than they had been four years earlier, Mercer G. Johnston desperately wanted "to put Labor on notice that Liberal cooperation was . . . indispensable to attain its objectives. . . . Labor really does need the help of advanced Liberalism." Progressives, therefore, had to "make good . . . in the eyes of those who look to us with the confidence to lend a strong hand in putting the job through."[74] At the same time, Johnston hoped his progressive colleagues would recognize the AFL's endorsement of La Follette and Wheeler as "a great advance over anything ever done before." Though neither the federation nor the railroad brotherhoods had made a permanent commitment to a third party, their support broke a thirty-nine-year tradition of strict nonpartisanship. If liberals minimized the importance of this action, Johnston believed it would "add at least a decade to the ten, twenty, or thirty years within which we hope to build a party in America comparable to the British Labour Party."[75] So, there were practical as well as idealistic reasons motivating progressives. They now had a cause and a candidate worthy of the cause, but few liberals denied that they still had "a nation sodden with sleep" on their hands.[76]

After participating in the birth of the La Follette-Wheeler ticket, many independent progressives experienced an unusual kind of detachment that had little to do with passivity or indifference. Men like Oswald G. Villard, Mercer G. Johnston, Amos Pinchot, and George L. Record (who was running for the Senate again) were untiring supporters of all progressive candidates; their actions and letters, however, reveal a penchant for indecently early postmortems. These sentiments also reflected the attitudes of progressive Republicans like Harold L. Ickes, who had spent much of his life trying to reform the GOP. Realizing that the few progressives left after Coolidge's election would have "no more chance . . . in that party than the proverbial snowball," Ickes contemplated a national and personal realignment that would leave the Republicans conservative and the Democrats progressive. Though he admitted "a very real hesitation in taking a step . . . that [was] likely to change radically [his] whole political life," he confessed an "inexpressible disgust and an almost overpowering inclination to pack [his] playthings and go off with the lunatic fringe."[77]

The immediate source of that disgust was a statement signed by some fifty former followers of TR's 1912 campaign questioning La Follette's right to use the "Progressive" label. In enthusiastically supporting Coolidge, such ex-Bull Moosers as James R. Garfield, Raymond Robins, Chester H. Rowell, and Edwin A. Van Valkenburg attacked the senator as "a most sinister enemy of democracy" and "a dangerous man" with a "wild" following. Van Valkenburg, publisher of the Philadelphia *North American*, was particularly offensive, smearing La Follette as "an extreme radical whose program . . . [was] thinly disguised sovietism."[78] If there was a more symbolic and less important controversy in the campaign, one would be hard pressed to find it. Republican charges that La Follette was the "Bolshevik" candidate deserve mention, as does the GOP allegation that a deadlocked electoral college would place Charles W. ("Brother Charlie") Bryan, the Democratic vice-presidential candidate, and "an even more sickening name to many than La Follette's" in the White House.[79] But neither of these two issues stirred the progressive faithful more than their own family feud.

"I have been keeping on the side lines," Ickes wrote Hiram W. Johnson, "but a sizzling statement is beginning to ferment in my bosom and I am afraid I will have to give it expression one of these days." Despondent that many of his colleagues "who stood together and went down together in 1912 and 1916 . . . [were] falling on their bellies to lick the hand that has struck them," Ickes resolved to leave the Republican party. First, however, was the matter of answering the attack on La Follette by those self-proclaimed, "outraged" progressives whom Hiram W. Johnson accused of being "so anxious for office and so mad to bask in the sunlight of power, they will accept anything." He attributed Rowell's and Robins's support of the administration to "egregious vanity" and egotism and accused them of discarding a lifetime's views after a voyage on the presidential yacht *Mayflower*. The California senator, who had been Roosevelt's running mate back in 1912, believed that these Coolidge supporters were "heartily ashamed of having been irregular once in their lives, and are atoning for their offense by an added subserviency."[80]

In a campaign notably devoid of substantive issues, it is not surprising that the most excitement was engendered by slander, innuendo, Red-baiting, and deception. In drafting a reply to the statement of the former Bull Moosers, Amos Pinchot candidly admitted that their document though "shameful . . . was . . . the kind of thing which our group should give out."[81] Led by Pinchot, Ickes, Record, Gilson Gardner, J. A. H. Hopkins, Jane Addams, and Paul Kellogg, some forty-two La Follette progressives countered their former colleagues' accusations with charges of their own. Coolidge progressives were dismissed as "tired out stragglers, backsliders, and quitters of the progressive army" who could be divided into two classes: those who never had any progressive convictions and had hoped to "ride into power on Roosevelt's back" and those who had long since "lost their stomach for the big fight."[82] Much energy was expended, old speeches dug up, memories recalled, mud thrown, and history manipulated all in the name of progressivism. Republicans contended that TR, if alive, would be "on the firing line for Coolidge," while La Follette supporters countered with copies of a Roosevelt article (*Outlook*, May 27, 1911) praising the senator and the Wisconsin experiment in political democracy. When both sides disagreed, each accused the other of having an "exuberant imagination" or of suffering from "marked intellectual and ethical deterioration."[83]

Outspent and out-organized by their rivals, abandoned by both the
railroad brotherhoods and the AFL who saw their worst fears realized,
many progressives watched the ineptitude of the La Follette campaign
with undisguised horror. "I am so damned discouraged and disgusted,"
New York Congressman Fiorello H. La Guardia observed in early September, "that only my interest and love for Senator La Follette keeps
me going." Upset by the "five o'clock pink tea drinkers" in charge who
had no experience with urban and ethnic politics, the "Little Flower"
pleaded with national campaign chairman John M. Nelson to "loosen
up" with the money. "You must realize that both Democratic and Republican parties have Italian captains in [my] district holding jobs as
Prohibition agents, Internal Revenue agents, Deputy Marshals, and the
like with money to spend, handing out all sorts of lies and misinformation. . . . We cannot conduct a campaign in a city of six million people
by parlor discussions in the homes of amateur politicians."[84] But the
money needed to grease the electoral process was unavailable, particularly when the entire labor movement contributed barely $50,000.

What went wrong with the liberal-labor alliance? The question itself
is misleading because it presumes a mutual commitment when only the
most tenuous relationship ever existed. The railroad brotherhoods and
AFL leadership deserted the La Follette movement for practical political
reasons. During the campaign, when a Progressive victory appeared
more and more of a fantasy, trade unionists reconsidered their relations
with the Coolidge administration. The Republicans' antilabor stance, so
evident from 1921 to 1923 in the Justice Department's advocacy of the
open shop and compulsory arbitration, began to show signs of change.
Attorney-General Daugherty's dismissal removed the symbolic wielder
of the sweeping antilabor injunction of the 1922 railroad strike. President
Harding's role in eliminating the twelve-hour day in the steel mills,
Commerce Secretary Herbert Hoover's support for the maintenance of
industry-wide collective bargaining in the Central Competitive coal field,
and Calvin Coolidge's willingness to reform the antiunion Railroad Labor
Board convinced trade unionists that their immediate and long-range
interests would best be served within the political mainstream rather
than in radical politics.

There were many other problems—not the least of which was merely
getting on the ballot—that appeared equally unsolvable given the temporary nature of the campaign. The candidates' speeches often fell victim
to poor advance work, and an inexperienced staff was not improved by
the tripartite campaign leadership fragmented between Chicago, Washington, and New York, nor were these deficiencies compensated for by
the enthusiasm of progressive volunteers.[85] An equally perplexing problem with practical considerations concerned the public perception of the
campaign. Was it a "party" or a "movement"? Though La Follette in-

tended his candidacy to represent a progressive movement, even he initially contemplated devoting some effort to congressional races. When it became evident that neither time, expertise, nor money permitted such action, progressives agreed that state and congressional campaigns would be the responsibility of state chapters of the CPPA and AFL. In certain states La Follette organizers even promised not to interfere in local fights, yet state election laws placed the La Follette-Wheeler ticket alongside candidates running on the Socialist, Independent, Farmer-Labor, and Labor party lines. In those cases, progressives received few of the benefits of a permanent organization but many of the headaches associated with a minor party.[86]

One of the more encouraging developments of the campaign was the creation of a National Women's Division within the La Follette-Wheeler organization. Largely the work of lobbying efforts spearheaded by the Woman's Committee for Political Action (WCPA), the division and its impressive array of left-liberal feminists, veteran suffragists, and peace activists sought access and influence first within the CPPA and then the Progressive party. Drawing its leadership from both the National Woman's Party and the rival League of Women Voters, the WCPA's letterhead included some very familiar names within the liberal community: Mrs. Mabel C. Costigan, Mrs. Matilda Gardner, Elisabeth Gilman, Mrs. Marie Manly, Mrs. Eleanor Marsh, and Ruth Pickering (Mrs. Amos Pinchot). Not surprisingly, when the WCPA called its first national conference in Washington, D.C., in early May 1924, its delegates were addressed by such prominent progressive activists as Norman Thomas, George L. Record, Father John A. Ryan, and CPPA chairman William H. Johnston. Unfortunately, neither the WCPA nor its representatives in the La Follette organization seem to have had any real influence during the campaign. No women served as state chair-persons, only two of the Progressive party's fourteen-member executive committee were women, and the auxiliary nature of the Women's Division effectively excluded women activists from discussions of general policies and decision-making.[87] Ironically, the frustration and disappointment these women experienced paralleled their spouses' own tribulations during the campaign. In view of the extraordinarily active lives which professional publicists and lobbyists such as Basil M. Manly, Benjamin C. Marsh, Gilson Gardner, and Amos Pinchot led, it is not surprising that their wives were equally involved and just as committed to the cause. While their mutual participation has much to tell us about the eternal dilemma of balancing marriage, family, and career, it is also suggestive of the homogeneous, parochial, and insular nature of independent liberalism during these years.

The election results accurately reflected the Progressives' organizational, financial, and ideological difficulties. The senator's 16.5 percent of the popular vote, 4.8 million votes, and the thirteen electoral votes of his home state placed him a distant third behind Coolidge and Davis. The two GOP slogans, "Keep Cool with Coolidge," emphasizing Republican prosperity, and the closely related "Coolidge or Chaos," suggesting the economic and political dangers of a La Follette presidency, possessed an emotional appeal that Progressive attacks on monopoly could not match. Few of the independent progressives were surprised by the returns; many had voiced their own disappointments and doubts at various stages of the campaign engaging in a kind of self-fulfilling prophecy. Men like Amos Pinchot, who had been drawn into the struggle because of an interest in government ownership, regretted the senator's "running away from the railroad issue" and was especially disappointed that La Follette had been unable to prevent his antimonopoly rhetoric from appearing antibusiness as well. Though aware of the producer and job-oriented concerns of American workers, Pinchot remained adamantly opposed to class legislation. He believed the Progressive campaign had focused too narrowly upon the question of labor and wages. "Not that it is not a right plea," he hastened to add, "but where La Follette is weak is with the middle class, the small business man and the clerk, who fear him because they think he is going to bust up big business and that will mean less business, less jobs, less pay."[88] Such progressives felt betrayed and abandoned; they continued to demand an obsequious labor movement and dismissed trade union demands as evidence of misplaced arrogance and an undesirable sign of class consciousness.

Other progressives who came into the La Follette movement from outside labor circles had their own personal grievances. Morris Hillquit, the token Socialist representative on the campaign executive committee, predictably regretted the "one-man" campaign, the decision to postpone consideration of a third party until after the election, and the candidates' dependence upon "well-worn phrases about the 'predatory interests' ... and other familiar expressions from the middle-class vocabulary of the congressional Progressive or Insurgent bloc."[89] Oswald G. Villard, assistant national treasurer of the campaign, bemoaned the absence of a "thorough-going" attack on privilege that would not only oppose corruption and war but also encompass tariff reform and pacifism.[90] Villard also brought another perspective to the campaign which complicated his life and threatened to compromise his journalistic integrity. As editor of the *Nation*, he naturally used his journal to endorse La Follette's candidacy. As a journalist committed to diversity of opinion and free speech, however, he often had to walk a fine line between his totally committed campaign associates and his more cynical professional colleagues.

Among the *Nation*'s writers few matched William Hard's folksy but caustically analytical style. Hard, as one of his colleagues observed, was "a real character" with such a "rare individuality" that his friend sometimes wondered why he had not been lynched. Unfortunately for both Villard and La Follette, Hard frequently directed his attention at the senator. In 1920 he had been one of La Follette's strongest supporters, hopeful that the senator might lead progressives toward an American version of the British Labour Party. During the summer and fall of 1924, however, his "Weekly Washington Letter" aimed its barbs and insights at the left. His columns were neither vicious nor one-sided, but they were never uncritical puff pieces. He repeatedly emphasized the traditional, moderate, even obsolete nature of La Follette's solutions for the nation's economic ills. He quoted Communist William Z. Foster's observation that the Progressive platform was "the most reactionary document of the year" and concluded that it would be equally repugnant to both the Soviet Union and the U.S. Steel Corporation because they were "modern."[91] Such observations naturally aggravated the La Follette staff, the more so because they appeared in the *Nation*. Rumors circulated that Hard had "fallen for the social game" and had become a "warm and intimate" associate of Albert Lasker, the brilliant Republican advertising executive and chairman of the U.S. Shipping Board.[92] Basil M. Manly called Hard's articles "the most poisonous anti-La Follette and pro-Coolidge propaganda . . . now being written" and asked Villard to use his influence to effect a change. The *Nation*'s editor was an unabashed La Follette supporter, but the prospect of twisting Hard's arm was personally distasteful. Still, he tried, pleading with his colleague to "pick out something in [La Follette's] strategy, or in the man himself that you can really commend and be nice and kind to him. That would help you and us and him, and make a nicer feeling all the way around."[93] To Hard's credit he ignored the advice and continued to write columns which left people wondering whether he was a "reactionary or a wild radical." He reminded his readers that "the world is not governed by great men who calculate the world. It is governed by great men who are sufficiently themselves to imagine that what they want the world wants too."[94]

   This same child-centered view of the world, replete with its innocence and dogged persistence, was evident in the postmortems which a number of Progressives sent La Follette. "I hope you are not discouraged," wrote George L. Record, himself a loser in the New Jersey Senate race. "Everytime I go through one of these fights, I come out with an increased sense of the tremendous size of the task to which we have put our hands. It calls for the highest courage and the greatest possible patience." Record ended his letter, characteristically, with a call for a "series of conferences of those who have borne the brunt of this battle to determine what is to be our future course."[95] That same day the senator heard from another veteran colleague, J. A. H. Hopkins, who already was planning the permanent organization of a Progressive party. Typically optimistic and always able to find some good in even the worst disasters, the 48er chairman read the election returns as a "tremendous endorsement" of La Follette and his program "by a cross-section of society that comes from no special section or class."[96]

Publicly, La Follette was equally defiant and optimistic, apparently buoyed by the numerous congratulatory notes which came flooding into his Madison farm. "The Progressives will not be dismayed [by Coolidge's landslide victory]," he declared. "We have just begun to fight. There is no compromise on the fundamental issues for which we stand. The loss of this one battle in the age-long struggle of the masses against the privileged few is but an incident."[97] Privately, however, the senator might well have agreed with William Hard's preelection observation that the Progressive party represented "fortuitously joined members of a body of clay."[98]

Similar thoughts were echoed three days after the election by Hiram W. Johnson. "The idea of a third party," he wrote Harold L. Ickes, "has gone glimmering." The California senator, who was more a bystander than participant in the campaign's late stages, did not think that labor, farmers, and liberals could "be brought together under any one banner again. . . . The outlanders, Pariahs, and outcasts like yourself and myself," he told his Chicago friend, "have the choice between devoting ourselves to our private occupations, becoming a part of what we know is the crooked political machine, or speaking when opportunity offers our fruitless opposition."[99]

Ickes's "Dear Chief" letter a few days later left no doubt as to which of the three roads he would follow. In one of those delightfully biting and cynically disdainful letters that won him a reputation as a curmudgeon, Ickes dismissed Coolidge as "the manikin from Northampton" and a mediocrity whose campaign was designed to bring about "subnormalcy." "It was a great day for reaction and the saviors of the Constitution," he added. "The victory was sweeping and complete and since reaction was to win I am glad that it won overwhelmingly." The prospects for a third party did not seem to hold "any present hope," and his political future, Ickes concluded, lay in the past.[100] At the age of fifty, with a checkered and irregular political career behind him (he actually voted for John W. Davis in 1924), there was no reason to suspect that his prognostications would prove only half correct.

Reluctant acceptance of a less active political future was typical of many of Ickes's contemporaries. Historians are unusually fond of pointing to Frederic C. Howe's autobiographical *The Confessions of a Reformer* (1925) as evidence of the general malaise which affected the most dedicated liberals in the wake of La Follette's defeat. Seven years Ickes's senior, Howe's career encompassed a quarter-century of public service from the front line of urban politics with Tom Johnson in Cleveland to secretary of the CPPA and research assistant for the senator's last campaign. Unlike most of his progressive colleagues, Howe successfully submerged his own class bias and immersed himself in the labor movement. The 1924 election was especially disappointing because he had accompanied La Follette on the campaign trail and had witnessed the packed halls and cheering crowds. For the first time since 1919, prospects for fundamental change had seemed promising. There was corruption in Washington, anger over the Harding-Coolidge administration's high tariff policy, and widespread agrarian discontent. Yet less than a year later, Howe was putting the finishing touches on his autobiography's last chapter, "Beginning Again," while living in a farmhouse on Nantucket Island. "This long history of changing viewpoints may seem to argue that I am disillusioned with former convictions and hopes," he wrote. "But the reverse is true. I still believe in liberalism. . . . I believe in reform, but prefer the reform that is taking place within myself." Though acknowledging a still-troublesome conscience, Howe nonetheless looked ahead to summers on Nantucket and winters in Europe. "A lifetime spent in making good in materialistic ways, in political struggle, and moralistic reform," he concluded, "leaves me aware. . . . [that] I have more to learn than the time that is left suffices for. Yet I realize that only a beginning is possible to any man."[101] Eight years later, having rallied progressive support for Governor Franklin D. Roosevelt's campaign, Howe returned to public service as Consumer's Counsel within the Agricultural Adjustment Administration.[102]

For every Frederic C. Howe, however, there were countless others who permanently left progressive ranks, some to resume professional careers, and still others, like the Coolidge "progressives" of 1924, to emerge as defenders of the status quo. We would do well to heed Otis L. Graham, Jr.'s admonition that "reform was tedious, hard, disappointing work."[103] Yet the causes that would rally future progressives did not appear suddenly after the Great Crash. There was as much liberal political activity between 1925 and 1929 as there had been in the four years between Harding's and Coolidge's elections. The issues raised may not have been as glamorous as those of past years, but progressives continued to counter conservative initiatives with liberal alternatives, convinced that their ideas remained untested.

The lessons which most independent progressives took away from the La Follette movement reveal much about the strengths and weaknesses of American liberalism. The unseemly haste with which organized labor deserted their cause encouraged many reformers, who needed no excuse, to question the likelihood of future liberal-labor cooperation. It was not merely a distaste of class politics or the AFL's tepid support which underlay such mistrust. Progressives, who were powerless without union participation, still could not accept an equal or subordinate role in sharing that power.[104] For their part, trade unionists had little faith or respect for progressives who espoused the merits of the "public" interest but decried the need for special interest legislation. In a campaign intended to emphasize current economic problems, laborites grew impatient with progressives' familiar denunciations of special privilege. Fearful of political retaliation by the two major parties and skeptical of any movement that diverted labor from basic economic goals, the CPPA's union leaders saw no advantage in tying themselves to a handful of discredited intellectuals. From organized labor's perspective, there was nothing remotely "progressive" about the La Follette-Wheeler movement except its self-proclaimed name, and even that was in dispute.

Developments between 1921 and 1924 also revealed basic inadequacies in progressive tactics. Just as politicians often enjoy campaigning more than governing, the Harding years exposed the limitations in progressives' political strategy. Reformers received their greatest pleasure from the behind-the-scenes battling, lobbying, and maneuvering which preceded the actual campaign. Their influence diminished once a candidate was selected and platform approved. They functioned best in small, elite, and homogeneous groups and were notably less successful when mixing with others holding divergent views. Though progressives paid lip service to the idea of a liberal-labor coalition and could wax eloquent over an alliance of "hand and brain," they demonstrated no real commitment to the ideal of organization or cooperation. Such a partnership required the sharing of decision making, an acknowledgment of intellectual parity, and a willingness to accept and reconcile differences to the satisfaction of all parties. Most independent progressives could bring themselves to do none of these things because they refused to accept organized labor as an equal.

NOTES

1. Basil M. Manly to Robert M. La Follette, Sept. 15, 1920, Series B, box 86, La Follette Papers.

2. Robert M. La Follette to Lynn Haines, editor, *Searchlight on Congress*, Dec. 15, 1920, box 35, Haines Papers.

3. H. R. Mussey, executive secretary, PLS, to Mrs. Agnes Brown Leach, May 9, 1921, Document Group 4, box 3, American Union Against Militarism Papers, Swarthmore College Peace Collection.

4. "The League's Plan of Work for the People's Program in Congress," PRL Pamphlet, box 42, Amos Pinchot Papers; see also Benjamin C. Marsh, *Lobbyist for the People: A Record of Fifty Years* (Washington, D.C.: Public Affairs Press, 1953), 69–70.

5. Benjamin C. Marsh to Warren G. Harding, Sept. 14, 1921, box 1, Benjamin C. Marsh Papers, Library of Congress, hereinafter cited as Marsh Papers.

6. Benjamin C. Marsh to Amos R. E. Pinchot, Feb. 26, Mar. 17, 1921, box 42, Amos Pinchot Papers. Benjamin C. Marsh to Harry Daugherty, June 27, 1921, box 1, Marsh Papers. Benjamin C. Marsh to Warren G. Harding, June 28, Oct. 15, 1921, Jan. 3, 1922, and June 24, 1922, *ibid*. See also George B. Christian, Jr. (Harding's personal secretary) to Benjamin C. Marsh, July 5, 1921; Harry Daugherty to Benjamin C. Marsh, July 11, 1921, and Benjamin C. Marsh to Commerce Secretary Herbert Hoover, Jan. 27, 1922, *ibid*.

7. J. A. H. Hopkins, News Article #15, Committee of Forty-Eight, National Bureau of Information and Education, Aug. 1, 1921, box 151, Amos Pinchot Papers, and News Article #16, Aug. 8, 1921, *ibid*. George L. Record to Amos R. E. Pinchot, Sept. 7, 1921, box 43, *ibid*. Pinchot and Record had a very strong interest in political change and hoped that William G. McAdoo might declare his candidacy for the Democratic presidential nomination on a government ownership platform; see also K. Austin Kerr, *American Railroad Politics, 1914–1920: Rates, Wages, and Efficiency* (Pittsburgh: Univ. of Pittsburgh Press, 1968), 170.

8. Mark Perlman, *The Machinists: A New Study in American Trade Unionism* (Cambridge: Harvard Univ. Press, 1961), 39–73; John H. M. Laslett, *Labor and the Left: A Study of Socialist and Radical Influences in the American Labor Movement, 1881–1924* (New York: Basic Books, 1970), 172–177, and Gary M. Fink, ed., *Biographical Dictionary of American Labor Leaders* (Westport, Conn.: Greenwood Press, 1974), 178–179.

9. William H. Johnston, cover letter announcing CPPA meeting, Feb. 4, 1922, box 47, Johnston Papers.

10. Nathan Fine, *Labor and Farmer Parties in the United States, 1828–1928* (New York: Rand School of Social Science, 1928), 401.

11. Mercer G. Johnston to Edward Keating, Feb. 7, 1922, box 47, Johnston Papers.

12. "Declaration of Principles Adopted by the CPPA," Feb. 20–21, 1922, *ibid*.

13. Frederic C. Howe had been an aide to Mayor Tom Johnson in Cleveland, an Ohio state senator, commissioner of immigration during the Wilson administration, and secretary of the All American Farmers' Cooperative Commission. He served as chairman of the CPPA's Committee on Organization, charged with responsibility for transforming the organization's disparate elements into a unified whole. Basil M. Manly headed the Committee on Declaration of Principles. See Kenneth Campbell MacKay, *The Progressive Movement of 1924* (New York: Columbia Univ. Press, 1947), 63.

14. William H. Johnston, "A Call to Action," Mar. 15, 1922, box 47, Johnston Papers. See also David Brody, "On the Failure of U.S. Radical Politics: A Farmer-Labor Analysis," *Industrial Relations* 22:2 (Spring 1983), 150.

15. Mercer G. Johnston to Edward Keating, Mar. 16, 1922, *ibid*.

16. Frederic C. Howe, form letter, Apr. 19, 1922, *ibid*. See also "Producers of Wealth Unite: Use Your Ballot for a Better America," a CPPA pamphlet in the Johnston Papers. A special effort was made to appeal to women who "suffer the most from privilege . . . and have to make the greatest sacrifices."

17. Harry A. Slattery to Amos R. E. Pinchot, May 13, 1921, box 42, Amos Pinchot Papers; Harry A. Slattery to Gifford Pinchot, June 21, 1921, Harry A.

Slattery Papers, Duke Univ., hereinafter cited as Slattery Papers; Hiram W. Johnson to Hiram W. Johnson, Jr., and Archibald M. Johnson, May 10, 1921, Part IV, box 3, Johnson Papers.

18. Mercer G. Johnston to Alabama Congressman George Huddleston, vice chairman of the PLS, July 21, 1921, box 46, Johnston Papers.

19. Amos R. E. Pinchot, "Direct Action," *Freeman* 3 (Apr. 20, 1921), 136–137. See also the excellent analyses of Record and Pinchot by Robert H. Zieger, *Republicans and Labor, 1919–1929* (Lexington: Univ. of Kentucky Press, 1979), 169–172, and Paul W. Glad, "Progressives and the Business Culture of the 1920s," *Journal of American History* 53:1 (June 1966), 75–89.

20. See "Form of Platform" n.p., n.d., box 148, Amos Pinchot Papers.

21. Amos R. E. Pinchot to V. I. Lenin, Nov. 29, 1921, marked "not sent" in box 42, *ibid.*

22. "Discussion of Major Objections to Possible Platform Planks," n.p., n.d., box 148, *ibid.*

23. *Newark Sunday Call*, Mar. 19, 1922; Mt. Holly (New Jersey) *Mirror*, May 24, 1922.

24. Robert K. Murray, *The Harding Era: Warren G. Harding and His Administration* (Minneapolis: Univ. of Minnesota Press, 1969), 306–308.

25. Joseph S. Frelinghuysen to George L. Record, June 12, 1922, marked "not sent," in Joseph S. Frelinghuysen Papers, Rutgers University, hereinafter cited as Frelinghuysen Papers; also Newark *News*, July 12, 1922.

26. George L. Record to Joseph S. Frelinghuysen, May 20, 1922, *ibid.*

27. Amos R. E. Pinchot to Frederic C. Howe, May 29, 1922, box 43, Amos R. E. Pinchot Papers; Amos R. E. Pinchot to Charles Crane, June 10, 1922; Record's suggested letter for Pinchot to send Senator La Follette can be found for Apr. 4, 1922; George L. Record, to Amos R. E. Pinchot, *ibid.*, and Amos R. E. Pinchot to Lynn Haines, Apr. 5, 1922, *ibid.*

28. The 1922 congressional elections produced a Senate with 51 Republicans, 43 Democrats, and 2 Farmer-Laborites. The House returns allowed for 225 Republicans, 205 Democrats, and 1 Socialist. See John D. Hicks, *Republican Ascendancy, 1921–1933* (New York: Harper & Row, 1960), 88–89; James H. Shideler, *Farm Crisis, 1919–1923* (Berkeley: Univ. of California Press, 1957), 221–230.

29. Murray, *The Harding Era*, 251–262; 271–280; and 317–321.

30. D. Joy Humes, *Oswald Garrison Villard, Liberal of the 1920s* (Syracuse, N.Y.: Syracuse Univ. Press, 1960), 138; Harry A. Slattery to Amos R. E. Pinchot, Nov. 10, 1922, Slattery Papers; William H. Johnston and Frederic C. Howe, form letter, n.d., box 47, Johnston Papers.

31. Harry A. Slattery to Amos R. E. Pinchot, Oct. 3, 1922, box 43, Amos Pinchot Papers.

32. Statement of Sen. Robert M. La Follette, Nov. 18, 1922, Series B, box 195, La Follette Papers.

33. Shideler, *Farm Crisis*, 235–236; MacKay, *The Progressive Movement of 1924*, 67; Murray, *The Harding Era*, 322; Hiram W. Johnson to Hiram W. Johnson, Jr., and Archibald Johnson, Dec. 9, 1922, Part VI, box 4, Johnson Papers.

34. Marsh, *Lobbyist for the People*, 77.

35. Fine, *Labor and Farmer Parties*, 403, and Marsh, 77–78.

36. David A. Shannon, *The Socialist Party of America: A History* (New York:

The Macmillan Co., 1955), 170; Fine, *Labor and Farmer Parties* 402–405, and MacKay, *The Progressive Movement*, 69–72; the quote is from 71.

37. "People's Legislative Service: Confidential," Dec. 17, 1922, Series B, box 195, La Follette Papers.

38. George L. Record to Edward Keating, Dec. 18, 1922, box 43, Amos Pinchot Papers.

39. Amos R. E. Pinchot to William B. Colver, Scripps Newspaper Alliance, Dec. 23, 1922, *ibid.*

40. Amos R. E. Pinchot to John Dewey, June 16, 1923, box 45, *ibid.*

41. Grenville S. MacFarland to Amos R. E. Pinchot, Mar. 13, 1923, *ibid.*

42. George L. Record to Robert M. La Follette, Mar. 26, 1923, *ibid.*

43. Shideler, *Farm Crisis*, 246–247.

44. Robert Morss Lovett, "The Farmer-Labor Fiasco at Chicago," *New Republic* 35:450 (July 18, 1923), 198–200. Lovett, a member of the Committee of Forty-Eight, was anything but an impartial witness. See James Weinstein's important article, "Radicalism in the Midst of Normalcy," *Journal of American History* 52:4 (Mar. 1966), 773–790, especially 775 and Theodore Draper, *American Communism and Soviet Russia* (New York: Viking Press, 1960), 38–48.

45. See Amos R. E. Pinchot to William Randolph Hearst, June 12, 1923, box 45, Amos Pinchot Papers. "Henry Ford," *New Republic*, 36 (Nov. 14, 1923), 301–304, and LeRoy Ashby's penetrating biography, *The Spearless Leader: Senator Borah and the Progressive Movement in the 1920s* (Urbana: Univ. of Illinois Press, 1972), 61–94, 117–139.

46. *Nation* 117 (July 25, 1923), 73.

47. Mercer G. Johnston to Bishop James S. Johnston, July 23, 1923, box 25, Johnston Papers.

48. Mercer G. Johnston to James Duncan, Nov. 19, 1923, box 48, ibid.

49. Mercer G. Johnston to Bishop James S. Johnston, Jan. 17, 1924, box 25, and also "Public Super-Power System: What It Will Do," a pamphlet of the Public Ownership League of America, Jan. 17–18, 1924, *ibid.*

50. Amos R. E. Pinchot to Victor Watson, Jan. 24, 1924, box 47, Amos Pinchot Papers, also Amos R. E. Pinchot to Karl Bickel, Feb. 1, 1924, *ibid.* See also J. Leonard Bates, *The Origins of Teapot Dome: Progressives, Parties, and Petroleum, 1909–1921* (Urbana: Univ. of Illinois Press, 1963) and James Penick, Jr., *Progressive Politics and Conservation: The Ballinger-Pinchot Affair* (Chicago: Univ. of Chicago Press, 1968).

51. Oswald G. Villard to Robert M. La Follette, Feb. 1, 1924, Villard Papers.

52. Thelen, *Robert M. La Follette and the Insurgent Spirit* (Boston: Little, Brown and Co., 1976), 176. Mercer G. Johnston to Bishop James S. Johnston, Apr. 6, 1924, box 25, Johnston Papers. See Robert H. Zieger's illuminating article on the coal situation: "Pinchot and Coolidge: The Politics of the 1923 Anthracite Crisis," *Journal of American History* 52:3 (Dec. 1965), 566–581.

53. Mercer G. Johnston to Bishop James S. Johnston, Jan. 29, 1924, and Apr. 30, 1924, *ibid.*

54. Amos R. E. Pinchot, "A Fair Deal for the Public," *Forum* 51:2 (Feb. 1924), 201–206; the quotation is on 206.

55. Thelen, *Robert M. La Follette*, 176–178. Progressives had discovered, however, that while government ownership benefited management and labor, the

consumer absorbed the wage and rate increases. See Kennedy, *Over Here*, 254–256.

56. Amos R. E. Pinchot to Gilson Gardner, Feb. 20, 1924, box 47, Amos Pinchot Papers.

57. Fine, *Labor and Farmer Parties*, 429.

58. Weinstein, "Radicalism in the Midst of Normalcy," 779. See also Millard L. Gieske, *Minnesota Farmer-Laborism: The Third Party Alternative* (Minneapolis: Univ. of Minnesota Press, 1979), 82–94.

59. J. A. H. Hopkins to William V. Mahoney, Feb. 11, 1924, Series B, box 98, La Follette Papers; also Draper, *American Communism and Soviet Russia*, 99–101; Weinstein, "Radicalism in the Midst of Normalcy," 775–779; MacKay, *The Progressive Movement of 1924*, 79–85; William Z. Foster, *American Trade Unionism* (New York: International Publishers, 1947), 136–140.

60. Draper, *American Communism and Soviet Russia*, 117.

61. Robert M. La Follette to Herman L. Ekern, May 26, 1924, Series B, box 119, La Follette Papers.

62. Thelen, *Robert M. La Follette and the Insurgent Spirit*, 182; Belle Case La Follette and Fola La Follette, *Robert M. La Follette*, vol. II (New York: The Macmillan Co., 1953), 1098–1102. For an opposing view stressing the importance of creating a third party, see Morris Hillquit, *Loose Leaves from a Busy Life* (New York: The Macmillan Co., 1934), 300–323, especially 316–319.

63. Milwaukee *Leader*, May 30, 1924, quoted in Weinstein, "Radicalism in the Midst of Normalcy," 787; Draper, *American Communism and Soviet Russia*, 113–114.

64. MacKay, *The Progressive Movement of 1924*, 90; Weinstein, "Radicalism in the Midst of Normalcy," 788–789; Draper, *American Communism and Soviet Russia*, 115–116, also 462, 66n. On July 10, 1924, six days after La Follette received the nomination of the CPPA in Cleveland, the Communist leadership of the National Farmer-Labor–Progressive Convention withdrew Duncan MacDonald's name and placed William Z. Foster at the head of a Worker's party presidential ticket, Draper, *American Communism and Soviet Russia*, 117–118.

65. Committee of Forty-Eight, Press Release, National Bureau of Information and Education, May 29, 1924, Series B, box 98, La Follette Papers.

66. Amos R. E. Pinchot to Robert M. La Follette, June 28 and July 2, 1924, box 46, Amos Pinchot Papers.

67. Amos R. E. Pinchot to Robert M. La Follette, June 28, 1924, *ibid.*

68. Arthur M. Schlesinger, Jr., and Fred L. Israel, eds., *History of American Presidential Elections, 1789–1968*, III (New York: Chelsea House Publishers, 1971), 2517–2523.

69. Harry A. Slattery to Cornelia (Mrs. Gifford) Pinchot, July 5, 1924, Slattery Papers.

70. Progressives like Mercer G. Johnston hoped that the election would leave the Republicans and Democrats as a conservative party. See Mercer G. Johnston to Bishop James S. Johnston, July 10, 1924, box 25, Johnston Papers.

71. Harold L. Ickes to Hiram W. Johnson, June 13, 1924, box 33, Harold L. Ickes Papers, Library of Congress, hereinafter cited as Ickes Papers.

72. Hiram W. Johnson to Harold L. Ickes, July 14, 1924, *ibid.*, and Ashby, *The Spearless Leader*, 138.

73. Mercer G. Johnston to Elisabeth Gilman, Aug. 9, 1924, box 30, Johnston Papers.

74. *Ibid.*

75. Mercer G. Johnston to Elisabeth Gilman, Aug. 23, 1924, *ibid.* See also Mercer G. Johnston to Dr. D. R. Hooker, Aug. 23, 1924, box 49, *ibid.*, on the importance of reaching a compromise with conservative labor leaders in order to "get this important aggregation out into the field." Also, Robert M. La Follette to the Non-Partisan Political Campaign Committee of the American Federation of Labor, Aug. 16, 1924, Series B, box 119, La Follette Papers, and MacKay, *The Progressive Movement of 1924*, 150–155.

76. Mercer Johnston to J. A. H. Hopkins, July 24, 1924, box 49, and Mercer G. Johnston to Bishop James S. Johnston, Aug. 16, 1924, box 25, Johnston Papers.

77. Harold L. Ickes to Hiram W. Johnson, Sept. 9, 1924, box 33, Ickes Papers.

78. *New York Times*, Sept. 15, 1924; Belle and Fola La Follette, *Robert M. La Follette*, II, 1120–1121; Edwin A. Van Valkenburg, "La Follette's Challenge," *Philadelphia North American*, July 7, 1924, 10; see also Alan R. Havig, "A Disputed Legacy: Roosevelt Progressives and the La Follette Campaign of 1924," *Mid-America* 53:1 (Jan. 1971), 44–64, and the same author's "The Poverty of Insurgency: The Movement to Progressivize the Republican Party, 1916–1924," (Ph.D. diss., Univ. of Missouri, Columbia, 1966), 305–312.

79. The quotation is from a letter of Ann Hard to Oswald G. Villard, Sept. 14, 1924, Villard Papers. The likelihood of Charles W. Bryan ending up in the White House was remote, but such a development could have occurred if La Follette's progressive supporters in the House of Representatives prevented both Coolidge and Davis from obtaining a majority of the votes of the state delegations. With the decision then shifted to the Senate, it would have been possible for the insurgents voting with Democrats to elect Bryan vice-president, and since no president had been elected, the Nebraskan would have become the occupant of 1600 Pennsylvania Avenue. See MacKay, *The Progressive Movement of 1924*, 167.

80. Harold L. Ickes to Hiram W. Johnson, September 9, 1924, and Hiram W. Johnson to Harold L. Ickes, Sept. 13, 1924, box 33, Ickes Papers. Hiram W. Johnson to Harold Ickes, Oct. 8, 1924, Part III, box 7, Johnson Papers.

81. Amos R. E. Pinchot to Harold L. Ickes, Oct. 13, 1924, box 46, Amos Pinchot Papers.

82. Amos R. E. Pinchot to Burton K. Wheeler, a public letter signed, Sept. 27, 1924, released on Sept. 30, 1924, box 49, Johnston Papers. The statement by pro-La Follette supporters can be found in the *New York Times*, Oct. 24, 1924, 3. See also, "Five Thousand Clergymen for La Follette," Oct. 26, 1924, in Kirby Page Papers, Southern California School of Theology.

83. Amos R. E. Pinchot to Edwin A. Van Valkenburg, Oct. 25, 1924, box 46, Amos Pinchot Papers.

84. Fiorello H. La Guardia to John M. Nelson, Sept. 6, 1924, Series B, box 99, La Follette Papers.

85. Belle and Fola La Follette, *Robert M. La Follette*, II, 1127–1147; MacKay, *The Progressive Movement of 1924*, 175–196; Oswald G. Villard, *Fighting Years: Memoirs of a Liberal Editor* (New York: Harcourt, Brace, and Co., 1939), 503; Oswald G. Villard to Robert M. La Follette, Sept. 13, 1924, Villard Papers; Arthur

G. Hays, *City Lawyer: The Autobiography of a Law Practice* (New York: Simon and Schuster, 1942), 269–270, and Fred Greenbaum, *Robert Marion La Follette* (Boston: Twayne Publishers, 1975), 216–220.

86. Robert M. La Follette, Jr., to John M. Nelson, Aug. 7, 1924, Series B, box 119, La Follette Papers, and James H. Shideler, "The La Follette Progressive Party Campaign of 1924," *Wisconsin Magazine of History* 33:4 (June 1950), 450–454.

87. I am indebted to Nancy F. Cott for drawing my attention to the existence of the WCPA and for generously sharing with me her own research based upon work in the Alice Park Papers. See the WCPA's "Statement of Principles," Apr. 9, 1924, its "Program" for the national conference, May 8–11, 1924, a "Report" on the conference, as well as press releases and internal memoranda, box 23, Alice Park Papers, Hoover Institution Archives. Isabelle Kendig, the WCPA's executive secretary, and an active participant in the Progressive party's Women's Division, discusses her experiences in "Women in the Progressive Movement," *Nation* 119 (Nov. 19, 1924), 544.

88. Amos R. E. Pinchot to George F. Peabody, Oct. 2, 1924, box 46, Amos Pinchot Papers. David P. Thelen discusses the appeal of Coolidge prosperity and its relationship to voters' job orientations in *Robert M. La Follette and the Insurgent Spirit*, 191–192.

89. Hillquit, *Loose Leaves*, 319–321.

90. Humes, *Oswald G. Villard*, 140–143.

91. William Hard, "That Man La Follette," *Nation* 119 (July 16, 1924), 65–66.

92. Basil M. Manly to Oswald G. Villard, Aug. 13, 1924, Villard Papers, and "In the Driftway," *Nation* 119 (July 9, 1924), 46.

93. Oswald G. Villard to William Hard, Sept. 2, 1924, Villard Papers.

94. William Hard, "La Follette's Strategy," *Nation* 119 (Sept. 10, 1924), 261.

95. George L. Record to Robert M. La Follette, Nov. 5, 1924, Series B, box 98, La Follette Papers.

96. J. A. H. Hopkins to Robert M. La Follette, Nov. 5, 1924, *ibid*. The point is not that Hopkins's assessment of the voting was incorrect but that his willingness to form a permanent new party still was predicated on his classless view of American politics. For an analysis of the 1924 vote see Allan J. Lichtman, *Prejudice and the Old Politics: The Presidential Election of 1928* (Chapel Hill: Univ. of North Carolina Press, 1979), *passim*.

97. *New York Times*, Nov. 7, 1924, quoted in Belle and Fola La Follette, *Robert M. La Follette*, II, 1148.

98. William Hard, "La Follette's Party—Will It Last?" *Nation* 119 (Aug. 6, 1924), 142–143.

99. Hiram W. Johnson to Harold L. Ickes, Nov. 7, 1924, box 33, Ickes Papers.

100. Harold L. Ickes to Hiram W. Johnson, Nov. 11, 1924, *ibid*.

101. Frederic C. Howe, *The Confessions of a Reformer* (New York: Charles Scribner's Sons, 1925), 337–338, 339–340; the quotation is on 342–343.

102. Otis L. Graham, Jr., *An Encore for Reform: The Old Progressives and the New Deal* (New York: Oxford Univ. Press, 1967), 106.

103. Otis L. Graham, Jr., *The Great Campaigns: Reform and War in America, 1900–1928* (Englewood Cliffs, N.J.: Prentice-Hall, Inc., 1971), 119.

104. Zieger, *Republicans and Labor*, 188–189.

VII

The Wilderness
Years, 1925–1928

The La Follette movement failed to transform the intense emotional energy of the 1924 campaign into a sustained commitment for permanent political survival. The swiftness with which a movement could decline, even one which had drawn nearly five million votes, was not as readily apparent as the Progressives' postmortems might indicate. Almost immediately, "acting" campaign directors and "provisional" chairmen began churning out publicity releases to "keep up the fight." The campaign's Washington office was kept open as if to suggest that a desk, chair, and mimeograph machine guaranteed life after defeat. There were promises of future meetings and conventions, and the faithful were encouraged to keep their contributions coming to pay off Progressive debts. "We must hang together now," was the unfortunately phrased observation of one form letter, "or be separately hanged later." Postelection talk consistently referred to "the next skirmish" in the development of a "new movement" in which the " 'Spirit of 1924' would bring ... government back into the hands of the people."[1]

Senator La Follette, though visibly exhausted after the campaign, doggedly fired off letters and telegrams, solicited information on campaign contributors, and requested lists of committeemen and women down to the precinct level. He attributed the Republican landslide to an unlimited slush fund and to voter intimidation with threats of price hikes, unemployment, mortgage foreclosure, and loss of consumer credit. Though the "industrial, financial, and commercial strength of the nation" had been mobilized against them, La Follette predicted that Progressives would close ranks for the next battle. "We are enlisted for life. ... We will not quit and we will not compromise." These sentiments were heartfelt, but had the senator looked around he would not have found Progressive legions marching "forward for the campaign of 1926."[2]

La Follette chose not to look back except with nostalgia. Ensconced on his Madison farm, physically weakened by recurrent bouts with pneumonia and bronchitis, and protected by his family, the senator chose only to see the good side. It was not difficult when supporters around the country testified to their undying affection. "Millions of people believe in you," wrote a former Progressive national committeeman. "Come back Senator and visit America 50 years from now and hear the school children tell of your great struggles for real democracy."[3]

There were others, of course, who would have written a much different history lesson. Expressing little surprise at the election results, Amos Pinchot directed his anger squarely at La Follette for failing "to inject into the campaign a program that would outlast [his] defeat. . . . [His] performance was essentially a selfish one; he sacrificed any beliefs he may have had to get as big a count as T.R." It no longer was enough to say that conditions were bad and had to be improved; Progressives had to tell the public what they were going to do, how it would be done, and what the implications would be. If the real problems were plutocracy and monopoly, as La Follette declared and as Pinchot believed, then Progressives had to formulate a step-by-step plan. "We . . . do not seem to be able to realize," he wrote a friend, "that, as a matter of tactical common sense, we have got to play an entirely different game from the conservatives."[4] Predictably, Pinchot did not share his views with La Follette.

For veteran newspaperman Gilson Gardner, La Follette's defeat had little to do with the failure to offer a specific agenda. "The mind of the average voter," he wrote Pinchot, "is a twelve-year-old mind. It thinks politically and in kindergarten terms. It understands nothing that can't be put into a catchword or phrase." What good was the development of an elaborate progressive program when voters "can't understand a movement to take the government away from the few rich." Progressives, he believed, should continue to channel discontent and offer alternatives without expecting to accomplish much in their lifetime. "In other words," he concluded, "we may not feel called upon single-handed to save the world."[5] Pinchot's disappointment lay less with the voters, who rejected "La Follette's hot air warmed over from 1912," than with the progressive "political crowd" in Washington who were "fundamentally uninterested . . . in any real issues that might make trouble in their constituencies. "I think," he observed, "we have got to look for comfort outside of Congress."[6] Characteristically, however, Pinchot remained on good terms with Washington's surviving Progressive officeholders, realizing that they were too valuable a resource to alienate.

There were always more generals than privates in the Progressive army who were willing to enlist for the long haul of forming a new party. If the 1924 La Follette campaign had been only half formed, with a head (the senator) and a tail (the railroad labor brotherhoods), the postelection progressive movement was both headless and tailless. "How absurd it is," noted Pinchot, "indeed how puerile, to imagine that a new party, without money, without prestige, and above all, without a definitive program . . . can overthrow the power of the enemy in one short political engagement."[7] The fact was not lost upon those who presumed to lead the way toward a new party. J. A. H. Hopkins urged creation of statewide Progressive parties and personally launched a skeletal organization, the "Provisional Organization Committee," which he operated out of the same New York office that had housed such other ill-fated ventures as the "National Party" and the "Liberal Party."[8]

This puttering around was of much less concern to Senator La Follette than organized labor's future role in third-party politics. Throughout November and December 1924, rumors circulated that the railroad brotherhoods were likely to return to nonpartisan political activity rather than support the call for a permanent new party many liberals hoped would result from their scheduled February conference.[9] Writing to William T. Rawleigh, the Freeport, Illinois, patent medicine king and Progressive sugar daddy, Robert M. La Follette, Jr., predicted the railroad unions' withdrawal from independent political action but announced his father's support for a representative gathering of "unorganized liberals." That phrase, clearly distinguishing independent progressives from the union-dominated Conference for Progressive Political Action, reflected two main concerns. First, it realistically acknowledged the CPPA's expected withdrawal from the Progressive coalition; second, however, it revealed an underlying fear that the Socialists might have sufficient strength to turn the Chicago meeting into a referendum on a group (class) as opposed to an individually composed party.[10] Convinced that labor was not interested in progressive political action and aware of the railroad brotherhoods' and AFL's intentions, Senator La Follette argued that a new party must be "representative of all the people and not of any section, group, or class." He disavowed any interest in a "federation of organizations . . . owing their allegiance to other causes and liable at any time to develop divergent views."[11]

The Progressive party convention which met in Chicago in February 1925 proved to be more of a wake than a revival. The railway brotherhoods attended as a courtesy to former colleagues and then interred the CPPA before allowing independents to go on record in support of a permanent third party.[12] The remaining independent Progressives created a National Executive Committee (NEC) and made it responsible for bringing the new party to fruition. This task seemed insurmountable for the four men and women whose selection by party chairman William H. Johnston owed more to their physical proximity to the Progressives' Washington headquarters than to any national experience.[13]

Under Johnston's leadership, however, the NEC did all it could to maintain Progressive morale. In March it announced a "Program of Public Service" as a foundation upon which a third party might evolve. Reflecting progressive traditions of a quarter-century, the committee placed federal abolition of monopoly at the top of its fourteen-point program. Public ownership of water power, natural resources, and the railroads occupied a prominent position, as did promotion of public works, surtaxes on excess profits, and a total revision of Republican legislation restoring taxes on inheritances, stock dividends, and estates. The new party publicly eschewed occupational and special interest representation, but its program spoke to the needs of farmers with proposals for the direct public control of money and banking, promotion of government marketing corporations, and to the needs of workers with proposals guaranteeing the right to organize and bargain collectively, abolition of injunctions in labor disputes, as well as a prohibition against punishment of union leaders for contempt without trial by jury. Other measures echoed long-standing progressive concerns for a child labor amendment, election of federal judges, and equal rights for women without the loss of special protective legislation. There were other more current proposals dealing with payment of the veterans' bonus, a deep waterway from the Great Lakes, abolition of conscription, disarmament, and a strongly worded condemnation of American foreign policy that drew upon the antimilitaristic sentiment of prewar progressivism. Reflecting Gilson Gardner's desire for simple catchwords and phrases, the statement assailed the "mercenary system of degraded foreign policy under recent administrations" which catered to the interests of "financial imperialists, oil monopolists . . . international bankers [and] concession seekers." It called upon all nations to outlaw war and proposed public referendums on peace and war.[14] The program touched most of the familiar bases but failed to create much excitement. "Nothing very startling has happened," Gilson Gardner wrote Harry Slattery early in April. "There is nothing going on except the quiet stealing by the landlord and the quiet suffering of the tenant."[15] Most Progressives seemed content to ride out the Coolidge honeymoon with sarcastic allusions to "King Kal the Silent" and "Sir Herbert Hoover" of the "Chamber of Horrors and Commerce," the "Knight of the Fat-Boys," and the "Order of Trade Combinations by a New Name."[16]

Others suffered less good-naturedly, and their bitterness was all the more evident because it was directed at fellow Progressives. Congressman John M. Nelson, the former national chairman of the La Follette-Wheeler ticket, was one of the most embittered of those still active. Saddled with responsibility of paying off campaign debts, he tried to rally fellow Progressives in the House who were being "read out of [Republican] councils, thrown off committees, and threatened with political destruction." Material support required financial angels, and Nelson organized a new committee to save congressional liberals. Fundraising letters were sent to proven contributors, a headquarters office was leased, and donors were encouraged to save the "Congressional end of the Progressive Movement, which is the heart and brains of it."[17] The response was so negligible, however, that Nelson occasionally charged some of his group's expenses against remaining assets of the 1924 campaign treasury. It was indicative of the pettiness to which Progressives had succumbed that National Treasurer William T. Rawleigh, the Illinois millionaire, felt no obligation to cover the debts of another Progressive party committee. A very bitter correspondence ensued between the Rawleigh Company and Nelson revealing the Progressives' propensity for nitpicking. "It is true," the congressman observed, "that I had to charge some things to the National Treasurer because I did not have the funds, but what is this money for in Mr. Rawleigh's hands? Is it not to carry on the Progressive Movement?"[18] There was something tragically comic about Progressives clashing over $488.54 left in their campaign treasury while their Republican rivals enjoyed the luxury of a multimillion-dollar campaign organization. That situation, however, was a fair approximation of both groups' relative position in national politics.[19]

Progressives spent more time fighting themselves than their enemies, and each rival group had a different principle to which it was attached. J. A. H. Hopkins, self-proclaimed chairman of the Provisional Organization Committee, attacked congressional Progressives and William H. Johnston's National Executive Committee for their lack of progress in moving toward a national convention. He accused liberal congressmen of cowardice and self-interest. No one, Hopkins declared, wanted to take a risk; Progressive senators and congressmen would accept what their party could do for them in the future but were notably absent when time came for present leadership. Though "read out of the Republican party . . . cast out of Congressional councils, [and] regarded as renegades by the Republican National Committee," they were still quite willing to "crawl back to office through the underground channels of the Republican primaries."[20] Hopkins's displeasure was sincere and his pot shots well intentioned, but they served no constructive purpose. The NEC had not acted because there was no support for a formal Progressive convention, and congressional liberals fighting for their political lives had no choice but to seek the legitimacy which major party affiliation provided. If Hopkins was justified in emphasizing the need for statewide leadership, he must have recognized that without strength at the top, Progressives were doomed to decentralized hit-and-run tactics. A realist would have concluded that the situation was dismal; even an optimist would have been depressed.

Eight months after the Progressives' defeat, the little black cloud which seemed to follow them around was still there. On June 18, 1925, Robert M. La Follette died at his Washington home.[21] His passing brought forth the usual eulogies and testimonials. "I predict that the nincompoop who was wished on us instead of your great father," Mercer G. Johnston wrote Robert La Follette, Jr., "will be remembered (as Pontius Pilate is) because he happened to live in the era in which a Great Soul gave his life for the people."[22] Many of the tributes were linked to current political conditions and to what the future might hold. In an important sense the senator's death gave Progressives a chance for a new beginning. The personal ties of a quarter-century were severed, and longtime followers did not fail to note the event as the end of an era. "It is almost a different world we have to face and fight in with Senator La Follette gone," Johnston wrote Basil Manly. "I feel somewhat as those Britishers did who marched out of Yorktown . . . to the tune of 'The World's Turned Upside Down.' "[23]

It was not only La Follette's death or their overwhelming repudiation at the polls that so distressed Progressives. A much deeper, more fundamental problem troubled them, one that extended beyond election reversals and personalities. Liberals questioned their own faith and many found their colleagues lacking in commitment. "Our fellows here have lived too long in political luxury," observed Senator Hiram W. Johnson. "Ease and comfort have them flabby . . . " Always the cynic, the California progressive blamed the decade's prosperity and the attractions of "easy profits which came from exploiting people and governments." He was particularly embittered by the actions of those "who once called themselves Progressives . . . who can be corrupted with a breakfast at the White House or an overnight trip upon the [presidential yacht] *Mayflower*. He did not blame the voters for wishing to "avoid all of the bitterness and heart-burning of the long struggle" rather than follow "fair-weather Progressives who . . . have little sense of guardianship of the people's rights and no courage either to safeguard or maintain them."[24] It is not difficult to find other equally pessimistic assessments of the Progressives' future. Evidence of liberal disaffection is abundant and offers a convincing case for a much weakened reform movement. All of these observations, however, cannot disguise the existence of sustained progressive activity on a number of fronts. The truth is that these were not glamorous times for political liberals, and those who remained active received little acclaim or glory.

One of many aggravations Progressives endured during the 1924 campaign was a Senate investigation of vice presidential candidate Burton K. Wheeler, which grew out of an indictment for fraud brought by a federal grand jury in Montana. Though Senator William E. Borah's committee found no evidence of wrongdoing and nothing to indicate that Wheeler had illegally accepted compensation from oil man Gordon Campbell, the Justice Department obtained a second indictment from a Washington, D.C., grand jury alleging that the senator, along with Campbell and Edwin S. Booth, former solicitor for the Interior Department, illegally conspired to obtain oil and gas permits on government land. Few Progressives thought it coincidental that the twin indictments came less than a year after the senator had helped lead a probe into the misconduct and indiscretions of the then Harry Daugherty-led Justice Department. Wheeler himself characterized the second indictment as "another evidence that the administration is attempting to discredit its political enemies or anyone who dares attempt to uncover corruption in governmental departments."[25] Sympathetic independent and Democratic newspapers called the government's action "disgraceful," "vindictive," "crookedly partisan," and "outrageous." Others, less certain about the senator's ethics, pointed out that he had used his influence in behalf of a client (Campbell) from whom he received a $10,000 retainer. Wheeler's acquittal by a Great Falls, Montana, jury could not protect him from those who recalled "the strictness of the moral principles" by which he had judged the Republican party a year earlier. "Mr. Wheeler is about the last person who ought to pose as a stickler for orthodox procedure," noted the editors of the *Detroit Free Press*. "His own record as a 'prosecutor' in the [Teapot Dome] oil scandal investigation carries no suggestion that he ever troubled himself to observe any nice ethical limitations."[26] It says a good deal about the Progressives' capacity for indignation that few considered Wheeler's behavior even remotely analogous to the disgraced former Secretary of the Interior Albert Fall's actions during the Teapot Dome inquiry.

It also was indicative of the general malaise affecting the liberal community that the Wheeler indictments, rather than some pressing national issue, had to provide a tonic for sagging Progressive spirits. The movement's custodians, however, could not afford to pass up any opportunity that channeled their energy toward some useful purpose. In early April 1925, Basil M. Manly and Mercer G. Johnston, the "mud-sills" of the undertaking, took the initiative in planning the Wheeler Defense Committee. Johnston's Baltimore-based Christian Social Justice Fund set aside $1,000 for the effort and began canvassing influential liberals to serve on a national committee.[27] The latter's purposes, as Johnston told soon-to-be chairman Norman Hapgood, were to provide Senator Wheeler a first-rate defense and to conduct and publicize the results of an independent investigation. The committee hoped to raise $25,000, $10,000 of which was expected to come from the fund-raising efforts of such New Yorkers as John Haynes Holmes, Norman Thomas, Harry W. Laid-

ler, Oswald G. Villard, and other prominent liberals. All committee
members would be volunteers, and substantial assistance was expected
from the American Fund for Public Service.

The fund's mere existence offers a strong testimonial to the hardiness
of liberalism in this putatively reactionary decade. Created in July 1921
when Charles Garland, a young Harvard dropout, refused to accept a
million-dollar inheritance which he considered morally and socially rep-
rehensible, the Garland Fund represented the left's modest answer to
the Rockefeller and Carnegie foundations. It was administered by a
who's who of American liberalism including Roger N. Baldwin of the
American Civil Liberties Union (ACLU), radical economist Scott Nearing, former Wobbly Elizabeth Gurley Flynn, Rabbi Judah Magnes, radical
labor leader William Z. Foster, James W. Johnson of the NAACP, and
many other illustrious members of the American left. The fund underwrote a variety of minority causes, cooperative and educational movements, and labor defense committees.[28]

Mercer G. Johnston placed the Wheeler committee's $5,000 request to
the Garland Fund in a context larger than that of one individual. "If the
evil forces that deliberately set out to 'get' Wheeler... succeed," he
wrote fund secretary Roger N. Baldwin, "it will be an extraordinary
member of the Senate or House indeed who lifts his voice against corruption in Washington."[29] Eleven days later Elizabeth Gurley Flynn, the
fund's assistant secretary, responded on behalf of the board of directors.
Even though several members of the board, especially Treas. Morris L.
Ernst, were intimately connected with the Wheeler committee, the fund's
directors agreed only to make available a $2,500 interest-free loan. "We
did not see our way clear," Flynn explained, "to make an outright contribution to a cause which ought to command much larger public support
than most of the causes we aid."[30]

The American Fund's decision accurately reflected progressive opinion. Many liberals sympathized with the senator's legal difficulties, but
his defense never became an all-consuming obsession. Wellesley College
professor Vida Scudder spoke for many by noting that her colleagues
thought Wheeler a lot richer than themselves, and most would rather
give to Sacco and Vanzetti.[31] Such indifference was not unusual, and
while prominent potential donors such as Bernard Baruch, Edward A.
Filene, and Joseph P. Kennedy were contacted, most of the money was
raised by committee members whose own solicitations grew more strident. "I don't care whether you Sons of Liberty have a Tea Party or a
Mass Meeting or just a plain Hold-up," Mercer G. Johnston wrote Morris
L. Ernst. "I know you can raise money for us."[32] Mercifully, the whole
inglorious episode ended in late December 1925 when the Washington,
D.C., Supreme Court dismissed the conspiracy indictment marking the
third time Senator Wheeler had been exonerated of the charges. It is

reasonable to assume (as Wheeler's supporters did) that former Attorney General Daugherty's friends at Justice and the Republican National Committee deliberately set out to "get" the senator, but Wheeler's own culpability received little attention. The Borah committee, a Montana jury, and District of Columbia court decided that no criminal offense had been committed, but the ethical question was consistently sidetracked, especially by Wheeler's defenders who ignored his association with a convicted felon, co-conspirator Gordon Campbell, who was sentenced to two years in prison.[33]

Victories had become so rare, however, that Progressives determined to make the most of Wheeler's acquittal by taking some pot shots at Calvin Coolidge, whom they held responsible for the witch-hunt. "Cal got sore because Wheeler kidded him during the campaign," Mercer G. Johnston wrote Oswald G. Villard, "and has been little and mean enough to sit with folded hands in the White House while the hounds of the Department of Justice chased (Wheeler) . . . across the country."[34] Some of the nation's most distinguished progressives paid tribute to the "unfaltering courage," "matchless skill," "unspotted record," and "unabated devotion" of Wheeler and his counsel, Senator Thomas J. Walsh, but there were more regrets than acceptances to the planned "Victory Dinner." John Haynes Holmes, Felix Frankfurter, William A. White, Clarence Darrow, Rabbi Stephen S. Wise, and Norman Thomas agreed that their joy was tempered by the public's lack of indignation over Wheeler's prosecution. "In a day when the public conscience seems to be deader than in a decade . . . and millions seem to be indifferent to everything except jazz and money," observed Josephus Daniels, "it is heartening to see that there are those who have kept the faith." Keeping the faith, however, was a very lonely affair even "if the company was good."[35]

Progressives met Wheeler's vindication with relief rather than jubilation. Most realized how small a victory it actually was. Perhaps it was a reflection of the times or of repeated electoral setbacks, but Progressives appeared beaten. There was no unifying force, no injustice that might lead La Follette's almost five million supporters to march again. There was still a La Follette in the Senate after Bob, Jr., won a special election to succeed his father in September 1925. But the issues he confronted seemed more complex, less reducible to questions of right and wrong, and many Progressives seemed convinced that he would play "a role very inferior to that of his father."[36]

Veteran progressives manning Washington's liberal lobby never gave up the cause. They continued to peck away at administration policy and at President Coolidge's appointments to federal agencies such as the Federal Trade Commission. Other activists devoted their time to protesting the lingering incarceration of Sacco and Vanzetti and convicted labor leaders Tom Mooney and Warren Billings, but there was none of the fire or intensity that might lead one to Armageddon to battle for the Lord. There also were many notable emotional lows which independent progressives experienced during the 1920s. One of the most serious occurred in October 1925, when William H. Johnston, the dynamo behind the International Association of Machinists' political activism and the CPPA's liberal connection, suffered a disabling stroke. His absence was immediately felt by the fledgling Progressive National Executive Committee, which he almost single-handedly had kept in existence. Bereft of their most experienced and respected leader, committee members decided to continue their activities with Johnston as the nominal head. Meanwhile, friendly rivals—like Basil M. Manly's People's Legislative Service and J. A. H. Hopkins's Committee of Forty-Eight—waited impatiently for the chance to eliminate another competitor. It may strike one as unseemly and uncollegial for one liberal organization to root for another's demise, but there were a limited number of liberal contributors, and Washington lobbyists would cut their mothers' throats to meet the next payroll or finance the next mailing. Moreover, the NEC's commitment to a permanent third party represented an increasingly unpopular view. Rather than risk embarrassment by holding a poorly attended national convention, the committee hoped to save face, money, and the third-party idea by sponsoring a "National Conference" for early December in Cleveland.[37] Even that modest proposal met opposition, however. J. A. H. Hopkins, writing in his role as vice president of the New York State Progressive party, argued that a conference would be perceived as a convention, and a sparsely attended meeting "will place us in a worse position than if we had not held it at all."[38] The conference was held, and acting national chairman Mercer G. Johnston felt relieved that "nothing hurtful happened." In fact, nothing at all happened, and a disheartened and frustrated Parley P. Christensen vented his despair and impatience. The Farmer-Labor party's forgotten presidential candidate of 1920 felt Progressives were merely "whistling in the graveyard." The situation was "gloomy"; Progressives were "floundering [and] frittering away . . . precious time." He saw no sense in calling a conference to call a conference. "The Home Folks have been waiting for a call . . . to action!" Thus, while Christensen demanded action—"lay aside strategy, forget quorums, issue a call with a thrill to it"—Mercer G. Johnston was dismantling the committee's Washington headquarters, eating brown-bag lunches, trying to save rent money, and doing everything possible to keep the official party apparatus out of the hands of both Christensen and Hopkins.[39]

Whether Johnston retained any lingering hope for a genuine third-party movement is difficult to determine. When pushed by Progressives disappointed at the lack of progress, he fell into his familiar role as the good pastor, a comfortable position for this ex-minister. "The birth even of one baby does not come without much pain," he reminded one colleague. "To bring about . . . a new birth of political and industrial thinking and acting—that takes enormous long-suffering patience and head pain and heart pain . . . something much like crucifixion." Though he paid lip service to the possibilities of achieving a new political alignment, Johnston's day-to-day handling of party affairs left him with severely scaled-down expectations.[40] By year's end the Progressives' last "national chairman" had sold the committee's office furniture and supplies to the People's Legislative Service, whose staff he joined as Basil Manly's top assistant.[41] Once welcomed into the elite if dwindling ranks of Washington's professional Progressives, Johnston found himself the caretaker of an almost extinct movement. Fearful for their political future, leaders such as Burton K. Wheeler and Robert M. La Follette, Jr., advised caution, patience, and moderation.[42] Frontal assaults in the form of Progressive conventions were discouraged rather than provide grist for the conservatives' propaganda mill or embarrassment for liberals. Johnston was advised to do the "sensible thing," which he took to mean holding periodic conferences, maintaining a paper front "partly as a bluff to the enemy, partly as a banner of hope to the scattered hosts," supporting hit-and-run guerrilla warfare on the Coolidge administration, and issuing a "middle-of-the-road" Progressive declaration of faith.[43] That Progressives seemed only to be going through the motions became evident when the first Progressive National Committee *Bulletin* did little more than resurrect memories of Teapot Dome and the persecution of Senator Wheeler; nor did the PLS organ, the *People's Business*, attempt much more.[44]

Amidst this confusion and despair, veteran reformers Oswald G. Villard and Peter Witt labored to bring life to a declaration of Progressive faith in anticipation of a hoped-for but still unscheduled national convention. Their final draft, submitted to Mercer G. Johnston and members of the executive committee, illustrated their movement's limited strengths and glaring weaknesses. The prose style was remarkably similar to the 1892 Populist party platform. "Privilege stalks abroad in the land; governmental favors are openly bought and sold; more and more the government enters into partnership with private individuals to fix their profits. . . . Public confidence . . . has so far ebbed that only fifty percent of our people care to vote. . . . Free speech, liberty of press and of assembly are strangled. . . . The machinery of government is breaking down."[45] Such observations compare favorably with the Omaha platform's sentiments some thirty years earlier: "We meet in the midst of a nation brought to the verge of moral, political, and material ruin. Corruption dominates the ballot-box, the Legislatures, the Congress. . . . The people are demoralized . . . public opinion silenced . . . labor impoverished, and the land concentrating in the hands of capitalists."[46] One might argue that nothing much had changed and that comparability was not coincidental but the result of inequities grown worse from neglect, indifference, and the failure of traditional progressive prescriptions. If conditions remained as bad or worse than those confronting the Populists, despite a generation of progressive legislation, maybe the answer was not more reform or the creation of still more progressive organizations. All the evidence seemed to call for a permanent liberal-labor coalition that would mobilize support within the political mainstream. It is unlikely, however, given their ties to the progressive past, that such a conclusion would have been acceptable to Villard—whose progressive pedigree extended back to the mugwumps—or to Witt, who personified a fiercely independent political tradition.

Their solutions for "striking off the shackles of politics, business, and privilege" encompassed a quarter-century of progressive ideas. Free trade would eliminate tariffs, which were the source of economic nationalism. Abolition of the military would lead to the outlawry of war. Government ownership of natural resources and nationalization of railroads would eliminate the inequities which created monopolies. Direct nomination and election of the president would place power in the hands of the people; a national referendum on public issues would curb machine influence on the democratic process. Prohibitions against the indiscriminate use of labor injunctions and affirmation of workers' right to organize would help balance labor-management relations. Support for producers' and consumers' cooperatives would solve problems of production and distribution. Enforcement of nondiscriminatory legislation would help guarantee equality of opportunity. If much of this sounds familiar, it was no less important in 1926 than when such proposals were first advocated years before. Even the foreign-policy planks drew upon a tradition of pacifist and antiwar sentiment shared by many though certainly not all progressives. All "entangling alliances" were to be avoided. A new Latin American policy, beginning with troop withdrawals from the Caribbean, would replace the unilaterally administered Monroe Doctrine and Roosevelt Corollary. Sharp distinctions would be drawn between foreign-policy and business needs so that "the flag [would not] follow the investor."[47]

The Villard-Witt document was a provocative mix of traditional progressive causes with some new and unfamiliar wrinkles. It was not, however, a "declaration of faith" but a definitive point-by-point platform representing a marked substantive departure from the La Follette campaign. Not surprisingly, it was coolly received by "those who [had] played a conspicuous part" in that movement. After presenting it to members of the Progressive NEC, Mercer G. Johnston reported back to Villard that his colleagues felt it unwise to endorse free trade or pacifism and questioned whether their "stop-gap committee" should present such a program to the "Progressives of the country." Better to deal in pleasant and harmless generalities, Johnston suggested, "after the manner of the first part of the Declaration of Independence" and other examples of inspirational literature.[48]

With Progressive leaders offering such advice and with enough references to "prima donnas" to serve as reminders of lingering jealousy, it is hardly surprising that "an extraordinary pessimism" pervaded reform circles. Frustrated by their inability to divert public attention from the blandishments of Coolidge prosperity or from the divisive and profitless battles of race and religion, progressives entertained one another with fatalistic predictions. "I think," Donald R. Richberg wrote Villard, "that when the so-called intellectuals come to the conclusion that appeals to religious prejudice and physical appetites are the only things that will stir the populace, they have given up the battle for democracy." That was far from being true, and Richberg, ever the diehard, admitted that though "the future may look dark," he was "not yet ready to confess defeat."[49]

Such sentiments were so widely shared by reformers in the late twenties that a clear pattern seemed to develop. There always were more lows than highs, but the exhilaration of participating in the next struggle or cause usually provided enough adrenaline and satisfaction to keep activists afloat and eager. Moreover, with the domestic scene an unlikely target for a successful progressive campaign, liberals rather easily redirected their attention to the Coolidge administration's Latin American policy, which seemed ready-made for a dose of progressive morality. In Nicaragua our government continued the heavy-handed, patronizing, totally insensitive application of dollar diplomacy anchored in a firm American military presence and manipulation of another nation's political affairs.

Since the days of the Taft administration, the United States had discouraged revolutions in Nicaragua by maintaining a legation guard of 100 marines in the capital city of Managua. Two Wall Street banking firms, J. and W. Seligman and Brown Brothers, managed the nation's railroad and bank, though the Nicaraguans gradually asserted economic independence over those sectors. The State Department's desire for stability was severely tested in October 1924 when national elections led to the defeat of the popular soldier-statesman Emiliano Chamorro's pro-American Conservative party, and the triumph of a conservative-liberal coalition headed by Carlos Solórzano and Juan Sacasa. Though aware of election irregularities, Secretary of State Charles E. Hughes chose to continue diplomatic relations and remove the marine guard whose presence long had been an unsettling factor. This was accomplished in early August 1925 over the protests of the Solórzano regime and Americans living in Nicaragua who feared the new government would not survive the troops' departure. Those fears were well founded, for within three months the Chamorristas had forced the liberals from the Solórzano coalition, placed the general in charge of the armed forces, and in January 1926 made him president. Liberal leaders were persecuted and removed from office. In spite of our publicized unwillingness to meddle in Nicaragua's internal problems, new Secretary of State Frank B. Kellogg announced that the U.S. would not recognize a Chamorro-led government even though American officials continued to monitor Nicaraguan finances. In August civil war broke out between Sacasa liberals and Chamorro conservatives with the former receiving military aid from Mexico. American neutrality gradually was replaced by pro-Conservative, though still anti-Chamorro, sympathies. This shift reflected our own strained relations with Mexico over the oil and land nationalization legislation advocated by its president, Plutarco Alias Calles; the latter's support for the Nicaraguan liberals; and Secretary Kellogg's conviction that Mexico's intervention was part of a Soviet plot to subvert American interests in Latin America.

Chamorro's withdrawal from office under strong State Department pressure in late October 1926 paved the way for Adolfo Diaz, a conservative, pro-American, former chief executive, to be elected president. On November 17, three days after his inauguration, the U.S. announced formal recognition of the Diaz government. The civil war did not end, however, and arms shipments from Mexico to Sacasa's liberal forces inside Nicaragua seemed to imperil the Diaz government's survival. Convinced of the threat to the nation's stability, Secretary Kellogg, acting on alarmist information from Nicaraguan officials, dispatched a legation guard of 160 marines to Managua during the first week in January 1927. Shortly thereafter, an additional 600 marines were dispatched and six warships arrived in Nicaraguan waters. President Coolidge's assertion that such action was necessary to support a friendly government against a foreign-inspired insurrection, and Kellogg's testimony before the Senate Foreign Relations Committee, blaming the hostilities on Communist subversion, placed the Nicaraguan situation on page one of every American newspaper. This development delighted the progressive community, whose outrage was mixed with pleasure at the administration's plight.[50]

From Washington, Senators George W. Norris and William E. Borah led the attack accusing the Coolidge administration of protecting American business interests and of using marines as a collection agency for Wall Street and as the underpinning of the Diaz regime. Displaying the bite of a rejuvenated bulldog, the *People's Business* denounced the government's "delirious diplomacy" and called for an end to our "blundering bullying."[51] In mass meetings across the nation thousands of

Americans protested administration policy with calls for immediate withdrawal, a negotiated ceasefire, investigation of American business and
banking activities in Nicaragua, and the dismissal of Secretary of State
Kellogg.[52] Uncomfortable in the role of bully and cognizant of the hypocrisy attendant with criticizing other nations for aggression and imperialism, reformers were distrustful and outraged with a policy they
considered indefensible. "Why do we have to land marines, censor
news, disarm inhabitants, and chase belligerents in Nicaragua," asked
Harold L. Ickes. "What concern is it of ours and what right have we to
decide for the Nicaraguans at the point of a pistol who their president
shall be?" Progressives were incensed by the administration's eagerness
to label Mexican support for the Sacasa liberals as part of a communist
plot. "All this talk," Ickes wrote Hiram W. Johnson, "gives me a feeling,
half of amusement and half of illness. Bolshevism is the most famous
red herring of all time."[53] The U.S. Senate evinced many of the same
concerns by overwhelmingly recommending arbitration with Mexico.
The Coolidge administration dismissed the proposal and seemed to take
an even harder line in late March 1927 with its announcement of an
arms and munitions sale to the Diaz government.[54]
    The arms sale coupled with the expanded American military presence
and news of a private bankers' one-million-dollar loan to the Diaz government were the precipitating events in creation of a "National Citizens'
Committee on Relations with Latin America" (NCC). George W. Norris
served as honorary chairman and Boston banker John F. Moors as titular
president, but the committee was run by its secretary, the ubiquitous
Mercer G. Johnston, with the active assistance of his PLS boss, Basil M.
Manly. Primarily a watchdog group, the NCC hoped to temper administration policy in Nicaragua and Mexico and "promote genuine good-
will between all the Latin American republics and the U.S." Its well-
wishers and members composed a who's who of surviving progressives.
In addition to Senators Borah, Thomas J. Walsh, Burton K. Wheeler,
and David I. Walsh, other distinguished supporters included journalists
William A. White, Oswald G. Villard, and Norman Hapgood; novelist
Zona Gale; labor spokesman Edward Keating; and Rabbi Stephen S.
Wise.
    Committee organizers were particularly anxious to attract the support
of prominent American Catholics as a signal to the Coolidge administration that its "solid" Catholic backing was an illusion.[55] The prize was
New York Governor Al Smith, a Catholic and likely presidential candidate in 1928, whose endorsement of NCC goals would conflict with
the Church's opposition to Mexico's revolutionary government. Some
progressives viewed Smith's position on Latin America as a litmus test
of his liberal credentials. His refusal to comply with anything less than
a no-holds-barred attack on administration policy would be proof of his

"spurious liberalism." "If Smith keeps silent about this iniquity," Johnston wrote Manly, "he can go to hell and fry there forever. Nothing he
could ever say would unconvince me that he was the Pope's little man
after all."[56] Smith was not prepared to issue the kind of blanket condemnation many progressives desired. Though declaring that "no country has a right to interfere in the internal affairs of any other," he defended
the Church's right to request American aid for "the oppressed of any
land" as had been the case, he carefully noted, when our government
"offered protection to Protestant missionaries in the Orient and [to] the
persecuted Jews of eastern Europe."[57] The presumption, if not the arrogance, of progressives in making such demands upon Smith seems
at odds with their public image of innocence and the altruistic goals of
their campaign. It also reveals a highly developed political ruthlessness
and a capacity for religious bigotry and treachery that hinted ominously
at future problems.

Having proven that the Coolidge administration had no monopoly on
bad taste, progressives proceeded to do what they did best—create another skeletal organization and quarrel. Within days of the NCC's founding, Mercer G. Johnston expressed regret at the organization of a
competing "Committee on Peace with Latin America." At the same time,
his friendly rival, J. A. H. Hopkins, proposed yet another committee to
prevent the U.S. government from guaranteeing or protecting its citizens
and their property in foreign countries.[58] While progressives engaged
in their petty jurisdictional disputes, President Coolidge sent former
Secretary of War Henry L. Stimson to Nicaragua in hopes of defusing
both domestic criticism and hostile world opinion. Dismissing this step
as nothing more than masking "an iron hand in a velvet glove," the
NCC contended that the Stimson mission promised "little more than a
beautiful funeral for Nicaraguan sovereignty." The committee called for
arbitration, a "square deal," the promotion of friendly relations, and the
rejection of the "misguided and blundering policy of dollar diplomacy"
in favor of "good neighborship."[59] It also contended that administration
policy was injuring our foreign trade with the rest of Latin America.

The Stimson mission and the subsequent appointment of Dwight Mor-
row as our ambassador to Mexico were widely praised throughout the
U.S. as evidence of a positive and welcome change in administration
policy. By questioning the motivation behind such efforts, the NCC
performed an essential role in a democratic system, but it also seemed
uncooperative and partisan at a time when most Americans supported
the change in policy. This public perception proved an uncomfortable
position for several committee members, including president John F.
Moors and former Secretary of War Newton Baker, who both resigned
in protest. These defections did not surprise Basil M. Manly or Mercer
G. Johnston, and it is likely that the NCC could not long have sustained

a broad-based coalition. Though the two veteran progressives initially sought bipartisan support, neither intended the committee to be anything less than a thorn in the administration's side, constantly probing for weaknesses to embarrass its adversary. They sought improved relations with Latin America, but that goal was often indistinguishable from the related concern of making life miserable for their Republican opponents. There was nothing conspiratorial in their making this connection, nor were progressives paranoid in their fears. Strong criticism from conservatives made the link between progressives' opponents and reactionism appear a logical conclusion.[60]

There was little room for compromise between liberals seeking a redirection of American foreign policy and their adversaries, some of whom believed our government "always . . . justified in exerting . . . moral and political influence and . . . military strength."[61] For their part, however, many progressives deliberately provoked extreme views, referring to Nicaragua as "Brown Brothers' Republic" and in so doing imputing to such views an unwarranted degree of respectability. In the end, though progressives in the National Citizens' Committee and other cooperative organizations played influential roles in temporarily moderating administration policy, they shared little of the credit. This was the result of their sustained and unremitting hostility to the Stimson mission and to the highly publicized attacks of leaders such as George W. Norris, who denounced U.S. policy as "indefensible," "disgraceful," and "inhuman."[62]

The resumption of civil war in Nicaragua, led by rebel leader César Augusto Sandino, prompting the presence of over 5,000 American troops in the country by July 1928, bolstered the administration and disheartened progressives. "I am frank to say to you that what we can do effectively with reference to Nicaragua is not . . . clear to me," an exasperated William E. Borah wrote Oswald G. Villard. Even Villard, the champion of pacifism and restraint, agreed that our troops were needed not only to insure free elections but probably to protect American property as well.[63] The presence of those troops, of course, provided an inviting target for the Sandinistas, and the shocking news of American deaths did not lead to demands for withdrawal. Most Americans were concerned over the loss of life and property, but few were convinced that Wall Street was ruthlessly exploiting Nicaragua.[64]

By the spring of 1928 a combination of disillusionment and interest in the upcoming U.S. presidential election put an end to the NCC's formal activities. "Candor compels me to confess," Mercer G. Johnston observed that April, "that we have not gotten very far with our protest. About all we have been able to do is to shoot the elephant in the tail with shots that do little more than slightly perforate the hide, if that, and make him wiggle his tail and snort a little.'"[65] Johnston's comments

underestimated the genuine influence progressives exerted, if only in a
negative way, on Coolidge administration policy. The NCC's efforts
allowed reformers to pursue their traditional role as gadfly and agitator,
keeping their constituents informed, ready to mobilize the faithful for
another battle. It is not the futility of the effort which stands out but the
stubbornness and refusal to acquiesce in defeat which should be remembered. The Nicaraguan episode captured the paradoxical nature of
progressivism in the late twenties—impotent yet unyielding, always
dependent upon outside events to stimulate political action. This rare
postwar venture into foreign policy proved that though progressives
were capable of achieving modest success within the framework of their
ephemeral organizations, they still showed no inclination to expand
beyond their own narrow group. The satisfaction which their efforts
produced stemmed from working *together*, but progressives seemed to
ignore the fact that they also worked *alone*.

Perhaps the most noticeable change in the progressive personality,
however, was a feeling of total helplessness which temporarily affected
the movement's top echelon. "Why is it that the people are deaf to the
cause of reform?" William A. White asked in June 1927. "What has come
over the spirit of the people to cause this worship of stability, this tremendous timidity toward change?" Even Mercer G. Johnston, the even-
tempered, steady editor of the *People's Business*, confessed he didn't
know. "I'm all unsettled and confused," he told his readers. Progressives
everywhere were bewildered by the lack of issues and depressed by
their obvious lack of power.[66]

Even issues on which progressives chose to make a fight seemed to
backfire. The devastating Mississippi River flood in the springtime of
1927, which produced untold property destruction and left over a million
people homeless and destitute, seemed ready-made for a liberal crusade.
Progressives quickly denounced Coolidge's refusal to call a special session of Congress as symbolic of Republican insensitivity to the plight of
voters in traditionally Democratic states. In a virtuoso display of intellectual gymnastics, Mercer G. Johnston accused the administration of
delaying action on flood relief out of fear that an investigation would
lead to unpleasant disclosures concerning American policy in Latin
America.[67] Commerce Secretary Herbert Hoover's masterful performance as chairman of the Special Mississippi Flood Committee, his ability
to generate substantial private funding and federal assistance for flood
damage and rehabilitation, quieted most progressive critics. Hoover's
reemergence as the "Great Humanitarian," recalling his universally acclaimed wartime services, also removed the flood as an issue and sent
progressives scurrying for another target.

Calvin Coolidge filled the bill perfectly. This "pitiful puppet of publicity . . . clownishly garbed in caricature cowboy costume" seemed part

of a circus performance. Critics assumed that the president's buffoonery was done reluctantly but intentionally to fool the people. The famous photographs of Coolidge pitching hay in Vermont with overalls covering his business suit, "jerking a tame fish out of a porcelain-lined lake" or stepping before the cameras "dressed in a ten-gallon hat, blue shirt, red necktie, and cowboy chaps with 'CAL' blazoned on each leg" seemed both deceitful and absurd. Coolidge was not trying to fool the people but reassure them that the traditional values of an earlier era would not be sacrificed before an urban-industrial future. It may well be that what progressives said in public and believed in private were two very different things. If Coolidge was "the first President to make himself the laughing stock of the multitude," his adversaries seemed unduly concerned about his winning reelection.[68]

It was typical of progressives in the summer of 1927 that when one issue failed they tried another, which also failed. "I have come to think," Mercer G. Johnston wrote Robert M. La Follette, Jr., "that in this imperfectly understood experience of ours on earth that it is more the way a man fights for the things he fights for, than the thing itself, or the result of the fighting, that is of prime importance." Such sentiments were comforting, but Johnston's combative nature sensed that the difficulty lay in framing an issue and lining up support "to stop the downsliding of the Goddess [of liberty] now that the reactionaries have her on the skids." Even though Coolidge would technically only be seeking reelection to a second term, Johnston told La Follette that the issue for 1928 should be the third term: "Third Terms for nobody—first-raters or third-raters." All hopes for a "militant move against the Third Term" went up in smoke less than a month later with Calvin Coolidge's brief announcement: "I do not choose to run for President in nineteen twenty-eight."[69]

Coolidge's withdrawal and Herbert Hoover's likely nomination—"The Amalgamated Society of Big and Little Babbitts are for him"—cast a pall of gloom over progressive ranks.[70] Few reformers held much hope of electing a president in 1928; most sensed they did not have a chance. "Anyhow," Johnston told the readers of the *People's Business*, "it is time to stop shooting at the moon and secure power where it will really count—in the Senate and House." Targeting the sixteen midwestern and western states where La Follette had captured more than 20 percent of the 1924 vote, Johnston proposed a "postcard" platform "that would command a strong following throughout the West." But aside from endorsing the McNary-Haugen farm bill—calling for federal price supports and the dumping of agricultural surplus abroad—as well as the public development and operation of governmental power and nitrate facilities at Muscle Shoals, and flood control on the Mississippi, progressives were content to echo familiar concerns. They attacked the

Coolidge administration's "imperialistic aggression" in Latin America, proposed revision of the Federal Reserve system to eliminate "control by international bankers," supported the Norris amendment to abolish lameduck congressional sessions, and resurrected calls for honesty in government and clean elections. This was one occasion when the actual program was less important than the willingness of progressives to remain active and publicly visible.[71]

The last concern was uppermost in progressive thoughts. Many noted the absence of "organized channels," the "breakdown of organization," the lack of leaders to take the place of Roosevelt, Wilson, Bryan, and La Follette, and "an almost complete destruction of all means of communication with . . . the people." Typically, however, independent progressives countered this pessimism with calls for a "new liberal, progressive organization." Many were quick to note that though this did not require a new party, a permanent organization with a "longtime program was essential." "Sooner or later," observed the *People's Business*, the American people "will turn aside from their present absorption in money, movies, radio, automobiles, and sports and respond wholeheartedly to a magnetic leader who will call them to the service of high ideals."[72] Some liberals placed more faith in a messiah than in the ideas which had nurtured the first progressive generation, but personality and policy continued to be inseparable in the minds of most reformers. The liberal situation in 1927 was pathetic and ironic because reformers were considering and actively formulating alternatives to current policy. That there were few listeners and that progressives lacked a broad power base outside Congress to espouse such concerns was unfortunate, but they had no one to blame but themselves. In many instances their new ideas seemed rather tired and old, echoes of previous unsuccessful struggles. Calls for liberal-labor cooperation, for example, were nothing new in 1927, having been voiced repeatedly since 1919. What distinguished such proposals from earlier pleas was the indifference with which they were met by organized labor, who had grown weary of progressives' quadrennial avowal of friendship. Still, enthusiasm for reform remained high among the nation's liberal elite. Reformers agreed that it would be exceedingly difficult "to find a basis upon which the liberal and progressive forces [could] be united," but all realized a way had to be found.[73] Inevitably, progressives believed organization to be the key. Their laments over the "breakdown of organization" and "destruction of all means of communication with . . . the people" were genuine but totally self-serving. For when they rhapsodized about a "new liberal, progressive organization," they had no one else in mind but themselves.

The progressives' peculiar view of cooperation was much in evidence in an exchange between Mercer G. Johnston, the caretaker chairman of the moribund Progressive National Executive Committee, and William

V. Mahoney, a veteran Farmer-Labor leader. The occasion was the Farmer-Labor Party's (FLP) call for a national convention in 1928 and Mahoney's request to meet with members of Johnston's committee. Both men knew each other from past ventures, notably the abortive FLP campaign in 1920 and the La Follette effort of 1924. Both shared a philosophical commitment that transcended doctrinal purity, yet each seemed wedded to organizational loyalty. Rather than providing the basis for future collaboration, their common experience was more of an obstacle than advantage. Concerned that his former colleague might " 'overlay' a Progressive committee meeting with Farmer-Labor sentiment," Johnston urged Mahoney that any suggestions should come "from the Progressive, and not from the Farmer-Labor side of your political personality." That this may have been "too fine a distinction," as Johnston acknowledged, did not prevent him from enforcing it "in fairness to those who voted the Progressive ticket."[74]

Farmer-Laborite interest in a third-party effort came at a time when most Progressives thought such an idea unwise. Neither a separate political party nor one "controlled by the common people" held much attraction for Johnston or his colleagues. "I cannot see that there is the slightest chance of making any progress politically at the present time," noted an unusually pessimistic J. A. H. Hopkins, "nor do I have any suggestions . . . in respect to the kind of political activities that . . . I would like to engage in."[75] Hopkins reflected the feelings of many liberals that there was no place in their immediate future for a third-party movement tied to the La Follette campaign. Thus, on November 3, 1927, with but three committee members present, Chairman Mercer G. Johnston joined his colleagues in concluding that continuing the life of the Progressive National Executive Committee "would serve no worthwhile purpose."[76] "We sought in vain to find facts more favorable than those that hemmed us in," he later observed. "Only by ignoring [them] could [we] have gone ahead." The committee's official demise had little historical or practical significance other than marking the disappearance of another sentimental tie to the La Follette campaign. Few veterans of that effort had ever placed much confidence in the committee; its very existence was confusing to some and embarrassing to others. Its only purpose, aside from publishing a few issues of the *Progressive Bulletin*, was to serve as a skeletal organization that would issue the call for the hoped-for but always postponed national convention. Johnston's brave contention that the committee's passing did not mean "the end of the Progressive Movement" was less an expression of faith than an acknowledgment of the continued liberal presence on Capitol Hill of other more successful lobbying groups. His final hope, however, that "sooner or later the principles for which the Progressives fought in 1924 will assume definite militant form" was merely a pipe dream.[77]

Progressive principles would triumph, but they were not ones closely identified with the 1924 campaign. The most notable new issue of the post-La Follette years concerned the "Power Trust." The battle against the nation's utility giants aroused traditional progressive hostility toward monopoly and raised an even more insidious specter of a conspiracy to "poison," "control," "bribe," and "deceive" the public.[78] Progressive lobbyists such as Judson King, director of the National Popular Government League, believed that the Power Trust's "Super-Lobby" in Washington would try to sidetrack any investigation into the utility industry's financial or lobbying practices. The focus of any inquiry would have been the lobby itself, officially known as the Joint Committee of National Utility Associations, an organization representing over 150 corporate clients including such powerful groups as the National Electric Light, American Gas, and American Street Railway Associations. Progressives contended that the Joint Committee, chaired by George B. Cortelyou of New York's Consolidated Edison, a former secretary of the treasury under Theodore Roosevelt and GOP national chairman, existed primarily to oppose the extension of federal regulation to the utility industry. Its chief counsel was another prominent Republican, former Senator Irvine L. Lenroot of Wisconsin. The Joint Committee also boasted the membership of John Spargo, onetime muckraker and advocate of municipal ownership, whose famous exposure of child labor, *The Bitter Cry of the Children* (1906), left him an easy target for liberal sarcasm. "Any man has a good right . . . to change his mind," observed Judson King, "and pass from radicalism to reaction . . . Mr. Spargo should write another book entitled, 'The Bitter Cry of the Power Magnates.' "[79]

In 1927, Senator Thomas J. Walsh introduced a resolution proposing an investigation of the utility industry that remained buried in the Interstate Commerce Committee. Fearful of providing a political forum for Walsh, George W. Norris, or some other presidential aspirant, the Coolidge administration lobbied to transfer the proposed inquiry from the Senate to the Federal Trade Commission. Under the conservative leadership of its chairman, William T. Humphrey, a Coolidge appointee, the FTC apparently had abandoned its prewar commitment to investigate and curb unfair business practices for conciliatory, nonadversarial relations with corporate leaders. Progressives were much less charitable in characterizing Humphrey's influence. The *People's Business* accused him of "insolence," "trickery," "petty tyranny," "an overweening concern for special interests, and dereliction of duty to public interests."[80] The commission seemed to offer the administration and the electrical industry a more hospitable and friendly environment than the hostile confines of a Senate chamber.[81] Progressive lobbyists pulled out all the stops, first, in an effort to get the Senate resolution passed out of committee and, second, to keep it a legislative inquiry. "If you favor an investigation to find out why the American people pay three times as much for electric light and power as the people of Ontario," observed the *People's Business*, "if you want cheap electric light and power, write . . . the [Interstate Commerce] Committee that you want . . . this resolution [reported] promptly." The National Popular Government League encouraged its members to send in their old electric bills, utility rate schedules, power company propaganda, and any other material that would "get the truth to the people."[82]

In February 1928, much to the horror of progressives, the Senate approved a resolution which shifted the utility investigation into the hands of the Federal Trade Commission. Blaming this result on the power lobby, "the most powerful group . . . of Special Interests that ever laid siege to Capitol Hill," progressives had little faith that the FTC had "the will [or] the power" to conduct an honest investigation.[83] What happened, however, to liberals' amazement, was that the commission took its inquisitorial role very seriously. Under the leadership of Chief Counsel Robert Healy, the FTC "confounded" its liberal critics and "dumfounded the . . . Power Trust" by exposing the interlocking, monopolistic nature of the utility industry and the almost conspiratorial scope of its propaganda campaign.[84]

"Keep your eyes and ears wide open during the day," warned the editors of the *People's Business*, "watch every mouthful of intellectual food and drink you take, and when you go to sleep put your fingers in your ears and keep your mouth shut tight. This is no joke. We are in dead earnest." Though obviously sarcastic in tone, this editorial was far from being entirely tongue-in-cheek. People's Legislative Service Director Mercer G. Johnston strongly denounced the "Superpower Poison Squad" whose "high-powered, ruthless propaganda [was] backed by the biggest slush fund yet dragged into the light."[85] The extent of the utility industry's media assault was soon evident, and if not immoral or unethical, its sheer scope, had it been widely known, would have been cause for public concern. Harry A. Slattery, one of Washington's most astute progressive watchdogs, informed Senator Norris that the National Electric Light Association (NELA) spent nearly a million dollars for lobbying during 1927, while dispensing its funds to twenty-eight public information bureaus across the nation.[86]

Even more ominous from the progressives' viewpoint was the carefully orchestrated deception and misinformation which characterized the power lobby's "message." This casual regard for the truth comes through clearly in the industry's tortured defense of its educational campaigns. No aspect of the FTC's investigation aroused more liberal indignation than the "poisoned propaganda" which utility interests disseminated to the nation's public schools. Paul S. Clapp, the NELA's managing director, denied that his organization "directly" furnished pamphlets to

teachers for school use "except on special requests" and never directly
to students though "hundreds of teachers commended their value." The
pamphlets, Clapp assured directors of the National Education Association (NEA), "contain nothing in the way of propaganda . . . and consist
merely of a truthful, plain, accurate, and simple recital of the facts." He
hastened to add, presumably to buttress his argument, that "the merits
of private versus municipal operation are not discussed."[87] The NEA,
however, called such power lobby propaganda "a crime against youth,"
while the American Federation of Teachers (AFT) termed it "the greatest
crime against civilization." Both organizations joined with concerned
citizens to establish the "Save-Our-Schools Committee" in an effort to
keep special interest propaganda out of the classroom.[88]

The NELA and other industry spokesmen did generate enormous
amounts of literature for external distribution, but reaching a broader
audience required a national campaign. Eager to win a part of the power
lobby's lucrative advertising budget, Victor Whitlock, vice-president of
the *U.S. Daily*, forerunner of the *U.S. News and World Report*, wrote to
Philip H. Gadsden of the Joint Committee of National Utility Associations with a major proposal. This memorandum is suggestive of how
potentially corruptive a force the power lobby's money could be. It also
reflected the type of professional obfuscation which distressed progressives. Whitlock proposed an educational campaign emphasizing the merit
of local responsibility, community development, state regulation, and
the evils of federal interference. Community prosperity and efficient
utility service would be linked to private initiative and local control. All
advertising copy would be subject to the Joint Committee's approval,
as would the fifty-two companies selected as the focus of this year-long
campaign. "The cumulative effect would be [to argue] that the public
utility problems of today are entirely local and that any other method
of handling them would mean chaos . . . as well as serious interference
with community development." Whitlock concluded his sales pitch by
noting, somewhat incredibly, that the *U.S. Daily* was "a fact newspaper,
containing no editorials or interpretation of its own being absolutely
nonpartisan."[89] Oswald G. Villard observed, however, that soliciting a
156-page contract "from the only side with funds available for advertising" hardly constituted impartiality.[90]

The tremendous importance of the utility issue, its links to the prewar
antimonopoly and municipal ownership movements, and present and
future ties to the development of hydroelectric power, gave the 1928
presidential campaign a definite Progressive cast. But this was not 1924,
and few La Follette veterans could help noticing that their advice and
assistance, even when invited, often went unacknowledged. Still, that
had never stopped reformers from offering unsolicited advice, and it

did not do so now. Rumors that Governor Smith might appoint the General Electric Company's Owen D. Young as Democratic National Chairman sent waves of distress through liberal ranks. Identifying himself as the "last" national chairman of the Progressive National Committee, Mercer G. Johnston wrote Smith aide Henry Moskowitz that Young's appointment would make it impossible for Progressives to believe in the sincerity of the Democratic program.[91] Such threats had little influence because Smith's position on the power issue, the determining factor for Washington's liberal lobbyists, was much closer to their own than was Herbert Hoover's. Moreover, the governor's staff took pains to cultivate progressive support. Invitation-only audiences with the candidate did much to dispel doubt and generate enthusiasm. "You will be surprised to hear, confidentially," Harry A. Slattery wrote a friend in early July 1928, "that I was up . . . at the Executive Mansion with Hon. Alfred Emanuel Smith. . . . He is certainly the most outstanding personality I have met since T.R."[92]

If the usually levelheaded Slattery was more impressed than many of his colleagues, they, too, eagerly awaited an invitation to Albany. There would still be a good deal of hedging, and many progressives expressed concern over Smith's Catholicism and antiprohibition stance, but these were the necessary preliminaries of any political courtship. "It may be," Mercer G. Johnston wrote George W. Norris, "that the election of Al Smith will have to be accepted as the summit of the hope of a liberal or progressive with his feet on the ground for the years just ahead of us." As for the choice between "liberalism in politics and compulsory sobriety," Johnston "would cast his vote for the former."[93] Even Norris, who disagreed with Smith on the prohibition question, did not let that misunderstanding overshadow his sympathy for the governor's public power position. "I would hate to see the American people go off on a tangent," the senator wrote Gifford Pinchot, "even though the tangent was very important, and then wake up later to find that we had sold our natural resources for a mess of pottage."[94]

But the *People's Business*, voice of the People's Legislative Service and congressional progressives, did not rush to embrace Smith's candidacy. In August 1928, director Mercer G. Johnston considered neither major party candidate "a real champion of a living Progressive issue." Smith was probably "the best we could do, in bad Progressive weather, for the cause of human rights." The tepidness of that endorsement was underscored when Johnston advised PLS members that it mattered little whether they voted for Smith, Hoover, or Socialist Norman Thomas. "The all important thing is to stabilize and increase the power of the . . . Progressive forces in Congress."[95] Such sentiments reflected the very delicate relationship the PLS director shared with his superiors—Washington's progressive officeholders—some of whom, such as Norris and Robert M. La Follette, Jr., had enough difficulty within the Republican party without adding to it by endorsing Smith.

Though colleagues such as Basil Manly, Frederic C. Howe, and David Niles assumed key roles in the "Progressive League for Alfred E. Smith," Johnston initially eschewed an official connection. He participated, but his behavior was marked by an uncharacteristic degree of restraint. Whether Smith's religion, "wet" stance on prohibition, or party affiliation contributed to this situation is difficult to pinpoint. One might surmise from a letter to his wife that Johnston never quite overcame an antiurban (New York) prejudice and all which that entailed. Describing a walk back to his hotel after a day of politicking in the city, the PLS director noted the crowds, "badly dressed" men and "absurdly painted" women, and the shop windows "stacked with things [he] was glad not to count among [his] possessions."[96] By October, however, such memories were less vivid and the prospect of four more years of Republican rule more disturbing. "Much water has flowed under the bridge and some down our back since August," Johnston observed, "when we said, 'neither Smith nor Hoover is a real champion of a living Progressive issue.' " Anything less than an enthusiastic endorsement of Smith, he believed, would be a serious mistake, especially now that the "Governor has met Progressive issues not only squarely but, we think, satisfactorily."[97] Proof of Smith's progressivism, Johnston assured PLS members, was support of his candidacy by "the greatest living Progressive," Senator George W. Norris, whose campaign speeches clearly praised the governor's positions on hydroelectric power, farm relief, and foreign policy. "Perhaps," Johnston concluded, "that is as much as the Republican chairman of the Senate Judiciary Committee should be expected to say."[98]

The more enthusiastic leaders of the Progressive League for Alfred E. Smith aimed their campaign propaganda at the almost five million La Follette voters for whom Norman Thomas represented the only third-party alternative. The league message was twofold: the Progressive vote could be decisive and Smith "was the best hope for the . . . cause." Veterans of the La Follette-Wheeler movement were reminded that Smith supported public ownership, development of hydroelectric power, nonintervention in Latin America, curbs on the use of unwarranted injunctions, conservation of natural resources, child welfare protection, and legislation "for the advancement of workers." No mention was made of the governor's stance on prohibition or his belief that "Government should interfere as little as possible with business."[99]

The ideal league spokesman would have been a Republican who had followed TR into the Bull Moose party, then turned to Woodrow Wilson, supported La Follette in 1924, and was now a Smith supporter. Finding someone with this political history was not difficult, nor were candidates bashful. Amos Pinchot was one of the best-known volunteers who declared for Smith in a public letter to Democratic National Chairman John J. Raskob, whose own ties to General Motors and DuPont aroused little progressive criticism. For Pinchot, as for most progressives, Smith's denunciation of the "Power Trust" and support for public ownership of hydroelectric power was sufficient proof of his progressive credentials. "In almost every case," Pinchot observed, "he has . . . taken the position that Roosevelt, La Follette, or, for that matter, Wilson would have . . . in the same circumstances." Unlike Hoover, who progressives believed would "quietly or openly oppose" public ownership, operation, and distribution of electric power, Smith's position paralleled "the plan which Senator Norris, Gifford Pinchot, and the liberals in . . . Congress [had] been trying to put over during the Coolidge administration."[100]

The power question never became as consuming a subject for the general public as it was for some progressives. This was especially true of lobbyists such as Judson King, who had devoted years to the fight for public ownership and operation of Muscle Shoals, Boulder Dam, and to future projects on the St. Lawrence and Columbia rivers. King's organization, the National Popular Government League, contended that had it not been for Smith the St. Lawrence and Niagara rivers would "today be in the hands of Alcoa, General Electric, and the DuPonts." It was not conservation or public ownership alone, however, which motivated reformers. Judson King, Mercer G. Johnston, Basil M. Manly, and Benjamin C. Marsh feared the political influence the Power Trust exerted on both major parties. They believed the differences between Smith and Hoover would have long-term consequences. These progressives may have been obsessed with the "Super Power" issue but they were not naive. They realized that most Americans would vote on the basis of other questions, notably prohibition and religion, without ever realizing the Power lobby's influential role in American life. "The investment bankers, holding companies, etc.," King observed, "will be quite pleased to have the voters pay exclusive attention to beer, theology, race, and states rights, while they operate on a national scale and hence are against any federal regulation to say nothing of federal operation."[101]

Other progressives, less attuned to the utility question, perceived fewer differences between the two major party candidates and thus no compelling reason to vote Democratic. "It is an occasion of real tragedy," veteran social reformer John Haynes Holmes wrote Amos Pinchot, "to find so many of my admired comrades of the old days hitching themselves on as tails to the rottenest political party with which this country was ever cursed." As able and as fine a man as Smith was, Holmes did not believe that the New York governor could redeem his party any more "than a master carpenter can use rotten timber to build a house."

What was to be gained in the long run by Smith progressives, Holmes asked, after their candidate had been thoroughly repudiated? How would Smith's defeat strengthen progressives for the work which lay ahead? The only realistic choice in 1928, he told Pinchot, was Norman Thomas. "You have got to support him or the political interests which he represents tomorrow, if you are not to abandon the progressive cause altogether."[102]

Pinchot viewed socialism much as he did special privilege; both were destructive of free competition. His support for such socialistic propositions as public ownership of water power, railroads, and other natural resources was part of a traditional attack upon industrial or, what he called, "artificial" monopoly and not a blanket endorsement of government ownership. Convinced of the basic soundness of the free enterprise system, he desired governmental intervention only when competition had proven undesirable or impossible to maintain. None of this was a surprise to Holmes, who had known and worked with Pinchot for almost twenty years on a variety of political issues. He knew his friend was not a socialist but contended that one did not have to be a party member or sympathizer to support Norman Thomas.[103] Holmes, one suspects, may have been confusing Pinchot's notorious disregard for party regularity with a much different commitment to doctrinal purity. Party loyalty had never been one of his colleague's main concerns, but ideological consistency always represented a matter of honor.

More importantly, Pinchot did not share Holmes's misgivings about Smith. He considered the governor's willingness to support government ownership "a great educational service... [that would] revitalize politics, stimulate a nationwide debate, and do something toward breaking the hold of plutocracy."[104] Other progressives, while sharing Pinchot's enthusiasm for the educational value of a Smith campaign, were less than enthralled with the candidate. "I am not saying that Smith is a great man," Mercer G. Johnston observed, "but I have come to think that he is a whale of a fellow morally and humanly as compared with Hoover." Such sentiments became more prevalent as the campaign entered its final weeks. "I have never said or thought that Smith was the kind of a Progressive that the rank and file... could vote for... with joy and melody in their hearts," the PLS director noted a few days before the election. "My position... is that Hoover is so completely sold, sealed up, and delivered to the big interests, especially to the Power Trust, that it would be infinitely worse to have him in the White House than Smith." Johnston confessed that he still felt a tug at his heart when friends (like Holmes) chided him for ignoring the Thomas campaign. Had he not been connected with "men in public positions of some power, whose program... is to get the practical best out of any given situation," he might have voted for Thomas. "If I did so, I would be yielding to my idealistic side. That is what I have been doing most of my life, but for the time being, I am . . . fighting along what seems to me to be more practical lines."[105]

However practical those lines may have seemed, it was political defeat which stared progressives in the face. On the day after the election they would "gather up the debris," as one reformer put it, and begin anew as they had for the last eight years. Given the limited roles which most independent progressives played in the Smith campaign, it is not surprising that most accepted Hoover's landslide victory with relief rather than despair. They had never really embraced Smith as one of the family. In spite of his admirable reform record, he was a product of the notoriously corrupt Tammany Hall machine, an Irish Catholic whose education ended in the eighth grade, and the son of immigrant parents. He came from a much different world than most of these liberal activists. Their participation in his campaign was less a labor of progressive love than an obligation to be endured. His defeat opened the way for a favorite progressive pastime. "It is a matter of infinite comfort to me," John Haynes Holmes observed the day after the election, "that I have already received a call to attend a meeting in December to take up the organization of a third party in 1932."[106] There was hope after all, for as the *People's Business* facetiously noted: "it might have been worse. It was just a landslide." Moreover, the special circumstances surrounding Smith's defeat made it easier for progressives to assume that fundamental economic issues once again had been ignored, this time because of "Protestantism, Prohibition, and Prosperity." Liberal second-guessers concluded that millions of Americans had voted against Smith not knowing and not caring what Hoover stood for.[107] Many progressives assumed that the Democratic party's defeat and current state of hopeless division afforded a reasonable opportunity for the formation of a new party.

That was an assumption which stirred the independent progressive soul. Eager to be present at this as yet unformed and unnamed party's creation, reformers vied for the ear of prominent insiders. Inevitably, as though a biological clock was ticking inside his body, George L. Record fired off a letter to Oswald G. Villard, one of those increasingly linked to a third party. Naturally, the veteran New Jersey progressive emphasized the value of "a single, central, and paramount idea." The abolition of privilege remained his choice for a campaign issue that acknowledged the failure of governmental regulation while stressing the advantages of public ownership and free competition. Hoping to strike a practical note, Record suggested that the 1930 New York City mayoralty campaign might be an opportunity for the new party to attract national attention. "My idea," he wrote Villard, "is that we . . . put up a candidate . . . some man like Amos Pinchot . . . and that the issue should be the taking over by the City of the entire subway system." This proposal was remarkably similar to one Record had made fifteen years earlier when the mayoralty also had offered an opportunity to chart a new course, and municipal ownership had seemed to hold the key.[108] It is difficult to know how seriously Villard took Record's proposal. The idea apparently struck him as sufficiently interesting to raise with his colleagues, but Record's peculiar and highly unorthodox political history made public association with him undesirable.

The selective nature of progressive political activity after the 1928 election offers a glimpse into internal liberal confusion and division. Many progressives, though unhappy with the way they had been utilized during the Smith campaign, remained unconvinced that a third party was the solution to their problems. Mercer G. Johnston, for example, agreed with Smith aide Henry Moskowitz that progressives would have "to accept the two-party system and infuse the party of the 'outs' with some content of liberalism."[109] Such comments reflected Johnston's involvement in the Smith campaign and his Washington connection with the People's Legislative Service.

For other liberals, however, especially those who had leaned toward Norman Thomas, the two major parties offered little hope. These reformers were committed to a party that would be "independent of voters' stupidity and special privileges' entrenched position." If such elitist sentiments seem odd coming from progressives, few intellectuals then trying to breathe life into the liberal movement claimed to be democrats. They were frustrated by a two-party system that used hero worship and the occasional candidacy of a "good man with some slight traces of progressivism . . . as a magnet" to draw support from the nation's independent and liberal leaders.[110] Progressives interested in third-party politics spoke with increasing frequency of setting aside immediate political ambition in favor of educational goals that would lead to long-term social change.[111] Typical of many ideas then circulating in intellectual circles was the suggestion that a small "very carefully selected committee composed . . . of economists, statisticians and other technically qualified persons" should meet and develop a strategy. From this nucleus would come a closed, dues-paying membership "like the [British] Fabian Society" that would "produce a body of trained thought . . . fit to inherit power." Many progressives, particularly those with academic ties, believed that past efforts had failed because of hasty, politically expedient decisions which compromised principles for the sake of mass appeal. As representatives of the American meritocracy, these intellectuals now wanted to run a campaign their way. "I think our failures all these years . . . have been due to trying to attract numbers," Constance Todd wrote University of Chicago economist Paul H. Douglas. "I want to start with a small nucleus representing intellectual ability and technical knowledge and let the work that they do attract its own following because of its incontrovertible accuracy and vision and importance."[112]

However naive or self-serving such sentiments may seem, they were the result of eight years in the political wilderness, the last four as outsiders excommunicated from the two-party system without a third party of their own. Under those circumstances it is not surprising that some reformers retreated inward or that the academics among them placed their faith in the solutions of the intellectual community. What progressive activity there had been between 1925 and 1928 was largely due to the daily efforts of Washington's professional lobbyists. These were extraordinarily trying times which really tested the liberal elite, yet they kept their faith alive.

They adapted their ideas to meet the issues raised by the major foreign and domestic questions of these years. When they acted, however, it always was in response to others' initiatives. They found themselves constantly on the defensive, reacting to rather than influencing policy, venturing out occasionally to engage opponents with guerrilla tactics, but rarely drawing even the attention of their target. One cannot help but feel that independent progressives were flailing about barely managing to keep their heads above water. They were undeniably weak, innocuous, limited in number and extraordinarily homogeneous. For all their collective urbanity, cosmopolitanism, and intellectual brilliance, they remained unattractively parochial. What they shared was a willingness to carry on, the attendance of meetings, the writing of letters to the editor, and the bolstering of progressives throughout the country. They also feared being ignored and sensed that without organization they would disappear. On December 15, 1928, over fifty of these men and women, veterans and newcomers alike but survivors all, gathered in New York City to renew their faith and to plan for a liberal renaissance in 1932.

NOTES

1. H. L. Brinson, acting director, National Progressive Headquarters, form letter, Nov. 10, 1924, box 49, Mercer G. Johnston Papers.

2. Robert M. La Follette to Edward D. Bieretz, Nov. 13, 1924, *ibid.*, and La Follette's postelection article, "Forward Progressives for Campaign of 1926," in *La Follette's Magazine* 16 (Nov. 1924), also in box 99, Series B, La Follette Papers.

3. Ray McKaig to Robert M. La Follette, Nov. 25, 1924, *ibid.*

4. Amos R. E. Pinchot to Gilson Gardner, Nov. 25, 1924, box 46, and Dec. 1, 1924, Amos Pinchot Papers.

5. Gilson Gardner to Amos R. E. Pinchot, Nov. 29, 1924, *ibid.*

6. Amos R. E. Pinchot to Gilson Gardner, Dec. 1, 1924, *ibid.*

7. Amos R. E. Pinchot to Darwin J. Meserole, Dec. 11, 1924, *ibid.*

8. J. A. H. Hopkins to Robert M. La Follette, Dec. 26, 1924, box 98, Series B, La Follette Papers.

9. For the "Call" to this conference mandated by the Cleveland convention of July 4, 1924, see William H. Johnston's form letter, Dec. 30, 1924, box 50, Johnston Papers.

10. Robert M. La Follette, Jr., to William T. Rawleigh, Dec. 29, 1924, Box 119, Series B, La Follette Papers.

11. Robert M. La Follette to Gilbert E. Roe, Feb. 3, 1925, *ibid.*

12. Kenneth C. MacKay, *The Progressive Movement of 1924* (New York: Columbia Univ. Press, 1947), 230–237; Morris Hillquit, *Loose Leaves from a Busy Life* (New York: Macmillan Co., 1934), 321, and "Report of National Progressive Convention," held Feb. 21–22, 1925, box 70, Johnston Papers.

13. The four members of the Progressive National Executive Committee were Mercer G. Johnston, Mabel C. Costigan, Marie Manly, and Gilson Gardner.

14. "To Progressives Everywhere," statement from National Progressive Headquarters of the New Political Party, n.d., box 70, Johnston Papers.

15. Gilson Gardner to Harry A. Slattery, Apr. 9, 1925, Slattery Papers.

16. Harry A. Slattery to Basil M. Manly, May 29, 1925, *ibid.*

17. John M. Nelson to Mrs. Lynn Haines, Apr. 19, 1925, box 35, Haines Papers.

18. Robert F. Koenig, Rawleigh Company treasurer, to John M. Nelson, May 4, 1925, box 51, Johnston Papers; Nelson to Koenig, May 6, 12, 1925, *ibid.*

19. John M. Nelson to William T. Rawleigh, Sept. 30, 1925, and Oct. 2, 1925; William T. Rawleigh to Robert M. La Follette, Jr., Oct. 5, 1925; William T. Rawleigh to Nelson, Oct. 16, 1925, *ibid.*

20. *Liberal* 4:6 (June 1925), box 70, *ibid.*

21. Senator La Follette described his postelection medical difficulties and treatment in a letter to Rudolph Spreckels, Mar. 25, 1925, box 119, Series B, La Follette Papers.

22. Mercer G. Johnston to Robert M. La Follette, Jr., July 3, 1925, box 51, Johnston Papers.

23. Mercer G. Johnston to Basil Manly, June 23, 1925, *ibid.*

24. Hiram W. Johnson to Harold L. Ickes, July 2, 1925, box 33, Ickes Papers, also in Part III, box 7, Johnson Papers.

25. Burton K. Wheeler with Paul F. Healy, *Yankee from the West: The Candid, Turbulent Life Story of the Yankee-born U.S. Senator from Montana* (Garden City, N.Y.: Doubleday & Co., Inc., 1962), 235–245; also see *Independent* 114 (Apr. 11, 1925), 426–427.

26. *Literary Digest* 85:6 (May 9, 1925), 13–14.

27. Basil M. Manly to Mercer G. Johnston, Mar. 31, 1925 and Mercer G. Johnston to Basil M. Manly, Apr. 1, 1925, box 50, Johnston Papers.

28. Mercer G. Johnston to Norman Hapgood, Apr. 10, 1925; Mercer G. Johnston to Roger N. Baldwin, Apr. 11, 1925, *ibid.* For background on the American Fund for Public Service, see Merle Curti, "Subsidizing Radicalism: The American Fund for Public Service, 1921–1941," *Social Service Review* 33 (Sept. 1959), 274–295, and Stephen J. Whitfield, *Scott Nearing: Apostle of American Radicalism* (New York: Columbia Univ. Press, 1974), 153–154.

29. Mercer G. Johnston to Roger N. Baldwin, Apr. 12, 1925, *ibid.*

30. Elizabeth G. Flynn to Mercer G. Johnston, Apr. 23, 1925, *ibid*.

31. Vida Scudder to Mercer G. Johnston, May 8, 1925, and Mercer G. Johnston to Elizabeth G. Flynn, May 11, 1925, *ibid*.

32. Mercer G. Johnston to Morris L. Ernst, May 13, 1925. Contributions ultimately exceeded defense committee expenses; hence each contributor received a check from the committee representing 22 percent of his donation. See Norman Hapgood to Contributors, May 3, 1926, box 52, Johnston Papers.

33. *Nation* 122 (Jan. 13, 1926), 25–26; *New Republic* 45 (Jan. 13, 1926), 200–201; *Outlook* 142 (Jan. 13, 1926), 43.

34. Mercer G. Johnston to Oswald G. Villard, Jan. 14, 1926, box 52, Johnston Papers.

35. See Mercer G. Johnston to Sen. Thomas J. Walsh, Dec. 29, 1925, box 51, *ibid*.; John H. Holmes to Mercer G. Johnston, Apr. 2, 1926, box 52; Felix Frankfurter to Johnston, Rabbi Stephen Wise to Mercer G. Johnston, Clarence Darrow to Mercer G. Johnston, Apr. 5, 1926; Josephus Daniels to Mercer G. Johnston, Apr. 13, 1926; and Harry W. Laidler and Norman Thomas to Mercer G. Johnston, Apr. 3, 1926, *ibid*.

36. Amos R. E. Pinchot to George L. Record, Oct. 10, 1925, box 48, Amos Pinchot Papers.

37. Belle Rankin to Mercer G. Johnston, Oct. 9, 1925, box 51, Johnston Papers. William H. Johnston's letter of resignation, dated Dec. 1, 1925, can be found in *ibid*. See also Mercer G. Johnston to Peter Witt, Oct. 31, 1925, *ibid*.

38. J. A. H. Hopkins to Mercer G. Johnston, Nov. 7, 1925, *ibid*.

39. Parley P. Christensen to Mercer G. Johnston, Dec. 8, 1925, and Mercer G. Johnston to Mabel C. Costigan, Dec. 7, 1925, *ibid*.

40. Mercer G. Johnston to J. Otis Watson, Dec. 8, 1925, *ibid*.

41. Mercer G. Johnston to Basil M. Manly, Jan. 1, 1926, box 52; also, Mercer G. Johnston to Donald R. Hooker, Jan. 3, 1926, *ibid*.

42. Mercer G. Johnston to J. Otis Watson, Sept. 4, 1926, box 53, *ibid*.

43. Mercer G. Johnston to Mabel C. Costigan, Jan. 9, 1926, box 52, *ibid*.

44. Progressive *Bulletin* 2 (July 1, 1926), box 70, *ibid*., and *People's Business* 1:1 (July 1926), People's Legislative Service Papers, Library of Congress, hereinafter cited as PLS Papers.

45. Draft, "A Declaration of Faith," Oswald G. Villard and Peter Witt, Sept. 9, 1926, box 53, Johnston Papers.

46. Richard N. Current and John A. Garraty, eds., *Words that Made American History Since the Civil War* (Boston: Little, Brown, 1965), 223.

47. "A Declaration of Faith," box 53, Johnston Papers.

48. Mercer G. Johnston to Oswald G. Villard, Sept. 2, 1926, *ibid*.

49. Donald R. Richberg to Oswald G. Villard, Mar. 16, 1927, Villard Papers; see also Basil M. Manly to Mercer G. Johnston, Nov. 12, 1926, box 53, Johnston Papers. Thomas E. Vadney discusses the mercurial nature of Richberg's relations with progressives during the 1920s in *The Wayward Liberal: A Political Biography of Donald Richberg* (Lexington: Univ. Press of Kentucky, 1970).

50. This background material is primarily drawn from Dana G. Munro, *The United States and the Caribbean Republics, 1921–1933* (Princeton: Princeton Univ. Press, 1974), 157–216; L. Ethan Ellis, *Republican Foreign Policy, 1921–1933* (New Brunswick: Rutgers Univ. Press, 1968), 252–256; Walter LaFeber, *Inevitable Rev-*

olutions: The United States in Central America (New York: Norton, 1983), 64–66; Robert Freeman Smith, *The United States and Revolutionary Nationalism in Mexico, 1916–1932* (Chicago: Univ. of Chicago Press, 1972), 232–241; and Douglas Little, "Antibolshevism and American Foreign Policy, 1919–1939: The Diplomacy of Self-Delusion," *American Quarterly* 35:4 (Fall 1983), 381–382. Secretary Kellogg's testimony can be found in the *New York Times*, Jan. 13, 1927.

51. *People's Business* 2:2 (Feb. 1927), box 53, Johnston Papers.

52. LeRoy Ashby, *The Spearless Leader: Senator Borah and the Progressive Movement in the 1920s* (Urbana: Univ. of Illinois Press, 1972), 208–214; Richard Lowitt, *George W. Norris, The Persistence of a Progressive, 1913–1933* (Urbana: Univ. of Illinois Press, 1971), 372–375; and "Resolutions on Nicaragua and Mexico Passed at a Mass Meeting, Baltimore," Jan. 16, 1927, box 53, Johnston Papers.

53. Harold L. Ickes to Hiram W. Johnson, Jan. 14, 1927, Part II, box 45, Johnson Papers.

54. Munro, *The United States and the Caribbean Republics*, 219; Ashby, *The Spearless Leader*, 210–211.

55. Mercer G. Johnston to Harry Emerson Fosdick, Apr. 16, 1927, box 53, Johnston Papers.

56. Mercer G. Johnston to Basil Manly, Mar. 25, 1927, *ibid*.

57. This quotation is from Governor Smith's reply to an open letter by Charles C. Marshall, a prominent attorney, who questioned whether a Catholic president would be independent of the Vatican. See Charles C. Marshall, "An Open Letter to Governor Smith," *Atlantic Monthly* 139 (Apr. 1927), 540–549, and Smith's rebuttal, "Catholic and Patriot: Governor Smith Replies," *ibid*. (May 1927), 721–728. The passage referring to Mexico can be found in a campaign biography, Norman Hapgood and Henry Moskowitz, *Up from the City Streets: Alfred E. Smith, A Biographical Study in Contemporary Politics* (New York: Harcourt, Brace and Co., 1927), 316–317.

58. Mercer G. Johnston to Norman Thomas, Mar. 29, 1927; Norman Thomas to Mercer G. Johnston, Mar. 30, 1927; J. A. H. Hopkins to Mercer G. Johnston, Mar. 30, 1927; Mercer G. Johnston to J. A. H. Hopkins, Apr. 21, 1927; and J. A. H. Hopkins to Mercer G. Johnston, Apr. 26, 1927, box 53, Johnston Papers.

59. John F. Moors and Mercer G. Johnston, form letter, May 9, 1927, box 54, Johnston Papers; and Ellis, *Republican Foreign Policy, 1921–1933*, 256.

60. John F. Moors to Mercer G. Johnston, May 16, 1927, box 54; Mercer G. Johnston to John F. Moors, May 18, 1927; Newton D. Baker to Mercer G. Johnston, May 18, 1927; Mercer G. Johnston to Newton D. Baker, May 29, 1927; Mercer G. Johnston to John F. Moors, June 11, 1927; and Mercer G. Johnston to Burton K. Wheeler, Aug. 1, 1927, *ibid*.

61. Congressman J. Mayhew Wainwright to Mercer G. Johnston, May 23, 1927, *ibid*.

62. *Good Neighborship* (publication of the National Citizens' Committee) 1:1 (July 1927); telegram, George W. Norris to St. Louis *Post-Dispatch*, July 30, 1927, box 54, Johnston Papers; *Good Neighborship* 1:2 (Aug. 1927), 1:3 (Sept. 1927), boxes 55, 70, Johnston Papers.

63. William E. Borah to Oswald G. Villard, Jan. 17, 1928, and Oswald G. Villard to William E. Borah, Jan. 20, 1928, Villard Papers.

64. *Good Neighborship* 1:5 (Mar. 1928), box 70, Johnston Papers; and Munro, *The U.S. and the Caribbean Republics*, 246–247.

65. Mercer G. Johnston to Harry M. Aubrey, Apr. 23, 1928, box 56, Johnston Papers.

66. *People's Business* 2:6 (June 1927), PLS Papers.

67. *Ibid.*, 2:5 (May 1927). Pete Daniel, *Deep 'n As It Come: The 1927 Mississippi River Flood* (New York: Oxford Univ. Press, 1977).

68. *People's Business* 2:7 (July 1927), PLS Papers.

69. Joan Hoff Wilson, *Herbert Hoover: Forgotten Progressive* (Boston: Little, Brown and Co., 1975), 121; Mercer G. Johnston to Robert M. La Follette, Jr., July 10, 1927, box 54, Johnston Papers.

70. *People's Business* 2:8 (Aug. 1927), PLS Papers.

71. *Ibid.*, 2:9 (Sept. 1927); 2:10 (Oct. 1927).

72. *Ibid.*, 2:10 (Oct. 1927).

73. *People's Business* 2:4 (Apr. 1927), PLS Papers.

74. Mercer G. Johnston to William V. Mahoney, Oct. 21, 1927, box 55, Johnston Papers.

75. J. A. H. Hopkins to Mercer G. Johnston, Oct. 31, 1927, *ibid.*

76. Minutes of the Executive Committee of National Progressive Headquarters, Nov. 3, 1927, box 30, *ibid.*

77. Mercer G. Johnston, form letter, to members of the Progressive National Committee, Jan. 3, 1928, *ibid.*; see also Mercer G. Johnston to Richard Hogue, Nov. 23, 1927, and Dec. 24, 1927, box 55, *ibid.*

78. Lowitt, *George Norris*, 362.

79. National Popular Government League Bulletin #115, "Who's Who in the Super-Lobby in Washington and Out," Nov. 25, 1927, King Papers.

80. *People's Business* 3:2 (Feb. 1928), PLS Papers.

81. G. Cullom Davis, "The Transformation of the Federal Trade Commission, 1914–1929," 49 (Dec. 1962), *Mississippi Valley Historical Review*, 437–455, and Lowitt, *George W. Norris*, 282–283; 360–361.

82. *People's Business* 2:12 (Dec. 1927), PLS Papers; "Status of the Power War," National Popular Government League, Jan. 28, 1928, King Papers.

83. *People's Business* 3:2 (Feb. 1928), PLS Papers.

84. *Ibid.*, 3:7 (July 1928).

85. *Ibid.*, 3:5 (May 1928).

86. Harry Slattery to George W. Norris, May 23, 1928, box 60, King Papers.

87. Paul S. Clapp to officers and directors of the National Education Association, June 29, 1928, box 56, Johnston Papers.

88. "Save-Our-Schools Committee," Bishop Francis J. McConnell, chairman; John Dewey, first vice chairman; and Mercer G. Johnston, secretary; to J. W. Crabtree, secretary, National Education Association, Oct. 22, 1928, *ibid.*

89. Victor Whitlock to Philip H. Gadsden, approximately May 1928, Villard Papers. *The U.S. Daily*, headed by conservative journalist David Lawrence, was intended to be an impartial source of information for members of Congress.

90. Victor Whitlock to Oswald G. Villard, May 31, 1928, and Villard to Whitlock, June 5, 1928, *ibid.*

91. Mercer G. Johnston to Henry Moskowitz, June 30, 1928, box 56, Johnston Papers.

92. Harry A. Slattery to John P. Grace, July 11, 1928, Slattery Papers.

93. Mercer G. Johnston to George W. Norris, Sept. 12, 1927, box 55, Johnston Papers.

94. George W. Norris to Gifford Pinchot, July 14, 1928, box 60, King Papers.

95. *People's Business* 3:8 (Aug. 1928), PLS Papers.

96. Mercer G. Johnston to Katherine Johnston, Sept. 10, 1928, box 26, Johnston Papers.

97. *People's Business* 3:10 (Oct. 1928), PLS Papers.

98. Lowitt, *George W. Norris*, 411–412; Mercer G. Johnston to Frank P. Walsh, chairman of the Progressive League for Alfred E. Smith, Sept. 15, 1928, box 56, Johnston Papers.

99. Progressive League for Alfred E. Smith, form letter, Sept. 16, 1928, *ibid.*

100. Amos R. E. Pinchot to John J. Raskob, Oct. 9, 1928, box 136, Amos Pinchot Papers.

101. National Popular Government League, Bulletin #122, "The Power War and the Presidential Candidates: The Power Records of Hoover and Smith," Oct. 11, 1928, King Papers.

102. John H. Holmes to Amos R. E. Pinchot, Oct. 17, 1928, box 51, Amos Pinchot Papers and Holmes to Mercer G. Johnston, Oct. 16, 1928, box 56, Johnston Papers.

103. John H. Holmes to Amos R. E. Pinchot, Oct. 19, 1928, box 51, Amos Pinchot Papers.

104. Amos R. E. Pinchot to John H. Holmes, Oct. 18, 1928, *ibid.*

105. Mercer G. Johnston to John H. Holmes, Nov. 2, 1928, and Mercer G. Johnston to Edward Bieretz, Nov. 2, 1928, box 56, Johnston Papers.

106. John H. Holmes to Mercer G. Johnston, Nov. 5, 1928, *ibid.*

107. *People's Business* 3:11 (Nov. 1928), PLS Papers.

108. George L. Record to Oswald G. Villard, Nov. 7, 1928, box 1, and Record to Villard, Nov. 21, 1928, Howard Yolen Williams Papers, Minnesota Historical Society, hereinafter cited as Williams Papers.

109. Mercer G. Johnston to Henry Moskowitz, Dec. 1, 1928, box 56, Johnston Papers.

110. John H. Holmes to Mercer G. Johnston, Nov. 5, 1928, *ibid.*

111. Benjamin C. Marsh to Harry W. Laidler, Dec. 13, 1928, box 1, Williams Papers.

112. Constance Todd to Paul H. Douglas, Oct. 21, 1928, *ibid.*

VIII

Rehearsal for Reform

At one time or another, we have heard or uttered George Santayana's famous observation that those who cannot remember the mistakes of the past are condemned to repeat them. The progressives who attended the December 15, 1928, conference in New York City were particularly sensitive to the historic nature of their meeting. Predisposed by training and custom to draw lessons from the past, these reformers concluded that the results of the recent election left "progressively spirited Americans with no satisfactory political alternatives." Though many were veterans of past campaigns and conscious of their own and predecessors' failures, few doubted the need for a national political realignment. Their current thinking and future direction was evident in the names—"Third Party League," "Labor Party League," "Political Education Society," "American Fabian Society"—they considered for this new political organization. The name they finally chose, the League for Independent Political Action (LIPA), clearly revealed their intention while leaving the party's actual creation to later developments.

Though cautiously launched as a clearinghouse and resource agency for existing liberal groups, the activists who headed the emerging movement, such as economist Paul H. Douglas and social evangelist Kirby Page, were eager to consider tactics, strategy, and platform planks for a new political party. Douglas, in particular, argued that the two major parties' "almost complete identity of opinion . . . on fundamental economic questions" rendered their distinctions "virtually nonexistent." He dismissed the possibility of "economic liberals" ever capturing control of the Democratic party and called upon "economic progressives" to build a new party along the lines of the British Labour Party. Such a party would reject laissez-faire; emphasize national economic planning, income redistribution, and democratic management of industry; and call upon the federal government to guarantee unemployment, old age and health insurance, and provide public works programs, employment exchanges, and a decent minimum wage. Labor would be freed from the legal restrictions imposed by yellow-dog contracts, injunctions, and prohibitions against picketing and boycotting. Farmers would be assisted through a lower tariff on manufactured goods, government-sponsored cooperatives, adequate farm credits, and disaster insurance. The league's initial draft of principles also included a strong interest in foreign policy. Disarmament, peace, and American participation in an international organization committed to the outlawry of war were endorsed as was a more humane and just policy in the Caribbean.[1]

There was little in Douglas's statement that seemed new; progressives and laborities had been espousing many of the same concerns for more than a generation. The fact that these calls remained familiar but unfulfilled was proof that a party based upon such goals faced innumerable obstacles, not the least of which was liberal impatience with the slow, unrewarding aspects of party-building. Douglas believed such a party could be formed but only if the country's small yet discordant left-wing elements—socialists, progressive farmers, middle-class liberals, and unorganized workers—were able to cooperate.

It did not take long for disagreement to surface as a reminder of progressive contentiousness. One week after the initial organizational gathering, John C. Bennett, a faculty member at Union Theological Seminary, wrote Kirby Page protesting that the Douglas statement presented "a very one-sided picture" in its intimation that LIPA members were unanimously behind a third-party venture. In fact, several participants, including John Dewey, Paul Kellogg, and Harry F. Ward, initially urged cooperation with sympathetic elements in the major parties. Others doubted whether there were enough liberal voters to sustain "an exclusive sectarian attitude" that ignored progressive realignments in the older parties.[2] Progressives outside the LIPA echoed similar concerns. People's Legislative Service director Mercer G. Johnston admitted that his organization, which was equally dependent upon fragile left-wing cooperation, was experiencing severe difficulties without organized labor's financial support.[3]

The union movement's indifference reflected a strong suspicion of liberals' third-party machinations, but it also revealed a bitter internal struggle within the labor community. Following the abortive La Follette campaign, the AFL positioned itself squarely within the nation's political center. Its leaders disavowed independent political action and directed their efforts at securing job security, higher wages, shorter hours and better working conditions, the unexceptionable but proven tenets of "pure and simple unionism." The federation championed craft unions and skilled workers. It represented tradition and respectability and eagerly identified labor with the status quo. Dissatisfaction with such policies coalesced around the left-liberal faculty at Brookwood Labor College, a residential coeducational training center for labor activists. These labor progressives urged independent political action and the organization of unskilled workers in America's mass-production industries.[4] Following the lead of Brookwood's director, ex-minister and labor organizer A. J. Muste, labor progressives pursued a vigorous, occasionally militant, and consistently reformist attack upon conservative trade unionism. While AFL President William Green struck the pose of a labor statesman and decried calls for industrial unionism, Muste and his supporters engaged in guerrilla warfare aimed at achieving a militant, radicalized labor movement. In February 1929, Muste publicly challenged the AFL to pursue industrial unionism and independent political action. He courted a broader audience with calls for old age and unemployment insurance, recognition of the Soviet Union, and condemnation of America's military and imperialistic adventures. This manifesto, which appeared in *Labor Age*, a socialist journal and voice of labor militancy, bears a striking similarity to Paul H. Douglas's draft of LIPA goals which had been released less than three months earlier.[5] Moreover, both Muste and Brookwood board member James H. Maurer were intimately linked with the league. Muste served on the LIPA executive committee while Maurer would soon be chosen one of the league's vice-chairmen. For one of the very few occasions since the Armistice, independent progressives and their labor colleagues seemed to be moving in the same direction toward compatible goals.

While the dream of a liberal-labor alliance appeared to be taking tangible form, there were still some progressives who questioned the wisdom of reducing the pool of potential supporters to a homogeneous nucleus. Why, Paul Kellogg asked, should "a small like-minded bunch of people . . . close the door at the start to the great belt of fairly independent, fairly dissatisfied people whom they want to muster into a new formation?" He did not discount the ultimate value of a third-party movement but emphasized the preliminary steps necessary to build a following. An extensive program of research and education had to be undertaken to crystallize the movement's purpose in the public mind. Legislators had to be converted, bills proposed in Congress, and candidates supported "whatever their party tags" before trying out "the muscle of the independents." Kellogg believed that decisions made by newcomers convinced by LIPA action and practice would be vastly different from decisions made by the handpicked group (mostly socialists, he added) who attended the first league meeting. The important thing was to keep all avenues open. "Whether the decision then would be for a third party, for merging with the socialists . . . or for joining hands with . . . an insurgent group split off from . . . the old parties, would be on the laps of the gods.'"[6] As labor historian Nathan Fine put it, when the "big parade [forms] some day . . . it is just as well that all the groups criss-cross. . . . We'll all have to take a hand and find out in trying and doing."[7]

An "open door" policy, however, presented its own problems. Socialists, who had been attracted by the LIPA's third-party emphasis, naturally believed their own party offered the best hope for independent political action. Many liberals, however, disliked what they perceived to be the Socialist party's "rigid philosophical dogma."[8] Men such as Oswald G. Villard, a "Wilson Democrat" who traced his liberal faith back to the halcyon days of Grover Cleveland, considered the very word "socialist" a barrier to progress.[9] Though put off by the LIPA's socialist connection, Villard remained a strong third-party advocate. Other progressives, less enamored of independent political action, saw things much differently. Veteran third-party activist Harold L. Ickes saw nothing in the situation to warrant the "heart burnings" such a "hopeless venture" would require, nor did he believe intellectuals capable of organizing an effective political party.[10] Another experienced reformer, onetime muckraker Ray Stannard Baker, then at work on his six-volume biography of Woodrow Wilson, also saw "no hope in a new party." Liberals, he believed, would be more effective working within the Democratic party.[11] North Dakota Farmer-Labor leader William Lemke voiced the feelings of many agrarians who had grown weary of social and political movements. "The outs want to be in," he noted, "and when they get in they are just about as bad as the ins." Still, he, too, favored taking over the Democratic party "on the theory that if we have not got sense and courage to take over the machinery of one of the old parties and make a progressive party, then we cannot establish and maintain a new party."[12] Then, of course, there were the cautiously enthusiastic veterans of progressive campaigns past. Notable among this group was Amos Pinchot who, though "heartily sympathetic" with the new movement, waited to see if it was founded upon "a dominant issue." He felt that all previous attempts "to line progressive people up behind leadership that was prolific in aspiration, but barren as to a dominant issue . . . has been nothing short of tragic."[13] To suggest, therefore, that there was a consensus on the third-party issue would be misleading.

In late May 1929, six months after its initial meeting, the LIPA officially entered public life with the announcement that philosopher-activist John Dewey had agreed to serve as national chairman. Other elected officials included the four vice chairmen: Paul H. Douglas, one of the movement's driving forces; W. E. B. Du Bois, editor of the NAACP organ, the *Crisis*; writer Zona Gale, a veteran of the American Union Against Militarism; and the longtime labor and Socialist party leader, James H. Maurer. Other prominent members of the inner circle were Oswald G. Villard, treasurer; Socialist party presidential candidate Norman Thomas (until his resignation in March 1931); Devere Allen, associate editor of the *Nation* and formerly editor of the *World Tomorrow*; theologian Reinhold Niebuhr; and League for Industrial Democracy executive director Harry W. Laidler. Howard Y. Williams, a former St. Paul Unitarian minister, social activist, and congressional and mayoral candidate of the Minnesota Farmer-Labor party, was chosen as executive director.[14]

During the same week that the LIPA's independent liberals announced plans to promote realistic alternatives to the nation's political and economic policies, labor progressives were making their own break with the trade union establishment. At an invitation-only conference on May 25–26, 1929, over 150 trade unionists, socialists, and liberals gathered in New York City. Under A. J. Muste's direction, and with *Labor Age*'s new editorial policy as basis for discussion, the participants created the Conference for Progressive Labor Action (CPLA) to promote industrial unionism, independent political action, and fundamental change within the AFL.[15] The distance which separated the CPLA from the AFL paralleled the LIPA's differences with major party liberals. Not surprisingly, both groups shared similar weaknesses and inadequacies. Neither organized labor nor Democratic and Republican liberals welcomed another progressive splinter group which threatened their already tenuous existence. The LIPA and CPLA had no real constituency or base of support, and while each seemed adept at organizing, such efforts sent them spinning off in competing, counterproductive pursuits. Despite shared experiences and interests in economic and social change, there was no certainty that the LIPA's independent liberals and the CPLA's labor progressives would ever agree on the constructive, practical steps necessary for achieving their grandiose vision. Though joined by common ties to the political left, they remained within their own comfortable circles emerging from their separate cocoons to engage the rest of the world. When they did venture forth, they eyed each other just as cautiously as they did their more conservative opponents.

During the four months which followed the LIPA's and CPLA's entrance into the public arena, the indicators of industrial activity and factory production had peaked and had begun their downward slide. The stock market crash provided the contemporary backdrop as members of America's liberal community informally gathered to discuss the league's proposals. Though John Dewey's statement of principles, announcing the LIPA's creation, had been drafted prior to the crash, the events of Black Thursday injected a special urgency to his call for a far-reaching political realignment to match the economic turmoil overtaking the nation. The program, which closely followed Paul H. Douglas's original proposals ten months earlier, emphasized the need for unemployment, old age and health insurance, public works spending, farm credit, guarantees of civil liberties, consumer and producer cooperatives, democratic control of industry, and income redistribution.[16] Though these proposals spoke to the realities of American life, they evoked little reaction. Thoroughly familiar to most followers of liberal and labor politics, they placed the LIPA far in advance of most Americans including most intellectuals, who evinced little immediate concern for the economic survival of the nation. The most remarkable aspect of the Wall Street collapse was the negligible impact it initially had on American behavior and thinking. It was not surprising that the intellectuals' response was so tepid. Liberal journals such as the *Nation* and *New Republic* seemed unusually reluctant to probe the full meaning of the financial collapse or to express alarm at governmental inaction, yet their readers had been exposed throughout the twenties to editorials warning of the dangerously unequal distribution of wealth. It took a good year for the liberal community to sense the seriousness and dimensions of the problem.[17]

Responses to the LIPA's proposals which have survived seem quite distant in tone from the depression to follow. Herbert Knox Smith, an old Connecticut Bull Mooser, agreed in principle with the need for a new political alignment but doubted whether such a party could be created. He offered his progressive successors a sour-grapes litany of suffering, sacrifice, and recrimination designed to discourage the younger generation from following in his footsteps. "The actual cost and labor in establishing a working political machine," he wrote the league office, "is something enormous and . . . I don't believe you have got the factors to do it." Smith seemed particularly embittered at the so-called fencesitters, critics, and the intellectuals of his time "who were in favor of theoretical reform, but wholly disapproved of the men who were in the rough and tumble in trying to get it done. . . . I would not be surprised," he added gratuitously, "if some . . . in your own group were then in that class."[18]

A much different response came from A. J. Muste, the activist director of Brookwood Labor College and chairman of the CPLA. Though a member of the LIPA executive committee, Muste seemed uncomfortable with his colleagues' posturing and intellectualizing. He hoped the movement would not limit itself to the "Good Government" crowd or promote a third-party "which is just a hodge-podge of various dissenting elements, without any broad and sound economic base." He was eager to attract industrial workers, whom he considered the roots of any sound party.[19]

Norman Thomas, another executive committee member, whose extensive commitments to the Socialist party precluded an active league role, raised attention to a future trouble spot. The Socialist party was both a direct competitor with the LIPA and potentially one of its most important collaborators. He was anxious to avoid direct league interference with his party's membership drives and uneasy over the potential overlapping of functions. "The LIPA has a unifying rather than a di-versifying function," he warned Devere Allen, "or it has no function at all."[20]

The divisiveness between the Socialists and the league could not alone have blunted this ambitious movement for social change. A much more serious blow, which reflected a decade of liberal-labor mistrust, was the notable absence of support from organized labor. Barely a decade earlier, John Fitzpatrick had made the militant Chicago Federation of Labor the vanguard of the National Labor party. "In doing this," he observed, "we swept aside all the old ideas and methods of labor in politics and started off with new ideals and new standards." It was ironic that this movement's remarkable success, achieved in spite of strong condem-nation from the AFL, ultimately fell victim to Communist infiltration and conservative Red-baiting. The ideological splits between left and right had become so acute, however, that the merest hint of Communist involvement doomed cooperative action. If political liberals and labor progressives accepted Communist support, they left themselves open to Red-baiting; if they refused such assistance, they played into their opponents' hands. Thus, although Fitzpatrick welcomed the LIPA and supported its goals, he no longer was willing to expose his union to the vagaries of political life. "Some one said that 'a burned child dreads the fire,' " he wrote Howard Y. Williams, "well we are the burned child so to speak."[21] There would be no union support.

Labor's lack of enthusiasm was not surprising and mirrored the opin-ions of many disaffected third-party veterans. Ever since the 1924 La Follette campaign, which ended its temporary infatuation with inde-pendent political action, organized labor decided that real power rested in the two-party system rather than in the pie-in-the-sky dreams of politically impotent independents. This sentiment was reinforced in the spring of 1930 when the AFL joined Senate liberals from both parties to help block President Hoover's nomination of Judge John J. Parker to the Supreme Court. Parker, a Fourth Circuit Court Judge from North Car-olina, had been identified with antilabor injunctions, the yellow-dog contract, and racial views approving the exclusion of blacks from the political process. Both the AFL and the NAACP successfully mobilized a bipartisan progressive coalition to block the nomination. Routine expressions of support and cooperation were forthcoming from the Peo-ple's Legislative Service and other liberal lobbying groups, but the LIPA was not involved, and with good reason.[22] The league had made a point of separating itself from insurgents in the major parties, including such potentially powerful friends as Senate Judiciary Committee Chairman George W. Norris, and of establishing new priorities based upon in-dependent political action. None of these factors endeared the league to organized labor, which confined its own nonpartisan political support to major party candidates. Most union leaders dismissed all other arrangements as exercises in intellectual futility.

The LIPA's call for a new party also stirred considerable unrest and anxiety among progressive officeholders. These reform mavericks had sufficient difficulties within their own parties without the added burden of a three-way struggle. In some states major party insurgents feared that their opponents might use the LIPA movement to split the liberal vote. This appears to have been true of Montana Democrat Thomas J. Walsh, who expressed misgivings about the formation of a local LIPA chapter in Butte. "While we have not at all times agreed upon matter of public concern," the senator wrote Oswald G. Villard, "I feel quite sure you would not become a party knowingly to any such purpose... and that... you would see no profit to the public in displacing me here."[23] Villard and other league founders considered such alarm a sure sign of progress. They pacified Walsh, however, by assuring him that the LIPA would not enter Montana during his reelection campaign.[24]

Though the league's actions appear properly circumspect in dealings with major party liberals, in public its pamphlets and news releases were unequivocally clear: it would not condone "incipient flirtation with Republican and Democratic machines," nor would it approve "the outworn and fruitless method of supporting 'good men' " within the major parties.[25] In theory, these sentiments were fine and no less so for being acted upon cautiously. But it was obvious that the league could not maintain this double-edged (or two-faced) policy for long. On the one hand, many progressives remained unconvinced that the time was auspicious for a new political alignment; while major party liberals questioned the efficacy of undermining credibility and influence it had taken them years to develop. The danger, as one progressive put it, was that the LIPA's leadership would find itself "a band of officers without soldiers."[26] League spokesmen such as John Dewey, Paul H. Douglas, and Howard Y. Williams did not believe they were cutting their own throats by ignoring major party liberals. They understood, however, that their movement had to move beyond the shadow of congressional progressives to establish its own identity. To that end they exerted every effort and concentrated their financial resources in behalf of third-party candidates. In Minnesota, the league endorsed the Farmer-Labor party ticket, and in Milwaukee and New York City, LIPA funds assisted Socialist party candidates. In Buffalo and Niagara Falls, New York, and New Bedford, Massachusetts, local LIPA chapters endorsed trade unionists and progressives running on third-party tickets. In all instances the league hoped that successful local and statewide movements would be a positive stimulus toward a "new political alignment on a national scale."[27] There is little doubt, however, that at this early stage, the league, rather than those it endorsed, was the chief beneficiary. Success, however, did not come cheaply. Though a nonprofit organization, the league charged a three-dollar membership fee and depended heavily upon generous member patrons such as Oswald G. Villard; Sherwood Eddy, the international secretary of the YMCA; and outside donors such as William T. Rawleigh, each of whom contributed $1,000 toward the 1930 budget. But $15,000 was needed to finance these various campaigns; the rank and file could not make up the difference, and with unemployment reaching the seven million mark, money was tight and in demand for many equally deserving causes.[28]

Two years after its inception the LIPA stood at an impasse. Its calls for national economic planning and a new political alignment were widely acclaimed but seldom acted upon. It had alienated some of its strongest liberal supporters and had failed to progress beyond the elite intellectual forum from which it had hoped to emerge. Economic conditions were worsening, criticism of President Hoover was growing, and something more was needed to get the league off dead center. That something, the league hoped, would be a letter from John Dewey to George W. Norris, released to the press on Christmas Day, 1930, which called upon the Nebraska senator to leave the GOP and lead a third-party movement. The Dewey-Norris exchange, particularly the senator's refusal to come out for a new party committed to social and economic planning, was front-page news throughout the country. The *New York Times* seemed especially pleased with Norris's rebuff and with the overwhelmingly negative response to the LIPA proposal. "If Professor Dewey has been reading editorial comments . . . brought forth by his suggestion," the *Times* smugly observed, "he knows that his idea fares no better with the press than with the Insurgents at Washington."[29]

If the Dewey invitation had done nothing more than generate publicity, the league would have considered it a success, but it did much more. Norris linked his refusal to lead a third party with a call for the elimination of the electoral college, an institution, he argued, which favored the two major parties at the expense of independent candidacies. The senator, however, did not address the specifics of the league's economic program. Judging from correspondence among LIPA leaders, few expected Norris to accept their invitation. His refusal, however, enabled them to release another statement explaining their program and making it part of the public debate.[30] Within days after the Dewey-Norris exchange, the league announced that a conference of economists would meet in early January 1931 to prepare a "practical plan . . . based upon social planning and control . . . in the interest of workers of hand and brain." Underconsumption was the temporary source of distress, noted Howard Y. Williams, but the underlying cause of the nation's problems was a "maldistribution of wealth and [a] policy favoring invested property at the expense of the consumer."[31]

The league's publicity blitz also produced some unintended conse-quences. A. J. Muste, a member of the national executive committee, CPLA chairman, and advocate of a class-based party, resented the over-tures to Senator Norris, whom he considered a symbol of liberal capi-talism. "A loosely constructed party with a nice program, built around a few prominent individuals," he contended, "will get us nowhere."[32] Flirting with men like the senator damaged the LIPA's credibility as an agent of fundamental social change. Muste's bitterness reflected his own organization's courtship of the liberal establishment. In much the same fashion as the LIPA, the CPLA had tried to broaden its base of support. Its rhetoric became less strident and less offensive to middle-class ears; the emphasis on news releases stressed working within the system to meet immediate problems. Correspondence with third-party activists such as Oswald G. Villard and William T. Rawleigh underscored the CPLA's interest in "rallying . . . all the progressive and liberal elements in the nation."[33]

The highlight of the CPLA's moderate strategy came in June 1930, with the announcement of a nationwide campaign in behalf of unem-ployment insurance and a shorter work week. Placing themselves within the mainstream of American liberalism, CPLA members lobbied state legislators to support their model bill which was patterned after that of the American Association for Labor Legislation; they staged rallies and a cross-country automobile trip to publicize their campaign and joined with other left-liberal groups to support Senator Robert F. Wagner's introduction of a national unemployment insurance bill in December 1930.[34] The CPLA's flirtation with traditional middle-class reform barely lasted eight months. Its leaders discovered that acquiring temporary respectability did not prove particularly gratifying. Hobnobbing with academics, social workers, and legislators might help win foundation grants, but it did not move CPLA goals further along. Moreover, sup-porting state and federal legislation and staging street corner rallies had little to do with the organization's primary aims of fighting for industrial unionism and an independent labor party. Organized for the purpose of being an active, militant minority, Muste believed the CPLA func-tioned best outside the liberal consensus. Such a separation required distancing his organization from the LIPA, and Muste knew where to start. He made it clear that the nation needed a labor party built from the ground up that would stand for industrial democracy, a planned economy under workers' control, and social ownership of national re-sources. When such a party developed its own vitality and working-class leaders, he predicted that prominent political figures would join "without being ceremoniously invited to do so. This was very different," Muste lectured LIPA leaders, from "seeking after Messiahs who are to bring down a third party out of the political heavens."[35]

The league received a somewhat different but equally troublesome comment about third-party politics from Norman Thomas. The Socialist party leader considered it ridiculous for such men as Norris and Robert M. La Follette, Jr., to think that they could function as individuals regardless of party labels. The real question was whether major party insurgents would help build a new political movement. Even if they did, however, Thomas was not sure what kind of a party it would be or whom it would represent. Several commentators pointed to the potential conflict arising from a coalition of western farmers, urban laborers, and middle-class intellectuals. If prohibition was removed as a potential source of discord, these groups still were bound to disagree over tariff protection and farm subsidies which affected the price of food and raw materials. "The moral of all this," Thomas told socialist readers of the *New Leader*, "is that . . . we may not indiscriminately assume that everybody is progressive who attacks Hoover or that any and every type of third party is one which we can support."[36]

By the spring of 1931, the LIPA's third-party idea was no closer to fulfillment than it had been two years earlier. Neither organized labor, major party progressives, nor Washington's liberal lobbying groups seemed particularly interested in embracing independent political action. Progressives were not insensitive to the steadily deteriorating economic conditions or to the resulting personal tragedies. Realistically, however, few believed that another party would make an immediate difference. Rather than waste time, money, and energy on another lost cause, most liberals adjusted their expectations to attainable goals. This kind of thinking brought close to 200 reformers to Washington on March 11–12, 1931, for a Progressive Conference. Sponsored by a bipartisan coalition of Senate liberals and endorsed by all of the lobbying organizations except the LIPA, which was not invited, participants hoped to develop a legislative agenda around the issues of unemployment, industrial stabilization, utility regulation, farm credit, tariff protection, and representative government.[37] Resolutions were passed calling for unemployment relief and insurance, public works and anti-injunction legislation, tariff reduction and corrupt practices reform, as well as two of Senator Norris's pet proposals for abolition of the electoral college and a lameduck amendment changing both inauguration day and the first session of Congress from March to January. The conference may have been more notable for what it did not accomplish. Participants were unable to agree upon a coherent antidepression program and left Washington no more unified than when they first arrived.[38] The conference's senate sponsors were partly responsible for this situation. Having promised everyone that third-party action did not lurk in the background, they went out of their way to avoid any attempts at formalizing the group into a permanent organization. Beyond sharing Senator Norris's views that a Hoover administration doomed passage of any progressive legislation and that the country needed "another Roosevelt in the White House," participants left empty-handed.[39]

Historians and contemporaries alike have found it easy to castigate progressives for failing to solve the depression's problems. Given the gravity of the situation and the misery and hopelessness which pervaded the lives of millions, it is understandable how people's expectations exceeded liberal accomplishments. Progressives, of course, were convinced that the public overestimated their influence and demanded more than any mortal could provide. "One of the most difficult tasks in the capacity in which we serve here," noted Senator Gerald P. Nye, "is that to which friends subject us day after day."[40] George W. Norris seemed to have been particularly overwhelmed by requests, demands, and favors which taxed his patience and strength to the breaking point. On more than one occasion the senator suffered hours of depression, which left him despondent and his friends "dreadfully worried." Writing to Burton K. Wheeler in April 1930, Oswald G. Villard described a "perfectly extraordinary memorandum" which Norris had shown him. "I am being killed by my friends," Norris wrote. "I have pleaded with them in vain to let me live, but it seems to me as though the end is almost here, I am nothing but a living shell—a nervous wreck." The senator recounted all-night walks on the streets of Washington and physical exhaustion which interfered with his work. "Others take vacations—go away for a few days—rest up. I am not able to do that. I am here and the work goes on day and night. I have almost reached the point of explosion and yet to all outward appearances I am in the pink of condition."[41]

The depression and frustration which prompted Norris's memorandum was the response of an overworked and underappreciated public servant. The LIPA's leaders experienced their own frustration and despair, but it was hardly attributable to constant demands upon their time. The Progressive Conference's modest accomplishments brought an added burden for league activists. Though liberal critics praised the attention accorded national economic planning, (a long-standing LIPA concern), the absence of interest in independent political action, the league's primary goal, made a third-party movement highly unlikely in the immediate future. Still, however improbable, league officials worked out a scenario in which the Democrats would nominate a conservative such as General Electric's Owen D. Young for the presidency, forcing major party liberals to form a third party rather than accept the choice of a Hoover-Young campaign. The LIPA's executive secretary, Howard Y. Williams, did not believe a progressive could be elected but hoped that the expected Democratic victory would prove that voters "had nothing more to gain from conservative Democratic leadership than from conservative Republican leadership." By 1936, the third-party movement would be in a much stronger position to make an effective campaign. Few progressives, not even Williams and his league associates, placed much faith in such a development. A more likely and, from their standpoint, undesirable turn of events would have the Democrats nominate Alfred E. Smith or Franklin D. Roosevelt, neither of whom qualified in the league's judgment as "real progressives." Williams did not doubt, however, that millions of progressives and radicals would line up behind Roosevelt. After learning that Milo Reno planned to place his Iowa Farmers' Union behind FDR, Williams concluded that one of the league's first tasks in 1931 would be "to throw the searchlight on Roosevelt as a great straddler."[42]

What the league ultimately turned on the New York governor was not a searchlight but a microscope. Accusing him of trying to be all things to all people, the LIPA linked Roosevelt to the policy of dollar diplomacy through his authorship of the Haitian constitution. He was criticized for "extraordinary subservience" to Tammany Hall, condemned for his failure to fight vigorously for unemployment insurance, and chided for a public power policy which fell far short of supporting government production and distribution of electricity. Such criticisms always were followed by comments of grudging admiration for his honesty and an admission that he was "one of the better men in the two old parties."[43] Though league officials were reluctant to admit it, most liberal voters paid scant attention to left-wing critics. Traveling around the nation in the spring of 1931, Norman Thomas concluded that it would be very difficult to deny FDR the Democratic nomination. Though the Socialist party leader attributed Roosevelt's popularity to "a large amount of . . . muddle headed liberal and progressive support," he was most concerned with the dangers Roosevelt's candidacy presented. He warned the league that it could ill afford to play a neutral role in the 1932 campaign, nor should it postpone political action until after the major party conventions. Since the LIPA could not endorse a Roosevelt candidacy without compromising its own principles, and since league members would undoubtedly vote Democratic, Thomas foresaw but one option: the league should join forces with the Socialist party to build toward the 1936 election.[44]

The option of merging with the Socialists was not seriously considered because LIPA leaders wished to use their autonomy and influence to create an entirely new party devoid of the underlying stigma they believed tarnished the Socialists. With Roosevelt's nomination a growing certainty, however, a new political movement embodying league principles seemed more distant a hope than ever. Still, league officials, notably Howard Y. Williams, devoted an extraordinary amount of time lobbying among potential third-party supporters, urging them to refrain from endorsing FDR's candidacy. Williams's prize target was the Minnesota Farmer-Labor party, the group he knew best, whom he envisioned as the vanguard of a movement that would turn its back on the old parties and help lay the foundations for a coalition representing "the farmers and the workers of brain and hand."[45] Excluding the jargon, however, Williams's as yet unborn party would also advocate a more equitable distribution of wealth, public ownership of natural resources and utilities, unemployment insurance, old age pensions, tax increases on income and inheritances, a decent minimum wage, workers' right to organize, anti-injunction legislation, tariff reduction, and government assistance for cooperative marketing, purchasing and credit. In short, whatever the name of this new party, its platform would embody the LIPA program.[46]

In the six months immediately following the March 1931 conference, progressives engaged in intensive discussion concerning the best ways to combat the depression's worsening condition. In some respects, this internalized exchange of ideas was a necessary preliminary to the 1932 campaign, but it also helped establish the parameters of legislative action during the last year of what many hoped would be Hoover's one-term presidency. With unemployment rising, bread lines lengthening, and suffering visibly etched in the faces of the American people, progressives took their case to the president and the public. Conditions alone were sufficient evidence of the widespread public despair and dissatisfaction with Hoover's antidepression program. Yet, as the human dimension of the tragedy unfolded, it seemed that the public's increasingly sarcastic sense of humor was being made at the president's expense. In some instances, he seemed to seek out adversity; his overly optimistic public predictions provided their own damning indictment. People living in makeshift shanty towns called "Hoovervilles," which dotted the urban landscape; or those who drove "Hoovercarts," the horse-and-mule-drawn teams pulling gasless automobiles; and those who turned their empty pockets inside out to wave "Hooverflags" could not forget the sight of the president feeding his dogs on the White House lawn or his statement to the U.S. Chamber of Commerce that "we have passed the worst."[47]

As the nation entered the second full year of the depression, the president still felt obliged to convey an upbeat, if not rose-tinted, view of the future. "Whatever the difficulties may be," he told the Indiana Editorial Association in June 1931, "we know they are transitory in our lives, and in the life of the nation." That observation prompted a bitter letter from John Dewey asking Hoover whose lives he had in mind. "Is it the lives of the ten million unemployed—and only partially employed, the millions more suffering from wage and salary cuts ... or is it the lives of the few hundred thousand whose investments are not bringing in the usual return?" Dewey, who was then the titular leader of both the People's Lobby (formerly the People's Reconstruction League) and the LIPA, warned the president that though he could ignore calls for a special session of Congress and veto needed legislation, "you cannot so easily postpone starvation."[48] The LIPA executive secretary, Howard Y. Williams, wrote the president in September that "hundreds of men and women are taking their lives every month . . . because they will not face little families that they cannot feed, and so they end their lives." He urged Hoover to call a special session of Congress and to support a three-billion-dollar appropriation bill for public works employment that would include a housing program for urban workers, road construction, river development, and the erection of electric power lines in rural regions. Funding for these projects would come from higher income and inheritance taxes on those in the upper brackets. "The issue is clear. No one in this crisis should have cake until everyone has bread."[49] Anticipating conservative objections, Benjamin C. Marsh, of the People's Lobby, accused Hoover of being the "White House lobbyist . . . of some 15,000 with incomes over $100,000 . . . who don't want taxes on their unearned incomes increased to care for the unemployed."[50]

Though progressive critics had little difficulty presenting a unified attack on the Hoover administration, they seriously disagreed as to whether unemployment relief or public works spending should be the cornerstone of their antidepression program. At one time, George W. Norris, FDR, and Senator Robert F. Wagner all favored public works programs, while Senator La Follette and Colorado progressive Edward P. Costigan led the fight for direct relief.[51] Even when major party liberals agreed on the necessity of direct federal assistance, the question remained whether that relief should take the form of an outright gift or interest-bearing loan. In addition to the objections of those who disliked any measure which placed added power in the hands of the federal government, the progressives' relief and unemployment proposals antagonized white southerners who saw these measures as opening wedges justifying future interference in their region's folkways.[52] These issues would assume the center stage of a raging congressional debate in January 1932, as House and Senate liberals responded to administration initiatives and introduced their own antidepression alternatives. Before, during, and especially after these discussions, however, most independent progressives busied themselves with their own economic and political ruminations, some of which were only tangentially related to the debate in Washington.

"There never was a time in my experience when the people were so ready for a fundamental program as they are now," George L. Record wrote Pennsylvania Governor Gifford Pinchot. The New Jersey progressive was especially upset that "nobody in . . . public life [was] offering any such program."[53] His own long-standing commitment to the abolition of privilege had been ignored, but calls for unemployment relief and public works programs awakened his older attachment to the single tax. Record was certain that widespread unemployment offered the opportunity of using idle land to put people to work. He agreed with Amos Pinchot, however, that because the "single-tax" guaranteed political defeat, the label would have to be discarded.[54] The two men were convinced, nonetheless, that "the land question must be brought up before even intelligent discussion of overproduction and unemployment can be had." It was not political senility but old-fashioned consistency which led these two veterans to reach such conclusions. With little else of any substance available, both men believed their ideas were as viable as any others. They even considered rewriting their old Committee of Forty-Eight platform adding "what is necessary to meet current demands."[55]

These two independent progressives maintained their self-respect and reputations, at least among liberal colleagues, because they were committed to promoting discussion and debate. There was nothing glamorous about such work, and rarely did they find themselves preaching to the already converted. On more than one occasion, Pinchot was forced to defend an unpopular opinion to a fellow Yale alumnus. These exchanges reveal an enormously sensitive man, worn down but not out by a lifetime of political struggle and yet neither too embarrassed to admit past mistakes nor unwilling to face future failure. "The main point which I make my apology for my existence," Pinchot wrote one former classmate, "is not that I have been right about things, but that I have tried hard to make people take an interest in public problems. . . . Nothing could be more obvious than the fact that I have had little if any success at all. The things I have been working on have generally lost out—been snowed under for the time being."[56]

Pinchot took comfort in knowing that he had often been right at the wrong time but was equally conscious of his growing political impotence. Not since the Wilson administration had independent progressives enjoyed personal access to a powerful political leader, and not since the elder La Follette's death in 1925 had they enjoyed even the illusion of importance. "It seems . . . there are only two things that we can do," Record advised his friend. "One is to cooperate as you are doing with the (Senate) Progressives, and the other is to follow my idea of trying to influence the political action of any public man whom we can reach."[57] There remained a nagging feeling which troubled many progressives about their potential influence in any major party effort.[58] Bull Moose veteran Donald R. Richberg captured the essence of this anxiety. Conservatives, he observed, could always agree on preserving the status quo, even if admitting that some of it needed change. Revolutionaries were equally capable of agreeing on the need for total change, even though admitting the virtue of some existing institutions. "But when liberal or progressive groups get together to work out an evolutionary program, the conservatives (among them) are so fearful that they will go too far and the radicals so fearful that they won't go far enough, that the total result is they wabble now forward and now backward and when the conservatives and revolutionaries get really to grips they brush the impatient liberals out of the way and have a pitched battle."[59]

Fearing that the LIPA might fall victim to this liberal dilemma, the executive committee accelerated its pursuit of a third-party campaign. In late October 1931, Howard Y. Williams invited Socialist party leaders to an informal meeting to decide whether a united third-party front was possible or if a joint Socialist party-LIPA presidential ticket was a more realistic objective.[60] The Socialists, however, had decided to stay clear of LIPA-sponsored events. Morris Hillquit advised Williams that his colleagues stood ready "to cooperate with any bona fide labor party that may spring up" but saw "no indication or promise of such a party" materializing in time for 1932. He made it clear that while the Socialists welcomed league support of *their* presidential candidate in 1932, any other third-party deliberations would "divert the attention" of the rank and file from their immediate task of supporting Norman Thomas.[61]

The left's internal squabbling, organizational weakness, and political impotence were dramatized even further when the CPLA purged its Socialist members who were not fully committed to the creation of a new labor party. This step had been coming for some time. Back in April 1931, shortly after the LIPA's offer to George W. Norris to lead a third-party movement, A. J. Muste's article, "Do We Need a New Political Party in the United States?" appeared in *Labor Age*. He insisted that a new party was necessary, that it must have a class base, that it be committed to a planned economy under worker control, that it have a "correct attitude" on industrial unionism, and that it resist the temptation of tying its fortune to "big-name" politicians.[62] He did not believe that the Socialist party could be transformed into a radical or revolutionary organization and feared that conservatives led by the "[Morris] Hillquit-Milwaukee-[*Jewish Daily*] *Forward* influence" would remain in control. [63] Since Muste also denied that the Communist party could be made into "the militant vanguard of American labor," the need for a new party remained. But first a small, elite, disciplined faction had to prepare the way. By October it was clear that those doing the most active work in the CPLA, such as executive secretary Louis F. Budenz, were essentially "revolutionists" who saw themselves as the "Political instrument for emancipating . . . American workers."[64]

These sentiments were reflected in the CPLA's revised "statement of purpose" which was released in November 1931. It committed labor progressives to militant industrial unionism and left-wing political activity; offered a labor party based on industrial workers; voiced opposition to all forms of militarism, imperialism, and discrimination; and demanded the building of a workers' republic. Interspersed throughout the jargon-laden manifesto were familiar liberal and labor proposals for national social insurance, recognition of the Soviet Union, worker co-operatives, and "genuine workers' education that does not aim to educate workers out of their class."[65] The heart of the document emphasized a new political orientation much different from the theoretical discussions which preceded the CPLA's founding just two years earlier. Whether this new militant image would be a more effective method of organizing industrial workers remained to be seen, as did the consequences of a gamble which alienated militant Socialists and moderate left-liberals, including many supporters of the LIPA.

The CPLA's intensified militance and impatience with its less radical liberal colleagues significantly limited the potential supporters for an independent political party. In the past, third-party movements (such as the 1912 Bull Moose campaign) and even those with varying amounts of labor support (such as the 1920 Farmer-Labor party and the 1924 La Follette candidacy) possessed a strong middle-class character. That was precisely what the CPLA intended to avoid, and Muste's resignation from the LIPA executive committee reflected this rejection of middle-class respectability. Rather than create a labor party in name only that would be "a bulwark of capitalism" instead of a means to eliminate it, the CPLA pledged to become a left-wing political group around which "realistic revolutionary elements" might create a new political alignment. The elements that Muste had in mind would be working-class, and their activities would not be "political" in the electoral or legislative sense but primarily organizational, promoting strikes and industrial unionism in the basic industries.[66]

By the fall of 1932, the CPLA had moved as far to the political left as possible without publicly embracing communism. Its original support for an independent labor party patterned on the social democratic elements of the British model had given way to calls for a revolutionary workers' organization. Earlier campaigns for unemployment insurance were replaced by aggressive organizing of the unemployed into local centers of militant protest.[67] The CPLA's emphasis upon action rather than education alienated potential supporters. Militant advocacy of radical political and labor policies isolated it from the trade union movement, independent liberals, and Socialists. Its leaders arrogantly turned their backs on compromise and preserved ideological purity at the expense of real achievement; isolated themselves from the LIPA and Socialist party, the two groups with whom they had the most in common; and ignored and ridiculed their liberal colleagues and thus doomed whatever slim hope may have existed for a liberal-labor alliance in 1932.

The CPLA should not be expected to shoulder the complete responsibility for such failure. Their colleagues in the LIPA displayed the same arrogance and pride in refusing to cooperate with major party liberals. They, too, ignored and ridiculed their potential allies and, by repudiating the system, ended up its victims. Convinced that they could operate outside the liberal mainstream, LIPA leaders continued to lay the groundwork for a third-party effort. John Dewey, Paul H. Douglas, and Howard Y. Williams never stopped exhorting, propagandizing, and organizing in behalf of a major realignment of the American political system. Toward that end a conference of economic experts would be held on January 9, 1932, and its recommendations announced to the public as the LIPA's "Four-Year Presidential Plan." Simultaneously, the league would sponsor a series of conferences bringing together union, farm, and progressive leaders to consider statewide action. Finally, a national convention of third-party groups was planned for the spring of 1932 to consider the problems of the upcoming campaign.[68] This flurry of activity, designed to generate maximum publicity, overshadowed the league's more realistic options. Franklin D. Roosevelt's likely nomination and the Socialist party's lukewarm interest in a new party left the LIPA with two reasonable alternatives: it might remain neutral in the national election, emphasize a grass-roots approach, concentrate on electing third-party legislators, and peak for the 1936 campaign; or it might endorse Norman Thomas as being nearest to its position and submerge its pride for the left's greater good.[69]

The league's year-ending review of 1931's major events cried out for fundamental social and political change. In a prose style that was heavy on gloom and melodrama, the situation was described as "probably the darkest in the lifetime of anyone now living . . . [indicating] the impending destruction of western civilization." Everywhere one looked— bank failures, abandonment of the gold standard, fascism, Japanese militarism—"dark failures outweighed the light." Domestically, there was "an appalling absence of reality in our politics." Over ten million Americans were out of work without an adequate government response. The only bright side was "the success of the Spanish revolution with [its] emphasis on liberty . . . and democratic processes, and the steady development of the Five-Year Plan in Russia which has conquered unemployment and brought added security to the workers." Praise for the Spanish revolution's commitment to social democracy and the Soviet Union's experiment in national planning provided a fitting and revealing backdrop to the league's much ballyhooed economic conference.[70]

More than one hundred economists, political and labor leaders, social welfare advocates, and farm spokesmen gathered in New York City on January 9, 1932. The one-day affair was divided into two sessions. The morning was devoted to the meeting of groups organized around seven major issues: unemployment; people's rights; money, banking and credit;

taxation and the tariff; agriculture; power and public utilities; and international relations. Participants had been encouraged to send suggestions to their chairmen prior to the conference who, in turn, were expected to present a tentative plan for discussion. The afternoon session was a collective meeting to review and consider each group's recommendations. The end product would be the league's Four-Year Presidential Plan, a set of proposals designed to show what could be accomplished over the next four years "if a real progressive was put into the presidency."[71]

Three weeks after the conference, the league released its plan amidst charges by John Dewey that the two major parties were "tools and servants of the forces and men who have largely brought on the crisis." Heading the Four-Year Presidential Plan were proposals recommending $250 million a year in federal relief for the duration of the emergency and an appropriation of $5.5 billion for public employment. These recommendations compare favorably with legislation proposed by Senators Wagner and La Follette that called for appropriations within the $2–5.5 billion range for public works.[72] Related league proposals, reflecting both the depression and traditional progressive goals, included calls for unemployment insurance and old age pensions (with government contributions), free labor exchanges, abolition of child labor, progressive taxes on income and inheritances, and tariff reduction and free trade (in twenty years). The league also advocated public ownership and operation of Muscle Shoals and other federal power projects, rural tax credits for debtors, reorganization of both the Federal Reserve and Postal Savings systems, and a prohibition against chain banking. The league proposed that the prohibition question be resolved through a constitutional convention where delegates might continue with the present system, provide for partial implementation exempting light wines and beer, create a system of federal liquor control under national ownership and operation, or permit state regulation. A sizable portion of the LIPA program dealt with foreign relations reflecting goals familiar to a generation of progressives. The league proposed American entry into the World Court and League of Nations (with participation confined to nonmilitary matters); recognition of the Soviet Union; Philippine independence; readjustment of war debts and reparations; repudiation of the war-guilt clause saddling Germany with sole responsibility for World War I; abolition of conscription and compulsory military training; safeguards for conscientious objectors, and a national referendum prior to any declaration of war.[73]

Though there was much in the Four-Year Presidential Plan, particularly in its antidepression proposals, anticipating the New Deal, there was also a good deal which the LIPA first endorsed at its initial meeting back in December 1928. In calling the program "the most advanced thinking that has been done in non-Socialist circles" since the Bull Moose and La Follette platforms, the *Nation*'s editors were offering an unintended comment on progressive inertia.[74] The document really served as a progress report of unfulfilled progressive goals and interests, some of which dated back to the prewar years.

Considering its target—independent liberals, third-party activists, and "leaderless" major party progressives—response to the league's program was at best mixed and in some cases hostile. Though the *Nation* and the *New Republic* bemoaned the program's absence of "a single compelling moral or economic issue," each warmly embraced the document as an essential preliminary step to any discussion of national planning.[75] Many citizens who felt strongly enough about the proposals to write the league office usually did so to expound the virtues of their own particular theories. Some progressive veterans, such as George L. Record, found the league's program offensive and impractical. "I can not conceive of a National Convention putting out this program," he wrote John Dewey, "and . . . I can not conceive of a rational campaign upon it." The New Jersey reformer objected to the platform's complexity (eighty-four recommendations), noting, as he had many times in the past, that "you can not take a hundred details to the mass of the people." He consequently dismissed the plan as one that merely "muddies the water, scatters the energy of . . . forward looking people, and confuses the public mind."[76] Another disgruntled correspondent, the local LIPA chairman from the single-tax community of Fairhope, Alabama, found nothing in the plan which distinguished the league from the major parties. What had happened to Dewey's pledge to meet the needs of socialists and single-taxers? Where was the experts' acknowledgment of the land problem? Surely, Georgists "could do better . . . than to accept such dubious and unintelligent assistance as that offered by the 'Hundred Experts' of the LIPA."[77]

Prominent Socialist politicians like Milwaukee Mayor Daniel W. Hoan refused to endorse the league program fearing that such action might divert attention from their own party's efforts to roll up "a stupendous Socialist vote."[78] Other correspondents praised the league's proposals but questioned why another party was necessary when others already were in the field. Such letters from both the influential and merely eccentric usually concluded with calls for cooperation if the league would drop its insistence upon another party, "I do wish to inform you that we already have a Third Party in the field and your views are all about the same as our platform," a Liberal party supporter wrote Dewey. Actually, however, the league shared little in common with the Liberal party save a mutual commitment to public ownership. The remainder of the latter's platform reflected the views of William Hope ("Coin") Harvey, its octogenarian presidential candidate and free silver advocate, whose "money crank" ideas had strong support in the western cities of Tacoma and Yakima, Washington.[79] Still, Howard Y. Williams corresponded with Harvey (whom he expected to join a united party movement) and with Father James R. Cox, the Pittsburgh priest who led thousands of hunger marchers to the nation's capital in January 1932. Though neither of these men's followings had much importance, the league invited the leaders of each to its national convention scheduled for July.[80]

This solicitous concern for the opinions of fringe groups was not merely evidence of the LIPA's thoroughness and attention to detail, but recognition that without Socialist party support the league would need all the friends it could muster from whatever quarter. The absence of the Socialists made the LIPA even more concerned about the role of the Minnesota Farmer-Labor party, one of the few remaining organizations left on which a national third party might be constructed. Once Minnesota Governor Floyd Olson mobilized moderate FLP support behind Governor Roosevelt, however, the league not only lost a key ally for the 1932 campaign, but the endorsement's long-term consequences would further erode left-wing militancy.[81]

The academics, intellectuals, and middle-class liberals who made up the heart of the LIPA delighted in their amateur status as politicians. Yet their attempt to disassociate themselves from the two major parties seemed to have confused purity and professionalism. In dealings with Republican and Democratic progressives and in negotiations with Socialists and Minnesota Farmer-Laborites, the league's incompetence was neither charming nor reassuring. The experts who helped draft the Four-Year Presidential Plan intended it to stimulate public discussion and serve an educational purpose. The LIPA's officials, however, seemed more preoccupied with putting a third party in the field than in promoting a serious public debate. Moreover, their public disdain for Roosevelt and refusal to work with major party liberals led to questionable political judgments. Chances for a new party depended, as the league well knew, upon a deadlocked Democratic convention and the nomination of a conservative. Alfred E. Smith's entry into the campaign early in February 1932 seemed to convince Howard Y. Williams that the Democrats might yet choose a conservative such as Maryland Governor Albert Ritchie or former Secretary of War Newton Baker. Faced with the choice of voting for Hoover or a conservative Democrat, Williams still believed that congressional progressives would bolt their own parties and unite behind a new alignment. Many people held this conviction, and Smith's early primary victories in New England lent temporary credence to a stop-Roosevelt movement.[82]

If the LIPA would have no part of a Roosevelt candidacy, quite the opposite was true of equally independent but perhaps more politically astute observers like Amos Pinchot and George L. Record. Neither of these two progressives had much influence on the future president, but their approaches and the candidate's reaction represent a textbook case in political education. "Like all really good letters," FDR wrote Record, "I put yours aside to read it over—and I have done this at least four times before finding a real opportunity to sit down and give you some of my thoughts." In this way, the governor brought his progressive colleague into the campaign, and both men benefited from the subsequent exchange. Roosevelt enjoyed being the recipient of some constructive political advice, and Record had the ear of a presidential candidate. "I agree with you, too," FDR continued, "that we have got to have a constructive program that is not based on an imitation of the Republicans or on subserviency to the same financial leaders who have brought about the present wreck." If Record would care to send along some ideas, the governor would be most interested. "It may be better to take up one subject at a time," FDR added, "because, as you know, the human mind can better grasp one thing at a time, just so long as the many things tie into a fairly concrete and understandable whole."[83] Record had been giving the same advice to unheeding politicians for over thirty years. This time, perhaps, things would be different.

A politically savvy Record wrote back in late March 1932 that conditions had changed so much since their meeting a year earlier that "there was no time to educate public opinion upon any new position, no matter how sound." Moreover, the governor's primary victories in New Hampshire and North Dakota required a more cautious policy to avoid endangering his nomination. "If that judgment is sound," he added, "then you should make as few speeches as possible and advance no new ideas or principles, but aim to emphasize what you consider the main issue." Record could not resist advancing a few ideas of his own, particularly on public power. Here he thought it wise to emphasize "the enormous stake in excessive rates which the power interests have in controlling our . . . legislatures, and particularly in having a President upon whom they can rely." Record advised caution, however, in discussing any ultimate remedy. "I consider regulation as absolute a failure as prohibition, but I would not advise your saying so at this time." On the other hand, reference to the Muscle Shoals and St. Lawrence power projects would "not unduly alarm the public mind," if the emphasis was upon the production of cheap electricity and the "experiment" in public distribution.[84]

One day after receiving Record's letter, Roosevelt heard from the other half of this unusual political alliance. Amos Pinchot was equally candid and typically less deferential in expressing his opinions. The governor was the only candidate strong enough to defeat Hoover, especially if business engineered a preelection economic revival. Pinchot unfolded an extremely informed and impassioned campaign strategy which drew heavily upon his own research for two books, "Big Business in America" and a *History of the Progressive Party*.[85] He urged Roosevelt to take advantage of the "extraordinary revival of muckraking" then portraying bankers and businessmen as "stupid, short-sighted, and incompetent" men unworthy of public trust. That perception should be combined with an emerging view of public utility companies as "hard-boiled, grasping interests" making unconscionable profits disproportionate either to their investment, production, or distribution costs. "Now, what I am getting at," Pinchot added, "is that . . . the banker with his exploitation of the public . . . and the utility magnate with his greedy and extortionate practices . . . stand out as one and the same person." The "banker-utility crowd" was the "mainstay" of the Hoover, Ritchie, Baker, and Smith candidacies and was "ready to move heaven and earth to prevent the election of a man whom they cannot own." He encouraged FDR to capitalize on growing popular hostility by portraying these interests as "malefactors of wealth, very much as TR did," holding them up to the public "as the people not merely responsible for the depression but for prolonging the depression by preying on the consumer in his hour of extreme weakness."[86]

Many times in the past, particularly in their relations with TR, Record and Pinchot had been accused of impracticality and idealism. It would be incorrect and misleading to argue that these two men had changed their views—but they had matured. They still were capable of engaging in ideological battles but were much more sensitive about maintaining their credibility with national progressive leaders. They understood that time was running out for their generation and consciously assumed a modest and more flexible public posture. They reserved their criticism and doubts for the privacy of their own studies and made every effort to appear cooperative and supportive. Their relationship with Senator La Follette, immediately prior to and following the 1924 campaign, reflected this more cautious behavior, and their letters to FDR in the spring of 1932 revealed this same mature approach. Record, who advocated an unusually strong single-tax position at the beginning and end of his political career, was a model of restraint with FDR. Even Pinchot, whose antibusiness sentiments were deemed politically dangerous by Governor Roosevelt in 1932, would see those ideas acted upon by President Roosevelt two years later.[87] The key to this episode is not that a presidential candidate admitted these men to his inner circle—he did not; nor did his advisers pay significant attention to their suggestions. One suspects that neither man held any serious illusions to the contrary. Perhaps the real key to this affair is that it occurred at all. Here were two very independent progressives, losers of more political struggles than they could recall, frequently on the periphery of power, trying to influence another generation's leaders. Roosevelt, the consummate professional, listened to them out of courtesy and respect. He made them feel that their ideas warranted consideration, and that was not an illusion but part of the give-and-take that is the lifeblood of every politician.

In many respects, the LIPA defied these very customs. Its middle-class academic and professional leaders eschewed partisanship, whether it involved amalgamation with the Socialists or cooperation with major party progressives. Independence was valued above collaboration and principle prized above compromise. These were not virtues, however, which were highly admired either in the academic or professional world. The league's disdain for "practical politics" was a repudiation of the expediency and sordidness with which its leaders associated the two-party system. If getting ahead meant getting along with special interests, the LIPA embraced impracticality. Men such as John Dewey and Paul H. Douglas believed that they were the true realists for having concluded quite early that the major parties were incapable of serving reform ends. What could be more "practical" than calling for an immediate realignment of American politics rather than waiting for some unlikely changes within the two-party system?[88] The LIPA never overcame public confusion over what it represented and where it stood. Its leaders relished portraying themselves as pragmatic, experimental, unselfish men meeting a challenge ignored by conventional politicians. The league's problem was that it did not fit into established categories. Progressives committed to the two-party system and those disillusioned with past third-party disasters found the LIPA's amateur status ominously familiar. Socialists and labor leaders, remembering liberal rebuffs in 1920 and 1924, remained suspicious of a solidly middle-class liberal and intellectual group which spent its time debating the type of society that "white collar workers want and with what groups they should affiliate."[89] While the league was eager to welcome workers' support, its proposals were not aimed in their direction. Frequent references to middle-class, white-collar professionals may have been an unintended indiscretion, but it reinforced traditional antagonisms and gained the LIPA few working-class supporters.[90] Distrust of the league's leadership was widespread and probably reflected a general hostility toward academics. "The very use of 'Dr.' " preceding John Dewey's name carried "a bad significance," observed a University of Chicago student named James D. Staver. Calling himself "another Communist casualty," Staver explained that he was withdrawing his membership and joining the Communist party because the LIPA was a bankrupt liberal movement. The only practical purpose a socialist-liberal movement could serve would be to provide a "respectable screen for more effective Communism . . . by evoking the right of free speech and so on—rights dear to the hearts of liberals and socialists, but only tools to be used by communists." If progressives and socialists could not defect to the Communist ranks en masse, they should do so individually as he had.[91] Staver's comments pointed up another side of the LIPA's dilemma. As a progressive organization on the left, it was a convenient whipping boy for major party progressives who viewed a split in their ranks as tantamount to insuring Hoover's reelection. On the other hand, the league's fashionably socialist but non-Marxist rhetoric won it no converts from the Communists and alienated Socialists whose support was essential to any serious third-party movement. If the LIPA moved closer to the latter, it risked the distinctiveness of its educational program; and if it cozied up to the Socialists without the possibility of a new third party, its very existence was in jeopardy.

The league's options were determined as much as anything else by FDR's nomination in late June. The third-party idea became less and less practical with the absolute refusal of the Socialists to participate and the Minnesota Farmer-Labor party's decision to cooperate with the state Democratic organization. Without the support of these two indispensable groups, the LIPA belatedly chose to compromise. Its executive committee endorsed the Socialists' presidential ticket headed by Norman Thomas, a onetime league member, and James H. Maurer, one of the league's original vice-chairmen. Cooperation, however, did not mean merger. The LIPA continued its nationwide educational campaign looking toward a third-party movement in 1936. It also assisted independent candidates whose positions compared favorably with its own.[92]

Perhaps the most surprising aspect of the LIPA's Cleveland convention on July 9–10, 1932, was the amount of excitement it generated though there were few surprises. Gathering together under the slogan "Jobs for the Jobless and Food for the Hungry," LIPA leaders gave the 100 delegates and 300 to 400 observers a dose of old-fashioned political rabble-rousing. Oswald G. Villard ridiculed the major parties for substituting the symbolism of the "full beer mug" for the "full dinner pail" when starvation stalked the land. Howard Y. Williams accused Republicans and Democrats of using prohibition as a "red herring" to divert attention from the real issues. "In one semi-hysterical period," noted John Dewey, "we adopted prohibition to win the war; in another time of hysteria we are going to abolish it in order to restore prosperity." It was suggestive of the league's minority party image that its leaders spent most of their time either attacking Roosevelt or Hoover. Roosevelt, in particular, had a curious fascination for these third-party liberals who were attracted by his personality but dubious of his intentions. Dewey announced that the LIPA would utilize the campaign to show "how little basis there was for the idea that FDR . . . was really progressive." The governor was a "gentleman of good, kindly, and amiable intentions," he observed, "but he lacks force. . . . I have never seen the slightest indication he has any ability to control his party." Roosevelt would lose the nomination, Villard claimed, if selection was based on "great intellectual capacity, or proved boldness in opposing issues and problems, or courage and originality in finding solutions."[93]

These observations reflected widespread skepticism of Roosevelt's qualifications, especially among prominent public spokesmen. Walter Lippmann was never allowed to forget his comment that Roosevelt was little more than a "kind of amiable boy scout. . . . A pleasant man who, without any important qualifications for the office, would very much like to be President."[94] The independent liberal view seemed to be that unless Roosevelt displayed "a vision, ardor, and courage which will amaze even his most optimistic friends," there was no reason to expect anything fundamental or significant to emerge from his election. In that case, the need for a new party which "recognizes the weakness of the present order [and] is willing to go far enough to revitalize it" was greater than ever.[95] It was much less clear, however, whether a new party reflecting LIPA goals or the Socialist party with LIPA support was the answer. For the moment, the league had no choice. Putting the best face on a bad situation, its delegates ratified the executive committee's endorsement of Thomas and Maurer and voted to call a national congress early in 1933 to create a united third party.[96]

The LIPA approached the 1932 campaign with at least three major goals. It wanted to survive Roosevelt's election as a viable and responsible voice on the left; it intended to gain the widest possible publicity for its own program; and it hoped to lay the foundation for the development of a genuine (league-dominated) third party. "I know you must feel as we do," Paul H. Douglas wrote potential contributors, "that this time of dark depression marks a virtual end of an epoch of unbridled expansion—that we must prepare to change our stride." He invited them to "join hands . . . in the fight for a new *American* party. The old parties were born and shaped as allies of an economy that has run its course and ended in the present morass of human tragedy. . . . The hour is epochal, the need desperate. Won't you join with us today?"[97]

There already were signals coming from the liberal camp, however, indicating that the league's call to action would fall on deaf ears. Even before the Cleveland convention, telegrams and letters full of hopeful enthusiasm inevitably contained regrets of nonattendance and more fundamental doubts about the efficacy of future third-party action. "I have been giving the matter . . . a great deal of thought," Fiorello H. La Guardia wrote John Dewey in late June, "and [as you know I] was one of the few strongly against disbanding after our 1924 attempt." The New York congressman believed, however, that an unprepared third party would only hamper the cause. Clarence Darrow, another nonparticipant, told Dewey that he would support an independent party "if it seemed to have any chance to make a showing, but I am afraid it will not."[98] A more troubling rejection, at least from Howard Y. Williams's perspective, was William V. Mahoney's refusal to support a third-party movement. As much as anyone, Mahoney, the new mayor of St. Paul, symbolized the Minnesota Farmer-Labor movement. He had deep roots in labor and socialist circles and had played a major role in trying to integrate farmer-laborism into the 1924 La Follette campaign, only to fall victim to communist infiltration and Red Scare tactics. He wrote, therefore, as an insider, veteran third-party activist, and as an established politician. He had no illusions that Roosevelt was a radical but believed the governor to be a practical politician with strong progressive tendencies. Like 90 percent of his fellow Farmer-Laborites, he would vote for FDR because four more years of Hoover, "would be a calamity that might precipitate a revolution." The most disturbing aspect of Mahoney's letter was not merely his resignation from the LIPA executive committee, but his unqualified rejection of the league's leaders. Though four years had elapsed since its founding, Mahoney could see little accomplishment and nothing to offer hope of any future success. Had the league done its job, he suggested, there would now have been a "powerful Farmer-Labor Party in practically every state." Instead, "all sorts of Third Party fragments [were] conducting farcical campaigns for the Presidency." Wanting no part of "such silliness," Mahoney still believed millions of progressives were waiting to be organized, but he did not expect the leadership to come from LIPA intellectuals in New York City.[99] Once again, independent progressives' much acclaimed commitment to organization and cooperation was revealed to be strikingly parochial and narrowly conceived.

Throughout the late summer and fall, league spokesmen spent as much time justifying postelection calls for third-party action as they did working to build up a big vote for Norman Thomas. "Why a separate LIPA?" was a question many voters asked, and the response always seemed inadequate. League leaders argued that the task of educating the public, particularly those "repelled by the name Socialist," could only be accomplished by a non-Socialist group. Though encouraging the Socialists' attempt to unite all progressive forces, the LIPA's self-assigned task was to win the maximum number of converts to its program as the first step toward forming a united third party.[100] League officials never pretended that their support of Thomas was anything but a temporary compromise. This independent stance, however, had immediate practical consequences that impinged upon future league success. If it adhered to a policy of noncooperation with major party progressives, then its support of independent, Socialist, and Farmer-Labor candidates would inevitably place the LIPA in opposition to prominent liberal politicians. The defeat of men such as Robert M. La Follette, Jr. or George W. Norris would, as Fiorello H. La Guardia warned, kill any chances of a third party capturing the presidency in 1936.[101] Local LIPA branches, therefore, were encouraged to back such men or, at least, to avoid outright opposition.

An equally troublesome matter stemmed from the league's identification with the Socialist party. If its objective was to attract and educate voters offended by the socialist label, what was to be gained from endorsing Norman Thomas's candidacy? The disadvantages were more clearly apparent. Supporting Thomas would automatically identify the league as socialist in leaning and eliminate some of the very voters it needed. On the other hand, the Socialists' unwillingness to participate in any future third-party movement and the unlikelihood of Thomas securing a respectable vote added further confusion to the LIPA endorsement. "Honest and brilliant as are the minds directing the present movement of the LIPA," one correspondent observed, "to follow their counsel in the present emergency, and throw away votes on a hopeless Socialist Presidential candidate, looks for all the world like a freak of momentary madness."[102]

Every third-party movement inevitably comes to grips with the "wasted vote" argument. In 1932, this was a particularly sensitive issue for the LIPA because the future success and credibility of its program depended upon Norman Thomas drawing a decent vote. The key question, Howard Y. Williams believed, was whether the Democratic party, its nominee, and its platform represented a genuine progressive alternative to the Republicans; in neither instance did he think this true. Williams's Democratic party was a bifurcated organization consisting of a conservative, utility-dominated Southern half and a machine-and-boss-controlled Northern half. He had a bit more difficulty explaining away the Democratic platform's call for federal relief and unemployment and old age insurance, but he managed to dismiss those progressive proposals as "vote catching devices." But what about FDR? Here, Williams's strong dislike for the Democratic candidate was barely disguised. No one, he noted, could stand up to the reactionary control of the Democratic party and win out. Roosevelt was a man "who wants to be liked but runs from a fight." New York had the largest number of unemployed of any state, yet the governor's response "has been pitifully inadequate and the results criminal." The best way to make your vote count, Williams argued, would be to cast it for Thomas, help build an opposition party representing farmers, workers, and "white collar folks," and eventually elect a Farmer-Labor president. Even if many progressives agreed with Williams that national economic planning was needed to bring about a more equitable distribution of wealth, most were more immediately interested in defeating Hoover than in pursuing the dream of the "co-operative commonwealth."[103]

During the campaign, the Democrats and their "progressive" supporters waged a verbal war against both the Republican and Socialist
parties and their "progressive" supporters. Eight years earlier, Coolidge
and La Follette had fought over the right to TR's Progressive mantle; in
1932, Thomas, Hoover, and Roosevelt renewed the battle with the latter
two having the most at stake. Democrats were concerned by statements
aimed at progressive Republicans intimating that there were few differences between the major party candidates. One issue in particular, public
power development, prompted Judson King's National Popular Government League (NPGL) to create a "Roosevelt Campaign Committee"
to publicize the candidates' power records. That comparison, the NPGL
hoped, would contrast the president's opposition to public development
of Muscle Shoals and the St. Lawrence project with Governor Roosevelt's
more positive positions. The league also issued campaign statements
rejecting the Republicans' "absurd claim" that Hoover was carrying out
the conservation policies of TR and Gifford Pinchot.[104] While Republicans
struggled to minimize the differences between Hoover and Roosevelt,
and Democrats worked equally hard to maximize them, it was the Socialists who had the last word. "If anyone is doubtful about the similarity
of the [two] parties," Devere Allen observed, "let him examine the way
in which each party cast its votes . . . during the last session (of Congress)." Allen, chairman of the LIPA executive committee, was running
on the Socialist ticket for the senate from Connecticut. Noting that legislators from both parties had coalesced to defeat major progressive
proposals, he dismissed the presidential election as "a great sham battle"
ending in "a friendly system of backscratching and respectable
plunder."[105]

Election results suggested that few Americans shared this view. Press
coverage of Roosevelt's overwhelming triumph over Hoover barely left
room for mention of Norman Thomas's disappointing 880,000-plus votes.
If the Socialists were upset, the LIPA appeared almost jubilant at the
outcome. Publicity releases poured out of league headquarters detailing
optimistic plans for the future. League officials were convinced that the
millions who shared their views but mistakenly voted Democratic soon
would become sufficiently disillusioned to join a new party. "It is part
of our job," John Dewey observed, "to catch these citizens on their
rebound and make them see that a New Deal . . . can be carried out only
through a new party." In the peculiar logic of defeat the league applauded the six-million-vote shift in the major party votes between 1928
and 1932 as confirmation "that faith and loyalty to the old parties [were]
disappearing."[106] Certain that neither their ideas nor organization had
really been tested, league officials were convinced that their opportunity
would come after the election. There were some signs which seemed to
bode well for the future. The Minnesota Farmer-Labor party's sweeping

statewide success, its election of four new congressmen, and third-party victories in Utah and Washington led a buoyant Howard Y. Williams to predict a united third party in place by the 1934 congressional elections.[107]

There were just as many signs indicating that all was not well, yet league officials seemed reluctant to accept that fact. No matter how much the LIPA wished to disassociate itself from the Socialists' poor showing, it could not afford to ignore the minimal support Thomas had received from organized labor and the urban working class. John Dewey was not alone in calling this a "sad commentary," but in the next breath he seemed reassured that "social workers, teachers, engineers, clergymen, [and] professional classes are with us, though they didn't vote that way." Though Dewey paid deference to the problems of farmer and laborer, his upbeat forecast for a new party still seemed dependent upon the support of the white-collar "skilled intellectual workers."[108] Such sentiments were fairly widespread throughout the liberal community. Amos Pinchot, who certainly qualified as one of Dewey's intellectual activists, had steered a wide enough course during the campaign to support Roosevelt's candidacy. Finding himself in the unaccustomed and, perhaps, uncomfortable position of being on the winning side, he offered his own postelection predictions. The country, he believed, was not headed toward either socialism or fascism, but the time had come for liberals to offer a comprehensive, clear-cut idea of the direction in which the nation should move. So often in the past liberals had finished a poor second in comparison with "both the dignified but glacial immobility of the conservative and the dramatic appeal of . . . the left wing." Yet, who else in the last generation had offered anything more constructive to the political process? Pinchot's own prescription—tariff reduction, income redistribution, free competition, unemployment relief, public works programs, civil liberties guarantees and "international friendship"—was an amalgam of familiar progressive ideas. Revived by the failure of conservatism and the need for positive action, he believed that the nation would once again turn to liberals for "progressive deeds in politics."[109]

Other progressives also came to view Roosevelt's election as an opportunity to pick up where they believed Wilson had deserted them fifteen years earlier. Like their LIPA counterparts, these independent liberals found themselves in a familiar position on the periphery of power. They were close enough to touch it, intimate enough to gain access, but destined to remain outsiders. Most had over twenty years experience in national politics; they were neither naïve nor idealistic. Few expected to have much impact upon the new administration, but many welcomed roles as the new president's conscience. "The American people did not acquiesce in our entry into the World War to make America safe for starvation," Benjamin C. Marsh wrote Roosevelt. He reminded the president-elect that the United States was the only nation

in the world with sufficient national income to provide every American
family with a decent standard of living, "if properly distributed." The
People's Lobby executive secretary, who was an old single-taxer, promised FDR that taxes on land values, income, inheritances, excess profits,
and estates would permit "both feeding the starving and balancing the
Federal Budget . . . without unbalancing the budgets of millions of American families." He dismissed as "economic agnostics" and "political ig-
noramuses" those "self-appointed spokesmen for the Democratic Party
who clownishly prate about attaining prosperity" when 2 percent of the
nation's families controlled four-fifths of the national wealth.[110] Like so
many independent liberals, Marsh had a unique capacity for rubbing
people, especially his friends, the wrong way. After lecturing Roosevelt
on the gross inequities of power and wealth in the United States, he
could not resist one last dig. "You took your well-earned vacation on
the yacht of Vincent Astor, representative of a ruling family in New
York, which has pocketed scores of millions of dollars of ground rents,
only because it and similar families have been able to control successive
state legislatures."[111] Needless to say, such gibes won Marsh few friends
in the White House.

Marsh's arrogance represented an extreme manifestation of progressive misgivings about Roosevelt that other liberals shared to a certain
degree. "I am glad to see that you are not taking things for granted, as
so many progressives are," Judson King wrote George L. Record, "and
I can assure you that your apprehensions are well grounded."[112] Just a
year earlier the New Jersey reformer had corresponded with FDR and
advised caution on all questions including the power issue. At an Albany
dinner party, however, Record had listened as the governor "presented
some ideas which . . . seemed to show a complete ignorance of economics."[113] Anxious to provide Roosevelt with a crash course in political
economy, Record discovered it was much harder to see the president-
elect than the presidential candidate, and the harder he tried the more
difficult it became. "The fact is I have no tact," he confessed. "It hand-
icaps my work in dealing with men, but I seem to be built that way."[114]

Though many progressives remained as apprehensive as Record during the four-month interregnum between Roosevelt's election and inauguration, they were soon swept up in the infectious enthusiasm
generated by the new administration. After twelve years in the wilderness, progressives had friends in Washington's inner circles, even in
the cabinet. Many things which liberals had fought years to achieve
were coming true. "It's a wonderful and encouraging thing to see how
the country responds to a brave and honest spirit in the White House,"
Amos Pinchot observed. He was pleased that Roosevelt was attacking
both the psychology of the depression and the conditions themselves,

and doing so without "highbrow explanations or oratorical thunder." He had few illusions that the country's economic woes were over; his own personal problems caused nagging concern, and yet he could not help but be optimistic. "Most of us do feel, even the pessimists, that we are on the eve of a better era in this country. Honesty and common sense at the top is what we have needed right along in business as well as in politics."[115]

Gradually, the unalloyed happiness which characterized some liberals' feelings toward Roosevelt gave way to a more balanced admiration and, in some cases, to undisguised opposition. Progressives praised the president's actions in warding off a total cataclysm and the swiftness with which the administration proposed remedial measures. But the nation's troubles were not entirely psychological. Purchasing power had to be increased and money if not wealth more equitably distributed. Pinchot remained enthusiastic and hopeful but not overconfident. "I'm all for this person Roosevelt," he wrote an old colleague. "I think he may be a great man, and certainly he is an honest and able one. But he is in a position of tremendous danger, for the simple reason that the banking crisis which he has met so well has apparently . . . sidetracked his attention from . . . major problems."[116] Other liberals refused to allow the president to be diverted for long. John Dewey kept hammering at the nation's inequitable tax system and maldistribution of wealth as major causes of unemployment and poverty. "The real hoarders today," he wrote the president, "are not alone hoarders of gold . . . they also include the few hundred corporations with twenty-billion dollars of surplus and undivided profits." Dewey thought it futile and inhumane for the government to enact relief measures and then ask those barely above the poverty level to bear most of the cost. "Redistribution of the national income through taxation is the only immediate feasible and just method to abate our depression. . . . The rights of producers transcend the claims of accumulated wealth."[117]

Shortly after the end of Roosevelt's first hundred days in office, the LIPA released a report card on New Deal progress. Considering that Congress had just enacted fifteen major pieces of legislation covering agriculture, banking, relief, public works, and regional as well as industrial planning, league spokesmen confined themselves to constructive criticism. Praise for the Tennessee Valley Authority, federal regulation of securities, and creation of the U.S. Employment Service was countered, however, with regrets over the failure to nationalize the banks, the potential weakness of the National Industrial Recovery Act's labor provisions, and the use of the military in operating the Civilian Conservation Corps camps. "This half-year reveals as no other six months in history," Howard Y. Williams observed, "that we are going to have economic planning in the world. The future will tell," he ominously added, "whether it is to be fascist planning in the interest of the few, or social planning in the interest of all."[118]

Four months was barely enough time to get accustomed to a new administration, much less one led by a man with extraordinary spiritual and mental energy who seemed to launch a new rapid-fire program every week. Still, the first hundred days were an important time in crystallizing independent progressives' views. Some like Pinchot and Record concluded that while Roosevelt's attack on the depression was genuine, it did not embody their program, and that meant all the difference to these two ideologically consistent reformers. Others like John Dewey and Howard Y. Williams, who were committed to a third party, were destined to demand more radical social change than New Dealers considered expedient. A number of scholars, notably Otis L. Graham, Jr., in his excellent study, *An Encore for Reform*, have delineated the variegated nature of the older progressives' responses to the New Deal. It seems clear that liberals did not react to the Roosevelt administration in easily compartmentalized ways. What is most striking from the perspective of the New Deal's first summer was the confusion which accompanied the exhilaration of these first hundred days. The spring of 1933 was an unforgettable time for progressives whose activism spanned the two Roosevelt eras. "We live in a queer time," Gilson Gardner wrote a friend. "I feel terribly out of touch. Most of the things that are happening I don't believe. I think results are going to be good, but I have not personally felt any of the rising tide. A friend of mine—a life-long Democrat—and a man who has supported this President, replied to my question: 'I feel as well as anyone can who has seen all the landmarks of economies and the law which I have believed in for fifty years swept away down stream.' "[119]

It was testimony to the New Deal's extraordinary impact on the nation's political climate that within four months of its launching millions of Americans were reading about and discussing programs for economic and regional planning that previously had been the province of a few hundred academics and progressive activists. Less than five years separated the first tentative steps of the LIPA and the first hundred days of the New Deal, but in that short time the nation's political agenda changed dramatically. Whether the New Deal would have evolved its solutions to the Great Depression differently had there not been constant prodding from liberal groups like the LIPA and the People's Lobby is unresolvable. One might well ask whether this was another example of academics and middle-class liberals talking to and at one another while the nation concentrated on more practical matters. Most Americans were unfamiliar with these and other progressive groups, and the percentage either acquainted with or readers of prominent liberal journals such as the *Nation, New Republic, Common Sense,* and the *World Tomorrow* was incalculably small. But for future New Dealers, government officials, labor leaders, and those interested in public service, these journals were required reading. The Roosevelt administration may not always have endorsed their views, but it could not afford to ignore them. In that respect, the independent progressives who wrote for such an audience were helping to shape the public policy that would affect the lives of millions of Americans for generations to come.

When the fifty-odd participants in the LIPA's first organizational meeting gathered in New York City in December 1928, no depression ravaged the country, and there was no New Deal to lift the flagging spirits of the people. Yet their discussions centered around proposals for national planning, income redistribution, public ownership, and government responsibility for the elderly, the unemployed, and the indigent. That it took the depression to attract public attention to these issues makes what took place before March 4, 1933, no less an accomplishment. It seems unreasonable to expect a group of progressives who rarely agreed among themselves to respond with overwhelming enthusiasm to everything New Dealers tried. It is true, of course, that only a handful of these older progressives played active roles in the New Deal. Most gradually found themselves at odds with the new administration on major policy questions. Perhaps, we should be less concerned with how they reacted to the New Deal than that they responded at all. The handful of independent progressives who operated the LIPA, the People's Lobby, and the National Popular Government League kept issues alive. They made public power, public works, and unemployment relief an important part of the political debate, and they refused to be silenced. Those progressives whose health and desire permitted them to stay politically active remained just as opinionated and just as impossible to ignore. That had always been their major role and their greatest public service.

NOTES

1. League for Independent Political Action (LIPA), box 1, Williams Papers. Several scholars have considered the importance of the league's activities on intellectual and political currents. See R. Alan Lawson, *The Failure of Independent Liberalism, 1933–1941* (New York: Putnam Sons, 1971), 39–46; Donald R. McCoy, *Angry Voices: Left-of-Center Politics in the New Deal Era* (Lawrence: Univ. of Kansas Press, 1958), 1–27; and Karel Denis Bicha, "Liberalism Frustrated: The League for Independent Political Action, 1928–1933," *Mid-America* 48:1 (Jan. 1966), 19–28.

2. John C. Bennett to Kirby Page, Dec. 23, 1928, and Kirby Page to John C. Bennett Dec. 26, 1928, box 1, Williams Papers.

3. Mercer G. Johnston to William T. Rawleigh, Jan. 9, 1929, box 57, Johnston

Papers. The People's Legislative Service ended its operations at the end of Jan. 1932; see Mercer G. Johnston to Sen. Bronson Cutting, Jan. 9, 1932, box 58, *ibid.*

4. James O. Morris, *Conflict Within the AFL: A Study of Craft Versus Industrial Unionism, 1901–1938* (Ithaca, N.Y.: Cornell Univ. Press, 1958), 89–128; Jo Ann Oiiman Robinson, *Abraham Went Out: A Biography of A. J. Muste* (Philadelphia: Temple Univ. Press, 1981), 32–48; and Charles H. Howlett, "Brookwood Labor College and Worker Commitment to Social Reform," *Mid-America* 61:1 (Jan. 1979), 47–66.

5. "The Challenge to Progressives, An Editorial Statement," *Labor Age* 18 (Feb. 1929), 3–7.

6. Paul Kellogg to Kirby Page, Jan. 9, 1929, box 1, Williams Papers. See Kellogg's refusal to join the LIPA in his letter to Howard Y. Williams, Feb. 20, 1930, box 2, *ibid.* The editor of *Survey* declined membership because of the league's refusal to admit insurgent Democrats and Republicans while welcoming Socialists and Farmer-Laborites.

7. Nathan Fine to Kirby Page, May 23, 1929, box 1, *ibid.*

8. Alfred Hayes to Kirby Page, Dec. 26, 1928, *ibid*; See also John P. Burke, president of the International Brotherhood of Pulp, Sulphite, and Paper Mill Workers to Kirby Page, Apr. 4, 1929, *ibid.*

9. Oswald G. Villard to Ray S. Baker, Apr. 17, 1929, Villard Papers.

10. Harold L. Ickes to Kirby Page, Apr. 18, 1929, box 1, Williams Papers.

11. Ray S. Baker to Oswald G. Villard, Apr. 20, 1929, Villard Papers.

12. William Lemke to Howard Y. Williams, Oct. 21, 1929, box 1, Williams Papers.

13. Amos R. E. Pinchot to Oswald G. Villard, May 14, 1930, Villard Papers.

14. LIPA, "To Members of the National Committee and Executive Committee," May 29, 1929, box 1, Williams Papers. Other influential members included Nathan Fine, Paul Brissenden, Robert M. Lovett, Paul Blanshard, and John H. Holmes.

15. *New York Times*, May 26–28, 1929; Leonard Bright, "C.P.L.A. Organizes," *Labor Age* 18 (June 1929), 3–4; and "Statement of Policy of the C.P.L.A.," *ibid.*, 6–7.

16. John Dewey to Devere Allen, Oct. 2, 1929, box 1, Williams Papers.

17. See Richard H. Pells's important insights in *Radical Visions and American Dreams: Cultural and Social Thought in the Depression Years* (New York: Harper & Row, 1973), 43–45.

18. Herbert K. Smith to LIPA office, Nov. 26, 1929, box 2, Williams Papers.

19. A. J. Muste to Devere Allen, Nov. 29, 1929, *ibid.*

20. Norman Thomas to Devere Allen, Nov. 30, 1929, *ibid.*

21. John Fitzpatrick to Howard Y. Williams, Dec. 17, 1929, *ibid.* Theodore Draper discusses Fitzpatrick's disillusionment in *American Communism and Soviet Russia* (New York: Viking Press, 1960), 50–51.

22. Richard L. Watson, Jr., "The Defeat of Judge Parker: A Study in Pressure Groups and Politics," *Journal of American History* 50:2 (Sept. 1963), 213–234. See also William Green to Mercer G. Johnston, Apr. 2, 1930, box 57, Johnston Papers; "Spare the Supreme Court," press release of the People's Legislative Service, Apr. 10, 1930, *ibid.*; William Green to George W. Norris, April 29, 1930, *ibid.*; and *People's Business* 5:5 (May 1930), PLS Papers.

23. Thomas J. Walsh to Oswald G. Villard, Apr. 24, 30, 1930, box 3, Williams Papers.

24. Oswald G. Villard to Devere Allen, Apr. 28, 1930, *ibid*.

25. Devere Allen, "Night Letter," June 19, 1930, *ibid*.

26. E. A. Ross to Howard Y. Williams, July 22, 1930, box 4, *ibid*.

27. Howard Y. Williams to Paul H. Douglas, Aug. 28, 1930; and Howard Y. Williams and John Dewey to Howard Reel, Aug. 18, 1930, *ibid*.

28. See Howard Y. Williams to William T. Rawleigh, Jan. 4, 1930, box 2, Williams Papers; and the latter's refusal to make further contributions, William T. Rawleigh to Howard Y. Williams, Sept. 6, 1930, box 4, *ibid*.

29. *New York Times*, Jan. 14, 1931, in box 36, *ibid*.; see also John Dewey to George W. Norris, Dec. 23, 1930, George W. Norris Papers, Library of Congress; Norris to Dewey, Dec. 27, 1930, *ibid*.; also New York *World*, Dec. 27, 1930, box 36, Williams Papers; and "The Political Party of the Philosophers," *Christian Science Monitor* (Dec. 29, 1930), box 36, *ibid*.

30. Howard Y. Williams to Oswald G. Villard, Jan. 5, 1931, box 6, *ibid*.

31. Howard Y. Williams, "A Plan for the Nation," *Minnesota Union Advocate*, Jan. 1, 1931, box 36, *ibid*.

32. A. J. Muste to Howard Y. Williams, Dec. 28, 1930, box 2, *ibid*.

33. A. J. Muste to William T. Rawleigh, Apr. 5, 1930, and Muste to Oswald G. Villard, Apr. 5, 1930, box 28, folder 9, Brookwood Labor College Papers, Archives of Labor and Urban Affairs, Wayne State University, hereinafter cited as BLC Papers.

34. News Release, June 3, 1930, box 28, folder 11, BLC Papers; Louis F. Budenz, "Outline of CPLA Program of Action—Nationally and in New York City in Particular," for A. J. Muste, undated but probably mid-May 1930; and A. J. Muste to Louis F. Budenz, June 6, 1930, box 28, folder 12, BLC Papers. For a discussion of the unemployment insurance issue see Daniel Nelson, *Unemployment Insurance: The American Experience, 1915–1935* (Madison: Univ. of Wisconsin Press, 1969), 155–156; Roy Lubove, *The Struggle for Social Security, 1900–1935* (Cambridge: Harvard Univ. Press, 1968), 168–174; Morris, *Conflict Within the AFL*, 133–134; "Unemployment Insurance—The Next Step," *Labor Age* 19 (June 1930), 21–22; "Our Unemployment Insurance Bills," *ibid*., 19 (Dec. 1930), 21–23.

35. A. J. Muste, "Do We Need a New Political Party in the United States?" *Labor Age* 20 (Apr. 1931), 10–13.

36. Norman Thomas, "The Lucas-Norris Episode," *The New Leader* (Dec. 27, 1930) and *Chicago Journal of Commerce* (Dec. 31, 1930), box 36, Williams Papers. See Norman Thomas's letter of resignation, Mar. 6, 1931, box 7, *ibid*.; "The Need for a New Party," *New Republic* 65 (Jan. 7, 1931), 203; and "Toward a New Party," *Nation* 132 (Jan. 14, 1931), 32, box 36, Williams Papers. See also John Dewey, "Who Might Make a New Party?," *New Republic* 66 (Apr. 1, 1931), 178, and "Policies for a New Party," *ibid*., 66 (Apr. 8, 1931), 203–205.

37. Form letter announcing the conference and signed by Senators George W. Norris, Edward P. Costigan, Bronson Cutting, Robert M. La Follette, Jr., and Burton K. Wheeler, Feb. 27, 1931, box 58, Johnston Papers. That progressive ideas were very much in ferment is evident from the intellectual debate then embroiling the *New Republic*. See Edmund Wilson's, "An Appeal to Progres-

sives," *New Republic* 65 (Jan. 14, 1931), 234–238, and his fellow editor George Soule's "Hard-Boiled Radicalism," *ibid.*, 65 (Jan. 21, 1931), 261–265. Cletus E. Daniel makes some insightful observations about liberal intellectuals in the early 1930s in *The ACLU and the Wagner Act: An Inquiry into the Depression-Era Crisis of American Liberalism* (Ithaca: New York State School of Industrial and Labor Relations, 1980), 2–9.

38. Albert U. Romasco, *The Poverty of Abundance: Hoover, the Nation, the Depression* (New York: Oxford Univ. Press, 1965), 216–219. Details of the Progressive Conference can also be found in Ronald L. Feinman, *Twilight of Progressivism: The Western Republican Senators and the New Deal* (Baltimore: The Johns Hopkins Univ. Press, 1981), 23–25; Patrick J. Maney, *"Young Bob" La Follette: A Biography of Robert M. La Follette, Jr., 1895–1953* (Columbia: Univ. of Missouri Press, 1978), 85–87; and Richard Lowitt, *George W. Norris: The Persistence of a Progressive, 1913–1933* (Urbana: Univ. of Illinois Press, 1971), 509–511.

39. Maney, *"Young Bob" La Follette*, 86.

40. Gerald P. Nye to Oswald G. Villard, Apr. 23, 1930, Villard Papers.

41. Oswald G. Villard to Burton K. Wheeler, Apr. 21, 1930, *ibid.* Senator Norris's sentiments were extraordinarily similar following the 1931 conference; see Maney, *"Young Bob" La Follette*, 87.

42. Howard Y. Williams to Clarence Senior, May 5, 1931, box 8, Williams Papers.

43. Howard Y. Williams to Harriet Mills, May 18, 1931; and Howard Y. Williams to William V. Mahoney, June 2, 1931, *ibid.*

44. Norman Thomas to Kirby Page, May 22, 1931, *ibid.*

45. Howard Y. Williams to William V. Mahoney, June 2, 1931, *ibid.*

46. See Howard Y. Williams, article in the *Minnesota Union Advocate*, July 18, 1931, box 36, Williams Papers, in which the LIPA executive secretary transfers the league program directly on to the skeleton of a "National Farmer-Labor Party."

47. Joan H. Wilson, *Herbert Hoover: Forgotten Progressive* (Boston: Little, Brown and Company, 1975), 146.

48. John Dewey to Herbert Hoover, June 25, 1931, box 1, Marsh Papers, and Harris G. Warren, *Herbert Hoover and the Great Depression* (New York: Oxford Univ. Press, 1959), 296. In April 1928, the People's Reconstruction League changed its name to the People's Lobby.

49. Howard Y. Williams to Herbert Hoover, Sept. 7, 1931, box 9, Williams Papers. For a further elucidation of this argument see Williams's article in the *Jersey Observer* (Hoboken), Sept. 14, 1931, box 36, *ibid.*

50. Benjamin C. Marsh to Herbert Hoover, Sept. 26, 1931, box 1, Marsh papers.

51. J. Joseph Huthmacher, *Senator Robert F. Wagner and the Rise of Urban Liberalism* (New York: Atheneum, 1971), 93–94; Warren, *Herbert Hoover*, 149; Maney, *"Young Bob" La Follette*, 83–84; and Lowitt, *George W. Norris*, 494–495.

52. Huthmacher, *Senator Robert F. Wagner*, 93; Benjamin C. Marsh to Sen. James Couzens, Mar. 15, 1932; and Sen. James Couzens to Benjamin C. Marsh, Mar. 16, 1932, box 1, Marsh Papers.

53. George L. Record to Gifford Pinchot, Nov. 10, 1931, box 52, Amos Pinchot Papers.

54. George L. Record to Amos R. E. Pinchot, Sept. 8, 1931, *ibid.*

55. Amos R. E. Pinchot to George L. Record, Aug. 24, 1931, *ibid.*

56. Amos R. E. Pinchot to Burhans Newcombe, Oct. 29, 1931, *ibid.*

57. George L. Record to Amos R. E. Pinchot, Apr. 18, 1931, *ibid.*

58. Amos R. E. Pinchot to George L. Record, Apr. 22, 1931, *ibid.*

59. Donald R. Richberg to Amos R. E. Pinchot, Oct. 7, 1931, *ibid.*

60. Howard Y. Williams to James H. Maurer, Oct. 22, 1931, box 9, Williams Papers. Other Socialists invited included Morris Hillquit, James Oneal, and McAlister Coleman.

61. Morris Hillquit to Howard Y. Williams, Nov. 26, 1931, *ibid.*

62. A. J. Muste, "Do We Need a New Political Party in the United States?" *Labor Age* 20 (Apr. 1931), 10–13.

63. A. J. Muste to Leonard Bright, Oct. 20, 1931, box 28, folder 13, BLC Papers. Bright was a militant Socialist and a member of the CPLA; see the series of letters between the two men: Muste to Bright, Aug. 1, 1931; Bright to Muste; Aug. 12, 1931, Oct. 5, 1931; and Muste to Bright, Oct. 14, 1931, *ibid.*

64. Confidential Memorandum on Relations between CPLA and the Socialist party, undated, box 28, folder 24, *ibid.*

65. CPLA, "Statement of Purpose," box 29, folder 11; see also CPLA Statement of Principles and Policy, undated, box 28, folder 24, *ibid.*

66. A. J. Muste to W. W. ("Bill") Biddle, Nov. 11, 1931, box 28, folder 14, *ibid.*

67. Roy Rosenzweig, "Radicals and the Jobless: The Musteites and the Unemployed Leagues, 1932–1936," *Labor History* 16:1 (Winter 1975), 52–77; and Daniel J. Leab, " 'Until We Eat': The Creation and Organization of the Unemployed Councils in 1930," *Labor History* 8 (Fall 1967), 300–315.

68. Howard Y. Williams to Jesse H. Holmes, Swarthmore College, Dec. 9, 1931, box 10, Williams Papers.

69. Howard Y. Williams, "Is a New Party Possible in 1932?," *Naked Truth* (Dec. 1931), box 36, Williams Papers; see also Howard Y. Williams to Norman Lermond, Jan. 4, 1932, *ibid.*, with Williams's observation: "If Roosevelt is nominated, I do not think that there is much hope for a united third party ticket in 1932."

70. LIPA newspaper release, Jan. 2, 1932, box 36, *ibid.*

71. Howard Y. Williams to Phillip Carlin, National Broadcasting Company, Jan. 6, 1932, box 10, *ibid.* John Dewey, the league's national chairman, served as leader of the session on unemployment; Alvin Johnson of the New School for Social Research directed the session on money, banking, and credit; the chairman on taxation and the tariff was Clair Wilcox of Swarthmore College; Benson Y. Landis, president of the Country Life Association, directed the session on agriculture; Amos Pinchot handled the public power and utilities panel; Paul Brissenden of Columbia University was the leader of the session on people's rights; and Devere Allen served as chairman of the session on international relations.

72. Maney, *"Young Bob" La Follette*, 93–94.

73. The league also endorsed a constitutional amendment for the rights of workers that would encompass substantial labor and social welfare legislation, repeal of syndicalist and espionage laws, and freedom for Tom Mooney, Warren

Billings, and the Wobbly defendants in the Centralia, Washington, case. See
Paul Brissenden, Draft on Labor Legislation and Civil Liberties, Mar. 2, 1932,
box 11, Williams Papers; and *New York Herald Tribune*, Feb. 1, 1932, box 36, *ibid*.
The full LIPA program can be found as a special supplement in the *Nation* 134
(Feb. 17, 1932), section II. Not to be outdone, the *New Republic* had published
its own special supplement on economic planning; see "Long-Range Planning
for the Regularization of Industry," *New Republic* 69 (Jan. 13, 1932), part two,
3–23.

74. *Nation* 134 (Feb. 17, 1932), 186.

75. *New Republic* 69 (Feb. 10, 1932), 335–336, and *Nation* 134 (Feb. 17, 1932),
185–186.

76. George L. Record to John Dewey, Feb. 11, 1932, box 11, Williams Papers;
see also George L. Record's letter to the editor, *Nation* 134 (Mar. 16, 1932), 313.

77. E. Yancey Cohen to John Dewey, Apr. 1, 1932, box 11, Williams Papers.

78. Daniel W. Hoan to John Dewey, Feb. 13, 1932, box 11, *ibid*.

79. A. R. Anderson to John Dewey, Feb. 8, 1932, and Howard Y. Williams
to Oswald G. Villard, box 12, Williams Papers.

80. *New York Times*, Jan. 6, 7, 8, 18, 1932; also in Warren, *Herbert Hoover*,
154, 225, and McCoy, *Angry Voices*, 13–14.

81. Howard Y. Williams, perhaps due to his strong personal ties to the
Minnesota FLP, refused to believe that his colleagues would support FDR. A
more realistic view can be found in a letter from Clarence Senior, executive
secretary of the Socialist Party of America to Howard Y. Williams, Apr. 14, 1932,
box 11, Williams Papers; see Howard Y. Williams to Clarence Senior, May 4,
1932, *ibid*.; and Millard L. Gieske, *Minnesota Farmer-Laborism: The Third-Party
Alternative* (Minneapolis: Univ. of Minnesota Press, 1979), 158–161.

82. Howard Y. Williams to Officers of LIPA local chapters, Mar. 17, 1932,
box 11, Williams Papers. William E. Leuchtenburg, *Franklin D. Roosevelt and the
New Deal, 1932–1940* (New York: Harper & Row, 1963), 4–7; and J. Joseph Huthmacher, *Massachusetts People and Politics, 1919–1933* (Cambridge: Harvard Univ.
Press, 1959), 234–238. See also LIPA founder Paul H. Douglas's, *The Coming of
a New Party* (New York: Whittlesey House, 1932).

83. Franklin D. Roosevelt to George L. Record, Mar. 16, 1932, box 53, Amos
Pinchot Papers.

84. George L. Record to FDR, Mar. 22, 1932, *ibid*.

85. See Helene M. Hooker, ed., "Amos R. E. Pinchot," *A History of the
Progressive Party, 1912–1916* (New York: New York Univ. Press, 1958), 76–78.

86. Amos R. E. Pinchot to FDR, Mar. 23, 1932, box 53, Amos Pinchot Papers.

87. By that time, however, Pinchot had broken with FDR. See Otis L. Graham, Jr., *An Encore for Reform: The Old Progressives and the New Deal* (New York:
Oxford Univ. Press, 1967), 74–77.

88. Lawson, *The Failure of Independent Liberalism*, 115, cites Dewey, "The
Irrepressible Conflict," *LIPA Bulletin* 1 (Jan. 1934), 4. Robert B. Westbrook discusses Dewey's interest in radical politics in "John Dewey and the Search for
Democratic Community," 15–16, in a paper delivered at a meeting of the Organization of American Historians, Apr. 1982, Philadelphia, Pa.

89. Paul H. Douglas to Howard Y. Williams, May 27, 1932, box 12, Williams
Papers.

90. Gieske, *Minnesota Farmer-Laborism*, 165.

91. James D. Staver to Howard Y. Williams, May 30, 1932, box 12, Williams Papers.

92. John W. Herring to Max E. Geline, June 30, 1932, *ibid*.

93. *Cleveland Plain Dealer*, July 10, 1932, box 36, *ibid*.

94. Quoted in Ronald Steel, *Walter Lippmann and the American Century* (Boston: Little, Brown and Company, 1980), 291–292.

95. Harry Elmer Barnes, "The Liberal Viewpoint," *New York World-Telegram*, July 18, 1932, box 36, Williams Papers.

96. *New Republic* 71 (June 20, 1932), 245, 258, called the LIPA decision to support the Socialist ticket "an acute sense of political reality." See also the *Nation* 135 (July 20, 27, 1932), 46, 80–82; also Howard Y. Williams, form letter to local chapters, Aug. 10, 1932, box 13, Williams Papers.

97. Paul H. Douglas to John W. Herring, July 18, 1932, *ibid*.

98. Fiorello H. La Guardia to John Dewey, June 29, 1932; and Clarence Darrow to Dewey, July 13, 1932, box 12, *ibid*.

99. William V. Mahoney to Howard Y. Williams, July 19, 1932, box 13, *ibid*.

100. John W. Herring to Mary S. McDowell, July 27, 1932, *ibid*.

101. John W. Herring to Fiorello H. La Guardia, Aug. 26, 1932, *ibid*.

102. William Benjamin Smith to John Dewey, Sept. 27, 1932, box 14, *ibid*.

103. Howard Y. Williams, "Making Your Vote Count," Devere Allen Papers, Document Group 53, Box C4, 1932, Swarthmore College Peace Collection, hereinafter cited as Allen Papers.

104. National Popular Government League, Bulletin #157, "Power Records of Hoover and Roosevelt," Sept. 9, 1932, King Papers; also "Roosevelt Campaign Committee of the NPGL," Oct. 17, 1932, *ibid*. Just as the Democratic party had attempted to attract disaffected progressive Republicans in 1928 by creating the "Progressive League for Alfred E. Smith," so, too, did it follow that pattern in 1932 with the "National Progressive League." In both cases, men such as Frank P. Walsh, Amos Pinchot, and Basil M. Manly played key roles. See the *New York Times*, Sept. 26, 1932, and Feinman, *Twilight of Progressivism*, 40–41. See also Harry A. Slattery to Edward L. Roddan, Jan. 27, 1933, Slattery Papers.

105. Devere Allen, Radio Address over WICC, Nov. 5, 1932, transcript in Document Group 53, Box C4, 1932, Allen Papers.

106. LIPA, News Release, Nov. 22, 1932, box 36, Williams Papers.

107. Howard Y. Williams to Mrs. Ethel Clyde, Nov. 15, 1932, box 16, *ibid*. Mrs. Clyde was a very prominent contributor to a number of liberal causes including the People's Lobby. See Marsh, *Lobbyist for the People*, 91; and John Dewey to Benjamin C. Marsh, Apr. 15, 1931, box 1, Marsh Papers.

108. John Dewey, "After the Election—What?" *LIPA News Bulletin* 1 (Nov.–Dec. 1932), 1. In his valuable study, *Angry Voices: Left-of-Center Politics in the New Deal Era*, Donald McCoy argues (25–27) that the league's leaders responded to the election results by deemphasizing intellectual concerns and switching emphasis to a grass-roots approach that would build support among the agrarian and working classes. It is unclear, however, whether this transformation took place as rapidly as he suggests.

109. Amos R. E. Pinchot, "The American Liberal and the Liberal Program,"

an address presented, Nov. 13, 1932, at the Community Forum, New York City, box 175, Amos Pinchot Papers.

110. Benjamin C. Marsh to FDR, Jan. 6, 18, 1933, box 1, Marsh Papers.

111. Benjamin C. Marsh to FDR, Mar. 3, 1933, *ibid*.

112. Judson King to George L. Record, Feb. 18, 1933, box 6, King Papers.

113. George L. Record to Judson King, Feb. 20, 1933, *ibid*.

114. George L. Record to Amos R. E. Pinchot, Feb. 11, 1933, box 54, Amos Pinchot Papers.

115. Amos R. E. Pinchot to William P. Eno, Apr. 18, 1933, box 29, *ibid*., and Pinchot to Allen McCurdy, May 6, 1933, box 54, *ibid*.

116. Amos Pinchot to Allen McCurdy, Mar. 22, 1933, *ibid*. Pinchot's public break with the New Deal is the subject of Richard Polenberg's, "The National Committee to Uphold Constitutional Government, 1937–1941," *Journal of American History* 52:3 (Dec. 1965), 582–598.

117. John Dewey to FDR, Apr. 6 or 10, 1933, box 1, Marsh Papers.

118. Howard Y. Williams, "Nation Convalesces in First Half of 1933; Semi-Annual Political Review," July 2, 1933, box 36, Williams Papers.

119. Gilson Gardner to Amos R. E. Pinchot, July 18, 1933, box 54, Amos Pinchot Papers.

IX

Conclusion

Political activists occupy a peculiar position in American life. We do not so much revere as respect them; we envy their energy, occasionally question their judgment, frequently wish they would go away, and are usually grateful for the necessary role they play. We rarely ignore them, since they will not be silenced.

American liberals between 1913 and 1933 experienced all these sentiments as they confronted their insurgent critics. These were men and women whose names graced the letterheads of countless organizations but were not "professional" liberals. They did not wear their progressivism on their sleeves in public and store it in their closets after hours. They were the managers, directors, technicians, and followers of independent organizations who relentlessly pursued the goals of equal justice and equal opportunity. But they were not saints; they distrusted power yet desperately sought it. They were suspicious of privilege though never hesitant to use it. They envisioned themselves as custodians of the democratic tradition and named their organizations accordingly— the National Popular Government League, the People's Lobby, the People's Legislative Service—yet they were most comfortable and effective in small, exclusive, elitist groups and most ineffective and awkward when dealing directly with the public. So they were neither perfect nor innocent, and few pretended otherwise. They failed far more often than they succeeded, yet they made a difference by forcing friends and adversaries to consider their views.

Many first came to political maturity as soldiers in the Bull Moose crusade. Struggling with the limitation imposed by the two-party system, they quite early demonstrated a disquieting willingness to sacrifice principle (loyalty to Robert M. La Follette) for glory. Shaken by TR's dismissal of them as "ultra-progressives," they nonetheless enjoyed the role of outsider and underdog. They seemed to thrive on adversity, positioning themselves on the periphery of power, constantly probing the leadership for recognition of their presence. The closer they came to Roosevelt and Wilson and the more they were rejected, the harder they tried to convert such men. Since their ideas were never really tested, they rarely doubted the appropriateness of their program. They tended to see everything solely through their own eyes. This made them extraordinarily convincing advocates but unusually poor collaborators.

These strengths and weaknesses became more apparent in the years immediately preceding World War I. Disturbed by the violence, lawlessness, and class animosity generated by labor-management disagreements, progressives placed their faith in proven methods of investigation. Prolabor in their sympathies, they visited strike sites and returned home denouncing the evils of monopoly and special privilege and preaching the gospel of economic democracy. True to their political principles, they linked the suffering they saw at Ludlow, Lawrence, and Paterson to the evils of monopoly and demanded government intervention. The creation of the United States Commission on Industrial Relations and its call for national unemployment insurance, government ownership of railroads and natural resources, and a more equitable distribution of wealth symbolized the zenith of the prewar progressives' faith in moral suasion and government by experts. It also marked the first significant degree of cooperation between liberal and labor leaders, and though the immediate results were disappointing, it was the beginning of a new direction in American liberalism.

When the war came, progressives who had been close to the labor situation insisted that the preparedness debate was inextricably linked to the prewar struggle for human dignity. Shifting the focus of their support from labor defense funds and strike relief, they created new organizations first to keep America out of the war and later to prevent the conflict from benefiting the few. They repeatedly stressed the connection between war and social injustice, relied upon their prewar experiences, and dutifully worked for change within the system. Though expecting to serve as Wilson's liberal conscience, they discovered that access to the White House reduced their effectiveness, increased their vulnerability to presidential persuasion, and rendered them politically impotent. For some this represented their first serious disillusionment with progressive leaders; for others it offered another lesson in power politics and convinced them that fundamental change could only be accomplished through the creation of a strong liberal-labor coalition.

When liberals finally were in a position to demonstrate their commitment to industrial democracy, most failed miserably. They grew arrogant, haughty, conceited, and patronizing. Many found it impossible to lay aside cherished beliefs in a classless society if doing so meant admitting the need for special labor legislation; others were unwilling to accept organized labor as the dominant or even equal partner in a new political alliance. But the major issues in the immediate post-Armistice years—democratic control of industry, government ownership of the railroads, and the restoration of free speech—depended heavily upon the labor movement's financial and organizational support. Some liberals, notably Frederic C. Howe, Frank P. Walsh, and Basil M. Manly, readily accepted labor's leadership. Others, including the majority of activists in the Committee of Forty-Eight, remained tied to an anachronistic preoccupation with the evils of monopoly or promoted a romanticized version of industrial democracy that fell far short of labor's needs. The 1920 campaign revealed the formidable barriers of class and ideology which continued to separate liberal and labor leaders. The more conservative 48ers, sensing it had been a mistake to seek labor's cooperation, turned inward refusing to compromise their commitment to a classless society. Union leaders saw things quite differently. After watching liberals desert and demean both the Labor Party and Farmer-Labor movements, they concluded that labor would be the controlling partner in any subsequent association of "hand and brain."

Both groups entered the 1920s in noticeably weakened positions. Progressives engaged in a flurry of organizational activity which inversely reflected their national strength. These were difficult years for liberal insiders who hoped to protect past gains, serve as watchdogs of Republican policies, function as a resource agency for congressional liberals, and do all these things on shoestring budgets. Progressive lobbyists harassed conservative adversaries, published newsletters for liberal constituents, and held periodic conferences to rally the faithful. But they lacked the financial resources, political leverage, and organizational commitment necessary to do more than survive.

Organized labor entered the decade shaken by a series of damaging strikes widely attributed to radicals within the union movement. The Red Scare, a well-financed open shop campaign, hostile public opinion, and the 1921 recession seriously impaired the progress labor had made during the war. Eager to solidify those gains and reverse the Harding administration's opposition to government ownership of the railroads, the railway brotherhoods invited independent progressives to join a new political movement. Many liberal and labor leaders still distrusted each other, but there were no other options. The union-sponsored Conference for Progressive Political Action needed the legitimacy, respectability, and recognition which came with liberal participation. Progressives depended even more upon their labor allies for any future attempt at launching a third-party movement. Many liberals maintained the illusion that they could educate union leaders and gain control of the CPPA. At the least they hoped to prevent laborites from following a socialist course.

Most progressives remained divided over the issue of independent political action. Even those who supported a third party did so with less enthusiasm than in years past. Embittered by earlier defeats, suspicious of the motives of both the unions and aspiring presidential candidates, progressive activists engaged in a series of cat-and-mouse games that belied their own internal differences. The 1924 La Follette campaign revealed once again that reformers were excellent campaigners but miserable organizers. They prided themselves on their political sophistication and experience but were amateurs at heart. Nothing revealed this more accurately than the fruitless battles engaged in by La Follette's and Coolidge's supporters over the right to the Progressive label. There was something ironic about these former Bull Moosers claiming to be political heirs of a man many had rejected years earlier.

In the years that followed, independent progressives witnessed a number of changes which gradually altered the direction of the liberal movement. First, the railway brotherhoods, eager to cut their financial and political losses, dismantled the CPPA, leaving what remained of independent liberalism lodged with a handful of veteran organizers who continued the struggle. Another link to the progressive past was broken with Robert M. La Follette's death in June 1925. His passing exposed the movement's dependence upon personalities, but it also stimulated a renewed commitment to issues. Progressives soon directed their energies to contemporary concerns and produced a provocative synthesis of old and new approaches that called for tax reform, public ownership, government cooperatives, public works spending, labor's right to organize, and a major new emphasis upon a more compassionate and just foreign policy in Latin America. A significant amount of time, energy, and money was expended in awakening the public to the Coolidge administration's bullying tactics in Nicaragua. Liberals served an invaluable, though unappreciated, role as critics of a foreign policy which an earlier progressive generation once admired. Though this issue seemed guaranteed to arouse public indignation, neither it nor the progressives' criticism of the utility industry's "Power Trust" evoked more than a negligible response.

The problem was not merely that progressives were leaderless or directionless; their ideas were sound and their organizations capable of offering collective leadership. What independent liberals lacked was power. Their temporary flirtations with third-party action had left them discredited. Independent political campaigns may have provided temporary gratification for a Roosevelt or La Follette, but a sustained commitment to such ephemeral causes left rank-and-file followers powerless. This was particularly true of the period between 1924 and 1928, when labor returned to a nonpartisan political position leaving independents to carry on alone. Frequently a major party campaign attracted reformers back into the fold; they were trotted out for an endorsement, encouraged to participate in "The Progessive League for . . . ," invited to submit campaign suggestions, and occasionally asked to meet the candidate, but this was all window dressing; they were helpful and supportive but clearly unessential.

Alfred E. Smith's defeat in 1928 reflected all these shortcomings, and while it disillusioned some progressives, it convinced others that prospects for a real political realignment still remained. The enthusiasm which pulsated through certain reaches of the liberal and socialist community early in 1929 was not notably different in tone from earlier third-party ventures. Like their predecessors in the Bull Moose and La Follette movements, the founders of the League for Independent Political Action were confident; they believed in the value of expertise and were themselves the cream of the nation's intellectual meritocracy. They offered classic liberal prescriptions but mixed them with approaches that spoke directly to the country's economic needs. National economic planning, income redistribution, and the democratic management of industry would provide the government with a much more active role; so, too, would the league's calls for national old age, unemployment, and health insurance. Ironically, when independent liberals finally did their homework and presented a reasonable set of proposals for public consideration, they were ignored by voters, held at arm's length by Socialists and organized labor, and co-opted by Democratic party liberals.

The interlocking nature of liberal-labor concerns was also underscored by the formation of the Conference for Progressive Labor Action. The CPLA's labor progressives, like their LIPA colleagues, drew support from the same "lib-lab" network which produced the U.S. Commission on Industrial Relations, the American Union Against Militarism, and the Conference for Progressive Political Action. Both the LIPA and CPLA experimented with conventional and more radical approaches. The more they set themselves apart from the liberal mainstream, the more such actions reduced their middle-class support. In the end, though both the LIPA and CPLA served an important role in stimulating public debate, both were anomalous and loosely conceived organizations whose personal rivalry kept them apart and politically ineffectual.

Persistence remains the key in understanding America's independent progressives during these years. Most liberals did their work far from the fanfare of parades and the applause of cheering crowds. They operated behind the scenes, lobbying and advocating policies which had stirred them to action in the first place. Only a handful sustained their commitment over an entire generation, and one must wonder how often their efforts reached beyond the confines of their own small group. But what a group it was! If we could chart the frequency of interaction among progressive activists between 1913 and 1933, a very distinguished set of

names would constantly reappear. People like Amos Pinchot, George
L. Record, Frederic C. Howe, Harry A. Slattery, Basil M. Manly, Benjamin C. Marsh, J. A. H. Hopkins, and Mercer G. Johnston did not lead
lives that are readily measured or easily evaluated. They have been called
"second-line" progressives, reflecting their position a step or two below
the leadership, but they should more accurately and deservedly be placed
in the front line because they were the heart, soul, and conscience of
political liberalism between the First World War and the Great Depression. I believe it is a mistake to dismiss them as the progressive footnote
in any discussion of American politics immediately prior to the New
Deal. Their contribution extends far beyond their organizational enthusiasm and lobbying skills. Much of their lives was taken up with the
clutter of professional detail; but they did far more than answer tele-
phones, crank out newsletters, or buttonhole legislators. They were the
founders, mainstays, and publicists of new and relevant progressive
concerns that set the tone for liberal politics down through the Great
Depression. They organized and wrote, debated and complained, but
because they rejected the traditional path to power through the two-
party system, their triumphs were few.

It is difficult to write about them without feeling a good deal of ambivalence. "I sometimes try to fathom the motive which compels me to
make these foolish attempts which I have been doing for thirty years,"
George L. Record wrote an old friend in 1932. "I am getting old in reality,
and figuratively speaking paralyzed so far as any power is concerned,
but I think until the end of my life if any of these privileged interests
which I have fought . . . come within reach so that I can bite them I will
try to do so, at least I hope so."[1] We have all known and grudgingly
admired such people. They annoy us with their persistence, embarrass
us with their tirelessness, and occasionally affront us with their rude-
ness. But they will always be with us because they are organizers and
survivors.

NOTE

1. George L. Record to James Kerney, Dec. 21, 1932, quoted in Ransom E.
Noble, Jr., "George L. Record's Struggle for Economic Democracy," *American
Journal of Economics and Sociology* 10:1 (Oct. 1950), 83.

Bibliographic Essay

Anyone who has ever written a "term" or "research" paper knows that one of the last decisions to make concerns what to include in the bibliography. I have chosen not to duplicate all of the entries cited in the footnotes but rather to describe some of the more important primary and secondary literature which might be of interest to both specialists and general readers. I hope that this essay will also acknowledge my profound respect for the scholarship of other writers whose own work made my labors so much more enjoyable.

PRIMARY SOURCES

Sometime in the mid-seventies, while on a research trip to the Library of Congress (LC), an archivist introduced me to the Amos R. E. Pinchot Papers. The better part of the next decade was spent studying that collection, following leads to other repositories, and making frequent stops back to the LC to mine Pinchot's papers. I believe this collection represents one of the richest sources of information on the major political questions of the early twentieth century. It is indispensable for understanding the group of activists I have referred to as "independent progressives," and my frequent references to it testify to its centrality in this study.

I gained a clearer understanding of Theodore Roosevelt's, Robert M. La Follette's, and Woodrow Wilson's relations with the "radical Progressives" from the three men's own papers (LC), as well as from the William Kent Papers (Yale University), the Charles E. Merriam Papers (University of Chicago), the Harold L. Ickes Papers (LC), and the George W. Perkins Papers (Columbia University). The Theodore Roosevelt Association Collection (Harvard University) also contains a good deal of correspondence pertaining to the Progressive party.

Amos Pinchot's Papers contain numerous exchanges with progressive and union leaders testifying to liberal-labor interaction immediately prior to the First World War. The correspondence is particularly good on the Paterson and Colorado strikes and details efforts in behalf of various labor defense funds. I would

agree with a number of other historians that the single best source on labor-
management relations during these years is the published reports of the United
States Commission on Industrial Relations (Washington, D.C., Government
Printing Office, 1915, 15 volumes). These reports offer testimony by a host of
distinguished contemporaries on the labor violence of this period. Readers also
will wish to consult the papers of W. Jett Lauck, the commission's Managing
Expert, at the University of Virginia's Alderman Library.

The antipreparedness, antiwar, and "pay-as-you-go" movements of these
years offer a wonderfully rich written legacy. The American Union Against
Militarism (AUAM) and People's Council of America (PCA) papers in the Swarthmore College Peace Collection provide a first-rate source of information. Other
collections which proved very helpful include the Lillian Ward and Norman
Thomas papers (New York Public Library); the Pinchot, La Follette, Roosevelt,
Wilson, and John Haynes Holmes papers (LC); and the oral history memoirs
and reminiscences of Roger N. Baldwin and A. J. Muste at Columbia University's
Oral History Research Office. Here, as throughout the book, I also relied upon
contemporary periodicals such as the *Nation*, the *New Republic*, the *Freeman*, the
Public, and *Survey*.

Manuscript material on the postwar "reconstruction" era, the rise of the Committee of Forty-Eight, and the Labor Party is abundant and easily accessible.
Once again, the Pinchot and La Follette papers (LC) are excellent, but the single
best source may well be the Mercer G. Johnston collection (LC). Johnston, a
Baltimore-based social activist and former minister, was the moving force behind
the Christian Social Justice Fund. An articulate and prolific correspondent, his
papers provide an invaluable source on the 48ers and the 1919–1920 liberal-labor
efforts at cooperation. I also was aided by an examination of Judson King's
Papers (LC) and his role as the head of the National Popular Government League,
an organization which was extremely active in the first optimistic months after
the Armistice. The John Fitzpatrick Papers (Chicago Historical Society) provide
a laborite perspective on these events and shed light on the problems of the
Farmer-Labor party during the 1920 campaign. Other important collections relevant to this period include the Oswald G. Villard Papers (Harvard University)
and the Alice Park Papers (Hoover Institution Archives).

The years between 1921 and 1924 best exemplify the organizational side of
postwar liberalism. The activities of the Conference for Progressive Political
Action, the People's Legislative Service, and the People's Reconstruction League
can be followed through the personal papers of Lynn Haines (Minnesota Historical Society), Benjamin C. Marsh (LC), and Harry A. Slattery (Duke University). Like other historians who happened upon the Slattery collection, I found
his correspondence with Gifford Pinchot, George W. Norris, and other contemporaries extremely insightful. His unpublished autobiography, "From Roosevelt
to Roosevelt: A Study of Forty Years in Washington," deserves a wider audience
than the researchers who visit the Perkins Library of Duke University. The voice
of Washington's progressive officeholders, the *People's Business*, can be found
in the People's Legislative Service Papers (LC). Other very helpful collections
to consult include the George W. Norris, Harold L. Ickes, and William E. Borah
papers (LC); the Joseph S. Frelinghuysen Papers (Rutgers University); and especially the Hiram W. Johnson Papers (University of California, Berkeley).

Most of these same collections provided the bulk of the information for my analysis of the post-La Follette years between 1925 and 1928. Material relating to the progressives' legal and public relations efforts in behalf of Senator Burton K. Wheeler, their criticism of Coolidge administration policy in Nicaragua, and attacks upon the Power Trust can all be found in the Mercer G. Johnston and Judson King papers (LC). Information on independent liberal activity in Alfred E. Smith's campaign can be obtained from reading the papers of Harry A. Slattery (Duke University), George W. Norris, Amos R. E. Pinchot (LC), and Frank Walsh (New York Public Library).

Third-party activists eager for a liberal alternative after 1924 hoped that the League for Independent Political Action would be their salvation. Though publicly identified with its national leaders, John Dewey and Paul H. Douglas, it is historically appropriate that the league's records and major correspondence are a part of its executive secretary Howard Y. Williams' Papers (Minnesota Historical Society). Like Mercer G. Johnston, Basil Manly, Judson King, and Benjamin C. Marsh, Williams was one of those relatively unknown technicians who kept his organization functioning without much acclaim. His papers provide a very complete and informative analysis of third-party efforts and are especially good on the role of the Communists in the Farmer-Labor movement. Other collections which contain material on the LIPA include the Kirby Page Papers (Southern California School of Theology), the Devere Allen Papers (Swarthmore College Peace Collection), the Oswald G. Villard Papers (Harvard University), and the George W. Norris Papers (LC). The LIPA, of course, was not the only voice of liberal protest; John Dewey's other progressive organization, the People's Lobby (formerly the People's Reconstruction League), was also a thorn in the side of the Hoover administration. The latter's activities can be found in the papers of its executive secretary, Benjamin C. Marsh (LC).

Researching the progressive labor movement was particularly interesting and relatively easy to accomplish. The Walter P. Reuther Library's Archives of Labor and Urban Affairs at Wayne State University contains the Brookwood Labor College Papers as well as the papers of such Brookwooders as Arthur Calhoun and Katherine Pollak Ellickson. The Reuther Archives also house the Selma Borchardt Papers and a very helpful Labor Education collection. There are smaller collections of material on Brookwood and A. J. Muste at the Robert F. Wagner Labor Archives of the Tamiment Institute Library (New York University) and in the John Nevin Sayre and A. J. Muste papers in the Swarthmore College Peace Collection. The single most important collection of Muste's correspondence for the Brookwood period, however, is in the Reuther Library. Other collections helpful for understanding the split within the labor movement and its impact upon liberal-labor relations include the Powers Hapgood Papers (Lilly Library, Indiana University), the Edmund B. Chaffee Papers (Syracuse University), the Fannia Cohn Papers (New York Public Library), and the John Fitzpatrick Papers (Chicago Historical Society). The activities of the Conference for Progressive Labor Action represent an important part of the Brookwood Labor College Papers (Wayne State University), and a good grass-roots portrait of CPLA efforts can be found in the Elmer Cope Papers (Ohio Historical Society).

Aside from the well-known progressive or liberal journals of opinion such as the *Nation* and the *New Republic* mentioned earlier, I found some other periodicals very helpful in reconstructing contemporary sentiment. *Labor Age*, voice of the progressive labor movement in the late twenties, is an excellent source for the Museite perspective. The *World Tomorrow*, the house journal of the Fellowship of Reconciliation, edited by Devere Allen, Norman Thomas, Kirby Page, and others, provided good insights into the pacifist and antiwar movements. Organized labor's view of this era's major political and economic issues can be obtained from reading *Labor*, voice of the railway brotherhood unions, and the *New Majority*, the organ of the Labor Party movement.

SECONDARY SOURCES

The relationship between the Progressive Era and the New Deal is still a matter of dispute among historians. However, it has produced a very fruitful and provocative literature. Some of the following works will serve as an introduction: Richard Hofstadter, *The Age of Reform: From Bryan to F.D.R.* (New York: Random House, 1955); Russel B. Nye, *Midwestern Progressive Politics: A Historical Study of Its Origins and Development, 1870–1950* (East Lansing: Michigan State College Press, 1951); Arthur S. Link, "What Happened to the Progressive Movement in the 1920s?," *American Historical Review* 64 (July 1959), 833–851; William E. Leuchtenburg, *The Perils of Prosperity, 1914–1932* (Chicago: Univ. of Chicago Press, 1958); Herbert Margulies, "Recent Opinion on the Decline of the Progressive Movement," *Mid-America* 45 (Oct. 1963), 250–268; Clarke Chambers, *Seedtime of Reform: American Social Service and Social Action, 1918–1933* (Minneapolis: Univ. of Minnesota Press, 1963). Otis L. Graham, Jr.'s, *An Encore for Reform: The Old Progressives and the New Deal* (New York: Oxford Univ. Press, 1967) is a brilliant scholarly work which very deftly follows the surviving progressives into the New Deal era. I disagree with his view of liberal activity during the 1920s but owe much of this book's inspiration to issues he first raised. There are many other works which directly relate to the issue of continuity between the two reform eras, and several are mentioned later in this essay. Readers seeking a basic overview of the first reform period would benefit from an essay by Robert H. Wiebe, "The Progressive Years, 1900–1917," in William C. Cartwright and Richard L. Watson, Jr., eds., *The Reinterpretation of American History and Culture* (Washington, D.C.: National Council for the Social Studies, 1973), 425–442. Two other important articles include Dewey W. Grantham, "The Progressive Era and the Reform Tradition," *Mid-America* 46 (Oct. 1964), 236–251, and Peter G. Filene, "An Obituary for 'The Progressive Movement,' " *American Quarterly* 22 (Spring 1970), 20–34.

The remainder of this essay is devoted to works which had a direct impact upon my own thinking. For purposes of convenience, I have organized them according to the chapter titles in this study. Readers interested in learning more about the Bull Moose campaign and the "Radical Progressives" might begin with: John Gable, *The Bull Moose Years: Theodore Roosevelt and the Progressive Party* (Port Washington, N.Y.: Kennikat Press, 1978); Allen F. Davis, *Spearheads for Reform: The Social Settlements and the Progressive Movement, 1890–1914* (New York: Oxford Univ. Press, 1967), especially 194–217; George E. Mowry, *Theodore Roosevelt and the Birth of Modern America, 1900–1912* (New York: Harper & Row, 1958), and his earlier study, *Theodore Roosevelt and the Progressive Movement* (Madison: Univ. of Wisconsin Press, 1946). These are all meticulously crafted works and might be enjoyably complemented by a reading of Theodore Roosevelt's published correspondence; see Elting E. Morison, ed., *The Letters of Theodore Roosevelt*, 8 vols. (Cambridge: Harvard Univ. Press, 1951–1954), especially volumes VII–VIII. The best single volume biography of Roosevelt is William H. Harbaugh, *Power and Responsibility: The Life and Times of Theodore Roosevelt* (New York: Farrar, Strauss and Cudahy, 1961). David P. Thelen has written a short but provocative biography of Senator La Follette, *Robert M. La Follette and the Insurgent Spirit* (Boston: Little, Brown, 1976), which might be combined with the senator's autobiography, read—naturally—with some caution: Robert M. La Follette, *La Follette's Autobiography* (Madison: Univ. of Wisconsin Press, rev. ed., 1960), and the La Follette family's view as described in Belle Case La Follette and Fola La Follette, *Robert M. La Follette*, 2 vols. (New York: Macmillan, 1953). The roles played by the senator's insurgent colleagues, Amos Pinchot and George L. Record, are discussed in Helene M. Hooker's excellent biographical introduction to Pinchot's *History of the Progressive Party, 1912–1916* (New York: New York Univ. Press, 1958). Pinchot's difficulties with Bull Moose chairman George W. Perkins is explained by John A. Garraty in *Right-Hand Man: The Life of George W. Perkins* (New York: Harper & Brothers, 1957). Pinchot is the subject of Rex O. Mooney's doctoral dissertation, "Amos Pinchot and Atomistic Capitalism: A Study in Reform Ideas," (Ph.D. diss., Louisiana State Univ., 1973). George L. Record's mercurial career can be followed in several studies written by Ransom E. Noble, Jr., *New Jersey Progressivism Before Wilson* (Princeton: Princeton Univ. Press, 1946); "Henry George and the Progressive Movement," *American Journal of Economics and Sociology* 8:3 (Apr. 1949), 259–269; and "George L. Record's Struggle for Economic Democracy," *ibid.*, 10:1 (Oct. 1950), 71–83. Two volumes in Arthur S. Link's definitive biography of our twenty-eighth president are also must reading: *Wilson: Confusions and Crises, 1915–1916* (Princeton: Princeton Univ. Press, 1964); and *Wilson: Campaigns for Progressivism and Peace, 1916–1917* (Princeton: Princeton Univ. Press, 1965). A brilliant recent work which comes to terms with Roosevelt, Wilson, and their political legacy is John Milton Cooper, Jr., *The Warrior and the Priest: Woodrow Wilson and Theodore Roosevelt* (Cambridge: Harvard Univ. Press, 1983).

The best place to begin an analysis of liberal-labor relations prior to the First World War is Graham Adams, Jr., *Age of Industrial Violence, 1910–1915: The Activities and Findings of the United States Commission on Industrial Relations* (New York: Columbia Univ. Press, 1966); also helpful is Allen F. Davis, "The Campaign for the Industrial Relations Commission, 1911–1913," *Mid-America* 45 (Oct. 1963), 211–228. Melvyn Dubofsky, *When Workers Organize: New York City in the Progressive Era* (Amherst: Univ. of Massachusetts Press, 1968); and Irwin Yellowitz, *Labor and the Progressive Movement in New York State, 1897–1916* (Ithaca, N.Y.: Cornell Univ. Press, 1965) both testify to early difficulties when trade unionists and social reformers sought to collaborate. Other studies on this subject include Marc Karson, *American Labor Unions and Politics, 1900–1918* (Carbondale: Southern Illinois Univ. Press, 1958); and William Graebner, *Coal-Mining Safety in the Progressive Period: The Political Economy of Reform* (Lexington: Univ. Press of Kentucky, 1976). Two related studies emphasizing the working-class contribution to the Progressive Era include J. Joseph Huthmacher, "Urban Liberalism and the Age of Reform," *Mississippi Valley Historical Review* 49 (Sept. 1962), 231–241; and John D. Buenker, *Urban Liberalism and Progressive Reform* (New York: Charles Scribner's Sons, 1973).

There is a wealth of outstanding literature in the progressive response to the First World War or what I have called, "The Road from Henry Street to Wall Street." A good place to begin is with Charles Chatfield, *For Peace and Justice: Pacifism in America, 1914–1941* (Knoxville: Univ. of Tennessee Press, 1971); C. Roland Marchand, *The American Peace Movement and Social Reform, 1898–1918* (Princeton: Princeton Univ. Press, 1972); Charles DeBenedetti, *The Peace Reform in American History* (Bloomington: Indiana Univ. Press, 1980); and *Origins of the Modern American Peace Movement, 1915–1929* (Millwood, N.Y.: KTO Press, 1978). Other works pertaining to free speech, the labor movement, and pacifism include Gilbert C. Fite and Horace Peterson, *Opponents of War, 1917–1918* (Madison: Univ. of Wisconsin Press, 1957); Seward W. Livermore, *Woodrow Wilson and the War Congress, 1916–1918* (Seattle: Univ. of Washington Press, rev. ed., 1968); Donald Johnson, *The Challenge to American Freedoms: World War I and the Rise of the American Civil Liberties Union* (Lexington: Univ. Press of Kentucky, 1963); Frank L. Grubbs, Jr., *The Struggle for Labor Loyalty: Gompers, the A F. of L. and the Pacifists, 1917–1920* (Durham, N.C.: Duke Univ. Press, 1968); William Preston, Jr., *Aliens and Dissenters: Federal Suppression of Radicals, 1903–1933* (Cambridge: Harvard Univ. Press, 1963); Paul L. Murphy, *World War I and the Origin of Civil Liberties in the United States* (New York: Norton, 1979); and Harry N. Scheiber, *The Wilson Administration and Civil Liberties, 1917–1921* (Ithaca, N.Y.: Cornell Univ. Press, 1960). Three more recent works well worth close study are Michael D. Pearlman, *To Make Democracy Safe for America: Patricians and Preparedness in the Progressive Era* (Champaign: Univ. of Illinois Press, 1984); John F. McClymer, *War and Welfare: Social Engineering in America, 1890–1925* (Westport, Conn.: Greenwood Press, 1980); and Stephen Vaughn, *Holding Fast the Inner Lines: Democracy, Nationalism, and the Committee on Public Information* (Chapel Hill: Univ. of North Carolina Press, 1980). These works should be read in conjunction with David M. Kennedy's extraordinary synthesis, *Over Here: The First World War and American Society* (New York: Oxford Univ. Press, 1980). Several older essays which should not be neglected include Sidney Kaplan, "Social Engineers as Saviors: Effects of World War I on Some American Liberals," *Journal of the History of Ideas* 17 (1956), 347–369; Walter I. Trattner, "Progressivism and World War I: A Re-Appraisal," *Mid-America* 33 (1962), 131–145; and Allen F. Davis, "Welfare, Reform, and World War I," *American Quarterly* 19 (Fall 1967), 516–533. Biographical studies also deserve attention; some recent accounts include Stephen J. Whitfield, *Scott Nearing: Apostle of American Radicalism* (New York: Columbia Univ. Press, 1974); Ronald Steel, *Walter Lippmann and the American Century* (Boston: Little, Brown, 1980); Robert A. Rosenstone, *Romantic Revolutionary: A Biography of John Reed* (New York: Knopf, 1975); William L. O'Neill, *The Last Romantic: A Life of Max Eastman* (New York: Oxford Univ. Press, 1978); and Blanche Wiesen Cook, ed., *Crystal Eastman on Women and Revolution* (New York: Oxford Univ. Press, 1978). A classic study examining progressive opinion shapers is Charles Forcey, *The Crossroads of Liberalism: Croly, Weyl, Lippmann, and the Progressive Era* (New York: Oxford Univ. Press, 1961).

The immediate postwar activities of American liberals during the "Second

Reconstruction" also have elicited extensive historical inquiry. Several good studies may serve as an introduction: Burl Noggle, *Into the Twenties: The United States from Armistice to Normalcy* (Urbana: Univ. of Illinois Press, 1974); David M. Kennedy, *Over Here: The First World War and American Society* mentioned earlier; and David Burner, "1919: Prelude to Normalcy," in John Braeman, Robert H. Bremner, and David Brody, eds., *Change and Continuity in Twentieth-Century America: The 1920s* (Columbus: Ohio State Univ. Press, 1968), 3–31. Readers will also wish to consult Stuart Rochester, *American Liberal Disillusionment in the Wake of World War I* (University Park: Pennsylvania State Univ. Press, 1977); Robert K. Murray, *Red Scare: A Study in National Hysteria, 1919–1920* (Minneapolis: Univ. of Minnesota Press, 1955); and Robert H. Zieger's outstanding study, *Republicans and Labor, 1919–1929* (Lexington: Univ. Press of Kentucky, 1969). Three essays by Stanley Shapiro are crucial in understanding the "lib-lab" relationship during these years: "The Twilight of Reform: Advanced Progressives after the Armistice," *Historian* 33 (May 1971), 349–364; "The Great War and Reform: Liberals and Labor, 1917–1919," *Labor History* 12 (Summer 1971), 323–344; and "The Passage of Power: Labor and the New Social Order," *Proceedings of the American Philosophical Society* 120 (Dec. 1976), 464–474. Shapiro's "Hand and Brain: The Farmer-Labor Party of 1920," (Ph.D. diss., Univ. of California, Berkeley, 1967) is an excellent study of the conflict between the Committee of Forty-Eight and the National Labor Party and should be read with the contemporary account of Nathan Fine, *Labor and Farmer Parties in the United States, 1828–1928* (New York: Rand School of Social Science, 1928). K. Austin Kerr, *American Railroad Politics, 1914–1920: Rates, Wages, and Efficiency* (Pittsburgh: Univ. of Pittsburgh Press, 1968), is the best account of the struggle between the railway brotherhoods, management, and the government over nationalization. A superb essay by Paul W. Glad, "Progressives and the Business Culture of the 1920s," *Journal of American History* 53 (June 1966), 75–89, was a tremendous aid in understanding the activities of Amos Pinchot and George L. Record after their resignation from the Committee of Forty-Eight.

"Independent Progressives" were unusually active in the years leading up to Robert M. La Follette's presidential campaign in 1924. Kenneth C. MacKay, *The Progressive Movement of 1924* (New York: Columbia Univ. Press, 1947) still remains the definitive account. Related studies which provide a more complete picture include: Robert K. Murray, *The Harding Era: Warren G. Harding and His Administration* (Minneapolis: Univ. of Minnesota Press, 1969); John D. Hicks, *Republican Ascendancy, 1921–1933* (New York: Harper & Row, 1960); James H. Shideler, *Farm Crisis, 1919–1923* (Berkeley: Univ. of California Press, 1957); David A. Shannon, *The Socialist Party of America: A History* (New York: The Macmillan Co., 1955); James Weinstein, *The Decline of Socialism in America, 1912–1925* (New York: Monthly Review Press, 1967); and Millard L. Gieske, *Minnesota Farmer-Laborism: The Third Party Alternative* (Minneapolis: Univ. of Minnesota Press, 1979). Several political biographies also should be consulted since many have a great deal to say about the decade's larger issues. See two works dealing with the *Nation's* Oswald G. Villard: D. Joy Humes, *Oswald Garrison Villard, Liberal of the 1920s* (Syracuse, N.Y.: Syracuse Univ. Press, 1960); and Michael Wreszin, *Oswald Garrison Villard: Pacifist at War* (Bloomington: Indiana Univ. Press, 1965). One of the best studies of this era is LeRoy Ashby, *The Spearless Leader: Senator Borah and the Progressive Movement in the 1920s* (Urbana: Univ. of Illinois Press, 1972); equally important works worthy of study include Richard Lowitt, *George W. Norris: The Persistence of a Progressive, 1913–1933* (Urbana: Univ. of Illinois Press, 1971). There are two important biographies of Herbert Hoover: Joan H. Wilson, *Herbert Hoover: Forgotten Progressive* (Boston: Little, Brown, 1975); and David Burner, *Herbert Hoover: A Public Life* (New York: Knopf, 1979); William H. Harbaugh's *Lawyer's Lawyer: The Life of John W. Davis* (New York: Oxford Univ. Press, 1973) has much to say about Democratic party politics during these years. Organized labor's surge of interest in the La Follette campaign and the crucial role of the railway brotherhoods are discussed in a number of places. See Mark Perlman, *The Machinists: A New Study in American Trade Unionism* (Cambridge: Harvard Univ. Press, 1961); John H. M. Laslett, *Labor and the Left: A Study of Socialist and Radical Influences in the American Labor Movement, 1881–1924* (New York: Basic Books, 1970); Robert H. Zieger's *Republicans and Labor* cited earlier; Russel B. Nye, *Midwestern Progressive Politics: A Historical Study of Its Origins and Development, 1870–1950* (East Lansing: Michigan State College Press, 1951); and James H. Shideler, "The Neo-Progressives: Reform Politics in the United States, 1920–1925," (Ph.D. diss., Univ. of California, Berkeley, 1945). Several interesting essays also should be consulted: James Weinstein, "Radicalism in the Midst of Normalcy," *Journal of American History* 52 (Mar. 1966), 773–790; James H. Shideler, "The La Follette Progressive Party Campaign of 1924," *Wisconsin Magazine of History* 33 (June 1950), 444–457; Alan R. Havig, "A Disputed Legacy: Roosevelt Progressives and the La Follette Campaign of 1924," *Mid-America* 53 (Jan. 1971), 44–64. Havig's dissertation also is very informative on developments within the GOP; see Alan R. Havig, "The Poverty of Insurgency: The Movement to Progressivize the Republican Party, 1916–1924," (Ph.D. diss., Univ. of Missouri, Columbia, 1966). The other major party is the subject of David Burner's fine study, *The Politics of Provincialism: The Democratic Party in Transition, 1918–1932* (New York: Knopf, 1968).

Many of these scholars carry their analyses beyond the 1924 election and follow progressives through the "wilderness years" between 1925 and 1928. An early but still valuable essay is James H. Shideler, "The Disintegration of the Progressive Party Movement of 1924," *Historian* 13 (Spring 1951), 189–201. For background material on the independent progressives' criticism of Coolidge administration foreign policy, I utilized works by L. Ethan Ellis, *Republican Foreign Policy, 1921–1933* (New Brunswick: Rutgers Univ. Press, 1968); and *Frank B. Kellogg and American Foreign Relations, 1925–1929* (New Brunswick: Rutgers Univ. Press, 1961); Dana G. Munro, *The United States and the Caribbean Republics, 1921–1933* (Princeton: Princeton Univ. Press, 1974); Joan H. Wilson, *American Business & Foreign Policy: 1920–1933* (Lexington: Univ. Press of Kentucky, 1971); William Kamman, *A Search for Stability: United States Diplomacy Toward Nicaragua, 1925–1933* (Notre Dame: Univ. of Notre Dame Press, 1968); and Walter LaFeber, *Inevitable Revolutions: The United States in Central America* (New York: W. W. Norton & Co., 1983). Progressive interest in the "Power Trust" is discussed in Richard Lowitt's outstanding biography, *George W. Norris: The Persistence of a Progressive, 1913–1933* mentioned earlier and in Ellis W. Hawley, *The New Deal and the Problem of Monopoly* (Princeton: Princeton Univ. Press, 1966). An excellent essay on this issue is G. Cullom Davis, "The Transformation of the Federal Trade

Commission, 1914–1929," *Mississippi Valley Historical Review* 49 (Dec. 1962), 437–455.

Although I have called the emergence of the League for Independent Political Action and the actions of other progressives between 1928 and 1932 a "rehearsal for reform," I would not want their efforts evaluated only as a prelude to the New Deal. A number of scholars have accepted the struggles of these years as representing their own distinct period and I would agree. A good place to begin is with Donald R. McCoy, *Angry Voices: Left-of-Center Politics in the New Deal Era* (Lawrence: Univ. of Kansas Press, 1958); R. Alan Lawson, *The Failure of Independent Liberalism, 1933–1941* (New York: Putnam's Sons, 1971); Karel Denis Bicha, "Liberalism Frustrated: The League for Independent Political Action, 1928–1933," *Mid-America* 48 (Jan. 1966), 19–28; and Richard H. Pells, *Radical Visions and American Dreams: Cultural and Social Thought in the Depression Years* (New York: Harper & Row, 1973). Other studies helpful in understanding these years include Albert U. Romasco, *The Poverty of Abundance: Hoover, the Nation, the Depression* (New York: Oxford Univ. Press, 1965); Ronald L. Feinman, *Twilight of Progressivism: The Western Republican Senators and the New Deal* (Baltimore: The Johns Hopkins Univ. Press, 1981); Patrick J. Maney, *"Young Bob" La Follette: A Biography of Robert M. La Follette, Jr., 1895–1953* (Columbia: Univ. of Missouri Press, 1978); Martin L. Fausold and George T. Mazuzan, eds., *The Hoover Presidency: A Reappraisal* (Albany: State Univ. of New York Press, 1974); J. Joseph Huthmacher, *Senator Robert F. Wagner and the Rise of Urban Liberalism* (New York: Atheneum, 1971); Jordan A. Schwarz, *Interregnum of Despair: Hoover, Congress, and the Depression* (Urbana: Univ. of Illinois Press, 1970), and Elliot A. Rosen, *Hoover, Roosevelt & the Brains Trust: From Depression to New Deal* (New York: Columbia Univ. Press, 1977).

Readers interested in the struggles of the progressive labor movement from the " 'New Era' to the New Deal" will find the choices diverse and the literature generally excellent. The starting point for most students since its publication in 1960 is Irving Bernstein's, *The Lean Years: A History of the American Worker, 1920–1933* (Boston: Houghton Mifflin, 1960). That should be supplemented by James O. Morris, *Conflict Within the AFL: A Study of Craft Versus Industrial Unionism, 1901–1938* (Ithaca, N.Y.: Cornell Univ. Press, 1958); Walter Galenson, *The CIO Challenge to the AFL: A History of the American Labor Movement, 1935–1941* (Cambridge: Harvard Univ. Press, 1960); and especially by Melvyn Dubofsky and Warren Van Tine, *John L. Lewis: A Biography* (New York: Quadrangle, 1977). Works dealing primarily with Brookwood Labor College and A. J. Muste include Jo Ann O. Robinson's fine biography, *Abraham Went Out: A Biography of A. J. Muste* (Philadelphia: Temple Univ. Press, 1981); her 1972 thesis, "The Traveller from Zierkzee: The Religious, Intellectual and Political Development of A. J. Muste from 1885 to 1940," (Ph.D. diss., The Johns Hopkins Univ., 1972); Charles H. Howlett, "Brookwood Labor College and Worker Commitment to Social Reform," *Mid-America* 61 (Jan. 1979), 47–66; Joel Denker, *Unions and Universities: The Rise of the New Labor Leader* (Montclair, N.J.: Allanheld, Osmun, 1981); Nat Hentoff, *Peace Agitator: The Story of A. J. Muste* (New York: Macmillan, 1963); *The Essays of A. J. Muste*, Hentoff, ed., (Indianapolis, Ind.: Bobbs-Merrill, 1967); and Rita J. Simon, ed., *As We Saw the Thirties: Essays on Social and Political Movements of a Decade* (Urbana: Univ. of Illinois Press, 1967). Two essays exploring the more radical activities of labor progressives are Roy Rosenzweig, "Radicals and the Jobless: The Musteites and the Unemployed Leagues, 1932–1936," *Labor History* 16 (Winter 1975) 52–77; and Daniel L. Leab, " 'Until We Eat': The Creation and Organization of the Unemployed Councils in 1930," *Labor History* 8 (Fall 1967), 300–315. The Conference for Progressive Labor Action's activities in the mill towns and mining camps of the nation are better understood after reading two essays in Gary M. Fink and Merl E. Reed, eds., *Essays in Southern Labor History: Selected Papers, Southern Labor History Conference, 1976* (Westport, Conn.: Greenwood Press, 1977); Dennis R. Nolan and Donald E. Jonas, "Textile Unionism in the Piedmont, 1901–1932," 48–79, and David A. Corbin, " 'Frank Keeney Is Our Leader and We Shall Not Be Moved': Rank-and-File Leadership in the West Virginia Coal Fields," 144–156. Some closely related works include F. Ray Marshall, *Labor in the South* (Cambridge: Harvard Univ. Press, 1967); and Herbert L. Lahne, *The Cotton Mill Worker* (New York: Farrar & Rinehart, 1944). Two documentary studies which helped me considerably were Gary M. Fink, ed., *Biographical Dictionary of American Labor Leaders* (Westport, Conn.: Greenwood Press, 1974); and Bernard K. Johnpoll and Mark R. Yerburgh, eds., *The League for Industrial Democracy: A Documentary History* (Westport, Conn.: Greenwood Press, 1980). Finally, I would like to join a host of others in acknowledging the pioneer work of David Brody, most recently in a collection of significant essays, *Workers in Industrial America: Essays on the Twentieth Century Struggle* (New York: Oxford Univ. Press, 1980).

Index

Pinchot's liberal group, 144, 148; works with La Follette Progressives, 153; politics and marriage noted, 155; assesses Progressives' future, 168; as member of Progressive National Executive Committee, 198 n.13; attitude toward New Deal, 236
Gardner, Matilda, 155
Garfield, James R., 152
Garland, Charles, 174. *See also* American Fund for Public Service
Garland Fund. *See* American Fund for Public Service
Garretson, Austin B., 54
Gary Committee, 47
Gary, Elbert H., 47
General Electric, 191, 193
General Motors, 193
Gilman, Charlotte Perkins, 46
Gilman, Elisabeth, 118, 155
Glad, Paul W., 7
Gladden, Washington, 43
Gompers, Samuel: advisory member of Counsel of National Defense, 75; attacked by People's Council of America for Democracy and Peace, 88; denounces NLP, 103; relations with Democratic Party, 108, 118; opposed by CPPA, 134
Graham, Otis L., Jr., 6–7, 159, 236
Grand Jury, Montana, 172, 175
Grand Jury, Washington, D.C., 173
The Great Campaigns (Graham, Jr.), 6–7
Great Depression, 9, 11, 216–17, 236
Green, William, 205
Gronna, A. J., 91 n.21

Haines, Lynn, 119
Haitian Constitution, 215
Hallinan, Charles T., 73, 88
Hampton, George P., 123
Hapgood, Hutchins, 62 n.8
Hapgood, Norman, 35, 80; supports free speech, 62 n.8; chairman Wheeler Defense Committee, 173; supports NCC, 181, 199 n.32

Harbaugh, William H., 14, 20
Hard, William, 3–4; as supporter of Committee of Forty-Eight, 101; attends NLP convention (1920), 115–16; covers La Follette's 1924 campaign, 156–58
Harding administration: efforts to aid farmers, 4; attacked, 132-33; labor policy, 134; scandals in, 137, 146; tariff policy of, 159; opposition to government ownership of railroads, 247
Harding, Warren G., 104, 112, 122–23, 131, 141–42, 145
Harriman, Florence, 54
Harvey, William Hope ("Coin"), 223–24
Haverford College, 95 n.81
Hayes, Max, 103, 151
Hays, Arthur Garfield, 101
Haywood, William D., 27; participates in Paterson textile strike, 48–49
Healy, Robert, 189
Hearst syndicate, 120
Hearst, William Randolph, 112
Heney, Francis J., 25, 34
Henry Street Group, 83; antiwar group formed, 68; adopts policy statement, 69; organizational change, 70; influence on ACWF program, 76. *See also* Anti-Militarism Committee; Anti-Preparedness Committee; American Union Against Militarism; American Union for a Democratic Peace
Henry Street Settlement, 68, 70, 73
Hillman, Sidney, 123, 142
Hillquit, Morris: supports free speech, 62 n.8; NYC mayoralty campaign, 87, 94 n.75; cautions against separate labor party, 142; reacts to 1924 La Follette campaign, 156; advises LIPA of Socialist party commitment to Norman Thomas, 219
History of the Progressive Party (Pinchot), 27, 226

Henry Street group, 68; chairman
AUAM, 70–71; attacks militarism,
73; alarmed over AUAM emphasis
on CO issue, 83–84
Walling, William E., 46
Walsh, David I., 131, 181
Walsh, Frank P., 103, 243 n.104, 247;
chairman, U.S. Commission on In-
dustrial Relations, 44; endorses
staff report, 53; dismisses Charles
McCarthy, 54, 64 n.37; helps or-
ganize Committee on Industrial
Relations, 59; co-chairman War La-
bor Board, 64 n.36; mentioned as
possible third party candidate, 113;
meets with Senate progressives
(1920), 131
Walsh, Thomas J., 175, 181, 188,
210
Warbasse, James, 71
Ward, Harry F., 204
Washington, D.C., Supreme Court
of, 174–75
Weinstein, James, 14, 53, 58
Weinstock, Harris, 54
Welfare capitalism, 4
Weyl, Walter, 52, 62 n.8, 86,
101
"What Happened to the Progressive
Movement in the 1920s?" (Link),
5
"What is Progressivism?" (Hard),
3–4
Wheeler, Burton K., 214; elected to
Senate, 141; as vice presidential
candidate (1924), 151; under inves-
tigation and indictment, 172–74;
exonerated, 175; urges progressive
caution, 177; supports NCC,
181
Wheeler Defense Committee, 173–75,
199 n.32
"Where are the Pre-War Radicals?"
(Survey), 5
White, William Allen, 27, 175, 181,
184
Whitlock, Victor, 190
Why War (Howe), 75–76

Wilcox, Clair, 241 n.71
Wilcox, Delos F., quoted, 22
Williams, Howard Yolen, 209; executive director LIPA, 207; supports
third party candidates, 210; calls
for redistribution of wealth, 211;
looks to 1936 for third party, 214–
15; turns to Minnesota FLP, 216;
urges public works spending, 217,
invites cooperation with SP, 219;
pursues political realignment, 221,
224; addresses LIPA convention,
228; rebuffed by FLP, 230; criticizes
FDR, 231; predicts third party in
place by 1934, 233; offers opinion
of FDR, 235–36
Wilson administration: support for
social justice legislation, 53; responds to CIR report, 57–58; edges
toward war, 67; weighs loss of
AUAM support, 73; approves Senate revenue bill, 81; view of CO issue, 83; influences public opinion,
88; union unhappiness with, 102;
railroad regulation and, 104–5
Wilson-Seabury League, 35
Wilson Volunteers, 35
Wilson, Woodrow, 20, 25, 30, 88,
144, 186, 192–93, 246; differences
with TR, 16; relations with Record,
28, 31–33; appoints Brandeis to Supreme Court, 53; calls for preparedness, 69; meets with AUAM, 71–
72; peace candidacy of, 73; denounces filibuster against armed-
ship bill, 74; war message, 76;
signs 1917 Revenue Act, 81–82;
Fourteen Points mentioned, 83
Wisconsin Legislative Reference Library, 17, 54
"Wisconsin platform," 114–16,
119
Wise, Stephen, 35; lobbies for Industrial Relations Commission, 43–44;
member Henry Street group, 68;
AUAM meeting with Wilson, 71;
attends Carnegie Hall rally, 72; re-

ABOUT THE AUTHOR

EUGENE M. TOBIN is Associate Professor of History, and Director of the American Studies Program at Hamilton College. A native of Bayonne, New Jersey, he received his B.A. from Rutgers University and his M.A. and Ph.D. from Brandeis University. His articles have appeared in the *American Journal of Economics and Sociology, Labor History, New Jersey History*, and the *Historian*. He is the coeditor of *The Age of Urban Reform: New Perspectives on the Progressive Era* with Michael H. Ebner, and is currently working on a history of the National Lawyers Guild.